CORRECTIONAL TREATMENT
Theory and Practice

CLEMENS BARTOLLAS

University of Northern Iowa

Prentice-Hall, Inc., Englewood Cliffs, New Jersey 07632

Library of Congress Cataloging in Publication Data

BARTOLLAS, CLEMENS.
   Correctional treatment.

   Bibliography: p.
   Includes index.
   1. Corrections—United States.   2. Rehabilitation—
United States.   3. Prisoners—Psychiatric care—United
States.   4. Correctional psychology.   I. Title.
HV9304.B36 1985   364.6'0973   84-4702
ISBN   0-13-178328-9

Editorial/production supervision and
   interior design: Marjorie Borden and Sylvia Moore
Cover design: Wanda Lubelska
Manufacturing buyer: Ed O'Dougherty

Printed in the United States of America

10   9   8   7   6   5   4   3   2   1

0-13-178328-9   01

Prentice-Hall International, Inc., *London*
Prentice-Hall of Australia Pty. Limited, *Sydney*
Editora Prentice-Hall do Brasil, Ltda., *Rio de Janeiro*
Prentice-Hall Canada Inc., *Toronto*
Prentice-Hall of India Private Limited, *New Delhi*
Prentice-Hall of Japan, Inc., *Tokyo*
Prentice-Hall of Southeast Asia Pte. Ltd., *Singapore*
Whitehall Books Limited, *Wellington, New Zealand*

Dedicated to
my wife, Linda

Contents

Foreword

The new consensus on correctional treatment is simple. Program administrators, clinicians, and researchers have concluded that attempts to rehabilitate offenders are futile unless the individual to be rehabilitated desires that outcome enough to take the initiative. That principle is consistent with the American predilection for self-help—we are a nation convinced that God helps those who help themselves. Both experience and statistical evaluation support this ancient proverb.

There is also a woolly-minded consensus shared by people who fancy themselves as tough-minded hard-liners to the effect that the evaluation of correctional treatment shows that "nothing works." This second consensus is welcome to those who see no point in pouring money down rat holes for the benefit of criminals who deserve nothing from society but bunks in crowded cells and enough grub to keep them alive until they must be released from the edifying horrors of penitentiary life.

If I read this hard line right, all criminals except traffic violators deserve a term in jail or prison to spread the lesson that crime does not pay. Exactly what such jails or prisons will be like can be readily ascertained by a visit to almost any "correctional" facility in the land, all of them jammed to grotesque absurdity with idle convicts, most of whom are engaged in devising measures and sharpening weapons to ensure their survival. More such facilities are under construction. Few of them make provision for enough work or programs to keep convicts usefully occupied—or occupied at all.

It is characteristic of hard-liners that a one-line slogan—*"nothing works"*—is enough to establish a policy. They are sure that the search for supporting facts and observations will lead straight into needless confusion of their tough minds.

The policy that is emerging from the application of hard-boiled simplicities to the tough complexities of the crime problem is disturbingly close to general application. The consequences can be foretold by reference to any careful study of criminal careers, the most impressive feature of which is the persistence of recidivism.[1]

It is time to resuscitate the baby that the late Professor Martinson threw out with the bathwater.[2] It was true that the rehabilitation of convicts and juvenile delinquents as practiced during the fifties and sixties was a silly exercise in futility. A veteran of those times myself, I know something about the nonsense that went under the heading of correctional treatment in those days. A dollop of counseling here, a dab of group therapy there, and a diagnostic interview with a psychiatrist for those for whom dollops and dabs did not suffice to avert really serious trouble—and *presto!* there was correctional treatment. It convinced a lot of us that we were clinicians on the cutting edge of a new discipline. In spite of our efforts, our sincerity, and our dedication—all of which were real enough—our achievements were much more modest than our promises. By hindsight, it should have been expected that eventually someone like Martinson would come along to empty the tub of both bathwater and baby.

It is conventionally wise to assert that our error was in the application of the "medical model" to a condition that seemed to be analogous to disease but that in fact was fundamentally dissimilar. That was true as far as it went, but error had a longer history than that. We adopted the medical model because there were people around who were prepared to provide the various kinds of counseling services that were said to be needed. Counseling fit the medical model. The prison and the "training school" for juveniles were places where counselors could do their stuff, along with psychologists, psychiatrists, social workers, and other helping professionals.

The error was in the assumptions. We all assumed that the willingness to help would be balanced by the willingness to be helped. It took many years to establish that this balance could never be struck, especially by edict of a classification committee. We found ways for helping professionals to do what they had been trained to do, but prisoners did not often find the services of these helpers relevant to their special problems.

The complex question that was not asked until embarrassingly late in the history of the rehabilitative ideal was this: *What needs to be done?* Everyone but the convicts themselves could see the maladjustments that had propelled them into crime. Most prisoners did not find their maladjustments very distressing, but tended to acknowledge their need for change to satisfy an inquiring parole board.

We had glimmerings of new approaches to the therapy that we thought was

---

[1]For two recent studies, see Mark A. Peterson, Harriet B. Braiker, and Suzanne M. Polich, *Doing Crime: A Survey of California Prison Inmates* (Santa Monica, California: The Rand Corporation, 1980), and Stuart J. Miller, Simon Dinitz, and John P. Conrad, *Careers of the Violent; The Dangerous Offender and Criminal Justice* (Lexington, Massachusetts: D.C. Heath, 1982).

[2]See Robert Martinson, "What Works?—Questions and Answers About Prison Reform," *The Public Interest*, no, 35 (Spring 1974), 22–54.

so desperately needed. We thought that the culture of the prison had to support the individual's will to change. We talked about creating "therapeutic communities" in prisons, but we never took that idea much farther than organizing large groups to talk about community problems.[3]

Talk, talk, talk. Somehow we accepted the improbable notion that a weekly or even a daily group meeting under the auspices of a counselor would offset the hours and hours of talk in prison yards, day-rooms, and cell-block galleries about matters far less innocent than the topics discussed in professionally sanctioned groups. Relatively few prisoners really worked, and not many more were engaged in serious and effective educational programs. The assumption that therapy was the most important activity for a convict led to the equally silly assumption that the effectiveness of treatment could be discerned by comparing the recidivism of those participating in treatment with the recidivism of those who didn't. That led to Professor Martinson's finding that "nothing works."

What needs to be done? The formidable task is to create a culture of self-improvement. That objective calls for a lot more structure than the notion of a "therapeutic community." Prisoners should work for a living; those who don't should be viewed as odd and should enjoy none of the benefits of idleness.

That goal has eluded correctional administrators from the middle of the nine-teenth century on. There is never enough work to keep a convict population busy. There have always been plenty of reasons to tolerate the unemployment of offenders sentenced to terms of hard labor. First, there was the respectable argument that prison industries, employing unpaid or underpaid labor, could not be allowed to compete with private enterprise, thereby putting honest workmen out of their jobs. That argument can be met by paying prisoners regular wages and making use of federal and state markets for their products. A less respectable argument is the notion that work interferes with education and vocational training. To the extent that the interference is real, it can be eliminated by intelligent planning. Finally, there is the wrong-headed idea that prisoners should only be employed at work that can be found in the region to which they will be released. Far better that they should put in eight hours of work every day at any kind of work than that they should be swapping tall tales of crimes committed or planned, or conspiring to operate intra-mural rackets in narcotics or booze.

Time and facilities should be allotted for remedial learning and vocational training, and those who don't take advantage of these resources should be regarded as missing out on something of great value. Many, if not most, prisoners take this point of view now; those prisons that have competent educational and vocational training programs must administer long waiting lists for enrollment. The exertions of penal statisticians in the evaluation of correctional treatment have never been directed at education and training programs. There is a lot of anecdotal evidence

[3]Actually there have been some exceptions, the most important of which was the work of Elliot Studt and her colleagues in California in 1968: See Elliot Studt, Sheldon L. Messinger, and Thomasa P. Wilson, *C-Unit: Search for Community in Prison* (New York: The Russell Sage Foundation, 1968).

of their success, and I do not doubt that statistical support would be found if statisticians would bestir themselves to examine outcomes systematically.

All of us need counseling at some point in our lives—especially criminals. Prisoners will come to counselors if counselors will help with immediate but mundane problems in the outside world, inaccessible to men and women locked away from outside contacts. Very few will have the slightest interest in depth therapy of any type. The supposition that counseling can only be worthwhile if it thereby reduces recidivism is a simplicity that is unworthy of a thinking social scientist, but that simplicity has been gulped down by a generation of cost-benefit analysts. The work of a prison counselor is basic communication, and secondarily may be therapy, if not very deep therapy.

Correctional treatment can become a reality if the conditions are created to make it possible. Those conditions are not generally to be found in American prisons for reasons that I explore elsewhere in this book.[4] Innovative administrators can change all that. In doing so, they can transform the prison from an inferno in which all hope must be abandoned into a community in which prisoners can entertain realistic hopes for decent lives in the future that awaits nearly all of them after their release.

In this volume, Professor Bartollas has accurately laid out the possibilities for successful correctional treatment. Not only the treatment to be offered but also the organizational requirements for its success are clearly presented. Students who catch a note of excitement from this text will be correct. The challenge is nothing less than to rebuild American corrections. This book specifies the foundation on which this rebuilding must be undertaken. The rest is up to the hopeful and resourceful men and women who will carry out the reconstruction. Their rewards will mainly consist of the satisfaction of doing what has been thought to be impossible. For some wonderful people that will be satisfaction enough.

JOHN P. CONRAD

[4]See Chapter 13.

Preface

This book examines the role of treatment in American corrections. A new look at treatment is needed, because the changing currents of American corrections in the 1980s are leading to a treatment model that is likely to be much different than, and may be much better than, what existed earlier.

The decline and loss of confidence in the rehabilitation model became apparent in American corrections in the 1970s. Proponents of correctional treatment during the 1970s, attacked from all sides by critics and evaluators, defensively regarded themselves as "voices crying in the wilderness." But correctional treatment, as it has become less compulsory than it was under the older system of the indeterminate sentence and the parole board, is growing more varied in its approaches; more sophisticated in its technology; more concerned about improving theory, quality of interventions, and evaluation of programs; and more realistic about what can and cannot be achieved.

The study of correctional treatment is important. First, at a time when the public is concerned about crime being out of control and too many streets in our cities being unsafe, every effort must be made to provide opportunities for offenders to adopt law-abiding behavior. Second, correctional programs are still being conducted in every community-based and institutional facility, and it is important to understand what is taking place in these interventions. Third, two of the three basic approaches used in dealing with offenders uphold the feasibility of correctional treatment beyond mere confinement. Fourth, exoffenders sometimes credit the treatment received in community-based and institutional programs with helping them walk away from crime; that is, treatment appears to work for some offenders. Fifth, programs continue to play an important role in helping offenders do "easier time" in prison, and sometimes these programs enable offenders to gain valuable skills, insights about themselves, or a sense of purpose in life. Sixth, several exemplary programs in community-based and institutional settings show that improving the overall effectiveness of correctional treatment is possible. Seventh, individuals intending to work in corrections need training and preparation to become effective treatment agents.

In assessing correctional treatment, this book considers several questions: What are the basic correctional models being used to deal with juvenile and adult offenders, and what role does correctional treatment have in each model? What are the basic interventions being used in community-based and institutional settings. What common elements do effective programs have? What strategy can be developed to improve correctional treatment? How competent are treatment personnel? What are the basic job responsibilities of the main treatment agents in juvenile and adult corrections? What characteristics do effective treatment agents have in common? What kinds of people respond favorably to what types of treatment? Why do some correctional clients make it and others fail? How important to the effectiveness of treatment is the environment in which treatment is given?

This book attempts to take a new look at treatment by including material that is current or that has been slighted in other writings on correctional treatment. Treatment is examined within a broader context of the three correctional models used with offenders. In examining the overall quality of community-based and institutional programs, this book highlights the more innovative ones. Also, treatment is examined in the context of the role behavior of the main treatment agents, including their role expectations and pressures, and the characteristics of effective agents. The environment in which treatment takes place receives much attention in this text. The effects of treatment on offenders are examined, especially the reasons why offenders succeed or fail. Finally, the text explores strategies needed to improve correctional treatment.

The book is divided into four major units. The first deals with three basic ways to handle juvenile and adult offenders: the rehabilitative philosophy, the justice philosophy, and the utilitarian punishment philosophy. The role of correctional treatment is defined in each model. The second unit examines community-based and institutional programs in juvenile and adult corrections. This unit also considers common elements in effective programs and ways correctional treatment can be improved. The third unit considers the job descriptions and treatment responsibilities of several treatment agents in juvenile and adult justice. The fourth unit examines correctional environments and explores what elements should be present to make those environments more compatible with treatment, outlines the constitutional rights that inmates must have in these settings, considers why inmates succeed or fail, and explores how characteristics of offenders affect their receptivity toward treatment. The final chapter provides an overview of the book, projects what the future of correctional treatment may be, and makes specific recommendations for improving correctional treatment.

Students in corrections courses, as well as practitioners in the justice system, will find this book helpful in giving them a better understanding of the history, the frustrations and failures, and the potential of correctional treatment. Certainly, much has been wrong in the practice of correctional treatment; the yoke of coercive rehabilitative philosophy, especially the medical model, has sometimes done more damage than good to offenders. Yet considerable potential remains untapped in voluntary interventions based on sound theory and good research. We hope this book will make a contribution toward helping correctional treatment realize some of its potential.

Acknowledgments

Several individuals have made an invaluable contribution to this book. Foremost were the manuscript's two editors, Jean Kennedy and Judith Sutton. Jean Kennedy painstakingly reviewed the writing and organization of the manuscript and made appropriate, numerous, and invaluable contributions to making the manuscript more readable. As she has done with three of my other books, Judith Sutton did an outstanding job in copyediting the manuscript. I am also grateful to Ted Palmer, James Q. Wilson, David Fogel, Dr. Martin Groder, John P. Conrad, Rick Weider, Darrell Dierks, John Stepniewski, and Dr. Francis Tyce for their kindness in consenting to be interviewed for this book. Daniel R. Loutsch did an excellect job in preparing the index. Among the many friends and colleagues whose patience and expertise were critical for the completion of this work were Steve Smith, Steve Cuvelier, and Ron Amstrom. Julia Rathbone and Ruth Peterson typed many drafts, and Rosemarie Skaine performed other administrative tasks that enabled me to keep the manuscript moving without interruption. I would also like to thank Dean Robert Morin of the University of Northern Iowa for his assistance in providing the typing and xeroxing of this book. As always, I extend to Linda, my wife, my appreciation for her encouragement and patience during the years this project was underway.

Introduction

1

Objectives

1. *To examine the role that treatment has played in the history of corrections in the United States.*

2. *To present the status of correctional treatment today.*

3. *To describe the challenge that correctional treatment must meet to become more effective in community-based and institutional corrections.*

Criminal behavior presents a problem that is disruptive to the general welfare and threatening to the safety of citizens in American society. But crime, which is widespread today, is not a new problem. Some of the first written documents of Western society, indeed of most societies, set forth penalties for behavior that was against the good of society. The first approach to treating crime was punishment or isolation from the social group. Now, because of the burgeoning of crime, the problem of criminal behavior and of modifying that behavior so that the individual may become a productive member of society represents a major challenge. In addition, the American philosophy of recognizing the rights of the individual, as well as those of society, demands a humane approach in meeting the challenge.

The basic purpose of this text is to evaluate treatment of delinquent and criminal behavior in corrections today. Significantly, *corrections* is the term currently used to refer to both the programs and the agencies that have legal authority for the custody and supervision of offenders convicted of criminal acts.[1] The term itself indicates that the major thrust in dealing with offenders is to bring them to a recognition of their behavior as antisocial, as well as to motivate them to change their behavior so that it becomes more beneficial to the aims of society and perhaps to their own goals. Correctional treatment can be defined "as any measure taken to change an offender's character, habits, or behavior patterns so as to dismiss his [or her] criminal propensities."[2] The primary goal of treatment, then, is to alter an offender's attitudes and behavior so he or she is less inclined to commit crime again.

Correctional treatment in this nation takes place in a variety of preventive, diversionary, and correctional contexts. Some treatments are designed to identify and intervene in the lives of individuals or groups of persons who are in criminogenic circumstances so that their possible future involvement with the justice system can be minimized; but most correctional programs are designed to rehabilitate those individuals who have already been detected and convicted for delinquent or criminal acts.[3] Some of these programs show impressive results, while others leave a great deal to be desired.

Correctional treatment is a subject that stirs strong emotions among both supporters and critics. Even the interest of the general public in correctional treatment has waxed and waned from one generation to the next. Correctional treatment is certainly easily criticized, for in the past two hundred and fifty years method after method has been tried in the attempt to remodel, remake, reshape, and rehabilitate juvenile and adult offenders. Treatment as a means of correcting criminal and delinquent behavior has moved from penitence to reform to rehabilitation. The

---

[1]Robert M. Carter, Richard A. McKee, and E. Kim Nelson, *Corrections in America* (Philadelphia: Lippincott, 1975), p. 1.

[2]Andrew von Hirsch, ed., *Doing Justice: The Choice of Punishments* (New York: Hill and Wang, 1976), p. 11.

[3]Anne M. Newton, "Prevention of Crime and Delinquency," *Criminal Justice Abstracts* (June 1978): 246.

correctional panaceas of one generation all too frequently are seen as disasters by the next.

The purpose of this chapter is to review the role that correctional treatment has played in the history of American corrections, to present the current status of correctional treatment, and to discuss the challenges that correctional treatment must meet to become more effective. Later chapters will show the complex role of treatment in corrections by examining the rehabilitative philosophy and other correctional models advocated as alternatives, by looking at the diversity and overall quality of programs used in juvenile and adult corrections, by analyzing the role behavior of treatment agents, and by evaluating the response of offenders to the treatment process.

TREATMENT AND THE HISTORY OF CORRECTIONS

From the construction of the first prison to the emergence of recent correctional innovations, corrections has developed in stages, each representing an attempt to implement a new philosophy of treatment.

Treatment during the Colonial Period

Correctional treatment was minimal in America until the late eighteenth century because the colonists saw little possibility of eliminating crime from their midst. The prevailing Calvinist doctrines that stressed the natural depravity of the human race and the power of the devil did not allow optimism about reforming the criminal deviant. The colonists believed that only severe punishments held any hope for inspiring obedience. The fine and the whip were the two most widely used penalties, but the colonists did not hesitate to use the stocks and the gallows as well. The colonists usually relied upon noninstitutional means, partly because they did not believe confinement in jail could rehabilitate the offender.[4]

But after the War of Independence, ideas from the Enlightenment—which advocated boundless optimism about the perfectability of the individual and society—led to a spirit of reform.[5] In 1787, as part of this spirit, a group of influential Philadelphians gathered at the home of Benjamin Franklin to hear Dr. Benjamin Rush read a paper on new methods for treating criminals. Dr. Rush proposed that evening a prison program that would

1. Classify prisoners for housing.
2. Provide prison labor, which would make the institution self-supporting.

---

[4]David J. Rothman, *The Discovery of the Asylum: Social Order and Disorder in the Republic* (Boston: Little, Brown, 1971), pp. 46–53.

[5]Ibid., p. 57.

3.   Include gardens to provide food and outdoor areas for recreation.
4.   Classify convicts according to a judgment about the nature of the crime—whether it arose out of passion, habit, temptation, or mental illness.
5.   Impose determinate periods of confinement based upon the convict's reformative progress.[6]

Treatment and the First American Prison

In 1790, the reform ideas advocated by Rush led to the renovation of the Old Walnut Street Jail in Philadelphia to include a "cellhouse." This first American prison paid each male prisoner the same—or somewhat lower—wages as those paid for similar work in the community. Guards were forbidden to use corporal punishment, and inmates could be pardoned by the governor for good conduct. The silent rule was enforced in the shops, but prisoners could talk in the night room before bedtime.[7] The Walnut Street Jail program, as well as those of several other prisons established at this period of time, worked well for a few years, but this reform effort eventually collapsed "due to overcrowding, idleness, and incompetent personnel."[8]

The Penitentiary: The Great American Experiment

The next institution to be developed was the penitentiary, which used solitude and work to attain moral reformation. The theory behind the penitentiary was that crime was caused by a bad environment, in which young and impressionable offenders were led astray by the breakdown of community life. The purpose of the penitentiary was to make up for a bad environment by providing offenders with a properly structured environment, which would enable them to repent of their wrongdoings and become useful citizens upon their return to the community.[9]

The penitentiary was a product of the idealism of the Jacksonian period, which saw the young American nation as having an unlimited capacity to solve its social problems. The inspiration for the penitentiary came from the Philadelphia Society for the Alleviation of the Miseries of Public Prisons, which proposed a new prison that required complete solitude, with labor in the cells and recreation in a private yard adjacent to each cell. The society also proposed that a Bible would be furnished each prisoner for moral guidance.[10] The antecedents of the penitentiary, however, can be found in the Middle Ages, when the Roman Catholic Church developed

---

[6]Wayne Morris, ed., "The Attorney General's Survey of Release Procedures," in *Penology: The Evolution of Corrections in America,* ed. George C. Killinger and Paul F. Cromwell, Jr. (St. Paul: West, 1973), p. 23.

[7]Ibid., p. 27.

[8]Ibid., p. 33.

[9]Rothman, *Discovery of the Asylum,* p. 107.

[10]Ibid.

prisons called penitentiaries in which wrongdoers were expected to express penitence; in eighteenth-century France and England, the model was expanded to include the use of work along with solitude to achieve moral reformation.[11]

The Pennsylvania plan became reality when the legislature approved the construction of two prisons incorporating the Philadelphia Society's concepts to be opened in Pittsburgh in 1826 (Western Penitentiary) and in Philadelphia in 1829 (Eastern Penitentiary). The Eastern Penitentiary proved to be the more renowned of the two institutions. Here, extreme care was taken to keep prisoners separate from each other. Each prisoner had his own cell (nearly twelve feet long, seven and one-half feet wide, and sixteen feet high), work area, and exercise yard; even at Sunday worship services, prisoners were prevented from seeing each other.

David J. Rothman aptly expressed how the process of reform was intended to occur in the Pennsylvania penitentiaries:

> Thrown upon his own innate sentiments, with no evil example to lead him astray, and with kindness and proper instruction at hand to bolster his resolutions, the criminal would start his rehabilitation. Then after a period of total isolation, without companions, books, or tools, officials would allow the inmate to work in his cell. . . . The convict would sit in his cell and work with his tools daily, so that during the course of his sentence regularity and discipline would become habitual. He would return to the community cured of vice and idleness, to take his place as a responsible citizen.[12]

Meanwhile, a rival system of reforming prisoners, the "silent" or "congregate" system, had evolved in New York. In 1819, the Auburn State Prison was erected, and, influenced by Quaker thinking, administrators soon introduced the practice of total solitary confinement. When several prisoners attempted suicide and others suffered mental breakdowns, the decision was made to substitute a system which separated prisoners at night and involved them in a congregate work program in silence by day. The Auburn system permitted visual contact but no conversation among prisoners, so they could work and exercise together, thereby requiring much smaller cells than the ones in the Pennsylvania system.

Economics was the basic reason the Auburn silent system emerged victorious over the total solitude of its Pennsylvania rival. But as the Auburn system developed, prisoners were required to work long hours at unpaid labor, were subjected to a variety of humiliating degradations, and were frequently beaten. The rigorous discipline of the Auburn system was shaped by Warden Elam Elyds, who often informed visitors that the first step in the reform of criminals was to break their spirits. The Auburn legacy of wretched living conditions, poor food, extreme harshness, and a design of small cells and large, multitiered cellblocks marked prison life until well into the twentieth century.[13]

[11]Morris, "Attorney General's Survey of Release Procedures," p. 21.

[12]Rothman, *Discovery of the Asylum*, p. 85.

[13]John P. Conrad, "Correctional Treatment," in *Encyclopedia of Crime and Justice* (New York: Macmillan, 1983).

The Reformatory Model

A new wave of optimism concerning society's ability to rehabilitate offenders swept through corrections after the Civil War and led to the development of the reformatory model. Led by Enoch Wines, Franklin Sanborn, and Zebulun Brockway, the reformers were aware of the brutality and abuses of the existing penitentiaries and knew that a new design was necessary. A National Congress of Penitentiary and Reformatory Discipline met in 1870 at Cincinnati, and at this meeting the new reformatory model was developed. The evangelical mood that pervaded the Cincinnati conference led the participants to approve a Declaration of Principles, which contained the following recommendations:

> The progressive classification of prisoners, based on merit, and not on mere arbitrary principle, as age. . . . Since hope is a more potent agent than fear [we should establish] . . . a system of rewards . . . 1. A diminution of sentence. 2. A participation of prisoners in their earnings. 3. A gradual withdrawal of prison restraints. 4. Constantly increasing privileges . . . earned by good conduct. . . . The prisoner's destiny, during his incarceration, should be placed, measurably, in his own hands. . . . Preemptory sentences ought to be replaced by those of indeterminate duration—sentences limited only by satisfactory proof of reformation should be substituted for those measured by mere lapse of time.[14]

This declaration offered two new principles for the organization of the penitentiary. It urged that, first, "prisoner self-respect should be cultivated to the utmost, and every effort made to give back to him his manhood," and second, that the prisoner should determine his own destiny: "he must be . . . able through his own exertions, to continually better his own condition. A regulated self-interest must be brought into play."[15]

The basic principles of this reform model were derived from the penal experiments of Alexander Maconochie and Sir Walter Crofton. Although the notion of training prisoners for freedom had first been advocated by Cesare Beccaria and Jeremy Bentham, Alexander Maconochie put their ideas into practice at the Norfolk Island Penal Colony in Australia. Maconochie replaced the barbarous practices in effect before his arrival with a "mark" system that provided incentives for good conduct. Sir Walter Crofton, who later implemented the mark system in the Irish prison system, believed that prisoners must be trained for their return to society. Satisfactory work and performance in school were necessary to qualify the prisoner for transfer from the maximum security facility to an "intermediate" prison. Good behavior in these facilities entitled the prisoner to a ticket of leave, which meant release to community supervision.

In 1876, the Elmira Reformatory, the first and most ambitious attempt to

---

[14]*Transactions of the National Congress on Penitentiary and Reformatory Discipline,* cited in David Fogel, ". . . *We Are the Living Proof" : The Justice Model for Corrections* (Cincinnati: Anderson, 1975), p. 32.

[15]Ibid., p. 32.

fulfill the Declaration of Principles, was opened in New York State. Reformers believed this institution would be able to reform youthful offenders between 16 and 30 years of age. The basic reforms put into effect were: (1) a "mark system," by which prisoners could receive marks for satisfactory behavior; (2) the use of graded levels of accommodation and privilege; (3) programs of educational and vocational training, moral and religious instruction, military drill, and athletics and gymnastics; (4) the indeterminate sentence and parole; and (5) aftercare supervision. Zebulon Brockway, who was superintendent for twenty years, was responsible for deciding when a prisoner was ready for release; thus, anyone who failed to respond appropriately to the reformatory's programs would be retained.

Reformatories were built in twelve states in the next two decades, but the lofty principles of Elmira and the other reformatories fell far short in practice. Reformers soon realized these reformatories were still violent, stone-walled, multitiered fortresses, no more conducive to reform than were the old Auburn-type penitentiaries.

The Progressive Era: Individualized Treatment

Another wave of optimism swept through society during the Progressive Era— the period from 1900 to 1920—and led to the development of individualized treatment of offenders. The rise of community-based corrections, the use of the medical model to rehabilitate offenders, experimentation with inmate self-government, and the expansion of indeterminate sentencing all resulted from this emphasis on individualized treatment.[16]

The reformers' optimism during these years, which encouraged them to find new answers to old problems, can be traced to three influences. First, the new social sciences assured them that, through the approach of positivism, problems could be solved. The initial step in this new method was to gather all the "facts" of the case. Equipped with the data, reformers would then be able to analyze the issue in "scientific" fashion and discover the correct solution. Reformers also believed that the data would provide them with all the arguments necessary for winning approval of remedial programs from the legislature. Second, the Progressives had ultimate confidence in the benefits of the American system. The basic social goal was for all Americans to become middle-class citizens, abandoning Old World vices, becoming hardworking, and accumulating private property. Third, the reformers believed that the state could exercise its authority to correct imbalances, to bring about equality, and to realize the common good.

Armed with these beliefs, reformers set out to deal with the problem of criminality in American society. They were confident that they knew how to analyze the causes of criminality. The Progressives looked first to environmental factors, or poverty, as the most important cause of crime and concluded that no one raised

---

[16]This section on the progressive era is largely adapted from David J. Rothman, *Conscience and Convenience: The Asylum and Its Alternatives in Progressive America* (Boston: Little, Brown, 1980), pp. 32–60.

in poverty could be held strictly accountable for his or her actions. Some Progressives also were attracted to the doctrine of eugenics and argued that the biological limitations of offenders drove them to criminal behavior. But the psychological origins of crime eventually came to be more widely accepted than either environmental or biological origins.

Psychiatrists, the first proponents of the psychological origins of crime, contended that criminals were sick rather than bad, and that it was sickness that drove them to crime. They had little patience with the concept of personal responsibility, or culpability, of offenders because they were more concerned with finding cures than assigning moral blame. These founders of the therapeutic state promised that they could cure the disease of criminality by dealing with offenders on an individual basis, by prescribing the proper kind of treatment, and by implementing the ideal treatment plan.

Individualized treatment and the juvenile court.   The concept of the psychological origins of crime had been accepted in juvenile justice from the founding of the first juvenile court in Cook County (Chicago) in 1899. Based upon the philosophy of *parens patriae,* by which the state was established as a surrogate parent for children in trouble, the actions of the juvenile court were to be in the best interests of the child. Or to put it in the language of the 1905 *Commonwealth* v. *Fisher* decision, the purpose of the court "is not for the punishment of offenders but for the salvation of children . . . whose salvation may become the duty of the state."[17] Juvenile judges turned to professional social workers and psychiatrists to resolve through individual counseling the problems that drove the youth to crime.

Individualized treatment and community-based corrections.   Juvenile probation became receptive to psychological positivism at the turn of the twentieth century. Because the early growth of the juvenile court in Chicago coincided with the development of professional social work in that city, social work graduates who had been trained in the concepts of social diagnosis and social casework were attracted to positions as juvenile probation officers and were naturally receptive to psychological positivism. Several decades elapsed before social workers were able to adapt casework principles to adult probation, but by the 1920s, the impersonal professionalism of the counselor-therapist had replaced the image of the monitor of probation compliance and the friendly benefactor.[18]

Psychological positivism also influenced the development of parole in the early decades of the twentieth century. The growing acceptance of the parole board as the arbiter of whether or not criminals were resocialized or cured went hand-in-hand with the belief that it was indeed possible to cure offenders of their criminality. The parole board was charged with examining each offender's case history, in-

---

[17]213 Pa. 48, 62 A, pp. 198–200.
[18]Conrad, "Correctional Treatment."

cluding institutional behavior and earlier behavior, to determine his or her psychological readiness for release. The parole officer, like the probation officer, was expected to both watch over and treat correctional clients.

Individualized treatment and inmate self-government. In the second decade of the twentieth century, Warden Thomas Mott started the Mutual Welfare League at Sing Sing Prison in New York State. This league was based upon the Progressives' assumption that it was necessary to individualize and democratize the prison. As inmates became responsible for their own conduct, they believed, the prison would become a faithful model of society. As long as the Mutual Welfare League lasted, inmates elected a board of delegates, which in turn elected an executive board. The executive board constituted the prison's rule-making and enforcement body, subject to review by the delegates. Its members supervised prisoners in the shops and in the yard; they organized fund-raising efforts and used the proceeds to provide movies and additional recreational equipment. The executive board also elected a judiciary board to hear cases of infractions and levy penalties. In short, the League was intended to make prisoners "not good prisoners, but good citizens . . . [and] fit them for the free life to which, sooner or later they [were] to return."[19] The Mutual Welfare League soon met with sharp criticism and was one of the chief reasons that Mott was replaced as warden of Sing Sing. But the model of the prison as a community persisted through the 1920s and 1930s.[20]

Thus, by the end of the second decade of the twentieth century, all the basic ingredients of modern corrections were firmly in place. The medical model was established for curing the disease of criminality. Community-based corrections, with the development of probation and parole, competed with the dominance of institutionalization for dealing with the crime problem. The juvenile court, with its doctrine of *parens patriae,* was founded for treating youth in trouble. The next step, of course, was to implement the medical model in the prison setting.

The Medical Model and Rehabilitation in Prison

Under the leadership of psychiatrists, who were well established in prisons by the 1920s, the medical model was implemented in correctional institutions throughout the nation. Their basic goal was to make the prison into a hospital, or treatment center. One supporter of the medical model expressed how it could transform the prison:

We have to treat [inmates] as sick people, which in every respect they are. . . . It is the hope of the more progressive elements in psychopathology and criminology that the guard and the jailer will be replaced by the nurse, and the judge by the psychiatrist,

---

[19]Thomas Osborne, *Prisons and Common Sense,* cited in Rothman, *Conscience and Convenience,* p. 123.

[20]Rothman, *Conscience and Convenience,* p. 123.

whose sole attempt will be to treat and cure the individual instead of merely to punish him. Then and only then can we hope to lessen, even if not entirely to abolish, crime, the most costly burden that society has today.[21]

The first goal of advocates of the medical model in prison was to establish diagnostic centers for all new prisoners. They further urged the development of a variety of institutions, each serving the special needs identified at the diagnostic centers. But the psychiatrists' attention to the details of classification did not carry over into the design of the rehabilitative programs themselves. More attention was given to diagnosis, because psychiatrists were uncertain of how they would translate their broad explanations of criminality into specific recommendations for cure.[22]

The members of the treatment team were joined in the 1930s and 1940s by psychologists, psychiatric social workers, educators, and chaplains. Although chaplains had been involved in the rehabilitative process since the establishment of penitentiaries in the 1820s and educators had been involved since the implementation of the reform model at Elmira in the 1870s, they now became part of a team that would use the medical model to cure prisoners of the disease of criminality before they were paroled to their home communities.

There are many reasons for the popularity from the 1930s through the 1960s of the medical model in correctional institutions and in community-based corrections. Such rehabilitative treatment seemed far more humane than merely punishing juvenile and adult offenders for the harm they had inflicted upon society. The medical model also appeared modern and scientific. In contrast to the philosophy of "an eye for an eye and a tooth for a tooth," the basis of retribution of old, the medical model promised through professional intervention to restore society's misfits to useful and acceptable lives and activities. Furthermore, the medical model's focus on the individual's problems meant society had to deal with offenders, a far easier task than dealing with the social and economic factors that resulted in poverty, discrimination, and social injustice.

However, by the end of the 1960s, the medical model had largely been discredited in American corrections. First, there were claims that empirical studies had documented the inability of institutional treatment to prevent recidivism.[23] Second, critics asserted that the medical model's basic premises about change were questionable, arguing that the medical model not only overestimated the ability of the treatment agent to effect change but also made erroneous assumptions about human nature. Third, the critics charged that the brutal and inhumane prison environment was no place for treatment to take place. How could a group therapy session be efficacious when the inmate returned to a cell where he might be sexually assaulted and had to deal with the ever present tumult of prison life?

---

[21]Benjamin Kaysman, cited in Edwin Sutherland and Donald Cressey, *Criminology*, 9th ed. (Philadelphia: Lippincott, 1973), p. 605.

[22]Rothman, *Conscience and Convenience*, p. 125.

[23]See Chapter 2 for the findings of the various empirical studies.

The Reintegration Model
and Community-Based Corrections

An antiinstitutional movement in American society, as well as the growth of a spirit of receptivity to reform, led to the development of the reintegration model. The basic emphasis of the reintegration model was on keeping offenders in the community and on helping them reintegrate themselves within the community. "The task of corrections," according to the 1967 President's Commission on Law Enforcement and Administration of Justice, was to build or rebuild "solid ties between the offender and community life. . . . [24] This involved "restoring family ties, obtaining employment and education, securing in the large sense a place for the offender in the routine functioning of society."[25] The commission added that this form of rehabilitative philosophy was charged not only with changing the offender, but also with changing the community.[26]

Guided by the reintegration model, based on recommendations by a number of blue-ribbon commissions, and funded generously by federal dollars, community-based programs sprouted in nearly every state. The reintegration model proposed that the role of the probation officer—as well as of the parole officer—shift from caseworker to community resource manager. This new role was based on the premise "that the probation officer will have primary responsibility for meshing a probationer's identified needs with a range of available services."[27] The array of community programs also included residential facilities for probationers and parolees, community assistance services for parolees, daytime treatment interventions for delinquents, and youth service bureaus and other diversion programs for juveniles and adults.

Proponents of the reintegration model further proposed that offenders placed in short- and long-term correctional institutions required reintegration services. Work release was one such reintegration program instituted in jails across the nation at this time. Prisons and training schools, especially minimum security ones, began to offer a wide range of reentry programs, including prerelease, work release, educational release, and home furloughs.

However, the popularity of reintegration philosophy and community corrections dropped dramatically in the mid- and late-1970s when the public mood changed to support of a hard-line or a "get-tough-with-criminals" approach. The public became resistant to establishing new residential facilities in the community. Public pressure also encouraged legislatures and departments of corrections to upgrade the

---

[24]The President's Commission on Law Enforcement and Administration of Justice, *Task Force Report: Corrections* (Washington, D.C.: GPO, 1967), p. 7.

[25]Ibid.

[26]Ibid.

[27]National Advisory Commission on Criminal Justice Standards and Goals, *Corrections* (Washington, D.C.: GPO, 1973), p. 322.

criteria for eligibility for work release, educational release, and home furloughs, resulting in a significant reduction of the number of eligible offenders.

TREATMENT TODAY

The emergence of new treatment models from the ashes of the old has time after time restored hope in the rehabilitation of offenders. But in the mid-1970s, however, correctional treatment instead received the most biting attack in the history of American corrections. In 1974, the late Robert Martinson stunned correctional personnel and the public in general by announcing that, "With few and isolated exceptions, the rehabilitative efforts that have been reported so far have had no appreciable effect on recidivism."[28] This was quickly translated into the conclusion that "nothing works" in correctional treatment. Martinson's pronouncement, along with a 1975 book coauthored with Douglas Lipton and Judith Wilks—*The Effectiveness of Correctional Treatment*—persuaded many that the time had come to bury the rehabilitation model and to move on to more fruitful endeavors.[29] The instantaneous popularity of the "nothing works" thesis sparked an intense and spirited debate.

Ted Palmer, a highly regarded correctional researcher in California, challenged Lipton, Martinson, and Wilks' research by examining eighty-two studies mentioned in their study and showing that thirty-nine of them, or 48 percent, had yielded positive or partly positive results in terms of recidivism.[30] Palmer then used Martinson's own words to reject the "nothing works" thesis:

> These programs seem to work best when they are new, when their subjects are amenable to treatment in the first place, and when the counselors are not only trained people, but "good people" as well.[31]

Martinson sharply reacted to Palmer's review of his work:

> [I spent] the better part of four months struggling to decipher [Palmer's] research design, . . . to translate the footnotes, appendices, cross references, and tables from the original Egyptian. . . . Correctional treatment is about nine-tenths pageantry, rumination, and rubbish. . . ."[32]

[28]Robert Martinson, "What Works?—Questions and Answers about Prison Reform," *Public Interest* 35 (Spring 1974): 22–54.

[29]Douglas Lipton, Robert Martinson, and Judith Wilks, *The Effectiveness of Correctional Treatment: A Survey of Treatment Evaluation Studies* (New York: Praeger, 1975).

[30]Ted Palmer, "Martinson Revisited," *Journal of Research in Crime and Delinquency* 22 (April 1976): 180–191.

[31]Ibid., p. 137.

[32]Robert Martinson, "California Research at the Crossroads," *Crime and Delinquency* 22 (April 1976): 180–191.

But Martinson appeared to modify his opinion somewhat late in the 1970s when he conceded that by "disregarding the positive achievements of treatment, he threw out the baby but clung rigorously to the bathwater."[33] He also noted that the level of research technology was inferior in offender rehabilitation studies and stated that the apparent ineffectiveness of treatment could be related to inadequate research design rather than to lack of actual program success.[34] Martinson further indicated, "And contrary to my previous position, some treatment programs *do* have an appreciable effect on recidivism. Some programs are indeed beneficial; of equal or greater significance, some programs are harmful."[35]

Four Ideologies of Correctional Treatment

Today, four ideologies, or theoretical positions, concerning correctional treatment have crystallized in American society: (1) the reaffirmation of rehabilitation; (2) the position that a humane justice system requires treatment services for those offenders who want them; (3) the belief that the rehabilitation model has resulted in the coddling of criminals and the victimization of society; and (4) the position that treatment, as another piecemeal reform, actually encourages the continuation of the abuses of the existing correctional system. (The first three ideologies will be examined more extensively in Chapters 2 through 4.)

Reaffirmation of rehabilitation liberals.   Advocates of this perspective continue to support the efficacy of correctional treatment. They justify their support by claiming that rehabilitative programs remain a major goal of the correctional system and are conducted throughout the correctional process; that the ideology of rehabilitation protects society and the criminal against the increased repressiveness of the conservatives' position; and that rehabilitation has historically been an important motive underlying correctional reform and thereby has increased the humanity of the correctional process.[36] Some taking this stand claim that correctional treatment in the 1970s did make a number of impressive gains and that it is unfair to judge programs today against those in use prior to the 1970s. Most of those holding this perspective are content to retain indeterminate sentencing and the parole board, but there is some agreement that rehabilitative programs should become less a condition of release than they have been in the past.

Justice model liberals.   Those who hold this perspective contend that a humane justice system requires that treatment services be provided for those of-

---

[33]"It Has Come to Our Attention," *Federal Probation* 43 (March 1979): 86.

[34]Robert Martinson, "New Findings, New Views: A Note of Caution Regarding Sentencing Reform," *Hofstra Law Review* 7 (Winter 1979): 244.

[35]Ibid.

[36]Francis T. Cullen and Karen E. Gilbert, *Reaffirming Rehabilitation* (Cincinnati: Anderson, 1982), pp. 253, 257, and 261.

fenders who want them and can benefit from them.[37] Yet such treatment should be voluntary and have nothing to do with the length of an inmate's confinement. They also argue that the indeterminate sentencing system and the parole board should be replaced with a determinate sentencing structure. They claim that the basic goal of the correctional process should be justice and fairness rather than treatment— offenders deserve to be punished because they have broken the law. As part of their criticism of the rehabilitation, or medical, model, they accuse the model of contributing to the victimization of the offender. In the name of treatment, they assert, criminals have been victimized through the denial of their due process rights and prolonged incarceration in violent and inhumane institutions.

The conservative perspective. Proponents of the hard-line approach to crime are relieved that the rehabilitation model is no longer the primary goal of the correctional process because they believe that it has been ineffective in reducing recidivism and has contributed to the coddling of criminals and the victimization of society. Those who hold this position see punishment as more likely to deter crime and to provide protection to society.[38] They also claim that the establishment of law and order demands firm methods of crime control, such as a greater reliance on incapacitation, the use of the death penalty, the implementation of determinate and mandatory sentences throughout the nation, and a "get-tough" policy with juvenile criminals.

The radical perspective. Advocates of the radical perspective also want to dismiss correctional treatment, but for far different reasons from those of supporters of the conservative perspective. Proponents of the radical perspective hold that treatment is another piecemeal reform, which, in attempting to accommodate itself to correctional settings, actually encourages the continuation of the abuses of the existing correctional system. Those holding this position contend that fundamental change in prisons can take place only through radical change in society itself.[39] They argue that American society is plagued with crime and delinquency because delinquents and criminals form a subservient class that is alienated, powerless, and prone to economic manipulation.[40] In other words, it is society, rather than the criminal, that is in need of radical change.

---

[37]See Fogel, ". . . *We Are the Living Proof*" and David Fogel and Joe Hudson, eds., *Justice as Fairness* (Cincinnati: Anderson, 1981) for the development of the justice model perspective.

[38]See James Q. Wilson, *Thinking about Crime* (New York: Basic, 1975) and Ernest Van den Haag, *Punishing Criminals: Concerning a Very Old and Painful Question* (New York: Basic, 1975) for this conservative perspective. Both © Basic Books, 1975.

[39]Erik Olin Wright, *The Politics of Punishment: A Critical Analysis of Prisons in America* (New York: Harper & Row, 1973), pp. 313–314.

[40]Barry Krisberg and James Austin, *The Children of Ishmael: Critical Perspectives on Juvenile Justice* (Palo Alto, CA: Mayfield, 1978), p. 1.

Implications of These Perspectives
for Correctional Treatment

Those who reaffirm rehabilitation, those who advocate that a human justice system requires treatment programs for those who want them, and those who charge that rehabilitation has resulted in the coddling of criminals and the victimization of society are all affecting crime policy today. The hard-line mood of society, as well as the lack of proof of the effectiveness of rehabilitative programs, precludes the acceptance of treatment as the basic purpose of the criminal justice system. The rise of determinate sentencing requires that correctional interventions be voluntary rather than compulsory for release. The emphasis on justice and fairness in handling offenders mandates that treatment not perpetuate existing abuses in the juvenile and adult justice systems. The conflict perspective reminds proponents of treatment that economic, political, and social conditions of society influence who becomes a criminal; the way he or she is handled by the justice system; and the difficulties this individual faces in walking away from crime. Finally, the massive attack on treatment that surfaced in the 1970s compels proponents of rehabilitation to seek new models that are more effective than the medical model and to develop improved technologies in juvenile and adult corrections. But in order for correctional treatment to emerge in a different and vastly better form, the challenges discussed in the next section must be met.

CHALLENGES FACING TREATMENT
IN THE 1980s

Correctional treatment faces at least four major challenges today: to develop better theory and research; to provide improved programs for those receptive to change; to expand the resources in community-based and institutional corrections; and to create more humane correctional environments.

Develop Better Theory and Research

In the past decade, correctional researchers have begun to explore what works for which offenders in what contexts. As part of their inquiry, they have thus far concluded the following:

> A single cure (or intervention) cannot be relied upon to deal with the variety of complex problems leading to criminal behavior.
>
> Recidivism should not be the only dimension used to evaluate correctional treatment.
>
> There are certain characteristics competent treatment personnel appear to have in common.
>
> There are common elements in effective treatment interventions.

Offenders who exit from criminal careers appear to have certain experiences in common.

Improving on the elementary level of knowledge concerning what works for particular groups of offenders now requires that careful attention be given to the treatment process itself. Through research, a technique must be found (one is proposed in Chapter 9) to determine which treatment efforts are most effective with which particular group of offenders. The next step is to make certain that treatment interventions are based upon sound theoretical assumptions. Then, treatment plans must be designed with sufficient strength and integrity to accomplish the goals of the program. Finally, rigorous research methods must be used to evaluate what actually has taken place in the correctional intervention.[41]

Provide Improved Programs for Those Receptive to Change

Many criminal and juvenile offenders are unlikely candidates for profiting from treatment. They find the rationale, language, and process of treatment foreign to their world views. Many offenders also reject the notion that they need to change or to make improvement in their lives; as one stated, "Everyone is ripping off society; I just got caught."[42] Some juvenile and adult offenders also are still excited by the imagined thrills of the life of crime and cannot wait to get back to the real action on the streets. But even if an offender is determined to "go straight," the difficulties of finding a job may push him or her back to crime. Many offenders lack high school diplomas and have little or no viable job experience. Their lack of marketable skills, coupled with the label of criminal, means they are not considered good job risks. Furthermore, many adult and juvenile offenders have abused alcohol or drugs, and the stresses they face in returning to the community make it difficult not to resume the use of these substances.

In the development of effective programs for those offenders interested in self-improvement or change, the needs of offenders must be carefully considered. Offenders need a high school diploma or a G.E.D.; they need marketable skills so they can find jobs. They also need support groups in the community to help them deal with the stresses of community life. Finally, they need the hope that they can survive in the community without returning to crime.

The model programs discussed in later chapters show that correctional interventions can provide meaningful experiences for offenders. However, the overall quality of correctional interventions must be improved so that more programs provide positive experiences for correctional clients. The challenge is a double one at present because the rise of determinate sentencing nationwide means that treatment

---

[41]Susan Martin, Lee Sechrest, and Robin Redner, eds., *Rehabilitation of Criminal Offenders: New Directions for Research* (Washington, D.C.: National Academy of Sciences, 1981), p. 81.

[42]Interviewed in December 1981.

will no longer be required in many states, so that only those who are interested will elect to involve themselves in programs.

Expand the Resources in Community-Based and Institutional Corrections

Probation and parole agencies, as well as residential and institutional facilities, all lack adequate resources for effective correctional treatment. The meagerness of governmental support to juvenile and adult justice agencies is a major reason for these inadequate resources. The low level of funding is in part a result of the phasing out of the Law Enforcement Assistance Administration (LEAA), which was an important source of funding for juvenile and adult corrections. In a time of economic austerity, there is every reason to believe that juvenile and adult corrections will be forced to operate on even smaller fiscal allocations than in the past.

At the time of sentencing, judges are faced with inadequate resources to meet needs. A convicted defendant may need substance abuse counseling but there is none available. A probationer may need a "halfway-in" residential placement, but the only alternatives are continued probation, jail, or prison. A defendant may require mental health services rather than processing through the criminal justice system, but these services are not available or are too costly.

Probation and parole officers are severely handicapped by excessive caseloads, created by the inability or unwillingness of state or local governmental bodies to hire more officers. Some county probation officers may have to supervise as many as three hundred clients. Not surprisingly, little actual supervision takes place because the time and energy of the probation or parole officer is spread too thin, a situation which is made worse by copious reports for the court and by other paperwork, court appearances, trips to the jail or prison to see clients, and various other duties that are required.

Inadequate resources also present a problem in community-based residential facilities. Employment counselors, a critical treatment position in light of the employment needs of this population, are rarely found in residential programs. The lack of sufficient treatment staff also makes conducting ongoing individual and group therapy for residents nearly impossible. Line staff members typically are poorly paid, work long hours, and face hectic schedules. Consequently, they have high rates of burnout and job turnover. These factors lead to instability in the environments of residential programs.

Finally, inadequate resources are a critical problem in training schools and prisons. One of the reasons treatment has a marginal role in correctional institutions is that usually there are too few staff members to make an impact upon inmates. Many intervention programs also lack needed services and equipment. In addition, treatment often receives little support from institutional administrators and sometimes is sabotaged by custodial staff.

This challenge will not be an easy one for correctional treatment to meet at present, especially because of current fiscal austerity. But, as those in some juris-

dictions have found, continued lobbying in the political area has resulted in much better resources being allocated for criminal justice agencies.

Create More Humane Correctional Environments

Too many correctional environments are incompatible with effective correctional treatment. This criticism is more true of prisons, but criticism of community-based programs is not unjustified.

Big House prisons, especially, are violent and overcrowded jungles. New inmates learn very quickly that survival is their primary concern. In these facilities, there is more violence among inmates than ever before in the history of American corrections. In 1974, one in twenty-three California prisoners suffered a violent assault. Since most assaults do not come to the attention of officials, the true prisoner victim rate may be as high as one in ten.[43] The violence and brutality of prisoners toward one another is expressed far more often in sexual victimization than in stabbings or slayings. Paul Keve, former commissioner of corrections in two states, has expressed this well: "Prison is a barely controlled jungle where the aggressive and the strong will exploit the weak, and the weak are dreadfully aware of it."[44]

The increased use of confinement also has resulted in overcrowded prisons. In 1972, there were 196,000 prisoners confined in federal and state institutions; by December 31, 1982, there were 412,303. Significantly, the 42,915 inmates added to the population in 1982 represented the largest one-year increase in history. California, Texas, and Florida led the other states, each adding more than 4,000 inmates in 1982.[45]

Overcrowding has led to a number of problems that cripple treatment. Overcrowded institutions mean insufficient jobs and programs for inmates who want them. Overcrowding also means inhumane settings for treatment: Two or three inmates may be housed in a cell intended for one, basic services may be denied, and due process rights of inmates may be overlooked. Because overcrowded institutions are more difficult to manage, greater emphasis is placed on custodial concern and there is less concern for treatment. The tensions of overcrowded prisons also lead to violence, which results in inmates spending more time locked in their cells, with fewer opportunities to participate in programs. Finally, overcrowded institutions create more stress among staff; accordingly, both treatment and custody staff experience lower morale, reduced job satisfactions, and high rates of turnover.

Community-based correctional programs also have problems with inhumane environments. Frequently, facilities are located in undesirable neighborhoods, residents must live in dilapidated housing, and overcrowding is again a problem. The quality of life in these facilities is a further problem because of the lack of meaningful

---

[43]Lee Bowker, *Prison Victimization* (New York: Elsevier, 1980), p. 25.

[44]Paul Keve, *Prison Life and Human Worth* (Minneapolis: University of Minnesota Press, 1974).

[45]Stephen Gettinger, "The Prison Population," *Corrections Magazine* 9 (June 1983): 6. The statistics are taken from the 1982 prison census of the Federal Bureau of Justice statistics.

activity, particularly for those residents not on work release. Also, especially in diversion programs and drug therapeutic communities, due process rights are sometimes denied residents.

The challenge of improving correctional environments will be addressed in Chapter 13, and recommendations will be given for ways in which correctional environments can become more compatible with meaningful correctional treatment.

SUMMARY

It is important today to evaluate fairly where correctional treatment has been, where it is, and where it appears to be going in the future. To open this discussion, this chapter has reviewed the role of treatment in American corrections and considered the challenges that treatment faces. Nearly every new phase or cycle of correctional reform in the United States has begun with great optimism about making the prison into a community, a school, or a hospital; more recently, the community has been looked to as the ideal setting for delivering the services of correctional treatment. Indeed, the history of correctional treatment has been one of good intentions as one method after another has been employed to treat offenders.

Some of the traditional forms of treatment, such as the medical model, the use of indeterminate sentencing and the parole board, and compulsory treatment, appear to be on their way out. But this should be an enlightening time to study correctional treatment because, as subsequent chapters will show, the theoretical foundations and the ability of programs to deliver the services they are supposed to deliver are being examined, a variety of innovative programs are being developed and evaluated, and more attention is being given to the environments in which treatment takes place. Thus, correctional treatment may well be better in the present and the future than it has been in the past.

DISCUSSION QUESTIONS

1. "A history of good intentions" is how one scholar has defined the attempts of corrections to deal with offenders. Is this a fair assessment of the history of correctional treatment in this nation? Why?
2. "Nothing works," claimed Robert Martinson. What did he mean by this and how did Ted Palmer argue against it?
3. What are the basic ideological perspectives on correctional treatment?
4. Define the challenges facing correctional treatment at the present time. Which is the most serious challenge? Why?

2

Rehabilitative Philosophy

Objectives

1. *To indicate why treatment has a place in corrections, in an interview with Ted Palmer.*

2. *To discuss the underpinnings of rehabilitative philosophy in the medical, adjustment, and reintegration models.*

3. *To reveal the scope of rehabilitative philosophy in corrections in the United States.*

4. *To evaluate the strengths and limitations of rehabilitative philosophy for corrections today.*

The goal of rehabilitative philosophy is to change an offender's character, attitudes, or behavior patterns so as to diminish his or her criminal propensities.[1] As indicated in Chapter 1, rehabilitative philosophy came under increased attack in the 1960s and 1970s, but instead of conceding the burial that critics wanted to give it, proponents accepted the challenge to find new ways to improve offender rehabilitation. Whether the emerging form of rehabilitative philosophy will attain the respect and public acceptance rehabilitation had in the past is questionable, but, stripped of the medical approach, rehabilitative philosophy does promise to be more effective in achieving positive change with offenders.

This chapter begins with an interview with Ted Palmer, who rose to the defense of rehabilitative philosophy when its effectiveness was challenged by Robert Martinson and colleagues. The philosophy of rehabilitative philosophy then is examined, following which the scope, the defense, and the criticisms of the rehabilitative ideal are discussed.

Box 2-1 Interview with Ted Palmer

QUESTION: In terms of correctional treatment, you are acknowledged as one of the "defenders of the faith." Why do you believe that treatment has a place in corrections?

PALMER: First, I prefer the word *intervention* to *treatment*. By intervention, I include not only what is ordinarily thought of as treatment, such as counseling and vocational training, but also such means of external control as surveillance and specific restrictions. By intervention, I mean an overall effort which centers around programmed assistance and which, ideally, is both practical and personalized. Intervention need not necessarily seek to "rehabilitate" offenders in the sense of changing them in a deep or very broad way, though it may do so with some. Nonetheless, intervention should try to help offenders better cope with and adjust to their immediate environments; insofar as it achieves this goal, it can help society and offenders alike.

The *socially* centered goal of intervention is the reduction or elimination of illegal behavior. However, its *offender-centered* goal of intervention is to increase the individual's motivation and ability to pursue personally satisfying yet socially acceptable opportunities and to do so for extended periods of time. To achieve the latter goal, some individuals might need little more than encouragement or practical advice in terms of using the strengths or supports they already have. But individuals who have had numerous arrests might need additional resources to deal with pressures that could weaken their resolve or prevent them from making a serious effort in the first place. Still other offenders might need a combination of these approaches or an emphasis on specific incentives instead. Thus, each of these situations would involve the use of programmed assistance, though the degree of programming could vary from virtually none to quite a lot, and the type of programming could vary as well.

It is true many offenders want no assistance, either initially or later, even on a voluntary basis; these are not necessarily multiple offenders. In addition, most first-time offenders probably require—and, indeed, seem to desire—little if any intervention. Yet even if we eliminate these two sizable categories of offenders, a very large number or percentage remains. More specifically, I believe that many offenders—usually repeat of-

[1]Andrew von Hirsh, *Doing Justice: The Choice of Punishments* (New York: Hill and Wang, 1976), p. 12.

fenders, including many multiple offenders—*want* to broaden their social opportunities and personal horizons and recognize intervention as one way of doing so. These offenders sometimes describe this aim more in terms of "improving their miserable lot." It is especially, though not exclusively, toward these individuals that intervention could be profitably and appropriately directed. I think it would be difficult to maintain that offenders, simply because they are or have been offenders, do not genuinely seek assistance. Though some offenders do indeed "play the treatment game," this does not apply to the majority. Even some of those who "play the treatment game" become accepting and motivated, often increasingly so, once they experience concrete benefits from the program.

It should come as little surprise that a great many offenders are quite capable of recognizing the potential value of intervention and can keep this awareness uppermost in their minds. To assume that youthful and adult offenders cannot recognize or soon be brought to recognize and accept the potential value of vocational training, employment counseling, and individual or group counseling would be to look upon them as defective or thoroughly indifferent—more so, perhaps, than in the "medical model" itself.

Today's intervention programs, despite their many shortcomings by omission and commission, are the only approaches that show promise of helping a substantial portion of known offenders focus on their needs and life circumstances in concrete, individualized terms and on more than a fleeting or tangential basis. Programs that carefully focus on these areas should receive the support of society and its key decision-makers, especially if they show promise of meeting such needs and/ or reducing recidivism in a humane and relatively efficient way. In my opinion, society has no humane grounds for abandoning such programs as long as it has nothing to substitute for them; nor by abolishing them would society be serving its own interests with respect to self-pro-

tection via crime reduction—humane considerations aside.

Even apart from self-protection, society, by its professed, longstanding traditions and ideals, has a "responsibility" for providing at least some programmed assistance for offenders as human beings. This tradition relates not only to the general concepts of individual worth and potential, but to the more specific principle that every human being should have as much opportunity as possible to better himself and his existence, regardless of the past. This argument is not effectively countered or substantially weakened by instances of cold-blooded and/or mass murderers, etc. That is, even if one wished to rescind or limit the principle in question in the case of individuals who commit such crimes, little if any reason would exist to deny intervention to most offenders. In and out of prison, an offender should not be left, so to speak, on a barren island with little to do but pass time—certainly not if he *wishes* to better his lot.

The view that society has no humane grounds for abandoning today's more promising programs is valid despite recent developments with regard to "deserved punishments" or "deserts." By itself, the idea of making the punishment fit the crime and standardizing dispositions wherever possible does not address the specifics of an offender's future—his concrete needs and opportunities within an often demanding environment outside prison. Insofar as intervention can address the task of motivating or realistically helping an offender come to grips with that environment, it promotes society's own goal of self-protection as well, not just the *offender*-centered goal of intervention.

Fairness or fair treatment by the justice system can help create a tolerable, believable, sometimes supportive atmosphere for involvement and decision-making by offenders. Yet, by itself, fair treatment does not supply the direction, does not arouse the motivation, and does not provide the feedback or personal reward that must exist before realistic, satisfying decisions are made and maintained by those individuals. Thus, for many offenders, fairness without programmed assistance can be empty, even blind, and programs without fairness can be futile, even pathetic.

Finally, despite the controversial, highly coercive way correctional intervention has sometimes been used, its goal of providing assistance to offenders need not conflict with those of various reform movements that made substantial gains during the 1970s. In short, intervention need not be an obstacle to progress within such areas as determinate sentencing, deinstitutionalization of status offenders, and prisoners' rights. I believe that correctional intervention (1) can dissociate itself from the more questionable or undesirable practices of the past and be integrated with numerous social concerns and legitimate strivings of the present and future, and (2) can operate in a framework of humane interaction and exchange outside as well as inside the justice system, despite the unavoidable need for some degree of social control. Thus, correctional intervention need not reinforce the stereotypes that were often encountered in the 1970s: that it is rigid, self-serving, and passé. Eventually, intervention can and doubtlessly will take its place as one more valuable tool—another option for society and offenders alike, a tool which can be used appropriately without negating society's desire for punishment or even without contradicting the concept of "just deserts."

QUESTION: Is the treatment debate at the same place it was during the mid-1970s or has it shifted? Or, to put the question differently, is correctional treatment more or less popular than it was during the Martinson-Palmer debates?

PALMER: The treatment debate has moved a little. I would say that as of mid-1976, which was about a year and a half after Martinson's "What Works?" article appeared, intervention—with much more emphasis on "treatment" than "control"—was generally unpopular, say at "3" on a 10-point scale. I'd describe it as having been at "6" or "7" during 1965–1970. By 1978–1979, about midpoint in the debate, correctional intervention might have hit a popularity of "4"; and, as of now, it has probably edged back to "5." That is, it is almost considered acceptable and legitimate again—on pragmatic and probably ethical grounds—but still not quite.

In short, correctional intervention has not yet regained its pre-Martinson, even pre-Attica, popularity in an absolute sense. Nevertheless, it is increasingly viewed as: (1) having promise in terms of producing moderate-to-sizable reductions in crime for at least a moderate and possibly sizable portion of the correctional population, especially the "middle-risk" group, and as (2) being definitely legitimate—if only on humane grounds—provided that a minimum of coercion is involved. Moreover, I believe correctional intervention is no longer viewed as being destructive of or antithetical to individuality, personal dignity, or autonomy. But it still is largely associated with the medical model, in the minds of many concerned critics. I *don't* think it has to be based on that model; that association is still holding it back.

QUESTION: Has your thinking about correctional treatment changed in the past ten years? If so, in what ways?

PALMER: In the past ten years, my thinking about correctional intervention has changed somewhat, but not in terms of "basics." I presently consider intervention no less valuable than before, in terms of socially centered and offender-centered goals. However, I appreciate its relative value *more* than before because I saw what often happened when intervention programs were substantially reduced or even eliminated during the years following "What Works?" and after the first rounds of sizable budget cuts. My views as to *what* constitute promising approaches have been reinforced, but not changed, in light of the large-scale reviews of research that appeared during the past eight to ten years. Finally, I think my view of what correctional intervention ordinarily *cannot* do—its practical limitations—has not changed.

QUESTION: Are correctional treatment programs in the 1980s better than they were in the past ten years? If so, in what ways?

PALMER: Yes and no. There has been some reduction in the number of overly and unnecessarily coercive programs, and that is a clear and important improvement. Of course, as long as a correctional setting is involved, some coercion is inevitable. But the coercion need not be as extensive or oppressive as it sometimes was in the past. This view is apart from my belief that some forms of coercion and relatively moderate pressure can often contribute to desirable results, particularly if pressure is combined with positive approaches.

I see only slight change, possibly just the start of a trend, in the number or at least percentage of programs with clearly positive elements, or at least elements that are positive under given conditions or for certain clients. For instance, some forms of family counseling seem quite valuable for certain kinds of clients and problems. Yet, even if researchers were to observe more positive outcomes for most such programs it would be very difficult to determine if the *programs* were better than before, if the *research* was more sophisticated and sensitive than before, if the client/program *match* was better than before, or if the results were due to a little bit of each.

I do see substantially increased awareness and concern by academicians and researchers about what has long been called program quality and is now often described as "integrity," "intensity," and "avoidance of drift." But I've rarely heard of policymakers and administrators translating this concern into markedly different programs. This translation lag, if it doesn't reflect simple unawareness of the concern in question, is probably due to the higher priorities and various constraints of the policymakers, not to their lack of understanding or acceptance of what is being suggested.

QUESTION: Is recidivism an adequate measure of the effectiveness of correctional treatment or do you believe that other measures should also be used to evaluate treatment?

PALMER: Although it has several major definitional problems, recidivism is the most important effectiveness index from the public policy perspective, and it can be used in a meaningful, nonmisleading way. Yet, wherever possible, other indices should also be used to assess impact on offenders' lives, such as those which reflect vocational, educational, and personal/community-life adjustment. Together, such indices can provide a broader or better rounded picture of a program's impact.

Most programs are not designed to impact just one particular area; in fact, many focus on areas other than recidivism. Nevertheless, if the public and its policymakers are to support a program, especially in financially strapped times, they will doubtlessly prefer to see evidence of that program's impact on illegal behavior, not just on educational adjustment or attitudes. Despite what researchers, academicians, and others may say, recidivism cannot be brushed aside, since the public and its policymakers want correctional interventions to serve not just offender-centered but socially centered goals. In effect, though recidivism may not be "sufficient," because it does not tell the whole story, it can be meaningful and in a real sense "necessary."

Dr. Ted Palmer is one of the leading researchers in corrections. He was the principal investigator of the California Community Treatment Project, has studied group homes, and recently completed a statewide evaluation of juvenile diversion programs. He is the author of *Correctional Intervention and Research* (Heath, 1978) and many articles in professional journals. He is currently a researcher for the California Department of Youth Authority.
Source: Interview conducted in December 1982. Used with permission.

Ted Palmer makes several important points that are helpful in understanding the changes taking place in correctional treatment today. First, he prefers the word "intervention" to "treatment" and expands the meaning of intervention to include rehabilitative efforts, programmed assistance to help offenders cope more effectively with their environments, and such means of external control as surveillance and specific restrictions. Second, he describes the socially centered and offender-centered goals of intervention. While the purpose of the former is to deter or reduce illegal behavior of offenders, the purpose of the latter is to effect short- or long-range positive outcomes with offenders. Third, Palmer points out that offenders vary in their interest in and need for intervention. Fourth, he defines the need for intervention in a humane justice system, especially for those offenders who want to better their lot. Fifth, Palmer believes that intervention is almost considered acceptable and legitimate again, for it has regained some of the popularity it lost in the 1970s. Sixth, he does see some positive gains made in improving program quality or integrity, but he questions whether policymakers have translated these gains into improved programs. Seventh, although the index of recidivism has problems and does not tell the whole story about the effectiveness of intervention, Palmer holds that it is a necessary index and cannot be brushed aside.

PHILOSOPHY OF THE REHABILITATIVE IDEAL

The rehabilitative ideal traditionally has been identified with the medical model, but because the adjustment and reintegration models are also committed to changing the offender, they too should be included under the more inclusive term of "rehabilitative philosophy." The three models have some important similarities and differences.

Philosophical Underpinnings of the Medical Model

Donal E. J. MacNamara, in his noteworthy essay on the medical model, provides a definition of the model:

> In its simplest (perhaps oversimplified) terms, the medical model as applied to corrections assumed the offender to be "sick" (physically, mentally, and/or socially); his offense to be a manifestation or symptom of his illness, a cry for help. . . . Basic to the medical model, although rather surprisingly denied by many of its proponents, is that the criminogenic factors are indigenous to the individual offender and that it is by doing "something" for, to, or with him that rehabilitation can be affected.[2]

---

[2]Donal E. J. MacNamara, "The Medical Model in Corrections: Requiescat in Pace," *Criminology* 14 (February 1977):439–440.

Francis Allen, in an essay which has become a classic on the rehabilitative ideal, clarifies the basic assumptions of the medical model: (1) that "human behavior is the product of antecedent causes"; (2) that it is the obligation of the scientist to discover these causes; (3) that knowledge of these antecedent causes makes it possible to control human behavior; and (4) that measures employed to treat the offender "should be designed to effect changes in the behavior of the convicted person in the interest of his own happiness, health, and satisfaction."[3]

The American Friends Service Committee's *Struggle for Justice* defines the underlying rationale of the medical model:

> [T]he dispassionate behavioral expert displaces judge and theologian. The particular criminal act becomes irrelevant except insofar as it has diagnostic significance in classifying and treating the actor's particular criminal typology. Carried to an extreme, the sentence for all crimes would be the same: an indeterminate commitment to imprisonment, probation, or parole, whichever was dictated at any particular time by the treatment program. Any sentence would be the time required to bring about rehabilitation, a period which might be a few weeks or a lifetime.[4]

In short, proponents of the medical model believe that crime is caused by factors that can be identified, isolated, treated, and cured. Punishment should be avoided because it does nothing to solve offenders' problems and it only reinforces the already negative concept that offenders have of themselves. The medical model also assumes that the criminal lacks the ability to exercise freedom of choice or to use reason.

Advocates of the medical model further contend that the legal definition of delinquency and criminal behavior should be broad and that victimless crimes and status offenses for juveniles, as well as crimes against victims, should remain on the books. Those competent in diagnosis and knowledge of human behavior, according to the medical model, should have wide decision-making authority in the juvenile and adult justice system. This model also encourages a much wider use of mental health facilities.

Philosophical Underpinnings of the Adjustment Model

In the late 1960s and 1970s, some proponents of rehabilitation became dissatisfied with the medical model. Although they agreed with the medical model that offenders are different from nonoffenders, need treatment, and can be "cured" by the scientific expert (a person trained in a particular counseling technique), they

---

[3]Francis A. Allen, *The Borderland of Criminal Justice* (Chicago: University of Chicago Press, 1964), p. 26.

[4]American Friends Service Committee, *Struggle for Justice* (New York: Hill and Wang, 1971), p. 37.

claimed that offenders are still able to be responsible and to make law-abiding decisions.[5]

The adjustment model is based upon four assumptions. First, offenders need help, or treatment, to conform to societal expectations. They need to be shown that their maladjustive behavior, negative attitudes, or inappropriate interpersonal relationships led them to an involvement with crime. Second, offenders have the capacity to live a crime-free life and, therefore, the emphasis of correctional treatment should be on the belief that offenders are responsible for their present actions. That is, while offenders cannot change the facts of their emotional and social deprivations of the past, they can demonstrate responsible behavior in the present and can avoid using their past problems as an excuse for delinquent or ciminal behavior. Third, the larger social environment and the individual's interaction with this environment are important factors in understanding antisocial behavior. Individuals can be taught alternatives that will allow them to live crime-free lives. Finally, punishment is seen only to increase offenders' alienation and behavior problems.

Reality therapy, transactional analysis (TA), guided group interaction (GGI), positive peer culture (PPC), milieu therapy, the therapeutic community, and behavior modification all are used to help offenders cope more effectively with their personal problems, their peers, and their environment. Most of these therapies are based on gaining insight, usually in a group context, but behavior modification is a social learning approach that tries to modify behavior through positive reinforcement techniques.

The adjustment approach to rehabilitation accepts a broad legal definition of crime and holds that scientific experts should share in the authority to make decisions in the criminal justice system. But instead of emphasizing the pathology of offenders as the medical model does, this approach is primarily concerned with helping offenders make a more socially acceptable adjustment to society. Finally, this approach discourages the wide use of institutionalization for offenders.

Philosophical Underpinnings of the Reintegration Model

A basic assumption of the reintegration model is that offenders' problems must be solved in the community where they began. Another basic assumption is that society has a responsibility for its own problems and that it can partly fulfill this responsibility by helping law violators reintegrate themselves back into the social order. Thus, the community must offer the offender the opportunities to develop law-abiding behavior, and the offender must learn how to utilize these opportunities. A third assumption is that meaningful community contacts are re-

[5]Clemens Bartollas and Stuart J. Miller, *The Juvenile Offender: Control, Correction and Treatment* (Boston: Holbrook Press, 1978), pp. 14–15.

quired to achieve the objectives of reintegration. Offenders must be provided opportunities to assume the normal roles of citizens, family members, and employees. Offenders also need opportunities for personal growth in nonsecure environments. Finally, proponents of reintegration philosophy recommend community-based corrections for all but the hardcore criminals, and they would offer those offenders who must be institutionalized a wide variety of reentry programs, permit confined offenders to be brought into the decision-making process so that they may choose their prison programs, and provide the necessary services so that offenders can restore family ties and obtain employment and education.[6]

The process by which change takes place in the reintegration model is known as internalization. To achieve internalization, offenders must be presented with such options as education, employment, recreation, and any other activity needed to provide direct or indirect alternatives to criminal behavior. Proponents of this model reason that through a process of experimentation, offenders can learn how to meet their needs in law-abiding ways. Because such offenders choose their own means to achieve successful habilitation in the community, their change in attitudes and values reflect their new view of self. In other words, the change is internalized, and socially unacceptable values and behaviors are altered.

In 1973, the National Advisory Commission on Criminal Justice Standards and Goals, supporting the reintegration model, explained why it is necessary to keep offenders out of institutions:

> Prisons tend to dehumanize people. . . . Their weaknesses are made worse, and their capacity for responsibility and self-government is eroded by regimentation. Add to these facts the physical and mental conditions resulting from overcrowding and from the various ways in which institutions ignore the rights of offenders, and the riots of the past decade are hardly to be wondered at. Safety for society may be achieved for a limited time if offenders are kept out of circulation, but no real public protection is provided if confinement serves mainly to prepare men for more, and more skilled, criminality.[7]

In summary, the philosophy of reintegrating the offender back into the community clearly contains the mandate that the offender must be changed by community-based corrections so that he or she will become a law-abiding citizen. Proponents strongly support the notion that this change process is more likely to occur in community-based programs than in fortress-like institutions. Thus, the community is further charged with becoming involved in the change process.

---

[6]The President's Commission on Law Enforcement and Administration of Justice, *Task Force Report: Corrections* (Washington, D.C.: GPO, 1967), p. 7.

[7]National Advisory Commission on Criminal Justice Standards and Goals, *A National Strategy to Reduce Crime* (Washington, D.C.: GPO, 1973), p. 121.

SCOPE OF REHABILITATIVE PHILOSOPHY

Expressions of the rehabilitative ideal still guide most of what takes place in juvenile and adult corrections. The scope of rehabilitative philosophy covers the following areas:

1. *Parens patriae* (in juvenile justice): The purpose of the juvenile court is to become a surrogate parent and to save, or rehabilitate, children from a life of crime.
2. Indeterminate sentencing and the parole board: The parole board is charged with determining when an offender is rehabilitated and, therefore, ready to return to the community.
3. Diagnostic studies and classification of offenders: The purpose of these diagnostic and classification processes is to identify the needs of offenders so that they can be assigned (medical model) or can elect (reintegration model) those programs which will be most helpful to them.
4. The social study or the presentence investigation (PSI) reports: Probation officers are charged in these reports to diagnose the social backgrounds, behaviors, and attitudes of offenders and to prescribe treatment plans for their rehabilitation.
5. Individual, family, and group therapies: Offenders receive psychotherapy in both community and institutional settings, to resolve the emotional conflicts that drove them to crime or to help them improve their attitudes and interpersonal relations.
6. Diversionary programs: The completion of these diversion programs demonstrates offenders' rehabilitation and, therefore, charges are dropped and their cases are dismissed.
7. Medical and dental surgery: This means of rehabilitation could include everything from eliminating disfiguring blemishes with plastic surgery or eliminating stigmatizing tattoos to correcting a glandular imbalance with chemotherapy.
8. Survival programs: A wide variety of Outward Bound and other wilderness survival programs are conducted for juvenile offenders so that the skills gained and the improved self-esteem can lead to their rehabilitation.
9. Financial and symbolic restitution: The process of paying personally for the social harm an offender has inflicted upon society is seen as a good means of attaining rehabilitation because the law violator is able to extinguish the guilt internalized by his or her inappropriate behavior.
10. Reentry programs (prerelease, work release, educational release, home furloughs, and community assistance programs): These programs enable offenders to gain work skills, be reunited with their families, and gain community support needed to avoid future antisocial behavior.
11. Residential and day-treatment placements for probationers: These "halfway-in" placements provide another opportunity for rehabilitation for probationers as an alternative to imprisonment.
12. Educational, vocational, industrial, self-growth, and service programs in prisons and training schools: These programs give inmates a chance to gain skills or experiences that will be helpful to their rehabilitations.
13. Family visitation programs in prisons and training schools: These programs, which range from limited contact between inmates and families to conjugal visitation (whereby

inmates are permitted to spend a period of time alone with their spouses or family members), also are intended to facilitate the rehabilitation of offenders.

DEFENSE OF REHABILITATIVE PHILOSOPHY

The much-maligned advocates of the rehabilitative ideal have used various arguments in defense of correctional treatment: The widespread criticism of rehabilitation is unfair because the "nothing works" thesis is incorrect. Rehabilitation has not really been tried because it has never been given more than lip service in American corrections. Rehabilitation is a necessary part of a humane correctional process, and it is too compelling an ideal to give up.

Rejection of the "Nothing Works" Thesis

Ted Palmer reviewed Martinson's findings and found the following positive outcomes in the very research studies cited in claiming that "nothing works":

1. *Individual counseling,* e.g., in Martinson's words, this study suggests "there is something to be hoped for in treating properly selected amenable subjects"; another study indicates "a favorable outlook for . . . individual therapy . . . conducted by social workers. . . . "
2. *Group counseling,* e.g., "these programs seem to work best when their subjects are amenable to treatment . . . and when the counselors are not only trained people but 'good' [skilled] people as well."
3. *Individual psychotherapy in community settings,* e.g., one study, "a pragmatic psychotherapeutic approach which was marked by its small size and its use of therapists who were personally enthusiastic about the program, [led to] a decline in recidivism rates"; in another, arrest rates declined as a function of "intensity of treatment."
4. *Intensive probation or parole supervision, as versus imprisonment,* e.g., this latter category has "provided . . . encouraging reports on rehabilitative treatment [and indicates] that, by and large, intensive supervision does work—that the specially trained youngsters do much better according to some measure of recidivism."
5. *Milieu therapy,* e.g., "youthful males . . . over 16 appear to benefit more than those under 16" from residential milieu therapy.[8]

Palmer also indicated that at least thirty-nine individual studies (48 percent of those discussed in Martinson's study) were associated with positive or partly positive recidivism results. Of the remaining studies, 4 percent had ambiguous results and 49 percent showed negative finding or no reduction in recidivism. Palmer then arranged the favorable and unfavorable studies into treatment approaches and settings:

[8]Ted Palmer, *Correctional Intervention and Research: Current Issues and Future Prospects* (Lexington, Mass.: Heath, 1978), pp. 18–19. He was quoting from Robert Martinson's "What Works?—Questions and Answers about Prison Reform," *The Public Interest* 35 (Spring 1974):22–54.

a larger number of favorable than unfavorable ambiguous results were [mentioned by Martinson] in relation to the use of (a) probation rather than prison and (b) small caseloads and intensive supervision. The numbers were about equal in the case of (c) group counseling within residential settings and (d) psychotherapy within the community.[9]

Finally, Palmer noted three other significant patterns that appeared in Martinson's study. First, "the personal characteristics of offenders . . . were more important than the form of treatment in determining future recidivism." Second, the setting in which treatment occurs is an important variable: Martinson had observed that "for older youths who were deemed to be good risks for the future, a minimum security institution produced better results than a maximum security one." Third, the caseworker's characteristics, such as skill, level of enthusiasm, or professional orientation, were associated with a reduction in recidivism.[10]

Paul Gendreau and Robert R. Ross reviewed the literature published between 1973 and 1978 and found that 86 percent of the ninety-five intervention studies reported success.[11] In these programs more stringent research methods were used than previously to evaluate correctional treatment: 33 percent of the studies were random sample experiments, 23 percent employed baseline comparisons, and 23 percent used matched comparison groups. Most of the successful programs were based on a social learning concept of criminal behavior and focused on modifying inappropriate behavior.[12] According to Gendreau and Ross, this 86 percent success rate is "convincing evidence that some treatment programs, when they are applied with integrity by competent practitioners in appropriate target populations, can be effective in preventing crime or reducing recidivism."[13]

Sociologist Susan B. Long concluded from her examination of a major but unsuccessful rehabilitation project that the negative findings on treatment may actually result from the inability of investigators to measure the effects of treatment. She found that errors existed in the measurement of the recidivism data and that researchers had failed to "test for differential treatment effects." When she corrected these errors, she found sizable and significant treatment effects.[14]

Furthermore, proponents of rehabilitative philosophy are quick to remind critics that as mentioned in Chapter 1, Robert Martinson recanted his "nothing works" thesis in a 1979 article in the *Hofstra Law Review*. In the article, he noted

[9]Ted Palmer, "Martinson Revisited," *Journal of Research in Crime and Delinquency,* 12 (1975):133–152.

[10]Palmer, *Correctional Intervention and Research,* pp. 19–20.

[11]Paul Gendreau and Robert Ross, "Effective Correctional Treatment: Bibliotherapy for Cynics," *Crime and Delinquency* 27 (October 1979):463–489.

[12]Robert R. Ross and Paul Gendreau, "Offender Rehabilitation: The Appeal of Success," *Federal Probation* 45 (December 1981):46.

[13]Robert R. Ross and Paul Gendreau, eds., *Effective Correctional Treatment* (Toronto: Butterworth, 1980), p. viii.

[14]Susan B. Long, abstract, unpublished paper.

that "some treatment programs *do* have an appreciable effect on recidivism" and "some programs are indeed beneficial."[15] Advocates of rehabilitation think it is unfair that Martinson's "nothing works" pronouncement received nationwide publicity, but that his acknowledgment that "some programs do work" received little public attention.

Correctional Treatment Has Yet to Be Tried

Advocates of correctional treatment charge that rehabilitation has not been given an adequate chance. Seymour L. Halleck and Ann D. Witte put it this way:

> Correctional rehabilitation programs have generally been perfunctory, underfunded, understaffed and carried out in settings certainly not ideal. . . . With programs so limited in duration and quality, limited rather than dramatic changes in lifestyles would seem likely.[16]

Supporters of rehabilitation correctly surmise that programs are so few that they can serve only a small minority of inmates in adult prisons. Joan Petersilia, in reporting the findings of a national survey conducted by Rand, revealed that no more than 40 percent of the inmates in state prisons participate in a treatment program while incarcerated, and that only "one in four or five inmates with identified needs participate in prison treatment programs related to his needs."[17]

In addition, programs have been sabotaged by custodial staff in several ways. Staff members sometimes "forget" the days that certain inmates are to attend programs. Security staff members may recommend to prisoners that they not become involved in programs, and, at times, do not even permit treatment staff to see inmates on the cellblock or in other areas of the prison.

In addition, lack of follow-up in the community clearly negates the effects of treatment upon offenders. An offender may have profited from treatment and left the community-based facility or the prison intending to "go straight," but any number of debilitating factors, including a failure to receive adequate support services in the community, may unravel the good accomplished by correctional treatment.

Rehabilitation Is a Necessary Part of the Correctional Process

Halleck and Witt explain the rationale behind the defense of rehabilitation as a necessary part of corrections:

[15]Robert Martinson, "New Findings, New Views: A Note of Caution Regarding Sentencing Reform," *Hofstra Law Review* 7 (Winter 1979):244.

[16]Seymour L. Halleck and Ann. D. Witte, "Is Rehabilitation Dead?" *Crime and Delinquency* 23 (October 1977):375.

[17]Joan Petersilia, "Which Inmates Participate in Prison Treatment Programs?" *Journal of Offender Counseling, Services and Rehabilitation* 4 (Winter 1980):121.

Prisoners need the hope that rehabilitation brings. . . . There is good reason to fear . . . that a correctional program that doesn't include rehabilitation will be extremely difficult to implement, will be absurdly expensive, and will encourage us to ignore critical ethical issues.[18]

Francis T. Cullen and Karen E. Gilbert question what the criminal justice system would look like without rehabilitation. They contend that the state's handling of offenders would have been more repressive without the evolution of the rehabilitative ideal. Today, because of the increased acceptance of repressive methods to handle offenders, they argue, the retention of rehabilitation is necessary to maintain humanitarianism in the criminal justice system.[19] Indeed, they state that "rehabilitation is the only justification of criminal sanctioning that obligates the state to care for an offender's needs and welfare."[20]

Many offenders need the expert help provided by treatment because their past failures clearly indicate that they cannot make it on their own. This inability is especially true of repeat or multiple offenders and offenders involved in compulsive crimes. Unless repeat and multiple offenders make conscious decisions to walk away from crime and find support systems to help them succeed in this goal, they may end up spending a large portion of their lives in prison. Unless compulsive sex offenders, for example, receive intensive psychotherapy, they are likely to commit other sex crimes as soon as they are released from confinement.

Proponents of rehabilitation warn that without treatment, the victimization of society will increase. That is, society cannot afford to have untreated offenders released from correctional care because society needs the benefits of treatment for its own self-protection. Rehabilitation, in other words, serves the useful purpose of deterring property and personal crimes in American society.

Rehabilitation Is Too Compelling an Ideal to Give Up

The Panel on Research on Rehabilitative Techniques underlined the compelling nature of rehabilitative philosophy:

The promise of the rehabilitative ideal is so compelling a goal that the strongest possible efforts should be made to determine whether it can be realized and to seek ways to realize it before it is abandoned. Our society cannot avoid the perplexing and recurring problems of how to deal with criminal offenders and the consequences of its penal policy. It is crucial, therefore, that we avoid simplistic solutions and continue efforts to systematically develop, implement, test, and evaluate a variety of intervention programs in the search for a more humane and effective correctional policy.[21]

[18]Halleck and Witte, "Is Rehabilitation Dead?" pp. 379–382.

[19]Francis T. Cullen and Karen E. Gilbert, *Reaffirming Rehabilitation* (Cincinnati: Anderson, 1982), pp. 247, 253.

[20]Ibid., p. 247.

[21]Susan Martin, Lee Sechrest, and Robin Redner, eds., *Rehabilitation of Criminal Offenders: Directions for Research* (Washington, D.C.: National Academy of Science, 1981), p. 10.

Proponents argue that it is not necessary to give up on the compelling ideal of rehabilitation because correctional interventions made significant progress during the 1970s. In this decade, the reintegration and adjustment models largely replaced the controversial medical model, and compulsory programs received lessening support from advocates of rehabilitation. Equally as important, programs became more varied, especially in community-based corrections, and the technology of interventions became more sophisticated. Furthermore, the overall quality or integrity of programs improved, and far more adequate research methods were used to evaluate correctional interventions. Proponents are now predicting that it will soon be possible to predict more accurately what interventions will work for which offenders in what contexts.

CRITICISMS OF REHABILITATIVE PHILOSOPHY

The many criticisms rehabilitative philosophy has received can be grouped into three basic complaints: Its theoretical assumptions are in conflict with basic human values; it has been ineffective in reducing recidivism; and it has been a disaster in practice.

Rehabilitation's Assumptions Conflict with Basic Human Values

Francis A. Allen claims that the rise of the rehabilitative ideal resulted in matters of equal or even greater importance, such as deterrence, being ignored or insufficiently examined. This researcher also argues that the rehabilitative ideal has been used to disguise the true custodial and repressive nature of correctional institutions. Indeed, according to Allen, "the rehabilitative ideal has often led to increased severity of penal measures."[22] Finally, Allen believes that the rise of the rehabilitative ideal conflicts with the values of individual liberty and volition, both because this philosophy of change implicitly encourages procedural laxness and irregularity and because it tries to force offenders to change against their wills, which attempt they experience not as help but as punishment.

Other widely held viewpoints are that the basic assumptions about human nature held in rehabilitative philosophy are erroneous and that this reform model overestimates the ability of the scientific expert. Norman Carlson, director of the Federal Prison System, expressed this criticism well:

> Rehabilitation has been seen as the basic reason for incarceration, as well as for probation and parole. The medical model that evolved—a model that implied offenders were sick and could be cured of crime by a treatment program—was unrealistic.

[22]Allen, *Borderland of Criminal Justice*, pp. 28–38.

Rehabilitation was associated with humanness and we forgot that most inmates are not sick, that we do not know the causes of crime, and that we have developed no sure cures.[23]

Critics also assailed the three basic components of the rehabilitative ideal: individualization, indeterminancy, and discretionary power. Individualization, or focusing upon the criminal rather than the crimes committed, led to regarding the offender as sick and as different than noncriminals. Donal E. J. MacNamara tells what is wrong with this assumption:

For the basic flaw of the medical model is its basic premise: that the offender is "sick" when in fact he is far more likely to be as "normal" as most nonoffenders but inadequately, negatively, or contraculturally socialized, at war with a world he never made, a world in which he has been subjected to abuse, brutalization, discrimination, and exploitation. No program of education, vocational training, medical or psychiatric therapy is relevant to his "cure" and none is likely to reverse his twenty or thirty years of antisocial conditioning.[24]

The task of individually tailoring decisions to accomplish rehabilitation led to the indeterminate sentence whereby the offender is released only when "cured" of his or her criminality. But critics claim that a sentencing structure that depends on the rehabilitation of offenders lacks justice, fairness, constitutional safeguards, and reasonableness. For example, inmates have a right to know when they will be released from prison. In the California's indeterminate sentencing law, which was replaced by a determinate sentencing structure in 1978, the statutory limits were extremely broad: The most frequent sentence given was one to fifteen years. This meant an offender who was seen as a troublemaker by prison authorities could end up serving time for much longer than reasonable for the crime.

Finally, the wide discretionary power implicit in rehabilitative philosophy has been abused on at least two fronts: On one hand, rehabilitation has been too easy on offenders and, thus, has failed to satisfy the punishment-oriented mood of society at the present time. But on the other hand, rehabilitative philosophy has resulted in excessive power being given the parole board; the capricious and arbitrary manner in which parole boards typically decide when inmates are ready for parole has drawn strong criticism from prisoners, prison reformers, and the general public.

Rehabilitative Philosophy Does Not Work

In addition to the study by Lipton, Martinson, and Wilks, many others have questioned the efficacy of correctional treatment. Walter C. Bailey reported the results of one hundred empirical evaluations of treatment in 1957 and concluded

[23]Norman Carlson, "A More Balanced Correctional Philosophy," *FBI Law Enforcement Bulletin* 46 (January 1977):23.

[24]MacNamara, "Medical Model in Corrections," p. 441.

that there seemed to be little evidence of the effectiveness of correctional treatment.[25] He suggested that one or more of the following reasons explain the ineffectiveness of treatment: that treatment in and of itself may not be effective; that it may simply not be effective in a correctional environment; that much of what is called treatment is really not treatment; that some forms of treatment may be effective with some types of offenders but no measure of this phenomenon is available; and that treatment may be based on incorrect assumptions about the causes of delinquent and criminal behavior.[26] Robison and Smith added, in 1971, "that there is no evidence to support any program's claim to superior rehabilitative efficacy."[27] In the 1970s, Wright and Dixon questioned the efficacy of delinquency prevention programs, and Greenburg found that the overall results of rehabilitative programs have been disappointing.[28]

A six-year study of treatment in California adult correctional institutions, which included a three-year, postrelease follow-up of 1,000 clients, concluded that treatment had a negative effect upon participants, because they: "(1) were more hostile to staff than those in the control group; (2) committed more serious prison rules violations; (3) violated parole more frequently; (4) stayed out of prison a shorter period of time before violating parole; and (5) committed crimes more serious than their commitment offenses while on parole."[29] Other research conducted in California has also concluded that with rare exceptions treatment programs have had little or no effect on recidivism.[30]

A number of researchers who reviewed the empirical studies evaluating the efficacy of rehabilitation arrived at a similar conclusion:

> Despite an enormous investment of time, energy, and money, no approach, treatment, or rehabilitative framework has been demonstrably successful in preventing, reducing, and controlling recidivism. So great has been our failure in altering antisocial patterns and life styles that the entire people-changing enterprise has been condemned as both ineffective and, worse, as unjust. Many, if not all, serious concerned behaviorists now firmly believe that the total institution is an historical aberration and must be eliminated with all due haste.[31]

[25]Walter C. Bailey, "Correctional Outcome: An Evaluation of 100 Reports," *Journal of Criminal Law, Criminology, and Police Science* 57 (June 1966):153–160.

[26]Ibid.

[27]J. Robison and G. Smith, "The Effectiveness of Correctional Programs," *Crime and Delinquency* 17 (1971):67–80.

[28]W. E. Wright and M. C. Dixon, "Community Prevention and Treatment of Juvenile Delinquency: A Review of the Literature," *Journal of Research in Crime and Delinquency* 14 (1977):35–67; and David F. Greenburg, "Much Ado about Little: The Correctional Effects of Corrections," processed (Department of Sociology, New York University, June 1974), but the results of this study are found in von Hirsch, *Doing Justice*, pp. 14–15.

[29]David A. Ward, "Evaluative Research for Corrections," in *Prisoners in America*, ed. Lloyd E. Ohlin (Englewood Cliffs, N.J.: Prentice-Hall, 1973), pp. 190–191.

[30]Michael S. Serrill, "California: More Prisoners, More Programs, More Problems," *Corrections Magazine* 1 (September 1974):4.

[31]Harry E. Allen et al., "Sociopathy: An Experiment in Internal Environmental Control," *American Sociological Scientist* 20 (November-December 1976):215.

Rehabilitation Is a Disaster in Practice

Another criticism made about rehabilitative philosophy is that it has been a disaster in practice. First, critics claim that rehabilitative philosophy eventually results in punishment rather than treatment. In the name of treatment, the state has legitimized programming in offenders' lives, with fewer constraints on official behavior.[32] Because there is nothing in rehabilitative theory that places any limit on the amount of punishment given under the name of treatment, some proponents of the rehabilitative ideal have justified the use of aversive conditioning, electroshock therapy, heavy use of psychotropic drugs, and psychosurgery. One correctional jurisdiction went so far as to relabel the reduced diet used as a punishment for prisoners already being punished by segregation as "behavior modification meat loaf."[33]

Second, critics charge that rehabilitative philosophy has resulted in a more inhumane correctional process. In the name of treatment, the state has refused to release inmates until agents of the "therapeutic state" decided they were rehabilitated, and, for difficult inmates, this resulted in prolonged terms of imprisonment. But the anxiety of the parole process is one that every inmate receiving an indeterminate sentence faces. Another inhumane aspect of rehabilitation is related to the fact that some offenders get worse, rather than better, with treatment.[34]

Third, critics charge that rehabilitation did not belong in custodially oriented prisons in the first place. A letter from an exoffender tells why treatment seems inappropriate in prison environments:

> Prison for the most part is a dismal place of punishment and retribution, permeated with hatred, degeneracy, and always racism. Not one of these foregoing factors are conducive to establishing the desire nor attitudes in residents to promote or to become involved in positive programming.
>
> Involvement in prison is a desperate attempt by a resident to maintain a semblance of normality while living in a world of abnormality. There is a basic desire in all prisoners to maintain sanity and prove their worth.
>
> Most programs placed in prison fail because of disinterest and lack of participation. "Throw the key away attitudes" and "keep them locked up" syndromes are sicknesses which are the major cause of program failure. Such negative mentalities in correctional officials stop positive thought patterns in prisoners and prevent the atmosphere necessary for ideals to be born and bear fruit for inmates, prisons, and society.[35]

[32]Von Hirsch, *Doing Justice,* p. 12.

[33]Robert R. Ross and Bryan McKay, "Behavioral Approaches to Treatment in Corrections," in *Effective Correctional Treatment,* p. 45.

[34]Martinson, "New Findings, New Views," p. 258; Ward, "Evaluative Research for Corrections," pp. 190–191; Alexander W. McEachern and Edward M. Taylor, *The Effects of Probation,* University of Southern California Youth Studies Center, Probation Project Report no. 2 (Los Angeles, 1967).

[35]Letter received from Walter Danner in 1979. Used with permission.

EVALUATION OF REHABILITATIVE PHILOSOPHY

The rehabilitation of offenders so that they will diminish their propensities for criminal behavior is a compelling ideal. Yet, several criticisms of the rehabilitative ideal are valid. Rehabilitative philosophy as expressed through the medical model clearly was defective both in theory and practice. Indeed, this model was based upon several erroneous assumptions about human nature, and it overestimated the ability of scientific experts to cure offenders of the disease of criminality.

Compulsory rehabilitation is also in conflict with certain basic human values— at best, it violates human dignity and freedom; at worst, it represents cruel and unusual punishment. Compulsory rehabilitation has legitimized punishment in the name of treatment. The use of such methods as aversive conditioning and electroshock represents one of the saddest periods in the history of correctional treatment. Further, the point should be raised of how much conformity treaters have a right to insist upon and how much of the offender's individuality will be left untouched or untreated.[36] There is certain real question whether treaters have the right to attempt to manipulate unwilling offenders inside the perimeter of their conscious defenses.[37]

Critics also correctly question the effectiveness of rehabilitative philosophy. The expectation that the rehabilitative ideal, especially in psychotherapy, would have a major impact upon recidivism was completely unrealistic. Overcrowded and violent Big House prisons are the least likely place to expect positive results from rehabilitation. In addition, the lack of community support systems tends to unravel the positive contributions that rehabilitation does make.

But before dismissing rehabilitative philosophy, it is necessary to evaluate its strengths. First, proponents of rehabilitative philosophy make a good case for the argument that inmates' hope of improving themselves must remain part of the correctional process. The American system of justice is far too repressive now, and a justice system stripped of rehabilitative philosophy promises to become even more repressive. Thus, a humane justice system requires that correctional treatment be available for those offenders who are interested in change and self-improvement.

Second, sufficient evidence exists to demonstrate that some offenders have profited from correctional treatment. Indeed, some exoffenders look back to a correctional intervention as the turning point in their lives. Effective programs are more likely to take place when intervention is administered in humane environments, when offenders are genuinely interested in change and self-improvement in their lives, and when programs are led by dedicated staff.

Third, those who reaffirm rehabilitation make a good point that the changes taking place in correctional treatment promise improved interventions for the future. One positive trend is that the medical model receives little support today. A second

---

[36]Alexander B. Smith and Louis Berlin, *Treating the Criminal Offender,* 2d ed. (Englewood Cliffs, N.J.: Prentice-Hall, 1981), p. 93.

[37]American Friends Service Committee, *Struggle for Justice,* p. 146.

is that the concept of rehabilitation has been broadened to include programmed assistance to help offenders cope more effectively with their environments as well as to change their character, attitudes, or behavior patterns so as to reduce their criminal propensities. Also hopeful is the reduced support given to compulsory rehabilitation, because this has been so frequently abused in the past. In addition, more sophisticated technologies using multiple methods and differential treatment demonstrate that correctional interventions have improved in the past decade and promise to improve even more in the decades to come. Finally, the receptivity toward theory and research of many who reaffirm rehabilitation provides another hopeful sign.

SUMMARY

This chapter began with an interview with Ted Palmer, who answers some of the most pressing questions about correctional treatment. Intervention, as Palmer refers to treatment, has an important role in the correctional process. Rehabilitative philosophy is expressed through the medical, the adjustment, and the reintegration models. The medical model holds that the criminal is sick and needs to be cured of the disease of criminality. The adjustment model is more present-oriented and claims that offenders are able to be responsible and become law-abiding citizens. The reintegration model is based upon the belief that offenders' problems begin in the community and thus must be solved in the community. Expressions of the rehabilitative ideal show that this widely criticized correctional model still guides most of what takes place in corrections. Although rehabilitative philosophy has been both strongly supported and sharply criticized, largely stripped of the medical model and compulsory treatment and fortified with improved technology, it promises to provide even more meaningful services for those offenders interested in change and self-improvement.

To put the matter of rehabilitative philosophy in a larger context, three basic approaches are used in handling criminal offenders today: the rehabilitation model, the justice model, and the utilitarian punishment model. On the correctional left is the system of the indeterminate sentence, with the parole board requiring participation in rehabilitative programs for release from prison. In the center is the justice model, which does not have room for indeterminate sentencing or the parole board, but which accepts voluntary rehabilitative programs. On the correctional right is the utilitarian punishment model, which advocates the widespread use of imprisonment for those who violate the law; this repressive model has little or no room for rehabilitation.[38] The next two chapters explore more extensively the ways proponents of the justice and utilitarian punishment models believe criminal offenders should be handled.

---

[38]John P. Conrad, *Justice and Consequences* (Lexington, Mass.: Heath, 1981), pp. 156–157.

DISCUSSION QUESTIONS

1. How does Ted Palmer justify the continuation of interventions in corrections?
2. What are the differences among the medical, adjustment, and reintegration models?
3. List the main defenses of rehabilitation philosophy. Which defense do you believe is the strongest?
4. List the main criticisms of rehabilitative philosophy. Which criticism impressed you the most?
5. Based upon your reading of this chapter, what is your evaluation of rehabilitative philosophy? What role do you believe rehabilitative philosophy should play in the future?

The Justice Model

3

Objectives

1. *To indicate the history and development of the justice model, in an interview with David Fogel.*

2. *To discuss the basic philosophical underpinnings of the justice model.*

3. *To describe the main components of the justice model.*

4. *To evaluate the strengths and limitations of the justice model.*

Most corrections experts at the beginning of the 1970s agreed that corrections was confused and rudderless. But by the 1980s, many claimed that David Fogel's "justice model" provided a viable vision for corrections and a strategy to attain that vision. The justice-as-fairness perspective, as developed by Fogel, proposes the end of the indeterminate sentence and parole, the initiation of uniform sentencing, and the establishment of treatment programs based on the voluntary compliance of inmates.[1] Fogel summarized the basic approach of the justice model when he said, "If we cannot treat with reliability, we can at least be fair, reasonable, humane, and constitutional in practice."[2] In the following interview, Fogel defines more extensively the philosophy, the scope, and the implications of the justice model.

Box 3-1   Interview with David Fogel

QUESTION: What events, experiences, and concepts led you to form the justice model?

FOGEL: Having participated in the rehabilitation side of corrections and having observed it for quite a long time as a practitioner at both the juvenile and adult levels, I began to see problems emerging. First, I noted the Aesopian language that began to emerge; that is, when you say one thing but mean another. Probation officers, social workers, and psychologists began to talk as if the maximum custody settings could really provide "clinical treatment." They used odd language like "structured environment" to describe how a place like San Quentin might be used to "treat" when they should have known better.

I also found that rehabilitation was used to mask brutality in prisons. Rehabilitation was used by the most conservative types as window dressing for repression. In other words, if they had the proper clinical appendages—like group therapy, group counseling, the therapeutic community, or other programs that go under the rehabilitative umbrella—they could say they were up to date, while in fact they practiced brutality by leaving people in administrative segregation and isolation endlessly. They said that "clients" did not need due process safeguards because they were being "treated." I began to worry about all of this.

Second, because I had seen the serial violence of prison riots since Attica, I knew that new directions were needed in American corrections. I particularly noted the serial violence between May and September 1973 in the Midwest. All the maximum security institutions in the states of Ohio, Michigan, Minnesota, Indiana, Wisconsin, and Illinois had mass discipline problems at that time. I was struck by the Attica Commission report, which noted that uncertainty was a major problem as a cause of violence in prison.

Third, I was concerned about the inmate "conning" that goes on in American prisons. The parole decision-making process had turned out to be a big "con" game. Hans Mattick put it in capsule form by saying that the parole process had transformed the American prisons into centers of drama, in which the convicts are the actors and the parole board are the drama critics, handing out Oscars and Emmys in the form of paroles. The indeterminate sentence had turned out to be a tool for lengthening terms or punishing people who did not conform to prison programs. I saw the system as a degradation of justice by those who were charged to be agents of justice. I thought that a lot of the "conning" could be straightened out by telling people at the time they are coming *in* when they would be getting *out*

[1]David Fogel, ". . . *We Are the Living Proof*": *The Justice Model for Corrections*, 2nd ed. (Cincinnati: Anderson Publishing Co., 1979).

[2]David Fogel and Joe Hudson, eds., *Justice as Fairness: Perspectives on the Justice Model* (Cincinnati: Anderson, 1981), p. viii.

with a greater degree of certainty than was available when I first began to formulate the notion of the justice model.

QUESTION: What are the main components of the justice model?

FOGEL: I am going to list twenty points now. The first group were points I originally made in [my book] *". . . We Are the Living Proof,"* and the others paraphrase something I prepared for a book on the mission of probation:

1. The criminal law is the "command of the sovereign" [the right of a society].

2. The threat of punishment is necessary to implement the law.

3. People are socialized to respond to the commands and expectations of the ruling social and political power.

4. The criminal law has agencies which protect the power of the dominant prescribed morality.

5. In the absence of an absolute system of justice or natural law, no accurate etiological theory of crime is possible. Nor is a definition of crime ever stable.

6. Although free will may not exist perfectly, the criminal law is largely based upon its presumed vitality and forms the only foundation for criminal sanctions.

7. The criminal sentence represents a punishment embodied in the statutes that is invoked by a judge, who is constrained by procedural law, upon a person adjudged responsible for his or her unlawful behavior.

8. Although a sentence may have several intended purposes—that is, deterrence, retaliation, or rehabilitation—it is specifically a punishment proportionate to the harm inflicted by the criminal. The following are more specifically related to the mission of probation, but generally pertain to institutions as well.

9. Probation is a criminal sentence and should not represent an abstention of punishment. The guiding principle is, "No punishment exists without the crime and no crime without punishment."

10. The entire process of criminal justice must be played out in the milieu of justice. Justice-as-fairness represents a subordinate goal of all agencies of the criminal law.

11. When probation—or you can say the same thing for corrections—becomes mired in the dismal swamp of treating the client, it is in danger of becoming dysfunctional as an agency of justice. Probation officers should engage probationers as the law otherwise dictates, as responsible, volitional human beings.

12. Justice-as-fairness is not a program. It is an aspiration that insists that probation and all agencies of the criminal justice system perform their assigned roles with law violators lawfully. While individual probationers may need specialized, intensive services, probation officers should not be responsible for providing them. Nor should the probationer be judged for (purposes of revocation) on the basis of his or her success in heeding such treatments. The same thing would apply in the prison for that matter.

13. William Penn warned, "Where the law ends, tyranny begins." So does the exercise of discretion. Discretion is inevitable, but unbridled discretion undermines the rule of law. While discretion or professional judgments cannot be eliminated, the justice perspective seeks to narrow, control, and make such discretion reviewable.

14. Probation as a sentence must be made explicit. At present, probation exists as an indefinite legal sanction which invests large discretionary powers in a probation officer while giving vague and largely unexplicated reasons for the granting of such a sentence.

15. The presentence investigation should be treated as a legal document and discoverable by the defendant. Its focal concern should be on the victim and on the extent of the harm done. Since the defendant's legal culpability was established by the court, the presentence investigation now turns to the broader issue of how the offender may

assist in restoring the offended [victim] to the pre-crime status quo.

16. The judge should have flexibility in determining the actual individual conditions of the probation order. It is at this point that the perspective on what assistance the offender may furnish the victim comes into play. The order permitting the offender to remain in the community has to be balanced by whether nonincarceration would be likely to denigrate the law.

17. Probation is a summary sentence. It is not leniency; it does not replace another sentence, and it contains explicated conditions. The court should have statutory authority to sentence to probation and to set unambiguous conditions. The continuing relationship of the offender and the probation officer is always undertaken in the context of what conditions the probation order contains. The conditions are made explicit so that allegations of violations may be more objectively determined by the court.

18. Central to a justice model approach is a voluntary acceptance by the probationer of treatment, if treatment is to be provided at all. When treatments are "ordered," problems arise, such as coercion by the probation officer and manipulation by the probationer.

19. Revocation of probation represents a great intrusion into the offender's life and an interruption of assistance to the victim, where such assistance is ordered. Therefore, the standard of proof for revocation should be at least as high as the original finding which occasioned the sentence of probation— that is, beyond reasonable doubt—and must not be grounded upon nebulous assessment or attitudes.

20. The victim's needs, whether an individual or a community, should be explicitly reflected in any court order of probation. The probation officer's mandate from the court should be equally weighted with the concern for making the victim whole as much as it is with supervising the offender.

Restitution, that is financial and moral as well as community service, should be ordered whenever feasible as a portion of the condition of probation.

In addition to these twenty points, there are other programmatic components of the justice model. In prison, there would be provisions for a law library, civil legal assistance for inmates, due process for disciplinary procedures, and a semblance of self-government so that inmates feel they are agents of their own lives. I would go with the minimal standards of the ACA [American Correctional Association] but would extend these to include conjugal visitation and grievance procedures— ranging from early warning systems to the services of an ombudsman to have a separate, independent oversight over the system.

QUESTION: Are you encouraged by the nationwide acceptance of the justice model?

FOGEL: I'm encouraged by the rhetoric of the nationwide acceptance of the justice model, but there are precious few places that have accepted it as a mission. Most frequently, it has been forced upon prison systems by the courts. I am much more hopeful about the acceptance of the principles of the justice model by probation agencies. But even in prisons these days— and I get to a lot of prisons during the course of a year—tighter procedural practices are in place. When violations occur, there is a way to bring violations to court. A lot of prisons have monitors assigned to them as a result of suits, and a lot of prisons are gearing up for accreditation, so that they have at least a paper allegiance to due process. Before the interventions of the courts, people just did not pay much attention to due process. They [prison staff] threw someone in the "hole" [segregation] for a year or two, and they reviewed the case every ninety days. They would then say that he had not made enough progress to come out but did not give lawful reasons for keeping him in. Then, they used a caseworker or a psychologist on a review panel to legitimate such repression.

QUESTION: What gains have corrections in

the United States made in the past ten years? What losses has it incurred?

FOGEL: A number of gains took place during the post-Attica period. The ACA standards are one gain. But they are minimal standards put together by people in the field, and they are just barely passable on the basis of checks and balances. There has also been a lot of recent action asking for public oversight, and corrections is getting more and more responsive to this. Inmate self-governance is more acceptable than it has been in the past; the wardens voted it down before Attica, but just after Attica, they voted it in. The period after Attica has also seen the spread of the ombudsman, grievance procedures, tighter due process, and greater oversight both through the ACA accreditation process and, most importantly, as a result of the 1983 civil rights suits.

Unfortunately, most of the progress made during the first part of the 1970s was wiped out during the latter part of the 1970s as a result of severe overcrowding in prisons. I would say the greatest loss, and the one that is going to be felt for a while, is the Supreme Court decision in the *Rhodes* v. *Chapman* case. The Court said that double celling at the Lucasville prison in Ohio is not unconstitutional all by itself. The Court found that this facility built in 1972 is a topflight institution. Of course, it isn't, but the Court said it was. The Court also said prison represents pain that is reasonably expected to be imposed upon convicts. It is a "cost" of crime.[3]

In a Pontiac [Illinois] case, decided in the fall of 1981, Judge Baker found that overcrowding was a violation of the Constitution because people were being kept in their cells too long. Pontiac is an 1871 rather than a 1972 construction, but this decision has just been overturned by the Seventh Circuit Court of Appeal. I don't know whether this will be appealed to the Supreme Court, or whether the Supreme Court will hear it if it is. But I am afraid that the era when the courts would rule against overcrowding is coming to an end. As a matter of fact, President Reagan in his message to Congress on crime is asking for restrictions in the use of Section 1983 in prison cases.

QUESTION: You have been quoted as saying that probation is a great idea, but it has not yet been tried. What is needed to make probation work?

FOGEL: There is a progression in the process of criminal justice. There are front-end agencies like the police, the courts, and prosecution. After that, there are agencies identified with offenders, such as probation, jails, prisons, and parole, which are considered to be on the backline. You will note, the front end are identified with public safety and are usually funded at a much higher level than those dealing with the rear end of the system and the offender.

I would like to see probation move toward being a front-line agency. At the front end of the system probation would have as much concern with the victim of the crime as it does now with the offender. Right now, we are still wallowing around in the needs deprivation model. This model means the offender comes to the probation officer as a client, and corrections has to cater to the needs of the offender. Nothing is necessarily wrong with that, but it seems to me the reason for having a criminal justice system is to cater to the needs of the law-abiding victim of a crime at least as much as to the needs of the offender. The presentence investigation is a pivotal document and should be concerned as much with restoring the status quo for the victim of the crime as it is with the restoration of the offender. When victims are taken care of, society will probably be less retributive in mood than when victims are not taken care of by the criminal justice system.

QUESTION: What role does rehabilitation have in probation?

---

[3]Since this was written, Judge Battista, a federal circuit court judge, has ruled that the Mansfield Reformatory must be closed in 1984 because of overcrowding and conditions which constitute cruel and unusual punishment. The state of Ohio has accepted this ruling and is moving to implement it.

FOGEL: The pursuit of justice is a quite legitimate goal for probation. I think justice is a loftier goal than dealing with the elusive psyche of some offender, but perhaps more importantly, justice is a manageable goal for probation. Further, the pursuit of justice provides a thematic unity to the fragmentation of probation and to several reform formats now being advanced. Approaching the probationer as a truly responsible, volitional actor may produce some initial anxieties, since it requires some unlearning for probation officers. And it is true that, under a voluntary regimen, probation officers may have to be more imaginative than they are now, but, as Kay Harris has pointed out, the help they provide to offenders may seem more attractive and relevant on a voluntary rather than a forced basis.

QUESTION: What role does rehabilitative philosophy have in corrections?

FOGEL: It should be clear by now that I don't have anything against clinical rehabilitation as long as offenders enter treatment voluntarily, and early release isn't dangled as a reward for involvement in rehabilitation inside a prison. I would see rehabilitation having a more exciting role in corrections when participants are not coerced into using programs. When they come voluntarily, the therapist could be more sure that his services are actually sought and pertinent to the offender. What I believe the prisons can do is to offer opportunities for self-improvement. If we call that rehabilitation, all right, but I don't believe we ought to force people into it.

QUESTION: Stripped of its indeterminate sentence and parole board, will the rehabilitation model survive in American corrections?

FOGEL: The rehabilitation model may have quite a hard time maintaining itself when it is stripped of indeterminate sentences, the parole board, and its coercive power over inmates. The people who are interested in rehabilitation will need to reconceptualize how to deliver important casework, psychiatric, and psychological services without coercion; that is, providing these services without forcing them on anyone. Well, that scares people be-cause if they won't have captive audiences, they are afraid that their jobs may go. But having a captive audience does not tell you whether anything worthwhile is going on. But if nothing is taking place with that captive audience, the services are a waste of money anyhow.

QUESTION: Crime still seems to be out of control in our society. What needs to be done to make the crime problem more manageable?

FOGEL: I wish I knew the answer to that one. I would lean toward answers that are longer term; I don't have any short-term answers for anyone. I think the long-term answer has to do with the redistribution of wealth. I see the need for an internal Marshall Plan in this country to rebuild our cities, to strengthen the family, and to provide an opportunity structure for those who have been structured out of society.

QUESTION: What else needs to be added about the justice model that has not been covered in this interview?

FOGEL: What I am worried about is the role of criminal justice agencies in producing more violent people. My belief is that if you can't cure, you can at least treat humanely. I have just finished the year-long study in Europe of sentencing and alternatives to incarceration. A major difference with our society is that the Western European societies are simply not as punitive. I find a couple of reasons for this. One is the issue of racism, and we have not yet come to grips with that problem. It looks like we are continuing to harbor a time bomb in our inner cities. I made the suggestion of rebuilding the cities with an internal Marshall Plan in order to deal with racism and the lack of opportunity structures. A second problem the Europeans don't have is the ubiquitous presence of the handgun. I know that handguns are part of our tradition, but I think we are going to have to get much tougher on that issue. I think there is much less fear of crime in Western European societies because there is less violence and fewer weapons available.

European societies sentence offenders to months and fewer number of years. We rain bucketsful of years on offenders in this society. We sentence to five years, thirty, or a lifetime without turning a hair. I have run into people in prison who are serving five and six multiple lifetime sentences. We are not going to accomplish anything in thirty-eight years that we could not accomplish in twenty-eight years, or eighteen years, rather than eight years in prison except possibly make people worse. Everybody in criminal justice ought to be worried about turning convicts out of prison less safe than when they entered.

My reason for moving toward the justice model is to deliver greater degrees of certainty, to make behavior public, to let everybody know where they stand. I called for the abolition of the parole board because I was afraid if I called for the reform of the parole board, we would end up with a century of foot-dragging reform movements. The abolition of the parole board must be accomplished by a reduction in sentences; otherwise, prison populations will continue to balloon.

I think instigation of something in the order of a ten-year maximum sentence will eventually occur in this society; that is, a ten-year sentence for any crime short of premeditated murder. I believe that an offender might justifiably receive a life sentence for premeditated murder. The Committee on Incarceration, of which Andrew von Hirsh was director, came out with a top sentence of five years. Change is simply going to take time, but other Western societies similar to ours have been able to limit sentences to reasonable and safe terms. I have a feeling that there is a connection between caring for victims and reducing vindictiveness.

David Fogel received the doctorate in criminology from the University of California at Berkeley. Dr. Fogel has served as commissioner of the Minnesota Department of Corrections and as executive director of the Illinois Law Enforcement Commission. He has authored and coauthored four books and over forty articles on sentencing, correctional reform, probation, and comparative alternatives in incarceration. He is acknowledged to be one of the major voices in corrections, and the justice model, which is formulated in his writings, has been endorsed by state after state. Dr. Fogel is presently Professor and Director of Graduate Studies, Department of Criminal Justice at the University of Illinois at Chicago Circle.
Source: Interview conducted in September 1982. Used with permission.

PHILOSOPHY OF THE JUSTICE MODEL

David Fogel, as he indicates in *". . .We Are the Living Proof,"* was influenced by a number of philosophical concepts in developing the justice model.[4] First, Fogel acknowledged his indebtedness to philosopher John Rawls, who stated that the first priority of the justice system is to achieve justice. Rawls defines justice in this way:

. . . the first virtue of social institutions, as truth is of systems of thought, . . . a theory however elegant and economical must be rejected or revised if it is untrue; likewise laws and institutions no matter how efficient and well-arranged must be reformed or abolished if they are unjust.[5]

[4]These philosophical underpinnings are summarized and reprinted from Chapter 4 of David Fogel, *". . . We Are the Living Proof,"* 2nd ed. (Anderson Publishing Co., 1979), pp. 179–271.

[5]John Rawls, *A Theory of Justice* (Cambridge: Harvard University Press, 1972), p. 3, quoted in Fogel, *". . . We Are the Living Proof,"* p. 185.

Fogel is aware that justice must move from the philosopher's chair into the real world of the criminal justice system. From his examination of the system in action, Fogel concluded that justice is a much more viable goal for the criminal justice system than rehabilitation and that justice is achieved through fair, reasonable, humane, and constitutional practices.

Second, the concept of free will is a basic underpinning of the justice model. As Fogel indicated in his interview, he was influenced by a number of propositions, developed by Stephen Schafer, advocating a new-classical approach to justice; that is, offenders are regarded as having volition and, therefore, as responsible for their behavior. Schafer expressed it this way: "Although free will may not exist perfectly, the criminal law is largely based upon its presumed vitality and [free will] forms the only foundation for penal sanctions."[6]

Third, the concept of "just deserts" is a pivotal philosophical underpinning of the justice model. As volitional and responsible human beings, offenders deserve to be punished if they violate the law. The punishment shows that the conduct was wrong and that an offender is blameworthy for having committed it. Thus, the decisions concerning offenders should be based not upon their needs, but upon the penalties that they deserve for their acts.[7] However, the punishment that the state inflicts upon the offender must be proportionate to the seriousness of the offense or the social harm inflicted upon society. This "just deserts" position is also nonutilitarian; the punishment of the offender is not done to achieve any social benefits or advantages, such as deterrence or rehabilitation. In other words, the only reason to punish an offender is because he or she deserves it. Fogel feels that the "just deserts" model "provides a more rational ground for the construction of correctional policies" and offers a "set of principles for the rehabilitation of the correctional system itself"[8]:

> The retributive position, in contrast [to rehabilitation], is essentially nonutilitarian, holding that punitive sanctions should be imposed on the offender simply for the sake of justice. Punishment is deserved; the form and severity of the punishment must, however, be proportionate to the criminal act. The right of the state to impose treatments of one sort or another on the offender holds no place in this approach.[9]

Fourth, an uncompromising distrust of the power of the state is another underpinning of the justice model. Fogel claims that unbridled discretion in the justice system is one means by which the state misuses its power over citizens and is a central problem to be dealt with by justice-as-fairness.[10] The exercise of broad

---

[6]Fogel derived these propositions from Stephen Schafer, *The Political Criminal: The Problem of Morality and Crime* (New York: Free Press, 1974), quoted in Fogel, *". . . We Are the Living Proof,"* p. 185.

[7]Andrew von Hirsh, *Doing Justice: The Choice of Punishments* (New York: Hill and Wang, 1976), p. 98.

[8]Fogel and Hudson, *Justice as Fairness*, p. 1.

[9]Ibid.

[10]Fogel, *". . . We Are the Living Proof,"* p. 227.

discretion by judges results in offenders' serving various lengths of sentences for the same offense. Also, the discretion of the parole board forces inmates into trying to con the board into an early release. In *". . . We Are the Living Proof,"* Fogel quoted an inmate's view of the parole board: "If they ask is this yellow wall blue, I'll say of course it's blue. I'll say anything they want me to say if they're getting ready to let me go."[11] Correctional administrators also frequently abuse the authority given to them by denying the due process rights of inmates. Fogel believes that "one of the most fruitful ways the prison can teach the non–law-abiders to be law-abiding is to treat them in a law-abiding manner."[12]

Fifth, the justice model holds to the bankruptcy of the rehabilitative concept of justice. As a practitioner in the justice system, Fogel saw that rehabilitative philosophy actually perpetuated the abuses of the system and, at times, resulted in punishment rather than treatment. Thus, his experiences in corrections led him to question the rationale, methodology, and coerciveness of the rehabilitative ideal.

Sixth, a concern for the consumer of the justice system is another underpinning of the justice model. Fogel was influenced by Edmond Cahn, Paul Tappan, Edgar and Jean Cahn, Jonathan Caspar, and Philip Selznick in developing this concern.[13] Those who hold this "consumer perspective" advocate that all the participants who are acted upon by the justice process, including the victim, the juror, the witness, and the offender, receive justice-as-fairness. The "consumer perspective" emphasizes that it is necessary to guard against officials or processors of justice misusing their power.

Seventh, that offenders are to be treated with respect and dignity is another basis of the justice model. If offenders are not treated as responsible people who are entitled to opportunities to negotiate their fates, they will turn to violence, Fogel warns, as a means to achieve change.[14] Justice-as-fairness recommends treating offenders as responsible human beings by permitting them to choose programs voluntarily, by providing them with all the rights that the law dictates, by making certain that all the decisions made about them are made in a just and fair way, by creating mechanisms that permit them to bring grievance actions against unfair decisions made concerning them, and by giving them an opportunity to be involved in some degree of self-government within the prison.

Finally, that the fortress-like prison must be replaced is an underlying assumption of the justice model. Fogel's own experiences in corrections, as well as the violence in American prisons, convinced him that such prisons must be replaced. As he observed riots erupting in one major prison after another across the nation, Fogel began to question whether the fortress-like prison was indeed manageable, and, even if it was, whether prisoners would continue to put up with such environments. Also, Fogel was formulating the justice model during the period in the

[11]This quote is from American Friends Service Committee, *Struggle for Justice* (New York: Hill and Wang, 1971), p. 73.

[12]Fogel, *". . . We Are the Living Proof,"* p. 204.

[13]Ibid., pp. 188–189.

[14]Ibid., p. 206.

late 1960s and early 1970s when deinstitutionalization was a widely accepted concept in American corrections, and he was influenced by the philosophy of sentencing only criminals who had committed serious offenses to long-term prisons.

David Fogel used several of these philosophical assumptions as criteria for defining the mission of the justice model:

> To pursue justice-as-fairness rather than rehabilitation.
>
> To provide expanded opportunities for prisoner self-improvement rather than maintaining the coercive practice of herding prisoners into available slots, dangling the reward of possible early release in exchange for attendance.
>
> To develop "commonsense advocacy" services (e.g., classification, educational and vocational counseling, legal services, conjugal visiting, health and sanitation services).
>
> To provide state level corrections to care for only the residual, dangerous offender. The others [offenders] might be contracted with the growing private sector field.
>
> To abandon the fortress prison structure.
>
> To make an enormous commitment to line staff recruitment, training, safety, involvement, upgrading, and a salary to match their heroic effort.[15]

COMPONENTS OF THE JUSTICE MODEL

Fogel built the justice model upon the following components:

1. The indeterminate sentence and the parole board would be replaced by a determinate sentencing structure. This definite or flat sentence structure calls for different classes of felonies mitigated by substantial vested good time credit (good time is reduction of sentence given prisoners for good behavior in prison). For each felony class, a fixed sentence is proposed, with a narrow range in mitigation or aggravation allowed, either for the facts of a particular case or for the seriousness of the offense as compared to others in the same class. The theory of this sentencing structure is based upon the least restrictive alternative commensurate with the gravity of the criminal act. But whenever a judge finds imprisonment to be the appropriate disposition, he or she is expected to select a fixed sentence from within that range and impose it. The consequence of determinate sentencing is that when convicted offenders leave the courtroom, they know the actual sentence to be served, less good time.[16]

2. Probation is a criminal sentence and does not represent an abstention of punishment. Probation officers are to engage probationers as responsible, volitional human beings; the help they provide to probationers is voluntary and has nothing to do with revocation or the length of probation.

3. Officials of the criminal justice system are to have as much concern for victims of crime as they have for offenders. Financial restitution and community service sanctions are needed to restore victims to pre-crime status. Restitution and community service sanctions also contain the potential for fairness by giving offenders opportunities to make amends or atone for the damages they have done.[17]

[15]Fogel and Hudson, *Justice as Fairness,* p. x.

[16]Fogel, ". . . *We Are the Living Proof,*" p. 254.

[17]See Joe Hudson and Burt Galaway, "Restitution and the Justice Model," in *Justice as Fairness,* ed. Fogel and Hudson, pp. 52–65, for a more extensive commentary of the role of restitution in the justice model.

4. Inmate self-governance must be more fully implemented in American prisons. The ideal way to democratize the prison would be a joint venture between staff and inmates that would give prisoners some say in the decisions affecting their everyday lives.[18]

5. An adequate formal grievance process must be present in the prison. This formal grievance process would provide inmates an opportunity to negotiate the decisions affecting them, thereby serving as an effective means of conflict resolution.[19]

6. Legal aid in prison is a right that society must provide to enable prisoners to improve their circumstances lawfully.[20]

7. Administrators of correctional institutions can no longer keep the law out of prison; nor can they treat prisoners in capricious and arbitrary ways. Justice-as-fairness also involves having clear rules, insuring their promulgation, and following a procedure for determining and punishing rule violators based on due process safeguards.[21]

8. Participatory management techniques will be helpful in bringing correctional staff into the decision-making process. Unit management is one such technique that could be helpful in accomplishing this objective.[22]

9. An ombudsman, especially if he or she is not responsible to the department of corrections, is an effective means to ensure fairness in the prison. The ombudsman should be appointed by the legislature and should provide the legislature with information and recommendations concerning the operation of correctional institutions. This overseer of prison life can mediate with prison administrators concerning inmate grievances and can also recommend needed changes to prison officials.[23]

10. Programs in the prison should be totally voluntary and should have nothing to do with the length of confinement. Educational and vocational programs, especially, should be offered on a contractual basis after inmates have selected a program they believe necessary for their own self-improvement. New programs are to be added and old ones discarded in response to need.[24]

11. Prison guards need better training, a safe environment, upgraded job classification, and a better salary to match their difficult jobs.[25]

12. The emphasis in prison employment should be shifted from treatment to business. Prisoners need more adequate work environments and more fulfilling work. Five criteria for prison wage plans are as follows:

   a. The wage should constitute a sufficient incentive for creating and maintaining an acceptable level of worker productivity.

   b. The amount should be affordable by the industrial operation, expressed as a percentage of gross revenues.

   c. The minimum industrial wage should be set at a level above the basic institutional "welfare" payment to insure sufficient interest in the operation to maintain a stable work force.

---

[18]Fogel, ". . . *We Are the Living Proof,*" pp. 209–215.

[19]Ibid., pp. 215–221.

[20]Ibid., pp. 221–225.

[21]Ibid., p. 228.

[22]See Phyllis Jo Baunach, "Participatory Management: Restructuring the Prison Environment," in *Justice as Fairness,* ed. Fogel and Hudson, pp. 196–218, for a discussion of the application of unit management to the justice model.

[23]Fogel, ". . . *We Are the Living Proof,*" pp. 230–236.

[24]Ibid., p. 261.

[25]Ibid., p. 229. Refer also to Jess Maghan, "Guarding in Prison," in *Justice as Fairness,* ed. Fogel and Hudson, pp. 235–247, for a more extensive discussion of the correctional officer's role in the justice model.

    d.   Workers' earnings should allow for enough savings to be accumulated to assist in the transition period when the prisoner returns to the free world.

    e.   The wage plan should be generally congruent with institutional and political realities.[26]

13.   The residual offender, who is also known as the dangerous, organized, or repetitive criminal, must also be ensured of justice-as-fairness safeguards. Such offenders are to be protected from psychopharmacological and behavioral technology techniques and are to be provided with a safe environment.[27]

14.   The fortress-like prison, which is frequently overcrowded, violent, and inhumane, is to be dismantled. Newer and smaller facilities, with capacities not exceeding three hundred inmates, are to replace these prisons across the nation. They are to be constructed near urban centers because most prisoners come from urban centers and because prison staff will have more in common with inmates when both come from similar backgrounds and areas. These facilities, which may be distinguished by degress of security, should be subdivided into living units of thirty.[28]

15.   In order to bring more fairness to juvenile justice, it is necessary

> That the enormous discretion granted to juvenile justice practitioners be limited;
>
> That increasing numbers of youthful offenders be diverted from the justice system and to voluntary services;
>
> That common deficiencies in due process be remedied so as to ensure greater fairness in the transaction among the justice system, the family, and the juvenile offender;
>
> That curbs be placed upon the indeterminate sentencing practices of juvenile courts and that juveniles be given a fixed sentence by the court at the time of sentencing;
>
> That status offenses be decriminalized;
>
> That the governing principle of sentencing be one of "proportionality," which means that there must be a relation between the seriousness of the offense committed and the severity of the sanction imposed;
>
> That training schools be made safer and more humane;
>
> That programs offered in training schools be of a voluntary nature and have nothing to do with the release of a youth;
>
> That restitution and community service sanctions be required of more juvenile lawbreakers; these sanctions have the potential for fairness because they give youthful offenders opportunities to atone or make amends for the damage or harm they have inflicted upon others.[29]

DEFENSE OF THE JUSTICE MODEL

Its supporters argue that the justice model has many strengths. First, the justice model has appeal because it advocates the punishment of offenders, but in a humane way. Offenders are regarded as volitional and responsible human beings. If they

[26]Jack Schaller, "Normalizing the Prison Work Environment," in *Justice as Fairness,* ed. Fogel and Hudson, p. 229.

[27]Fogel, ". . . *We Are the Living Proof,"* pp. 275–276.

[28]Ibid., pp. 263–265.

[29]Charles Shireman, "The Juvenile Justice System: Structure, Problems and Prospects," in *Justice as Fairness,* ed. Fogel and Hudson, pp. 136–141.

violate the law, they deserve to be punished. The "just deserts" philosophy, according to its advocates, is a far more socially acceptable way of dealing with the crime problem than is rehabilitative philosophy, for society's "get-tough-with-crime" mood is no longer receptive to the idea of rehabilitation as the basic goal of the correctional process.

Second, the justice model draws endorsement because its emphasis on justice-as-fairness is a humane way of dealing with offenders. Whatever else is done during the correctional process, proponents of the justice model charge, fair play and due process of law must be primary concerns. On one hand, the justice model proposes a least-restrictive approach; that is, sentences to imprisonment should be reserved for offenders who have committed serious offenses. But on the other hand, offenders are to be sent to prison *as* and not *for* additional punishment and, therefore, they should be treated there in a humane and fair manner.

Third, the concept of justice-as-fairness is becoming widely accepted today among legal and corrections scholars, among policymakers in state capitals, and among practitioners in the justice system as a pivotal construct in dealing with the crime problem. For example, the recommendations of the report of the Committee for the Study of Incarceration have much in common with Fogel's justice model. Andrew von Hirsh reports the committee's recommendation that "deserts" be used as the guiding principle of the correctional process. Offenders are to be subjected to certain deprivations, or punishments, because they deserve them, and they deserve them because they have engaged in wrongful conduct. Also, the severity of punishment, according to von Hirsh, should be commensurate with the seriousness of the wrong. Furthermore, the committee, as Fogel does, recommends determinate sentencing, dismantling of rehabilitative procedures, limited use of confinement, and reduced length of sentences.[30] Thus, because of the growing acceptance of justice-as-fairness as a means of designing a more humane justice system, supporters claim that Fogel's model will have long-term impact on the correctional policy of this nation.

Fourth, the justice model is defended as the only reform strategy today encompassing a systemwide reform of the juvenile and adult justice systems. Fogel's justice model does deal with nearly every aspect of administering justice to offenders as well as with the needs of other actors in the justice process. The justice model also emphasizes the rights of victims, proposing that officials of the justice system should be charged with restoring the pre-offense status of the victims of crime. Compared to Fogel's justice model, supporters claim that other reform strategies are either piecemeal solutions or merely projections for change in the system.

Fifth, its supporters argue, the justice model deals with the performance rather than the promise of the criminal justice system. Justice model reforms consider the brutality of prison life, the anxiety of offenders trying to con the parole board into granting parole, the thankless and poorly paid job of guarding society's felons, the consequences of racism on the correctional process, the financial loss and emotional pain of being a victim, the abuses that have been inflicted upon inmates in the past, and the difficulties of effecting change in corrections.

[30]von Hirsh, *Doing Justice.*

CRITICISMS OF THE JUSTICE MODEL

Patrick D. McAnany has leveled three serious criticisms at the justice model. First, he claims that while the means of the justice model (provision of justice-as-fairness) are admirable, the relatively unexamined goals of the model become questionable when they are looked at more carefully.[31] For example, when the retributive features of the present justice reforms are examined ("just deserts"), McAnany believes that most individuals will "quail at proposing a system of punishment 'for its own sake.' "[32] Or, to put it another way, will society accept the basing of the justice process on retribution rather than some utilitarian principle, such as the deterrence or reformation of offenders?

Second, McAnany claims that deciding the seriousness of various offenses poses a serious stumbling block to implementing justice reforms because the responsibility for creating such a scale is not so much a matter of logic as it is a matter of politics.[33] Legislatures are likely to be influenced by the hard-line mood of society in creating more punitive and prolonged sentences than are humane or equitable. Critics of the justice model point out that this is precisely what has happened in states that have adopted determinate sentencing structures, where offenders are being sentenced to prison for longer periods of time.

Third, McAnany questions to what extent justice reforms can actually be attained in the criminal justice system. Procedural protections for prisoners will be slow to come because the Supreme Court and the highest state courts are reluctant to extend the full range of procedural safeguards to areas outside the adjudicatory process. Some evidence also exists that the Court has begun to undo earlier precedents where due process was accorded offenders. Such actors as the police and prosecutors are relatively immune to direct justice reforms. Furthermore, McAnany argues, the logic of the justice model is unlikely to change the present monolithic justice system because the system is too rigid and too entrenched in past practices to be penetrated by justice reforms.[34]

Francis T. Cullen and Karen E. Gilbert pose even sharper criticisms of the justice model. They claim that "a criminal justice system rooted in retributive principles will be neither more just, more humane, nor more efficient than a system that, at least ideologically, had offender reform as its goal."[35] For example, they question whether justice is served by determinate sentencing because this system of sentencing results in excessive rigidity, threatens to upset the checks and balances in the criminal justice system, leads to an expansion of prosecutorial power, and contributes to the crisis of overcrowded prisons.[36]

[31]Patrick D. McAnany, "Justice in Search of Fairness," in *Justice as Fairness,* ed. Fogel and Hudson, p. 40.

[32]Ibid.

[33]Ibid., p. 41.

[34]Ibid., pp. 29, 30, 39, 45.

[35]Francis T. Cullen and Karen E. Gilbert, *Reaffirming Rehabilitation* (Cincinnati: Anderson, 1982), p. xii.

[36]Ibid., pp. 159, 160, 164, 165.

Cullen and Gilbert further contend that discretion in the justice system is currently used to avoid injustice, not just to promote unfairness. The wide use of discretion at the time of arrest, especially of juveniles, spares some offenders from the questionable impact of the justice process. Even the discretion of the parole board enables most prisoners to shorten the length of their sentences. Officials of the justice system, as Donald Cressey has noted, often seek ways to soften the severity of statutory penalties in an effort to avoid imposing pain unnecessarily or unfairly.[37]

Finally, Cullen and Gilbert question those who do not trust the state to administer rehabilitation in a just and humane manner, but place total faith in the same state (through its legislature) to design just and humane determinate sentences. In fact, Cullen and Gilbert are so concerned about the future of rehabilitative programs in a justice-as-fairness system that they are proposing state-obligated rehabilitation.[38]

EVALUATION OF THE JUSTICE MODEL

A major contribution of the justice model rests in the idea of justice-as-fairness, which means that fair play and due process of law must be primary concerns of the justice process. The justice model also includes such positive aspects as regarding offenders as volitional and responsible human beings who must be treated with respect and dignity, suggesting procedural safeguards to reduce capricious and arbitrary discretion in the justice system, seeking the elevation of the role and job classification of the prison guard, and advocating the restoration of victims to their pre-offense status.

However, the justice model appears to have two serious flaws. First, the concept of "just deserts" or "just punishments," which affirms that criminals deserve punishment proportionate to the social harm they have inflicted upon society, seems to be a fatal weakness in the makeup of this model. Although punishment proportionate to the seriousness of the crime may be defended as a fair and humane standard for sentencing, retribution as the ultimate aim of the correctional process breeds a policy of despair rather than one of hope.[39] Indeed, the idea of "just deserts" has been around for centuries but has never totally dominated the penal policy of any advanced society. Thus, whether or not this theory could come to dominate the correctional policy of this nation at any time in the future is questionable.[40]

Second, the justice model may be widely accepted in theory, but little evidence exists that it is producing a more humane system. In fact, prisons are worse today

[37]Donald R. Cressey, "Doing Justice," *The Center Magazine* 10 (January 1977): 24.

[38]Ibid., p. 177.

[39]Willard Gaylin and David J. Rothman, "Introduction," in *Doing Justice,* by von Hirsch.

[40]Francis A. Allen, *The Decline of the Rehabilitative Ideal* (New Haven: Yale University Press, 1981), p. 69.

than in 1975, when Fogel began to gain the ear of administrators. A large part of the problem can be traced to "get-tough-with-criminals" politicians who use the concept of determinate sentencing to create more punitive sentences. Thus, in those states that have adopted determinate sentencing structures, prison populations have skyrocketed. Unfortunately, there is too much truth in the accusation that proponents of the justice model have launched a repressive "movement that assumes the values they have opposed."[41]

SUMMARY

The justice model's basic disavowal of the state's ability to administer rehabilitation signals the end of an optimistic era in American corrections. Instead of depending on the state to institute reform in corrections, the justice model seeks ways to limit the power of the state over the lives of offenders. Equally as important, the justice model wants to dismantle many of the reforms of the past: the indeterminate sentence and the parole board, the rehabilitative ideal and its positivistic underpinnings, discretionary justice, and even the fortress-like prison.

The justice model is growing in popularity today, as evidenced by the spread of determinate sentencing across the nation. But the justice model will likely have both short- and long-range problems. Change, especially systemwide change, has never been easy to effect in the criminal justice system, and with the current hard-line mood of society and tight fiscal constraints, change will be even more difficult to achieve today. Determinate sentencing is also being misused by policymakers to create a more oppressive system, in which inmates are serving more rather than less time in prison. In terms of long-range problems, it is questionable whether the idea of "just deserts," which has been around for centuries, will ever dominate the correctional policy of this nation.[42] In other words, while the ideals of the justice model are admirable and their achievement should result in a far more humane justice system, these ideals may be as difficult to implement effectively as those of rehabilitative philosophy were in an earlier era.

DISCUSSION QUESTIONS

1. Why did David Fogel become disillusioned with the rehabilitative ideal in prison?
2. How does Fogel want to change the mission of probation?
3. List the philosophical underpinnings of the justice model. How do they differ from those of rehabilitation?
4. Discuss the components of the justice model.
5. Evaluate the strengths and limitations of the justice model.

---

[41]Cullen and Gilbert, *Reaffirming Rehabilitation,* p. 138.
[42]Allen, *Decline of the Rehabilitative Ideal,* p. 69.

Utilitarian Punishment Philosophy

4

Objectives

1. *To examine utilitarian punishment philosophy, as expressed by James Q. Wilson and Ernest Van den Haag.*

2. *To discuss the historical development of the punishment approach to dealing with the crime problem.*

3. *To reveal the basic philosophical underpinnings of utilitarian punishment philosophy.*

4. *To list the main components of the utilitarian punishment model.*

5. *To evaluate the strengths and limitations of the utilitarian punishment model.*

In the mid-1970s, the United States returned to the philosophy of utilitarian punishment to deal with the crime problem. Utilitarian punishment philosophy, which was developed by the classical school of criminology in the early eighteenth century, is grounded on the assumption that punishment is necessary to deter criminals and to protect society from crime. Punishment, then, is justified because of its presumed social advantages. Advocates of this philosophy of punishment, the correctional right, make the argument: If we are unable to improve prisoners through rehabilitative programs, we can at least assure that they are imprisoned and that potential lawbreakers are deterred by the consequences incurred by those who break the law.[1] James Q. Wilson, a leading spokesperson for utilitarian punishment philosophy, here describes the main points of this hard-line approach.

Box 4-1 Interview with James Q. Wilson

QUESTION: Is the public mood more receptive to the punishment model than when your book *Thinking about Crime* was first published?

WILSON: The public mood was receptive to the argument presented in that book at the time it appeared, and the public continues to be receptive today. I am convinced that the essential argument of the book corresponds to the commonsense judgments of most Americans, at least when they give the matter a sober second thought.

QUESTION: Has your thinking about the punishment model changed since the book was first published?

WILSON: My thinking has not changed in any fundamental way. In the light of new research and a critical analysis of past research, I would qualify some of my statements. For example, the evidence supporting the view that modest changes in punishment will mean a change in the crime rate isn't as strongly supported by scientific evidence as it first appeared to be. Moreover, our estimates of the crime-reduction effects that might be attributed to incapacitation have been revised since I wrote my book. At that time I was relying essentially on the estimates provided by Shinnar. Current estimates are somewhat different, and higher.

QUESTION: How do you agree and disagree with Van den Haag about how criminal offenders should be handled?

WILSON: I think we are in essential agreement that the purpose of the criminal justice system is to punish offenders and that, if it fails to do so, society pays. It may be that Van den Haag is more persuaded of the evidence that appears to show that sanctions have a strong deterrent effect than I am; I believe that sanctions do have a deterrent effect, but it is not clear how much of an increased deterrent effect can be achieved by the increased probability of punishment. I think he tends to give less attention than I do to the potential crime reduction effects of incapacitation. By and large the differences between us are marginal.

QUESTION: What are the main philosophical underpinnings of the punishment model?

WILSON: The essential philosophical underpinning is that the purpose of the criminal justice system is to do justice—that is, its purpose is to assign a penalty for a violation of an agreed-upon behavior. But no theory of the criminal justice system can rest solely on any one justification. Though no one should be punished except for crimes he or she has committed, the amount of the punishment imposed can

---

[1]John P. Conrad, *Justice and Consequences* (Lexington, Mass.: Heath, 1981), p. 157.

and must be based on a joint consideration of "just deserts" and of the effects on the crime rate of any proposed sanction. The "just deserts" model sets the framework within which we can ask how much crime reduction, if any, is associated with different levels of punishment.

QUESTION: Crime still seems to be out of control in our society. What can be done to make the crime problem more manageable?

WILSON: I don't think anyone knows what feasible strategy can be adapted in this country at this time that will have more than a marginal effect upon the crime rate. In general, I would favor directing more attention to the way the criminal justice system processes juveniles and toward the way it identifies and handles serious or repeat career offenders. Moreover, if the prospect of the penalty has some effect upon the crime rate, then the prospect of having a legitimate alternative to crime ought also to have an effect upon the crime rate. As a result, society shouldn't choose between a "get-tough" policy on crime and a "job-creation" policy for reducing crime. Both policies should be pursued simultaneously, but it is important to bear in mind that neither policy is likely to operate in the absence of the other (if the punishment for crime becomes more severe but there are no alternatives to crime, crime rates may not go down very much; if jobs become more abundant but crime is only lightly punished, then many persons would prefer crime to jobs).

QUESTION: What can be done about overcrowded prisons?

WILSON: My view is that we have at present no reliable empirical evidence that exposure to prison increases the rate at which people commit crime when released from prison. No doubt it has that effect for some persons just as prison reduces the crime rate for other persons. The net effect of these two forces operating jointly probably leaves the crime rate for prisoners as a whole pretty much unchanged. There is no question that many prisons are overcrowded, violent, or inhumane, though it is appropriate to point out that there are also many prisons that aren't violent or inhumane. I think society has a moral obligation to reduce overcrowding, violence, and inhumanity. I think federal judges are quite right to close down prisons maintained by states that refuse to invest the necessary resources to bring these institutions up to adequate constitutional standards. We have been underinvested in prisons, and as a result we have created in many places brutal conditions that should not be tolerated.

QUESTION: What do you now feel about the possibility of rehabilitation programs in corrections?

WILSON: The effort to rehabilitate offenders should continue, but it should be accompanied by a most rigorous and objective evaluation of the effects of rehabilitation. A recent report of the National Academy of Sciences and the National Research Council sets forth guidelines for the development and testing of rehabilitation techniques. These guidelines should be followed.

QUESTION: What changes have you seen take place in rehabilitative philosophy?

WILSON: There is as yet no evidence that rehabilitation programs have improved. They may have improved, but we don't know because we have relatively little research that does an adequate job of measuring the rehabilitative effect, if any, of programs.

QUESTION: What is your evaluation of probation and parole?

WILSON: The only way to make probation and parole supervision consistent with the requirements of justice is to make certain that supervision in the community is accompanied by some restriction on individual liberty so that supervision becomes a serious form of punishment. This can be done by community service, by victim restitution, by close and detailed supervision by probation officers, or by some combination of all three.

Parole represents a slightly different matter—it isn't clear to me that we ought to have parole in the traditional sense. Persons should be sentenced to a given period of either probation or prison, and when their sentence is served, they should be released without further supervision. The proper function of parole, in my view, is to assist exoffenders in obtaining jobs and other means of reintegrating themselves in the community. Parole should not serve as a watchdog. If an offender needs to be closely watched, he should not be released in the first place. If he only needs to be watched somewhat, he should not have been sent to prison in the first place.

Professor James Q. Wilson is presently Henry Lee Shattuck Professor of Government at Harvard University. Dr. Wilson has served as vice-chairman of The Police Foundation and a member of the Attorney General's Task Force on Violent Crime. He is the author of *Thinking About Crime* and *Varieties of Police Behavior.*
Source: Interview conducted in June 1982. Used with permission.

Beginning with a brief summary of the history of the punishment model in the United States, this chapter discusses the philosophy, the scope, the defense, and the criticism of the punishment model.

THE HISTORY OF THE PUNISHMENT MODEL

The punishment model is as old as history itself, for the belief has been fixed from the earliest written records that criminals must be punished. The yoke of a harsh environment and the burden of natural disasters encouraged ancient people to strike out vengefully against wrongdoers. Religious laws also encouraged this reaction because it was believed that antisocial acts offended the gods. Tribal codes further advocated vengeance against wrongdoers; in the blood feud, for example, the victim's family retaliated in kind and took measures like "an eye for an eye" against the offender's family or tribe.

Punishment was also commonly believed to be good for the wrongdoer. In the following Greek dialogue, Plato conveys this thought as he speaks through Socrates:

SOCRATES: Where and to whom do we take the sick in body?
POLUS: To the doctors, Socrates.
SOCRATES: And the unjust and intemperate?
POLUS: To the judges, do you mean?
SOCRATES: To suffer punishment?
POLUS: Yes.
SOCRATES: Then money-making rids us of poverty, medicine of sickness, and justice of intemperance and injustice. . . . [O]f two who suffer evil either in body or in soul, which is the more wretched, the man who submits to treatment and gets rid of the evil, or he who is not treated but still retains it?
POLUS: Evidently the man who was not treated.

SOCRATES: And was not punishment admitted to be a release from the greatest of evils, namely wickedness?

POLUS: It was.

SOCRATES: Yes, because a just penalty disciplines us and makes us more just and cures us of evil.[2]

Retributionism has been widely accepted throughout modern history. In the Middle Ages, even the church justified the use of cruel punishments for deviants. Indeed, during the Inquisition, deviants and heretics were tortured, imprisoned, and put to death. The state also developed its own methods of punishment during the Middle Ages. Although most punishments given by the state were economic, taking the form of fines, confiscations, or restitutions, the state also invoked long-term imprisonment, torture, and the death penalty.

The old punishments were combined with new ones to make the eighteenth century one of the most brutal ages for punishment of criminals. Flogging was the most popular method of corporal punishment; the death penalty was also widely used, and over two hundred offenses were punishable by death. Prisoners were transported (deported) to colonies and other parts of the world during the seventeenth as well as the eighteenth century. Furthermore, abandoned or unusable transport ships were converted into prisons; brutal floggings and degrading labor characterized daily life on these floating hells.

Ernest Van den Haag has aptly summarized the horrors of the punishments used throughout history:

> In times past the variety of punishments inflicted on criminals would have satisfied the most exigent sadist. In modern times the wide range has been narrowed, the variety diminished. We no longer impose most of the harshest punishments. The ingeniousness that went into torture instruments now displayed in European museums and still in use two hundred years ago amazes us, and the cruelty seems stunning. Any pain that human beings can wreak on one another was used for punishment. Courts did not hesitate to prescribe horrifying physical tortures or gruesome bodily mutilations. The Middle Ages were as inventive as antiquity, the West as zealous as the East. Death, meted out for trifling offenses, was thought too mild a punishment for serious crimes or, perhaps, too dull. So dying was artfully drawn out into agony beyond belief by a succession of progressively more painful mutilations inflicted in multifarious ways.[3]

The Development of Utilitarianism

The classical school of criminology, a development of the eighteenth century, did much to rescue punishment from the brutal and sadistic practices of the Middle Ages. Cesare Beccaria's *Crime and Punishment,* which contains the essential principles of the classical school, states:

---

[2]E. Hamilton and H. Cairns, "Protagoras," in *The Collected Dialogues of Plato* (New York: Pantheon, 1961), pp. 308–352.

[3]Ernest Van den Haag, *Punishing Criminals: Concerning a Very Old and Painful Question* (New York: Basic, 1975), p. 196.

The purpose of punishment is to deter persons from the commission of crime and not to provide social revenge. Not severity, but certainty and swiftness in punishment best secure this result. Punishment must be sure and swift and penalties determined strictly in accordance with the social damage wrought by the crime. Crimes against property should be punished solely by fines, or by imprisonment when the person is unable to pay the fine. Banishment is an excellent punishment for crimes against the state. There should be no capital punishment. Life imprisonment is a better deterrent. Capital punishment is irreparable and hence makes no provision for possible mistakes and the desirability of later rectification.[4]

Jeremy Bentham further developed the philosophy of the classical school. He advocated the view that a rational human being would do what was necessary to achieve the most pleasure and the least pain. Bentham believed that if punishment were made appropriate to the crime, it would deter criminal behavior. He saw punishment as having four objectives: (1) to prevent all offenses, if possible; (2) to persuade a person who chooses to commit an offense to commit a less rather than a more serious one; (3) when a person has resolved upon a particular offense, "to dispose him to do not more mischief than is necessary to his purpose"; and (4) to prevent the crime at as cheap a rate as possible.[5]

Both Beccaria and Bentham reasoned that human beings were rational creatures who, being free to choose their actions, could be held responsible for their behavior. Thus, the doctrine that humans were rational beings with free will was substituted for the widely accepted theological determinism, which saw humans as preordained to certain actions. Punishment was no longer justified on the "barbarous" grounds of vengeful retaliation, nor was it seen by reasonable people as expiation on the basis of "superstitious" theories of guilt and repayment. In keeping with new ideas of the rising middle class, punishment was justified because of its practical usefulness. The aim was the protection of society and the dominant theme was deterrence. The theory was that, if the human being is a creature governed by a *felicific calculus* (pertaining to the ability to produce happiness for self) and oriented toward obtaining a favorable balance of pleasure and pain, then setting up a rational scale of punishments painful enough to deter the criminal from further offenses and others from following the offenders example of crime ought to be possible.[6]

Other important tenets of the classical school that contributed to the development of utilitarianism were that the sanctions of the criminal law should outweigh the rewards of crime, that sanctions should be proclaimed in advance of their use, that sanctions should be proportionate to the offense, that equal justice should be offered everyone, and that individuals should be judged by the law solely for their actions, not for their beliefs.[7]

[4]Harry Elmer Barnes and Negley K. Teeters, *New Horizons in Criminology,* 3d ed. (Englewood Cliffs, N.J.: Prentice-Hall, 1959), p. 285.

[5]Ysabel Rennie, *The Search for Criminal Man: A Conceptual History of the Dangerous Offender* (Lexington, Mass.: Heath, 1978), p. 22.

[6]Richard A. Ball, "Restricted Reprobation and the Reparation of Social Reality: A Theory of Punishment" (Paper presented at the Annual Meeting of the American Society of Criminology, Dallas, 1978), p. 6.

[7]Rennie, *Search for Criminal Man,* p. 24.

Contemporary Development of Punishment Philosophy

Utilitarianism, as advocated by many proponents for the next century, concluded that such considerations as criminal deterrence, social reform, and prisoner rehabilitation are justified because of their presumed social advantages. But, beginning with J. D. Mabbott's seminal essay "Punishment" in 1939, utilitarian theories came under increased criticism. Mabbott's central argument was that it is unjust to deprive a person of liberty as a consequence of that person's committing a criminal act for any reason other than that the act "deserves" to be punished and that the person committed the act.[8] This led to the "just desert" philosophy of punishment. Just desert advocates, such as David Fogel and Andrew von Hirsh, question the utility of punishment as a means of deterring crime and support the use of punishment only because those who commit crime deserve to be punished.[9]

However, in the 1970s, James Q. Wilson and Ernest Van den Haag articulated a neoutilitarian punishment philosophy.[10] Advocating punishment as a useful means of dealing with crime, Wilson and Van den Haag received an eager reception by a public that wanted to "get-tough-with-criminals."[11]

PHILOSOPHY OF UTILITARIAN PUNISHMENT

Proponents of utilitarian punishment philosophy display a great deal of diversity of backgrounds and beliefs, but they usually resent losses in the quality of American life caused by the widespread problem of criminality. They often express nostalgia for an earlier period of American society, when it seemed that values were clear, the moral consensus was overwhelming, and the future was predictable and inviting.[12] Advocates of the punishment approach also usually agree on most of the following underlying philosophical tenets.

First, they believe that a paramount duty of government is to provide a legal order that enables citizens to be secure in their lives, their liberties, and their pursuit of happiness. Governments protect the rights and liberties of citizens by specifying

[8]J. D. Mabbott, "Punishment," *Mind* 49 (1939), reprinted in Frederick A. Olafson, *Justice and Social Policy* (Englewood Cliffs, N.J.: Prentice-Hall, 1961), p. 39.

[9]Andrew von Hirsh, *Doing Justice: The Choice of Punishments* (New York: Hill and Wang, 1975) and David Fogel, *". . . We Are the Living Proof": A Justice Model for Corrections,* 2nd ed. (Cincinnati: Anderson, 1979).

[10]Van den Haag, *Punishing Criminals;* James Q. Wilson, *Thinking about Crime* (New York: Basic, 1975); and Wilson, "The Political Feasibility of Punishment," in *Justice and Punishment*, ed. J. B. Cederblom and William L. Blizek (Cambridge, Mass.: Ballinger, 1977).

[11]Part of the popularity of utilitarian punishment in the 1970s was related to the fact that it satisfied the public's need for vengeance as well as for reformation. Criminals would have to pay for their crimes and in the process be purified or cleansed because of the cost of punishment.

[12]Francis A. Allen, *The Decline of the Rehabilitation Ideal* (New Haven: Yale University Press, 1981), p. 62.

crimes through laws and by enforcing the laws. Laws prohibit some activities (crimes) on pain of punishment (penalties). Punishment is administered by many agencies, which form the criminal justice system. However, the rate of punishment declined in the decades prior to the mid-1970s because the moral justification and usefulness of punishment had been questioned. The reduced use of punishment coincided with a skyrocketing increase in such crimes as robbery, auto theft, and murder.[13]

Second, the basic purpose of punishment is to enforce the law and to vindicate the legal order. Punishment, like a debt, must be paid because it is owed by those who violate the law. But there is a difference between punishment and vengeance. Although vengeance is self-serving since it is arbitrarily taken by a person who feels injured and wishes to retaliate, punishment or retribution is imposed by the courts after a guilty plea or a trial in which the accused has been found guilty of committing a crime.[14]

Third, it is assumed that punishment will deter criminal behavior. Van den Haag, as Wilson suggested in the interview at the beginning of this chapter, is more convinced of the deterrent effects of sanctions than other proponents of utilitarian punishment philosophy. Van den Haag claims that the "first line of social defense is the cost imposed for criminal activity."[15] Thus, society should make the cost of crime high enough that it will deter most criminals. Van den Haag puts this well when he says:

> However, if a given offender's offenses are rational in the situation in which he lives—if what he can gain exceeds the likely cost to him by more than the gain from legitimate activities does—there is little that can be "corrected" in the offender. Reform will fail. It often fails for this reason. What has to be changed is not the personality of the offender, but the cost-benefit ratio which makes his offense rational. That ratio can be changed by improving and multiplying his opportunities for legitimate activity and the benefits they yield, or by decreasing his opportunity for illegitimate activities, or by increasing their cost to him, including punishment.[16]

Thus, punishment deters crimes because it is educative and moral; criminals are taught to not commit further crimes, and noncriminals see what happens to those who break the law. In other words, punishment deters crimes because it is a message to the criminal that there is a cost to crime and because it is a message to the public at large that "this will happen to you if you violate the law."[17] The effect of punishment depends largely on the stigma put on criminal activity as well as on the real sufferings inflicted on criminal violators and on the certainty and severity of punishment.

[13]Van den Haag, *Punishing Criminals*, pp. 1–5.
[14]Ibid., p. 11.
[15]Ibid., p. 57.
[16]Ibid., p. 59.
[17]Ibid., p. 60.

Fourth, although this punishment approach is designed around the social utility of punishment, support is also given to just desert punishment philosophy. Wilson states that the punishment imposed can and must be based on a joint consideration of just deserts and of the effects on the crime rate of any proposed sanction. He adds that the just deserts model sets the framework within which we can ask what crime reduction, if any, is associated with different forms of punishment. Yet the joint consideration that Wilson mentions is actually a submersion of just deserts to the concept of the social utility of punishment.

Fifth, proponents of utilitarian punishment philosophy believe that offenders can reason and have freely chosen to violate the law; that is, they are not controlled by any past or present forces. Because criminals are seen as having free will, advocates of utilitarian punishment philosophy conclude that offenders deserve punishment for the social harm they have inflicted upon society. Moreover, criminal behavior is not excused because of any internal temptation (motivation or inclination) or any external temptation (opportunity, stimulation, or deprivation).[18] Van den Haag expressed it this way:

> It is easy, though unfashionable, to see why justice must disregard the different needs and general disparities of temptation among persons and groups. A frustrated man rejected as repulsive by the sexual partner he craves may be more tempted to rape than another person better endowed or stimulated; an irritable person is more disposed to assault than a phlegmatic one; a poor and deprived man may be more tempted to steal than a wealthy one. But the prohibition against rape must be applied equally to repulsive (and frustrated) individuals and to attractive (and unfrustrated) ones; the prohibition against assault to the ill- and to the even-tempered; and the prohibition against stealing to rich and poor alike. Else the forbidden act would be prohibited only to those not inclined or tempted to commit it. Which won't help. The purpose of the law is to forbid what some people are tempted to do, by character or by circumstance. The threat of punishment is meant to discourage those who are tempted, rather than those who are not.[19]

Sixth, predatory street crime is a far more serious matter than white-collar crime and, therefore, should be the focus of the efforts of the criminal justice system. Although white-collar crimes victimize large organizations, street crime inspires fear, makes the maintenance of meaningful human communities difficult, and victimizes specific individuals, often the poorest ones.[20]

Seventh, advocates of this law-and-order philosophy believe that offenders are deterred from crime only when they become aware that unlawful behavior will result in a period of isolation from society. Hard-liners, not surprisingly, discourage the movement to deinstitutionalize juvenile and adult justice, because they claim that many offenders do not take the justice process seriously until they "do some time." James Q. Wilson explains why he believes it is necessary to isolate criminals:

[18]Ibid., p. 63.
[19]Ibid., pp. 44–45.
[20]Wilson, *Thinking about Crime*, p. xix.

. . . [W]e would view the correctional system as having a very different function—namely, to isolate and to punish. It is a measure of our confusion that such a statement will strike many enlightened readers today as cruel, even barbaric. It is not. It is merely a recognition that society at a minimum must be able to protect itself from dangerous offenders and to impose some costs (other than the stigma and inconvenience of an arrest and court appearance) on criminal acts; it is also a frank admission that society really does not know how to do much else.[21]

Eighth, advocates of utilitarian punishment philosophy are especially critical of making rehabilitation the purpose of sentencing. They feel that rehabilitation will not work, that there is insufficient evidence that rehabilitation reduces recidivism. Proponents are also indignant about the injustice of indeterminate sentencing, because offenders who have committed the same crimes under the same circumstances often receive very different sentences. They further question the ability of a parole board to know when a person has been rehabilitated. In addition, they question whether rehabilitation is a sufficient penalty for the social harm an offender has done.[22] Yet the punishment model still reserves some role for rehabilitation. Wilson says:

Now suppose we abandon entirely the rehabilitation theory of sentencing and corrections—not the effort to rehabilitate, just the theory that the governing purpose of the enterprise is to rehabilitate. We could continue experiments with new correctional and therapeutic procedures, expanding them when the evidence warrants. If existing correctional programs do not differ in their rehabilitative potential, we could support those that are least costly and more humane (while still providing reasonable security) and phase out those that are most costly and inhumane. But we would not do any of these things on the mistaken notion that we were thereby reducing recidivism.[23]

Ninth, hard-liners are particularly sensitive to the social harm that repeat offenders inflict upon society. Advocates of this model suggest that some offenders are "wicked" people and may require postpunishment incapacitation. Van den Haag goes a step further and proposes that some of these repeat offenders should be banished or exiled rather than returned to the community after they have completed their sentences.[24]

Finally, "prisons and jails are not intended to be country clubs." Wilson emphasizes this point:

Prisons and jails are not intended to be pleasant places. They are primarily institutions for punishment and, though conditions in them could no doubt be improved, the level of amenity there must always be less than its level in society at large else people outside will envy those inside and perhaps even try to break into prison.[25]

[21]Ibid., pp. 172–173.

[22]Ibid., pp. 171–172.

[23]Ibid., p. 172.

[24]Van den Haag, *Punishing Criminals*, pp. 256–257.

[25]Wilson, "Political Feasibility of Punishment," in *Justice and Punishment*, Cederblom and Blizek, p. 110.

However, as he said in the interview, Wilson feels society has a moral obligation to reduce overcrowding, violence, and inhumanity when they are present in correctional institutions. Van den Haag is more explicit about the conditions of the prison that lead to violence and inhumane conditions:

> In most cases, the prisoner's lot is worse than deliberate punitiveness would have made it. Once incarceration is no longer intentionally, officially, and directly meant to be punitive or penitential, the staff seems to have no more idea of the purpose of prisons than the inmates. And neither [group] has confidence in the proclaimed corrective purpose—if they [have] heard of it. Prisoners, then, are left at the mercy of an odd mixture of creaky bureaucratic regulations, individual abuses (sometimes well-meaning), and above all, laissez-faire. Laissez-faire has come to mean that prisons are effectively run by the prisoners. "Correctional officers" are content to enforce self-protective regulations without effectively protecting prisoners from one another. Hence prisoners who have achieved dominance—by virtue of strength, aggressiveness, organization, etc.—abuse other prisoners. Homosexual rape is commonplace. To avoid violence, injury, or death, most prisoners are compelled to submit to threats by bullying inmates. The effect is brutalizing and criminalizing—the very opposite of what benevolent reformers meant it to be. Attempts to structure the activities of prisoners meaningfully and to prepare them for law-abiding conduct upon release cannot be taken seriously under these circumstances.[26]

In summary, proponents of utilitarian punishment philosophy believe that it is the crime problem that is robbing citizens of the safety of the past. To "get tough with crime" will serve the social advantages of deterring criminals and protecting society. In declaring war on crime, proponents of utilitarian punishment philosophy recommend several strategies.

COMPONENTS OF THE UTILITARIAN PUNISHMENT MODEL

An increased use of incapacitation, a hard-line policy toward serious juvenile offenders, a greater use of determinate and mandatory sentences, more effective court systems, a get-tough policy with drug offenders, and the return of the death penalty are the main strategies behind the utilitarian punishment model.

Increased Use of Incapacitation

Proponents of this model believe that depriving a criminal of liberty will reduce the number of those free to violate the law, and, therefore, they recommend that most offenders should be imprisoned and that they should be held for longer periods of time. These advocates strongly emphasize the importance of incarcerating repeat offenders, who they claim now "suffer little or no loss of freedom."[27] And

[26]Van den Haag, *Punishing Criminals*, pp. 258–259.
[27]Wilson, *Thinking about Crime*, p. 200.

of course, it is also advantageous to incarcerate serious offenders because they are prevented during the period of their confinement from committing additional crimes.[28]

Hard-Line Policy toward Serious Juvenile Offenders

Hard-liners have little confidence in the *parens patriae* philosophy of the juvenile court in dealing with the serious problem of youth crime. Proponents of the punishment model believe that the present permissiveness of the juvenile justice system should be replaced by a tougher attitude and that violent juvenile offenders should be shifted from the jurisdiction of the juvenile court to face the adult court proceedings. They also contend that the commitment of more juveniles to training schools would act as a more effective deterrent to youth crime.

Greater Use of Determinate and Mandatory Sentences

Supporters of the punishment model advocate a wider use of determinate and mandatory sentencing. As previously indicated, they have little confidence in indeterminate sentencing and in the parole board. They believe that sentences fixed by the legislature will deal with the crime problem more adequately than those that depend on the discretion of judges and parole boards.

Development of a More Effective Court System

Proponents of the model see an overwhelmed and ineffective court system as partly to blame for the crime problem being out of control. They recommend that the court system be provided with dramatically increased financial and manpower resources so criminals will receive sufficient punishment. Wilson aptly states this position:

> Anyone familiar with the police station, jails and courts of some of our larger cities is keenly aware that accused persons caught up in the system are exposed to very little that involves either judgment or solemnity. They are instead processed through a bureaucratic maze in which a bargain is offered and a haggle ensues at every turn— over amounts of bail, degree of the charged offense, and the nature of the plea. Much of what observers find objectionable about this process could be alleviated by devoting many more resources to it, so that an ample supply of prosecutors, defense attorneys, and judges were available.[29]

[28]Ibid.
[29]Ibid., p. 205.

Get-Tough Policy with Drug Offenders

Both Wilson and Van den Haag are aware that drug addiction causes considerable criminal activity, especially in urban areas. But they refuse to regard addiction as a disease and thereby excuse the crimes that individuals addicted to drugs commit. Van den Haag believes that if "we punish becoming addicted, fewer persons do become addicted."[30] Wilson also notes that drug addicts, like other offenders, are deterred when a get-tough policy is enforced. He found that "when the cost declined sharply in 1961–1970 . . . the number of addicts in Boston increased about tenfold . . . the largest increases in the number of addicts tended to follow years in which the certainty and severity of law enforcement were the lowest."[31]

Return of the Death Penalty

Proponents of the utilitarian punishment model have been the most vocal supporters of the return of the death penalty. They argue that the death penalty is a proper and fitting penalty for some crimes, and should be more widely used. Wilson states, "The main issue remains that of justice—the point is not whether capital punishment prevents future crimes, but whether it is a proper and fitting penalty for crimes that have occurred."[32]

DEFENSE OF THE UTILITARIAN PUNISHMENT MODEL

The best defense of the utilitarian punishment model is its popularity today. Its main components have been widely accepted by policymakers throughout the nation. More than twice as many inmates are now confined in correctional institutions as were a decade ago. Many states have adopted determinate and mandatory sentencing systems, and many more violent juvenile criminals are being transferred to adult courts. In addition, the death penalty has been reinstated in many states; and, beginning with that of Gary Gilmore in 1977, a number of executions have taken place.

In short, the contention by advocates of the utilitarian punishment model that punishment should be tried because nothing else has worked with criminal offenders has been widely accepted by policymakers. There appears to be a consensus among policymakers in most states that an increase in imprisonment is necessary because community treatment methods do not work. Policymakers also commonly agree

---

[30]Van den Haag, *Punishing Criminals,* p. 127.
[31]Wilson, *Thinking about Crime,* p. 145.
[32]Ibid., p. 197.

that the public deserves protection, and, therefore, providing punishment for criminal acts is a just, feasible, and effective way to deal with crime.

Supporters of the utilitarian punishment model have used research on deterrence to validate the need for a harder line on crime. For example, in *Thinking About Crime,* Wilson gives considerable weight to the research on deterrence that Shlomo and Reuel Shinnar conducted in New York City. He says:

> Shlomo and Reuel Shinnar have estimated the effect on crime rates in New York State of a judicial policy other than that followed during the last decade or so. Given the present level of police efficiency and making some assumptions about how many crimes each offender commits per year, they conclude that the rate of serious crime would be only one-third what it is today if every person convicted of a serious offense were imprisoned for three years. This reduction would be less if it turned out (as seems unlikely) that most serious crimes are committed by first-time offenders, and it would be much greater if the proportion of crimes resulting in an arrest and conviction were increased (as also seems unlikely). The reduction, it should be noted, would be solely the result of incapacitation, making no allowance for such additional reductions as might result from enhanced deterrence or rehabilitation.[33]

Wilson also points to the study conducted by Marvin Wolfgang and associates in Philadelphia, Pennsylvania, in which they examined the delinquency records of all the males born in 1945 who lived in Philadelphia between their tenth and eighteenth birthdays.[34] The study on ten thousand boys showed that once a juvenile has been arrested three times, the chances of his being rearrested were over 70 percent. The researchers also found that around 6 percent of the sample committed over half of the serious youth crimes in Philadelphia. Thus, if a small percentage of the youth population had been isolated, Wilson reasons, much of the serious problem of youth crime in Philadelphia would have been prevented.

Van den Haag has used a number of other studies to support the notion that increased punishment would deter the amount of crime in society. He cites Gibbs, who found according to FBI data, that the greater the certainty and the severity of the punishment in forty-eight states, the lower the homicide rate.[35] Louis Gray and J. Martin, who used the same data for 1959 and 1960, concluded that the "certainty and severity of punishment have a demonstrable impact on the homicide rate. . . ."[36] George Antunes and A. Lee Hunt, analyzing 1960 data for all seven index crimes in forty-nine states, concluded that "the hypothesis that penal sanctions act as a general deterrent of crime finds support in our data."[37] Van den Haag also cites the

---

[33]Ibid., pp. 200–201.

[34]Marvin E. Wolfgang, Robert M. Figlio, and Thorsten Sellin, *Delinquency in a Birth Cohort* (Chicago: University of Chicago Press, 1972).

[35]Jack Gibbs, "Crime, Punishment, and Deterrence," *Social Science Quarterly* 48 (1968); 515–530.

[36]Louis Gray and J. Martin, "Criminal Homicide, Punishment and Deterrence: Methodological and Substantive Reconsiderations," *Social Science Quarterly* 52 (1971); 277–289.

[37]George Antunes and A. Lee Hunt, "The Impact of Certainty and Severity of Punishment on Levels of Crime in American States: An Extended Analysis," (Evanston, Ill.: Center for Urban Affairs, Northwestern University, 1972).

research of Isaac Ehrlich, who examined all FBI index crimes in the years 1940, 1950, and 1960, and measured the effect not of the actual legal threat but of the *credible* legal threat of punishment. Ehrlich concluded: "The rate of specific felonies is found to be positively related to estimates of relative gains and negatively to estimates of costs associated with criminal activity."[38] He adds, "The rate of specific crime categories, with virtually no exception, varies inversely with estimates of the probability of apprehension and punishment by imprisonment and with the average length of time served in state prisons."[39] Finally, Charles R. Tittle and Alan R. Rowe found that "certainty of arrests appears to be linked to the amount of crime in a negative direction when the level of certainty reaches 30 percent but not at all when certainty is below 30 percent."[40]

CRITICISMS OF THE UTILITARIAN PUNISHMENT MODEL

The most widespread criticism of the utilitarian punishment model is that a repressive response to crime will not work. Critics assert that a brutal treatment of criminals has not worked in the past and that a repressive response is no more likely to work now or in the future. They argue that the main reason why a repressive response to crime will not work is that the logic underlying the punishment model is fundamentally flawed. This neoclassical approach assumes that criminal acts take place after offenders have calculated rationally the costs and benefits of crime, but little evidence is available to support the existence of such a rational process of decision-making among offenders. More commonly, crime is committed by those who are poor, addicted to drugs, mentally unstable, or influenced by peers, and, rather than calculating rationally the costs and benefits of crime, offenders are merely responding to the needs or emotions of a particular situation.

Critics further question whether the efficacy of the punishment philosophy can be judged on the basis of the various deterrence studies, because most of these research findings are filled with speculation and methodological problems.[41] Several recent studies have specifically challenged the deterrence effects of incapacitation. For example, Van Dine, Conrad, and Dinitz—in their examination of violent crime in Franklin County, Ohio (Columbus)—found that incapacitation fails to prevent a significant amount of adult crime for two reasons. First, "over two-thirds of the persons in this study were first-time felony offenders" and "incapacitation could

---

[38]Isaac Ehrlich, "Participation in Illegitimate Activities: A Theoretical Investigation," *Journal of Political Economy* (May-June 1973), p. 560.

[39]Ibid., p. 545.

[40]Charles R. Tittle and Alan R. Rowe, "Certainty of Arrest and Crime Rates: A Further Test of the Deterrence Hypothesis," *Social Forces* 52 (June 1974): 455–462.

[41]See Stephen Van Dine, John P. Conrad, and Simon Dinitz, *Restraining the Wicked: The Incapacitation of the Dangerous Criminal* (Lexington, Mass.: Heath, 1979), pp. 17–33 for a review of the methodological problems of deterrence studies.

not have prevented their 1973 crimes," and, second, "the rate of recidivism for the recidivist group is too low to provide significant reductions in the incidence of crime through an incapacitation policy."[42]

Critics also assail the policy of increased confinement advocated by the utilitarian punishment approach, which is acknowledged to make more repressive a criminal justice system that is already viewed as one of the most repressive in Western society. Karl Menninger and others argue that imprisonment should be used only if criminals are incorrigibly dangerous. Menninger is bothered not only by the futility and expense but also by the motivations behind using imprisonment to punish offenders. He concludes that the state is acting as the vengeful agent of people who are content to let someone else do the dirty work for them.[43]

The fairness of the utilitarian punishment approach is further criticized. Although prisons and jails are not intended to be country clubs, many persons held in jail are awaiting trial and have not been convicted of any wrongdoing. Why should these persons receive "punishment"? In addition, critics claim that proponents of the utilitarian punishment model deny the widespread criminality in our society when they look upon the offender as an alien or an outsider. This view contradicts the various self-report studies, which have found that most individuals at one or more times during their lives involve themselves in some form of criminal behavior. Too, critics charge that hard-liners focus almost entirely on street crime while they minimize the social harm done to society by white-collar crime. Blacks, Hispanics, and those who commit street crimes usually (and often correctly) do not see the punishments they receive as just, when they observe white-collar criminals receiving a different brand of "justice."

Furthermore, the utilitarian punishment model is accused of limiting penal reform. Critics charge that the emphasis on repressive methods minimizes the impetus for reform of America's overcrowded, violent, and criminogenic prisons and could result in a return to a primitive conception of criminal justice.[44]

Finally, critics charge that proponents of the utilitarian punishment model neglect the social and structural conditions of society that lead to crime. The critics argue that, in blaming crime solely on offenders, advocates of the utilitarian punishment model encourage policymakers to continue neglecting social conditions such as poverty and unemployment that lead to crime.

Radical criminologists especially are critical of the way in which this conservative philosophy ignores the injustice and inhumanity of society. They charge that the utilitarian punishment approach solidifies the power of the ruling elites and, therefore, works against the structural transformation of an exploitative capitalist system. Richard Quinney, a major spokesperson for the radical criminology approach, puts this well:

[42]Ibid., pp. 64–81.
[43]Karl Menninger, *The Crime of Punishment* (New York: Viking Press, 1968).
[44]Allen, *Decline of the Rehabilitation Ideal*, p. 62.

As the "rehabilitation" ideal proves itself bankrupt in practice, liberals and conservatives alike (all within the capitalist hegemony) resort to the utilitarian of pain. . . . We have the reconstruction of a reality that takes as given the existing social order. Rather than suggesting an alternative order, one based on a different conception of human nature, political economy, and social justice, we are presented with schemes that merely justify further repression within the established order. The solutions being offered can only exacerbate the conditions of our existence.[45]

In sum, the shortcomings of this model clearly outweigh its strengths. Three criticisms leveled at the punishment model are particularly disturbing: (1) the repressiveness of the model will not work; (2) this approach will lead to a more inhumane and unfair justice system; and (3) this model encourages the ignoring of the social problems that lead to crime. Using repressive measures to declare war on crime may have dire consequences for American society.

COMPARING THE UTILITARIAN PUNISHMENT MODEL WITH THE JUSTICE AND REHABILITATION MODELS

The rehabilitation, justice, and utilitarian models differ in several significant ways. The rehabilitation model is based upon a deterministic outlook, which claims that crime is caused by some biological or psychological deficiency within the offender or some sociological factor within society. In contrast, the justice and utilitarian punishment models are based upon the concept of free will, in which offenders are looked upon as responsible individuals who deserve to be punished for their misbehavior. Although the concept of "just deserts" is the basic rationale for punishment in the justice model, the deterrence of offenders and the protection of society are acknowledged as the basic rationales for punishment in the utilitarian punishment models.

The purpose of sentencing in the utilitarian punishment model is to establish law and order in society. Doing justice, which means to minimize the harm done by the justice system and to ensure that the justice system does a better job of dispensing justice, is the basic purpose of sentencing in the justice model. But the rehabilitation model holds that the purpose of sentencing is to provide for the rehabilitation of offenders through individualized treatment, that is, the purpose of the justice system is to do good by providing opportunities for offenders to be cured of their propensity for criminal behavior. The rehabilitation model continues to uphold indeterminate sentencing and the parole board, while the justice and utili-

---

[45]Richard Quinney, *Class, State, and Crime: On the Theory and Practice of Criminal Justice* (New York: David McKay, 1977), pp. 16–17.

tarian punishment models propose the enactment of determinate sentencing systems throughout the nation.

The role of offender-rehabilitation is looked upon as the basic goal of the correctional process in the rehabilitation model. The justice model retains a role for treatment for those offenders who choose voluntarily to become involved in treatment. However, the utilitarian punishment model contends that treatment is ineffective and dangerous because it results in the coddling of criminals. Supporters of correctional treatment currently disagree on whether interventions should be voluntary or enforced, but advocates of both the justice and the utilitarian models strongly reject enforced rehabilitation during the correctional process.

The crime control strategy of the rehabilitation model is designed to eliminate the factors causing crime through a therapeutic environment or experience for offenders. Advocates of rehabilitation also maintain that the more programs are improved in design and quality, the more likely that offenders will be deterred from future criminal behavior. The justice model holds that offenders should receive "just deserts" or "just punishment" for their socially unacceptable behavior, but that once they are punished proportionately to the social harm they have inflicted upon society, they should receive humane and fair treatment by the justice system. The justice model also proposes that practitioners in the justice systems and victims of crime deserve justice-as-fairness. The basic crime control strategy of the utilitarian punishment model is to declare war on crime by instituting "get-tough" policies. Proponents of this model hold that increasing the cost of crime will deter the commission of criminal behavior and will protect the citizens of society. Table 4-1 displays the similarities and differences among the three models.

The danger today lies in the fact that the public mood and the decisions of policymakers are supporting repression. The utilitarian punishment model, unlike the classical school of old, leads to a repressive rather than a more humane approach to justice. Unfortunately, even the proposals for reform in the justice model are being used to create a repressive system. Since utilitarian punishment philosophy offers some tangible results and is consistent with the principles of our utilitarian society, it enjoys the support of the American public.

The role of correctional treatment in creating a more humane system is looming larger today. In the past, rehabilitation, especially the medical model, often contributed to the victimization of the criminal. Now, correctional treatment, largely freed of the medical or disease model, is mandated to join with the reforms of the justice model to preserve humanitarianism during the justice process. Although correctional treatment will not play the dominant role it has in the past, it is an essential and necessary part of the correctional process in a free and democratic society.

But the role of correctional treatment today must develop in the following context:

1. Punishment is acknowledged as the dominant purpose of the adult justice system and as an increasingly important function of the juvenile justice system.
2. Determinate sentencing will be enacted in many states.

TABLE 4-1   Comparison of the Rehabilitation, Justice, and Utilitarian Punishment Models

POLICY	REHABILITATION	JUSTICE	UTILITARIAN PUNISHMENT
1. Approach to the Offender	Deterministic or Positivistic Approach	Free Will Based upon the Classical School	Free Will Based upon the Classical School
2. Purpose of Sentencing	Establish Law and Order	Doing Justice	Doing Good
3. Type of Sentencing Advocated	Indeterminate	Determinate	Determinate
4. Role of Treatment	Basic Goal of the Correctional Process	Voluntary but Necessary in a Humane System	Ineffective and Dangerous because It Results in Coddling Criminals
5. Crime Control Strategy	Eliminate Factors Causing Crime through Therapeutic Intervention; Develop Improved Treatment Technologies	Justice-As-Fairness for Offenders, for Practitioners in the Justice System, and for Victims	Declare War on Crime by Instituting Get-Tough Policies

3. Correctional interventions will be made voluntary rather than enforced to a far greater degree than in the past.

4. Correctional treatment cannot ignore the importance of deterrence in validating its role in the correctional process.

5. Due process rights and procedural safeguards will continue to guide what is done with offenders during the correctional process.

6. Continued support of correctional treatment in a cost- and results-oriented society demands that interventions improve significantly throughout the correctional process.

SUMMARY

Clearly the punishment model of old has regained popularity today. Policymakers throughout the nation have come to the conclusion that increasing the punishment for criminal behavior will result in reducing crime. Utilitarian punishment, as articulated by Wilson and Van den Haag in the 1970s and early 1980s, is justified on the basis of its usefulness in protecting society and in deterring crime. These social advantages are to be achieved by an increased use of punishment, a hardline policy toward serious juvenile crime, a greater use of determinate or mandatory sentences, a more effective court system, a get-tough policy with drug offenders, and the return of the death penalty.

However, there is little evidence that longer criminal sentences, more punitive prisons, or a greater number of executions will result in less recidivism or in any other benefit. Proponents of utilitarian punishment philosophy want substantial proof that rehabilitation works before they will accept treatment as having a viable role in the correctional process, but, in a real sense, utilitarian punishment philosophy is grounded on no more secure theoretical or empirical foundation than is rehabilitative philosophy. Utilitarian punishment philosophy may have widespread acceptance in the public sector, but the danger is that this repressive response to crime may return the American society to the Dark Ages of corrections.

DISCUSSION QUESTIONS

1. What is the basic philosophy that James Q. Wilson articulates in the interview in this chapter?
2. Why has the public turned to utilitarian punishment time after time as the method for dealing with criminal behavior?
3. What are the major philosophical underpinnings of utilitarian punishment philosophy?
4. What are the main components of utilitarian punishment? Why do advocates of this model hold to each of these components?
5. How do Wilson and Van den Haag differ in their interpretation of the utilitarian punishment philosophy?
6. What is the major difference between just-deserts punishment and utilitarian punishment philosophies?
7. What is your evaluation of the utilitarian punishment approach?

5

Community-Based Programs: Juvenile

Objectives

1. *To describe the various programs for readjudicated and post-adjudicated juvenile offenders in the community.*
2. *To illustrate each type with one or more model programs.*
3. *To evaluate the strengths and shortcomings of each type of program.*
4. *To note the challenges to community-based corrections for juveniles.*

An impressive array of programs for youthful offenders exists in the community. These include delinquency prevention, runaway facilities, alternative schools, foster care, mediation with youth gangs, family therapy, diversion, restitution, day treatment, residential facilities, wilderness learning experiences, and therapeutic communities. The ongoing search for solutions, or panaceas, to the problem of delinquency and the popularity of deinstitutionalization in juvenile corrections probably best explain why there are so many programs for youthful offenders. Various studies of these community-based programs have found them to be vastly more humane, somewhat more economical, and at least as effective as institutions in reducing recidivism. It would seem to be beyond challenge that community-based corrections is a far better way for the United States to deal with its juvenile crime problem.

However, community-based programs must meet several challenges in order to provide even more effective treatment for juveniles. First, support of community programs declined in the 1970s because the hard-liners alarmed the general public about the extent and danger of youth crime. While there had been talk of closing all state training schools, as Massachusetts had done in the early 1970s, the shift in public opinion put community-based programs in a defensive and retreating position. Second, the end of LEAA funding in the late 1970s left many community programs unable to find sufficient funding to keep doors open. Third, most of the high-impact community-based programs for juveniles are led by charismatic and dedicated leaders and are strongly dependent upon the continued tenure of these leaders. So, unless bureaucratic agencies are capable of projecting the personal qualities of such leaders, many effective community-based programs for juveniles will disappear. Fourth, community-based programs for juveniles must develop a more elaborate network of services. As research in Massachusetts has indicated, communities with networks of services are more likely to have effective programs for juveniles than those that lack such networks.[1] Fifth, while mediating structures rooted in the community appear to offer a more effective way of dealing with urban youth crime, unless these mediating programs can be expanded to more urban neighborhoods, youths in these communities will continue to make urban areas unsafe for everyone.

This chapter examines the various nonresidential and residential treatment services for juveniles in the community. The more traditional services of probation and parole are considered together in Chapter 11. Beginning with delinquency prevention, runaway programs, alternative schools, mediation with youth gangs, foster care, and family therapy, this chapter then discusses diversion, restitution, nonresidential and residential interventions, Outward Bound, and therapeutic communities.

---

[1]Lloyd E. Ohlin, Alden D. Miller, and Robert B. Coates, *Correctional Reform in Massachusetts* (Washington, D.C.: GPO, 1977).

DELINQUENCY PREVENTION

Delinquency prevention is defined as any attempt to preclude delinquent behavior before it occurs.[2] Anne Newton has identified three levels of delinquency prevention:

Primary prevention is directed at modifying conditions in the physical and social environment at large.

Secondary prevention is directed at early identification and intervention in the lives of individuals or groups in criminogenic circumstances.

Tertiary prevention is directed at the prevention of recidivism (after delinquent acts have been committed and detected).[3]

An impressive number of primary and secondary prevention programs have been conducted since the beginning of the twentieth century, using as points of intervention neighborhood groups, the family and school environment, youth gangs, and social and mental health agencies.[4] Unfortunately, the results of most of these programs have been disappointing.[5] But two exceptions are the Chicago Area Projects and La Playa de Ponce, both programs showing success.

Chicago Area Projects

Clifford Shaw and Henry McKay, the founders in 1934 of the Chicago Area Projects, were committed to creating a community consciousness directed at solving social problems on the local level. The first projects were initiated in three areas: South Chicago, the Near West Side, and the Near North Side. Shaw and his colleagues recruited local leaders to promote youth welfare because they had lost confidence in official agencies. These local leaders supported indigenous community organizations and made a special effort to involve those who played important formal and informal roles in community life. Shaw was also able to get men with records to agree to work in the program because he made no moral judgment about what they had done previously. He regarded delinquency as a normal response to the situation of the inner city, believing that individuals did what they had to do

---

[2]J. David Hawkins et al., *A Typology of Cause-Focused Strategies of Delinquency Prevention,* Reports of the National Juvenile Justice Assessment Centers (Washington, D.C.: GPO, 1980), p. 3.

[3]Anne M. Newton, "Prevention of Crime and Delinquency," *Criminal Justice Abstracts* (June 1978), p. 4.

[4]Refer to John S. Wall et al., *Juvenile Delinquency Prevention: A Compendium of 36 Program Models,* Reports of the National Juvenile Justice Assessment Centers (Washington, D.C.: GPO, 1981) for examples of these programs.

[5]William T. Pink and Mervin F. White, "Delinquency Prevention: The State of the Art," in *The Juvenile Justice System,* ed. Malcolm W. Klein (Beverly Hills: Sage, 1976), pp. 5–26.

to survive, but that delinquency was no indication of an offender's true beliefs and commitments.[6]

Each project area has a committee, which operates as an independent unit under the guidance of a board of directors chosen by the local community residents. The Area Projects have also received support from the state of Illinois—at first, from the Illinois Department of Welfare through the Institute of Juvenile Research, then from the Illinois Youth Commission, and most recently from the Department of Corrections. Twenty Area Projects are now functioning in Chicago, and others have formed throughout the state. In addition, other groups in Illinois have taken the projects as the model for their own delinquency control programs.[7]

The Area Projects have three basic goals: First, the projects attempt to provide a forum so local residents can become acquainted with new scientific perspectives on child rearing, child welfare, and juvenile delinquency. Second, they initiate new channels of communication between local residents and the institutional representatives of the larger community, those influencing the life chances of local youth. Third, they intend to bring adults into contact with local youth, especially with those having difficulties with the law.

The philosophy of the Area Projects is based on the belief that instead of throwing youth so quickly to the justice system, the community should deal with its own problems and intervene on behalf of its youth. Citizens of the community show up in juvenile court to speak on behalf of the youths; they organize social and recreational programs so youths have constructive activities in which to participate. The leaders of the local groups, often individuals who were once in Area Projects programs, know how to relate to and deal with youths who are having problems at school or with the law.

The Chicago Area Projects have several noteworthy strengths: They have had far-reaching impacts on youths who have participated in their activities; they have encouraged communities to deal with their own social problems; and, dependent primarily on volunteers, they have been excellent sources of leadership development within local communities.[8] However, funding for the Area Projects has been reduced, and there is some question about the continued existence of the program in the years to come.

---

[6]The following description of the Chicago Area Projects is largely derived from Harold Finestone, *Victims of Change: Juvenile Delinquents in American Society* (Westport, Conn.: Greenwood Press, 1976), pp. 125–130.

[7]A book describing the organization and goals of the Area Projects on the Near West Side by one of these local leaders is Anthony Sorrentino's *Organizing Against Crime* (New York: Human Sciences Press, 1977).

[8]For the best evaluation of the Chicago Area Projects, see Solomon Kobrin, "The Chicago Area Projects—A Twenty-Five-Year Assessment," *Annals of the American Academy of Political and Social Sciences* 322 (March 1959):20–29.

La Playa De Ponce

La Playa, the port section of Ponce, Puerto Rico, has a population of more than 17,500. It has long been regarded as the "bad" section of town, dangerous to walk through and generally avoided by outsiders. Poverty, unemployment, drug addiction, an acute lack of social services, and physically deteriorated buildings have long plagued the area. But since 1968, Isolina Ferre, a sister of the Order of Missionary Servants of the Blessed Trinity, has worked to unite citizens in self-directed efforts against La Playa's many problems.[9]

Delinquency prevention has been one of the major goals of this community redevelopment project. Sister Isolina says, "Our aim is to prevent juvenile delinquency by helping the community provide self-help opportunities for their neighborhood youths."[10] She then adds:

> We have thirty-five ongoing programs. We began little; we began going to the courts, taking care of the youth affected by the courts. In 1969, for example, there were seventy juvenile delinquents found guilty by the courts. This year we only had eight cases in juvenile court. What has happened to the rest? We divert them. We go to the police station and pick them up there. The community brings them to us. We have all kinds of programs to involve them so they're not arrested and brought before the juvenile courts. These eight juvenile cases were given back to us, not sent to institutions. It is very seldom we cannot take care of a kid.[11]

Programs include vocational workshops to prepare youths for jobs in industry, home management workshops for girls, formal tutoring in academic subjects, and many nonacademic activities to help young people discover and develop their skills in horticulture, cosmetology, and photography, ceramics, and other art forms. There are also many activities directed toward general cultural development, such as excursions, a sports program, an equestrian club, a steel band, and a social club, with counseling on social relations and conduct.[12]

Part of the reason this community development project has caused a dramatic reduction of youth crime is that it has successfully involved youths in the affairs of the community. Youths take responsibility for caring for the children of the community. Furthermore, youths are accepted as valued members of the community and are expected to play important functions in the development of community life and activities.[13]

---

[9]Robert L. Woodson, *A Summons to Life: Mediating Structures and the Prevention of Youth Crime* (Cambridge, Mass.: Ballinger, 1981), p. 91.

[10]Robert L. Woodson, *Youth Crime and Urban Policy: A View from the Inner City* (Washington, D.C.: American Enterprise Institute for Public Policy Research, 1981), p. 17.

[11]Ibid., p. 18.

[12]Woodson, *Summons to Life,* pp. 91–92.

[13]Ibid., pp. 92–93.

La Playa de Ponce, which has similar strengths to the Chicago Area Projects, has been able to involve delinquency-prone youths in its programs, to deal effectively with the social problems infesting this economically depressed area, and to provide leadership development for community volunteers. But, in contrast to the now underfunded Area Projects, La Playa de Ponce is still thriving.

Evaluation of Delinquency Prevention Programs

The Area Projects and La Playa de Ponce can serve as exemplary models of what grassroots organizations in the community can achieve in preventing juvenile delinquency. But it must be remembered that these few successes are still greatly outnumbered by those programs which have had little or no success in curbing delinquency in their areas. The Juvenile Justice and Delinquency Prevention Act of 1974 and the Juvenile Justice Amendments of 1977 established the prevention of delinquency as a national priority, and the National Juvenile Justice Assessment Centers have developed a typology of cause-focused strategies of delinquency prevention (see Chapter 9 for this typology). As the technologies for delinquency prevention improve, these programs are likely to become more effective in preventing juvenile crime.

RUNAWAY PROGRAMS

Between 500,000 and 600,000 youths run away from home each year.[14] Some of these have been thrown out of their homes, but the majority choose to leave because of child abuse, unmanageable conflicts with parents, the influence of peers, or the thrills of being on one's own. Youths who are absent from home for a period of time must deal with survival, and about 50 percent of these runaways become involved in delinquent acts such as stealing, prostitution, and drug abuse.[15] Although the 1983 Missing Persons Act allows parents to list missing children with the FBI, runaway centers remain one of the few services that exist for runaway youth.

Runaway Centers

Under the Runaway and Homeless Youth Act, Title III of the 1974 Juvenile Justice and Delinquency Prevention Act, assistance was given states, localities, and nonprofit private agencies in order to operate temporary shelters for runaway youth, resulting in the creation of such centers throughout the nation. A staff member of

---

[14]Tim Brennan, David Huizinga, and Delbert S. Elliott, *The Social Psychology of Runaways* (Lexington, Mass.: Heath, 1978).

[15]Ibid.

the Covenant House, a twenty-four-hour drop-in crisis center located near Times Square in New York City, explains why these programs are needed:

> Thousands of runaway and nomadic adolescents are drawn to the Times Square area each year. These young people survive by panhandling, stealing, by exploiting and being exploited. Many, perhaps most, must touch at least temporarily the life of prostitution. . . . There is a total lack of service available to them in the Times Square area. There are no public or private agencies meeting the immediate and urgent needs of the runaway and delinquency-prone youth, hundreds of whom can be seen in Times Square at literally any hour of the day and night, drifting and wandering.[16]

The Door-A Center of Alternatives, also in New York City, was cited as a model program by the Department of Health, Education, and Welfare (now Health and Human Services) and is frequently mentioned at national conferences. The heart of this program is the S.O.S. Service, which provides emergency shelter, food, and clothing for desperate youths. It is one of the largest runaway programs in the United States, and four hundred or more youths are involved at any one time in such activities as drug-abuse counseling, job advising, prenatal counseling, dance or theater workshops, and martial arts classes. Group-Live-In Experience (GLIE), located in the Bronx, has expanded from a storefront location to an operation including three temporary care shelters, where 30 homeless youths can stay from three to eight months; two crash pads, where 19 youths can stay up to two weeks; and a reentry program, called Last Stop, where 14 youngsters can prepare for as much as a year for independent living. Hot Line Cares, located in Spanish Harlem, operates a telephone crisis line and referral agency; after screening them carefully, hot line workers place runaways in seven temporary safe houses, where youths can stay for seven weeks.[17]

A number of Safe Houses in St. Paul and Minneapolis, Minnesota, provide temporary placement for runaway youths with no place to go. The high rate of female and male prostitution in the Twin Cities, which are known as a national pipeline of prostitution, was a factor in the establishment of these houses. In addition to food and shelter, these programs also provide group and individual counseling.

Evaluation of Runaway Programs

Runaway centers contribute a great deal to youths who are receptive to these temporary placements. The centers provide runaways with food and shelter. Staff members furnish support and crisis counseling, and the larger runaway centers offer many helpful programs. Nevertheless, the impact of such centers on runaway youth is still minimal because they are considered undesirable places by most runaways

---

[16]U.S., Congress, Senate Subcommittee on the Constitution of the Committee on the Judiciary, *Homeless Youth: The Saga of "Pushouts" and "Throwaways" in America,* 96th Cong., 1980, p. 36.

[17]Ibid., pp. 35–44.

and because the few centers in existence are generally located in large urban areas. To lessen the involvement of runaways in youth crime, increased community services for them are clearly needed.

ALTERNATIVE SCHOOLS

Alternative schools are designed to serve those youths the public school cannot control or who are not doing satisfactory work in a public school setting. The juvenile court sometimes requires disruptive students to attend an alternative school, but more frequently, students are referred by the public school. A psychologist in an alternative school explains why public schools are unable to deal with disruptive students:

> In the public school setting disruptive students have ample opportunity and free time to get into trouble and, as a result, get themselves thrown out of school. I'm not very optimistic about these kids being able to progress in a public school situation. Public schools don't have the resources to deal with all the things they have to contend with. These students need supervision; they're used to ripping people off and to starting fights with other kids. It's tough for the people in the public school system to hold them in check.[18]

Public school administrators usually swiftly suspend troublemakers, thereby stigmatizing them as failures and reinforcing their negative behaviors. Alternative schools, which have smaller classrooms, usually deal with "turnovers" or acting-out behaviors by taking youths out of the classroom only until they have regained control over themselves. The ultimate goal of most alternative schools is to return students to their public school setting. The Alternate Learning Project in Providence, Rhode Island, and the Providence Educational Center (PEC) in north St. Louis are two of the most impressive alternative schools in the United States.

Providence Educational Center

An alternative school in north St. Louis for serious delinquents, PEC was started in 1972. It was selected as one of the LEAA's "exemplary" projects and received $1.7 million in federal funds. In 1976, when the LEAA's funding ended, PEC agreed to take up to seventy-five disruptive youngsters referred by the city's schools each year. This meant that thereafter all PEC students must be referred through the schools, rather than through the courts, and be certified as "behavior disordered."[19]

At PEC, each class has fourteen students and two teachers. Support staff members include two social workers, two truant officers, and a physical education

---

[18]Interviewed in March 1981.

[19]"In St. Louis, a Program Flip-flops," *Corrections Magazine* 2 (December 1976):29–30.

teacher. Individual educational goals are set for students in math, reading, and other subjects. Conventional grades are not given, and a variety of teaching techniques are used to make learning interesting. For example, one math class took a trip to a local used car lot and then to a bank to look into the financing of purchasing a car.

This program has been highly praised by judges and other court officials. One St. Louis probation officer who worked with PEC commented:

> I think the public school is failing a lot of kids. It is not developing a curriculum that meets the needs of inner-city youth. It takes a different breed of teacher, with patience and understanding, to do that. And I think that is what we have in Providence.[20]

Evaluation of Alternative Schools

A major advantage of alternative school programs is that they deal more effectively with disruptive students than does the public school system. They also relieve the public schools of the disruptive behaviors these youths display in regular classrooms, and they tend to reduce absenteeism and dropout rates. Their success appears to be largely related to their individualized instruction, small student population, low student-adult ratio, goal-oriented classroom environment focused on work and learning, and caring, competent teachers.[21] Yet, the increasingly difficult students that alternative school staff members must work with, along with declining federal funding, are reducing the overall impact of these programs.

MEDIATION WITH YOUTH GANGS

Youth gangs terrorize many urban communities today. The juvenile justice system has found it difficult, if not impossible, to deter the predatory and criminogenic behavior of these youth gangs. However, a number of community groups have effectively defused the violence of youth gangs within urban communities and have involved gang members in more constructive activities. The most noteworthy of these community projects are the House of Umoja (Philadelphia), Youth-in-Action (Chester, Pennsylvania), the El Control del Pueblo Community Center (New York City), the Inner City Roundtable of Youth (New York City), the Youth Identity Programs, Inc. (New York City), the South Arsenal Neighborhood Development Corporation (Hartford, Connecticut), and SEY Yes, Inc. (Los Angeles).[22]

Sister Falaka Fattah and David Fattah, founders of the House of Umoja, have played a remarkable role in defusing the gang violence in Philadelphia. Before the

---

[20]Ibid., p. 30.

[21]Wall et al., *Juvenile Delinquency Prevention*, pp. 18–19.

[22]See Woodson, *Youth Crime and Urban Policy*, for a description of these gang intervention programs.

House of Umoja started working with gangs, an average of thirty-nine black youths died on the streets and a hundred more were maimed each year.[23] Initially the founders invited gang members to live with them. Later they also sponsored citywide gang conferences. Box 5-1 contains an excerpt from a 1981 forum sponsored by the American Enterprise Institute.

Box 5-1   *American Enterprise Institute Forum*

MR. DALY: Sister Fattah, you started out with your husband discussing things with one street gang of fifteen in your home. You invited them to come in with you. You did all of this on a shoestring. Then you got some help from local community groups and churches and acquired a second home. You now have twenty-two of these homes for youngsters, about half of which are now in use and the other half in the process of repair so that they can be used; is that correct?

SISTER FATTAH: Yes, that is correct.

MR. DALY: You have said that you wanted to encourage in them an attitude like that of the African extended family. Would you explain what you have in view?

SISTER FATTAH: Yes, before Africa was colonized by the European powers, the African family was a social, political, and economic unit. Everything flowed from the family. There was a kinship, there were networks, there were tribal systems, there were rites of passage, and there was a clear role definition. This was the African family. Family was not necessarily based on blood lineage but on commitment to a goal.

MR. DALY: As I understand it, you have had 300 boys from some twenty-three gangs involved in the House of Umoja.

SISTER FATTAH: More than 500.

MR. DALY: And it has spread citywide?

SISTER FATTAH: Yes, it spread through the leadership of the gangs. At one time, there were more than 125 active gangs in Philadelphia. As the leaders came to our house, they were able to go back to the gangs and to influence others. Sometimes the gangs would have as many as 200 to 500 members [of the house of Umoja] in the street.

Source: "The Urban Crisis: Can Grass-Roots Groups Succeed Where Government Has Failed?" (Forum Sponsored by the American Enterprise Institute for Public Policy Research, Washington, D.C., 7 May 1981), pp. 4–5. Copyright © 1981, American Enterprise Institute. John Charles Daly (former ABC News Chief) was the moderator of the forum.

Evaluation of Mediating Groups

Mediating community groups have had remarkable success with youth gangs. The success of these programs in relating with gang members and in involving youth gangs in constructive activities owes much to the charismatic leadership of the programs. Such community programs show the potential of grassroots community groups in dealing with the problem of youth crime. But the future of such groups depends upon their gaining the support of city and state political leaders, and upon using local bureaucratic structures.

---

[23]Report by the Department of Public Health, City of Philadelphia, June 1973.

FOSTER CARE

The process whereby a juvenile or family court takes a child out of his or her natural home and places him or her in a substitute or foster home has been used a long time. Foster care placements include individual foster care homes, emergency foster care homes, and foster group homes. In an individual foster care placement, a child is placed in a foster home for an indefinite period of time. An emergency foster care placement is used only until a more permanent placement can be located, and a group foster group home provides a substitute home for several foster children. Foster parents are given subsidies for providing food, shelter, clothing, and expenses for their foster children. Though foster parents must meet state certification and inspection standards, the monthly allotment they receive from the state generally does not cover the expenses of raising foster children.

Foster care is often not considered part of juvenile corrections, but more delinquents are assigned to foster care than are placed in residential programs. In 1974, approximately 7,000 delinquents a day were assigned to foster care and 5,563 to residential programs.[24] Foster placements have recently received increased public attention; for example, the foster group homes started by Thomas Butterworth in rural Missouri were the focus of a television documentary.

There are few evaluation studies of foster care. Paula Van Der Waals did a follow-up study of 200 children in extended foster care and found that many of these children felt unsuccessful, dissatisfied, distressed, and emotionally maladjusted.[25] Yet, Elizabeth G. Meiser's findings were that most former foster children were self-supporting individuals who took care of their children adequately and were indistinguishable from their neighbors.[26]

Evaluation of Foster Care

Foster care is necessary for those youngsters who must be taken from their natural homes. The best foster homes provide a natural home-like environment for the child. They offer the promise of individualized care, attention, and affection in a family environment, thus avoiding institutionalization and its often destructive outcome.[27]

Yet, only a few foster homes adequately replace a real home, and many youths have negative feelings about foster care placement. Some youths are too

---

[24]Robert D. Vinter, George Downs, and John Hall, *Juvenile Corrections in the States: Residential Programs and Deinstitutionalization: A Preliminary Report* (Ann Arbor, Mich.: University of Michigan, November 1975), p. 62.

[25]Paula Van Der Waals, "Former Foster Children Reflect on Their Childhood," *Children* 13 (1960):29.

[26]Elizabeth Meiser, "Current Circumstances of Former Foster Children," *Child Welfare* 44 (1956):196–206.

[27]Yitzhak Bakal and Howard W. Polsky, *Reforming Corrections for Juvenile Offenders: Alternatives and Strategies* (Lexington, Mass.: Heath, 1979), p. 99.

destructive or disturbed to be placed in a family setting. Other youths are simply too delinquent to be placed in an open foster care situation; runaway behavior, the use of alcohol and drugs, and property offenses are common with these youths. Despite generally good selection criteria, some foster parents are simply poor parental figures. Other foster parents work well with certain types of youths, but sometimes a poor match is made between foster child and parents.[28]

FAMILY THERAPY

Juvenile judges often require that the entire family receive treatment before a child is returned home from a foster home, when a child is being subjected to abuse or neglect, and when family conflicts appear to be resulting in status offenses or delinquent behavior.

There are many types of family therapy, such as psychodynamic family therapy, family crisis counseling, family communication skills program, and the training of parents in behavior modification (see Chapters 7 and 8 for explanations of these technologies).[29] Evaluations have generally found that family treatment specifically focusing upon improving the communication skills of the family members does result in improved communication and improved behaviors.[30] The Sacramento 601 Diversion Project is an example of one such program.

Sacramento 601 Diversion Project

The first family treatment program to be evaluated was the Sacramento 601 Diversion Project, which was designed to test whether youths in need of supervision (truants and runaways) could be more effectively diverted from status offenses by providing short-term family crisis counseling than by using traditional juvenile court intake procedures. A random assignment was made of 803 youths to the treatment group and 558 youths to the control group. Those in the treatment group received from one to five counseling sessions involving the youth and his or her family. The counselor specifically attempted to help improve the communication processes used by the family to solve their problems. The results of the project were favorable: a significant difference was found between the percentage of youths who went through family counseling and were diverted—97 percent, compared with the control group—only 62.5 percent.[31]

---

[28]Ibid., pp. 113–114.

[29]Dennis A. Romig, *Justice for Our Children: An Examination of Juvenile Delinquent Rehabilitation Programs* (Lexington, Mass.: Heath, 1978), pp. 89–90.

[30]Ibid., p. 88.

[31]Ibid., p. 87.

Evaluation of Family Counseling

Dennis A. Romig reviewed twelve studies on family therapy and concluded that family treatment does not typically reduce delinquent behavior. However, he found that family treatment was effective when it focused upon teaching parents communication, problem-solving, and disciplining skills, and he went on to recommend that "all treatment programs involving delinquent youths and their families should provide the family and the youth training in [these areas].[32]

DIVERSION

In the late 1960s and early 1970s, diversion programs sprouted across the nation. Diversion can be attempted either through the police and the courts or through agencies outside the juvenile justice system. The main characteristic of diversion initiated by the courts or police is that the justice subsystems retain control over youthful offenders. A youth who fails to respond to such a program will usually be returned to the juvenile court for continued processing within the system. Police youth service bureaus and the 601 Project of the Sacramento Probation Department are good examples of diversion programs conducted by police and probation services. Substance abuse and shoplifters' programs also are used widely by juvenile courts and probation departments. The youth service bureau (YSB) is the most widely used diversion program outside the juvenile justice system; the St. Louis Experiment, which was hosted by the Jewish Community Centers Association, is another noteworthy diversion program outside the formal justice system.

The Youth Service Bureau

The major impetus to YSBs came in 1967 when the President's Commission on Law Enforcement and Administration of Justice recommended that such agencies be established to work with youths outside the juvenile justice system. Although Youth Service Bureau is the name most frequently used, other names used include Youth Resource Bureau, Youth Assistance Program, the Listening Post, or the Focus on Youth.

Sherwood Norman, who was highly influential in the development of youth service bureaus, identified the basic objectives of this diversion agency:

The Youth Service Bureau is a noncoercive, independent public [some are private] agency established to divert children and youth from the justice system by (1) mobilizing community resources to solve youth problems, (2) strengthening existing youth

[32]Ibid., p. 93.

resources and developing new ones, and (3) promoting positive programs to remedy delinquency-breeding conditions.[33]

From 1967 to 1973, one hundred and fifty YSBs were established throughout the nation. There are more YSBs in California than in any other state; Illinois has the second largest number. A 1971–1972 survey of 140 youth service bureaus conducted by the Youth Development and Delinquency Prevention Administration revealed that approximately 50,000 youths were diverted from juvenile court proceedings during that two-year period and that an additional 150,000 youths participated in YSB programs.[34] But the decline of federal funding in the late 1970s and early 1980s appears to be reducing the number of YSBs in this nation. In 1981, a director of YSB in Illinois noted, "There are now 54 YSBs in Illinois; there were 78 two years ago."[35]

Youth service bureaus offer a variety of programs. Drop-in centers, hotlines, truancy and school outreach programs, and twenty-four-hour crisis programs are common services. Some larger YSBs also make arrangements for temporary care for runaways, conduct programs for pregnant teenagers, and provide school dropouts with employment, for which they are paid a minimum wage.

Recently, YSBs have drawn criticism for several reasons. Critics see YSBs as coercive because a youth is likely to be returned to the juvenile court if he or she fails to cooperate with staff or to become involved in the program. Critics also claim that because of YSBs the net of the juvenile justice system is enlarged, arguing that youths referred to these agencies would have had their cases dismissed by the court before these bureaus existed. YSBs are further faulted for being so dependent on the approval of the juvenile justice system that it would be impossible for them to bring change to the system.[36]

Although these criticisms are generally accurate, YSBs have been helpful to some youngsters facing problems at home, at school, or with the law. Regardless, the future of YSBs is questionable at the present time because of the end of LEAA support.

Evaluation of Diversion Programs

The major strength of diversion programs is that they minimize penetration of youthful offenders in the juvenile justice system. However, diversion has come under increased criticism in recent years for enlarging the net of the juvenile justice

[33]Sherwood Norman, *Youth Service Bureau: A Key to Prevention (Paramus, N.J.: National Council on Crime and Delinquency, 1972), pp. 12–13.*

[34]Youth Development and Delinquency Prevention Administration, "The Challenge of Youth Service Bureaus," in *Back on the Street,* ed. Robert M. Carter and Malcolm W. Klein (Englewood Cliffs, N.J.: Prentice-Hall, 1976), p. 284.

[35]Interviewed in October 1981.

[36]See *Phase I Assessment of Youth Service Bureaus: Summary Report of Youth Service Bureau Research Group for LEAA* (Boston: Boston University, 1975), for an expansion of these criticisms of YSBs.

system, for ignoring the due process rights of juveniles, and for stigmatizing participants in these programs. Diversion programs must, above all, ensure youths of greater procedural safeguards in the future.

RESTITUTION PROGRAMS

Offender restitution for crime victims is becoming one of the most widely used sanctions in juvenile corrections. Such restitution can be defined "as a sanction imposed by an official of the criminal justice system requiring the offender to make a payment of money or service to either the direct or substitute crime victim."[37] Community service projects are much more widely used than financial restitution because juveniles frequently lack the economic resources to make payments to victims. Some probation departments have appointed restitution officers, and juveniles who are ordered by the juvenile court to restitution services are assigned to group projects. The Hennepin County Juvenile Court Work Squads is one of the most widely respected restitution programs in juvenile corrections.

Hennepin County Juvenile Court Work Squads

Youthful offenders in Hennepin County (Minnesota) find themselves very quickly dispatched by the juvenile judge to the Saturday work squads for a specified amount of community service: A first-time property offender will usually be given a sentence of forty hours. Each Saturday morning youths assigned to the work squad are required to be at the downtown meeting place at 8:00. The coordinator of the program, who is on the staff of the probation department, then assigns each to a specific work squad. Work details include recycling bottles and cans, visiting with patients at a nursing home, doing janitorial work, cleaning bus stops, planting trees or removing barbed wire fences at a city park, and working at a park reserve. This program, the fourth largest restitution granted funded by LEAA, sends out five trucks each Saturday, with ten youths and two staffs in each truck. By August 1981, 1800 youths had been involved in the program since its inception in the mid-1970s.[38]

Evaluation of Restitution Programs

Community service restitution orders are so widely used at the present time because they satisfy both hard-liners who want a tougher stance toward juvenile crime and officials of the juvenile justice system who observe juveniles committing one crime after the other without any real punishment. Restitution appears to work with some youths because it is a real reminder that there is a cost to socially

[37]Burt Galaway and Joe Hudson, *Offender Restitution in Theory and Actions* (Lexington, Mass.: Heath, 1978), p. 1.
[38]Information gained during an on-site visit.

unacceptable behavior. However, the amount of restitution service required now rests with the whims of individual judges, and the discretion allowed them certainly holds the possibility of abuse. Research must determine the proper amount and types of community service desirable for specific types of offenders.

DAY TREATMENT PROGRAMS

Day treatment programs, in which youngsters spend each day in the program and return home in the evenings, are in wide use in community-based juvenile corrections. These court-mandated programs are popular because they are more economical than residential placements as it is not necessary to provide living and sleeping quarters; they make parental participation easier; fewer staff members are required; and they are less coercive and punishment-oriented.

Nonresidential programs generally serve male juveniles, although California operates two programs for girls and several coeducational ones. Nonresidential programs have been widely used by the California Treatment Project, and the New York Division for Youth and the Florida Division of Youth Services operate several nonresidential programs. The nonresidential programs in New York, which are called STAY, are similar to many other nonresidential programs because they expose youths to a guided-group interaction experience. A nonresidential program involving the sea was established by the Associated Marine Institute (AMI) in Florida. The United Delinquency Service (UDIS) and Project New Pride are two other day treatment programs, both of which work with juveniles who have committed serious crimes.

Associated Marine Institute

The AMI is a privately operated, nonresidential program using the sea to stimulate productive behavior in youths referred by the courts or the division of youth services. Under the program, which is funded jointly by state, federal, and private donations, 130 trainees receive training in seamanship, diving, and other nautical skills, in addition to attending basic education classes. To be eligible for one of the five centers of AMI (Deerfield Beach, Jacksonville, Tampa, Miami, and St. Petersburg), a youth must be between fifteen and eighteen and of at least average intelligence, must have sixth-grade abilities in reading and math, and must not have been repeatedly involved with drugs or assaultive behavior. The trainees live either at home or in foster homes and attend an institute eight hours a day for up to nine months.[39]

Each youth must undergo a thirty-day evaluation period before he or she is accepted as a regular trainee. When a youth attains training status, and about three out of four do, a contract is drawn up between him or her and the institute. The

[39]"Can Delinquents Be Saved by the Sea?" *Corrections Magazine* 1 (September 1974):77–88.

contract sets individual goals for the training period in a dozen categories, including diving, seamanship, ocean science, lifesaving, first aid, and such electives as photography and marine maintenance. The major incentives for youths are the opportunity to earn official certification as scuba divers and to keep their diving equipment. Other incentives designed to maintain enthusiasm include sew-on patches; certificates awarded for short-term achievement in first aid, seamanship, and diving; trophies for trainees-of-the-month; and field trips, such as a cruise to the Bahamas or the Florida Keys.[40]

The AMI programs provide interesting activities and teach worthwhile skills to youths. For those who can qualify, these programs certainly are much preferred to placements in residential settings in the community or in long-term juvenile correctional institutions. Yet such programs are expensive, limited to certain parts of the country, and appear to be more suited to minor than serious offenders.

The United Delinquency Intervention Services

The UDIS, a Chicago-based program which began receiving referrals in October of 1974, primarily serves repeat offenders already on formal probation. Juvenile judges normally use the UDIS Project to divert probation violators from commitment to the Illinois Department of Corrections.[41] The major goals of UDIS are

1. To establish an adequate network of community-based services.
2. To reduce commitments to the larger institutional facilities of the juvenile division of the department of corrections, by 35 percent for the commitment rate in Cook County and by 50 percent for the commitment rate throughout the rest of the state.
3. To provide services at a cost much less than that of institutional placement with the Juvenile Division.[42]

The UDIS staff widely used purchases-of-service contracts, with services such as individual counseling, family counseling, vocational testing and job placement, education and tutoring, specialized foster care, group-home placements, temporary living arrangements, advocacy, wilderness programs, and intensive care units for residents. Most youths are involved with the UDIS Project for three to six months, although some offenders receive services for up to twelve months.

In 1976, the Rand Corporation released a very positive evaluation of the first-year results of UDIS in a report prepared for the National Institute for Juvenile Justice and Delinquency Prevention. The report said in part:

[40]Ibid.

[41]See Shirley Goins, "The Serious or Violent Juvenile Offender—Is There a Treatment Response?" in *The Serious Juvenile Offender: Proceedings of a National Symposium* (Washington, D.C.: GPO, 1977), pp. 115–129.

[42]Ibid.

UDIS appears to have good potential as a model of community-oriented corrections. It has demonstrated that it can offer alternatives to confinement for serious, as well as less serious, juvenile offenders without increasing the risk to the public. This is being achieved . . . at substantially reduced comparative cost. If continued, the achievements of UDIS will be most impressive.[43]

The report also indicated that "only 15 (7 percent) of the 221 youths who participated in UDIS during its first year had recidivated."[44]

However, the effectiveness of UDIS was questioned in an evaluation by the American Institutes for Research in Washington, D.C. Comparing matched samples of 317 youths who were committed to the juvenile division of the Illinois Department of Corrections and 266 youths who had participated in the at-home services of UDIS, Charles Murray and colleagues found two disturbing results: (1) UDIS did not do as well as DOC in reducing postrelease results; and (2) the UDIS at-home services fared worse than the residential placement and worse than the DOC placements.[45] The researchers concluded that "minimal intervention may be a good idea for less serious offenders, but for the serious juvenile offender, it is a bankrupt approach."[46]

Project New Pride

Another community program that offers services to youths who have committed serious offenses is Project New Pride in Denver, Colorado. Most of the youngsters involved in the project, which has been designated as an exemplary project by LEAA, are blacks or Chicanos. Each youth receives intensive services in the program for the first three months and then continues treatment geared to individual needs and interests for a nine-month follow-up period.[47] Academic education, counseling, employment, and cultural education are the four main areas of service provided in Project New Pride. For education, youths are assigned to classes in either the New Pride Alternative School or the Learning Disabilities Center. The goal of the counseling, which tries to match specific counselors and clients, is to enhance a youth's self-image and to help him or her cope with the environment. Job preparation is heavily emphasized, youths attend a job skills workshop and then receive on-the-job training. The purpose of cultural education is to expose youths to a range of experiences and activities in the Denver area.

---

[43]Dale Mann, *Intervening with Convicted Serious Juvenile Offenders* (Washington, D.C.: GPO, 1976), pp. 40–44.

[44]Ibid., p. 43.

[45]Charles A. Murray and Louis A. Cox, Jr., *Beyond Probation: Juvenile Corrections and the Chronic Delinquent* (Beverly Hills: Sage, 1979), p. 116.

[46]Quoted in Kevin Krajick, "A Blow for the 'Get Tough' Side," *Corrections Magazine* 4 (September 1978):20.

[47]The following materials on Project New Pride are taken from U.S. Department of Justice, National Institute of Law Enforcement and Criminal Justice, *Project New Pride* (Washington, D.C.: GPO, 1977).

Project New Pride has established four primary goals in working with its difficult clientele: (1) reduction of recidivism, (2) job placement, (3) school reintegration, and (4) remediation of academic and learning disabilities. The project has had impressive success in achieving the first three of these goals, and preliminary data on educational remediation indicate possible success. The success of this project has also been demonstrated by its replication in Chicago; Los Angeles; San Francisco; Boston; Kansas City, Missouri; Pensacola, Florida; Fresno, California; Washington, D.C.; Haddonfield, New Jersey; and Providence, Rhode Island.

Evaluation of Nonresidential Programs

Nonresidential programs appear to be a preferred way of handling minor youthful offenders. They are more economical, more humane (as they permit the juvenile to live at home), and less coercive and punishment-oriented than residential facilities. But the conflicting findings on their success with the hardcore make them a somewhat questionable placement for the serious juvenile delinquent. Some youths seem to require a secure placement to gain control over themselves and their antisocial behaviors.

RESIDENTIAL PROGRAMS

Residential facilities, which are known variously as group homes, group residences, halfway houses, and attention homes, provide twenty-four-hour care of juvenile offenders. Residential facilities fulfill several purposes in juvenile corrections: They provide an alternative to long-term placement in a training school; they serve as a short-term community placement while probation officers deal with youths' community problems; and they serve as a "halfway-out" placement for institutionalized delinquents who are reentering the community but lack a suitable home to which to return.

Intake criteria, treatment goals, length of stay, target population, services offered, physical facilities, specific location in the community, and house rules are extremely diverse in the residential juvenile facilities throughout the United States. Some facilities are very treatment-oriented and use a treatment modality like guided group interaction (GGI) to generate a supportive environment among residents and staff. In guided group interaction residents are expected to support, confront, and be honest with one another to the end that they will be helped in dealing with their own problems. Yet other group homes deliberately avoid providing a comfortable atmosphere, and staff members may even try to arouse anxiety.[48]

The Highfields Project and its variations, the California Youth Authority's Community Treatment Project (CTP), and the deinstitutionalization process in Massachusetts have all been closely examined by researchers.

---

[48]Oliver J. Keller, Jr., and Benedict S. Alper, *Halfway Houses: Community-Based Correction and Treatment* (Lexington, Mass.: Heath, 1970).

The Highfields Project and Its Variations

The Highfields Project is the best known of these residential placements. The New Jersey Experimental Project for the Treatment of Youthful Offenders—the official name for the Highfields Project—was established in 1950 on an estate once the home of Colonel and Mrs. Charles Lindbergh. The purpose of this residential program was to provide an alternative to an institutional placement for twenty youths; a control group of offenders with similar characteristics was sent to the reformatory. The youths involved in the Highfields Project worked during the day at the nearby New Jersey Neuro-Psychiatric Institute and met in two guided-group-interaction units five evenings a week at the facility. Empirical studies have indicated that this program was at least as effective in reducing recidivism as was sending youths to the Annandale Reformatory.[49]

The Highfields Project has been replicated at Southfields (Kentucky) and Essexfields (New Jersey). The Silverlake Experiment, also patterned after the Highfields Project, was established in Los Angeles County in the mid-1960s. This program, which is better known than the other two Highfields variations, was housed in a large family residence in a middle-class neighborhood and provided a group living experience for males between the ages of fifteen and eighteen. As at Highfields, only twenty residents at a time lived in the group home, and they all participated in daily group meetings.[50] A study of the impact of the Silverlake Project revealed very little difference one year after leaving between the Silverlake youths and those in the control group (who were institutionalized), even though the cost of the Silverlake program was one-third of the cost of institutionalization.[51]

A well-developed group home model is the teaching family group home concept, which was first adopted in 1967 with the establishment of the Achievement Place group home in Lawrence, Kansas. The teaching family group home model is currently in use in over forty locations in twelve states.[52] The Criswell Home, established in Florida in 1958, housed twenty-five youths on probation and parole and used GGI. During the 1970s, Florida developed a network of nine group homes based on the Criswell House model.[53] The Dare Program in Massachusetts, another widely used group home model, currently includes ten specialized facilities and thirteen community residences.[54] New York also has a network of group homes, the START centers (Short-Term Adolescent Residential Treatment).

[49]Ashley H. Weeks, "The Highfields Project," in *Juvenile Delinquency: A Book of Readings*, ed. Rose Giallombardo (New York: Wiley, 1976), pp. 535–547.

[50]LaMar T. Empey and Stephen Lubeck, *The Silverlake Experiment: Testing Delinquency Theory and Community Intervention* (Chicago: Aldine, 1971).

[51]William T. Pink and Mervin F. White, "Delinquency Prevention: The State of the Art," in *Juvenile Justice System*, ed. Klein, p. 21.

[52]D. L. Fixsen, E. L. Phillips, and M. M. Wolf, "The Teaching Family Model of Group Home Treatment," in *Closing Correctional Institutions*, ed. Yitzhak Bakal (Lexington, Mass.: Heath, 1973).

[53]Ronald H. Bailey, "Profile/Florida," *Corrections Magazine* 1 (September 1974):67.

[54]Contact Dynamics Action Residence Enterprise, Jamaica Plain, MA, for more information on DARE.

The California Youth Authority's Community Treatment Project

The California Youth Authority's Community Treatment Project (CTP), which took place between 1961 and 1969 and involved a total of 686 "experimental" youths and 328 control youths, has probably received more evaluations than any other juvenile corrections program. The initial evaluation showed that, overall, experimental youths returned to crime less often than did the controls.[55] Marguerite Q. Warren, one of the collaborators on CTP, concluded in 1966 that "the feasibility of substituting intensive community programs for incarceration of many juvenile delinquents has been demonstrated."[56] But Paul Lerman, in reexamining the findings of this study, concluded that "CTP did not have any measurable impact on youth behavior, in comparison to a traditional CYA [California Youth Authority] program. Using this standard of comparison, the program was relatively ineffective."[57] Lerman went on to say:

> The major findings of this study indicate that major goals of the community treatment strategy were not realized in practice. Community treatment was proposed as an effective alternative to traditional institutionalization and proved to be no more effective. Community treatment was proposed as a noncoercive substitute for state-delivered sanctions, and proved to be associated with increases in state and local social control. And community treatment was supposed to be less expensive, but proved to be associated with cost overruns.[58]

Deinstitutionalization in Massachusetts

The Harvard Center for Criminal Justice discovered no significant differences in recidivism rates in most regions between samples of youthful offenders paroled by the Department of Youth Services from training schools during the fiscal year 1967–1968 and comparable samples of youths released to residential and nonresidential programs in 1973 and 1974.[59] But in those regions of the state in which integrated networks of community-based programs replaced institutions, recidivism was reduced; for community programs lacking this integrated network, crime rates remained at previous levels or rose slightly.[60]

---

[55]Evaluation of CTP is derived from James O. Finckenauer, *Scared Straight! and the Panacea Phenomenon* (Englewood Cliffs, N.J.: Prentice-Hall, 1982), p. 21.

[56]Marguerite Q. Warren, "The Community Treatment Project: History and Prospectus," in *Crime and Justice: The Criminal in Confinement,* edited by S. A. Yefsky (New York: Basic, 1971), p. 309.

[57]Paul Lerman, *Community Treatment and Social Control: A Critical Analysis of Juvenile Correctional Policy* (Chicago: University of Chicago Press, 1975), p. 95.

[58]Ibid., p. 210.

[59]Robert R. Coates et al., "Exploratory Analysis of Recidivism and Cohort Data on the Massachusetts Youth Correctional System" (Cambridge: Center for Criminal Justice, Harvard Law School, 1975), pp. 1–2.

[60]Ohlin, Miller, and Coates, *Correctional Reform in Massachusetts.*

Evaluation of Residential Programs

The conflicting evidence on residential programs makes it difficult to support the conclusion that residential programs in the community result in lower rates of recidivism than institutional programs. Nevertheless, a convincing case can be made that residential programs are at least as successful as training schools, at far less trauma to youths and usually at less cost to the state.

OUTWARD BOUND

Outward Bound is an experiential learning situation that encourages participants to find new or unexamined areas of their personalities. Its goal is to place students in situations that will enable them to learn from their experience. This wilderness survival program uses "overcoming of a seemingly impossible task" to help the participant gain self-reliance, prove individual worth, and define selfhood.

The basic components of Outward Bound are defined as skill training, stress/hardship, problem-solving, service, reflection, and evaluation. Skill training develops skills enabling an individual to function with competence and safety in a particular environment. The stress/hardship component exposes participants to challenging experiences, compelling them to examine their own reactions and responses to new situations requiring action or decision—such as rappelling, rock climbing, or emergencies. The problem-solving component provides opportunities for participants and groups to analyze situations and arrive at solutions. The service component is designed to develop a sense of responsibility for others and for the environment through work projects, rescue expeditions, and work with groups of handicapped individuals. The reflection component encourages participants to think through their experiences in ways that provide new insight—i.e., patrol discussions, solo trips, and debriefing. The evaluation component is intended to sharpen the individual's response, thus encouraging critical assessment and constructive action.[61]

Outward Bound, which has involved delinquents since the first course was conducted at Colorado in 1962, is one of the most exciting treatment programs for juvenile offenders. Over one thousand programs presently exist, and Outward Bound programs or their variations are found in nearly every state. John Calhoun, former commissioner of youth services in Massachusetts, is positive about this wilderness experience, which is called Homeward Bound in his state:

That's done well; we love it. It probably is the single most consistently effective program we have. The problem is a kid comes back on his twenty-seventh day on a high, having battered the elements for his last solo. Then, he hits the hard streets. It's a magnificent temporary program, but where we have failed in that program is in the aftercare. These kids feel they're world beaters when they [get] back to the grim

---

[61]Outward Bound, "Instructor's Manual," n.d., p. 3.

reality of the projects. What we have to figure out is how to support that wondrous high.[62]

The need for aftercare showed up clearly in a study conducted by Francis J. Kelly and Daniel J. Baer. Sixty boys who attended Outward Bound schools and sixty boys who were treated routinely by juvenile corrections authorities were followed for five years. After the first few years, the youths who participated in Outward Bound programs had a much lower recidivism rate, but the differences in recidivism between the two groups nearly disappeared after five years.[63]

THERAPEUTIC COMMUNITIES

Therapeutic communities are used less frequently in juvenile corrections than in adult corrections because they tend to shut youthful offenders away from the network of community services. At present, Élan—the most controversial of this nation's therapeutic communities for juveniles—is stirring up considerable interest.

Élan

Joe Ricci, a former dope addict and one of the success stories of Daytop in New York City, and Dr. Gerald Davidson, a psychiatrist, started Élan in 1971 in Poland Springs, Maine.[64] Ricci, the executive director of Élan, has incorporated many of the concepts of the Daytop therapeutic community in a program which supporters think is exemplary and foes regard as brutal to participants. The program involves intense peer pressure, self-responsibility, hard physical and emotional work, and self-disclosure. Élan has grown into a finely tuned, million-dollar operation with more than 100 staff members, six buildings, and 250 residents. Parents are typically highly supportive of the program. One says about his son:

> In the length of time they had him, it's incredible. It was like he was heading north and they turned him south. Before, he was stealing cars. He pulled a shotgun on his aunt. He was in a high-speed chase. Now, he is sensitive. He is concerned about his mother. I'd recommend Élan to anyone.[65]

No external evaluation has been done on this program, but in-house evaluations indicate that 190 of the 500 individuals admitted to Élan since its inception have received "diplomas." Of this number, Élan officials claim that 78 percent have stayed out of trouble.[66] However, because therapeutic communities—which are

---

[62]Interviewed in June 1978.

[63]Joseph Nold and Mary Wilpers, "Wilderness Training as an Alternative to Incarceration," in *A Nation without Prisons*, ed. Calvert R. Dodge (Lexington, Mass.: Heath, 1975), pp. 157–158.

[64]Philip B. Taft, Jr., "Élan: Does Its Bizarre Regimen Transfer Troubled Youth or Abuse Them?" *Corrections Magazine* 5 (March 1979):18–28. Copyright 1979, *Corrections Magazine*. All rights reserved.

[65]Ibid., p. 20.

[66]Ibid.

discussed in more detail in the next two chapters—use coercive, and sometimes brutal, tactics on residents, it must be asked how the kindly parent, the state with its *parens patriae* philosophy can justify referring youths to these programs.

SUMMARY

Advocated by national commissions, supported by reintegrative philosophy, and funded largely by federal grants, community programs for juveniles expanded to include an impressive variety of situations during the 1970s. Some proponents of community-based programs for juveniles even backed dealing with all youthful offenders within the community and advocated closing all training schools. Often led by charismatic personalities who are assisted by community volunteers, para-professionals, and exoffenders, these community programs have typically been vastly more humane, somewhat more economical, and at least as effective as institutions in reducing recidivism. But community-based programs must meet several challenges, especially those posed by the demise of federal funding and the public mood of "getting tough on youth crime," to provide even more effective treatment for youthful offenders.

Yet the 1980s should be a good decade for community-based juvenile programs becaue the prohibitive expense of long-term institutions should lead to an increased use of alternatives to institutionalization. Perhaps deinstitutionalization to the extent desired by reformers in the 1970s will never be attained, but the economics of placing juveniles in long-term institutions will probably mean that these end-of-the line facilities will be reserved for hard-core and violent juvenile offenders.

DISCUSSION QUESTIONS

1. Which program in this chapter impressed you as most capable of dealing with today's youth crime problem? Explain your choice.
2. What advantages do community-based programs have over institutional programs?
3. What types of juveniles do you believe would benefit the most from which specific programs?
4. Which program do you consider potentially the most damaging to participants? Why?
5. Besides convenience, what benefits do you see from community-based programs for juveniles?

6

Community-Based Programs: Adults

Objectives

1. *To examine the Community-Based Corrections Act in Minnesota.*

2. *To discuss the Des Moines Project as an example of a locally co-ordinated community corrections program.*

3. *To discuss pretrial release programs.*

4. *To list and evaluate the main kinds of diversionary programs for adult offenders.*

5. *To focus upon the Port Corrections Center as an example of residential programs for adult offenders.*

6. *To evaluate reentry programs for exoffenders.*

7. *To discuss community assistance programs for exoffenders.*

Community-based programs for adults face several challenges today. First, the financial crunch affecting all levels of government, along with the demise of LEAA support of community programs, makes it difficult both to establish new programs and to sustain the ones already functioning in the community. Second, existing residential programs and the establishment of any new ones face mounting community opposition: The correctional truism that community programs are popular until they have a street address is more valid than ever before. Third, community correctional programs usually are located in areas of town less than conducive to the social rehabilitation of offenders. Pimps, prostitutes, and dope pushers frequently operate within sight of the facilities, and taverns, pawn shops, tenements, and vacant stores make up much of the neighborhood.

Yet the more than one million offenders involved in adult community-based programs each year still outnumber those incarcerated in jails and in state and federal correctional institutions. Also, community-based programs are at least as effective as, and far less expensive than, institutional confinement, according to evaluation studies. Participants in community-based corrections agree that these programs are more effective and more humane than institutional programs. Two residents of PORT in Rochester, Minnesota, put it this way:

> I feel the justice system has treated me fairly. If I was sent to prison, I don't know if I could make it. I feel losing your freedom is a terrible thing. I don't think God put us on this earth to be in cages.

> You've a chance to learn here. In prison, you just do your time and try to keep people away. In maximum security joints, you better get a weapon the first day if you want to survive.[1]

This chapter discusses state-administered community corrections acts, locally administered coordinated community corrections programs, pretrial release and diversion programs, halfway houses, and community assistance projects. Treatment programs in probation and parole are described in Chapter 11.

COMMUNITY CORRECTIONS ACTS

Minnesota, Kansas, and Oregon indicated support of community-based corrections by passing community corrections acts in the early and mid-1970s. In the late 1970s, California passed an act establishing the County Justice Subvention Program to replace the probation subsidy program. In a number of other states, community corrections legislation is on the drawing board; Michigan is one of the states in which a community corrections lobby is trying to influence legislation in that direction.

---

[1]Both interviewed in the summer of 1981.

Minnesota

Enacted in 1973, the Minnesota Community Corrections Act (CCA) is a broad and comprehensive act that was the model for the corrections acts later passed in Oregon and Kansas. The 1973 legislature appropriated $1.5 million for implementing the first phase in three pilot areas; the 1975 legislature appropriated over $7 million to continue the program in the pilot areas and to expand it to an additional eighteen counties over the subsequent two years; and the 1977 legislature provided $13.6 million to maintain the program in all the counties in which it was already established and to extend it to an additional nine counties.[2]

The purpose of the CCA is: (1) to reduce the number of commitments to state adult correctional facilities; (2) to encourage local units of government to take responsibility for offenders whose crimes are not serious (those who would receive a sentence of less than five years in a state facility); (3) to promote community corrections planning at the local level; and (4) to improve coordination among local components of the criminal justice system.

The Minnesota act requires county commissioners of participating counties to set up local corrections advisory boards. Each board, which has local representatives from the criminal justice system and other community groups, develops a comprehensive plan that identifies correctional needs and defines the programs and services required to meet these needs. The completed plan is submitted to the county board (or to a joint board in multi-county units) for final approval. The plan is then sent to the state department of corrections, and when the commissioner has approved the comprehensive plan, the county or multi-county unit becomes eligible for a state financial subsidy. Figure 6-1 shows how the CCA operates.

By 1980 70 percent of Minnesota's counties were participating in the community corrections project. Counties with community corrections programs are charged about $30 a day from their subsidies for any adult committed to a state institution for less than five years; the actual cost is determined by a formula that reflects the county's population, its corrections needs, and its financial resources.

The Minnesota Community Corrections Act succeeded in its goal of discouraging commitments to state institutions. Minnesota has the second lowest commitment rate in the nation based on inmates per 100,000 residents. The CCA also succeeded in persuading counties to take responsibility for their corrections needs, and as a result Minnesota has the greatest variety of community corrections programs of any state. Adult programs include halfway houses, nonresidential programs, substance abuse programs, therapeutic communities, predetention centers, work- and study-release centers, restitution programs, and in- and out-patient psychiatric care.

However, there is evidence that some counties comply with the CCA by

[2]Refer to Stephen Gettinger, "Community Corrections Begins to Pay Off," *Corrections Magazine* 5 (June 1979) for a more extensive description of the Minnesota Community Corrections Act.

Figure 6-1   The Minnesota Corrections Act

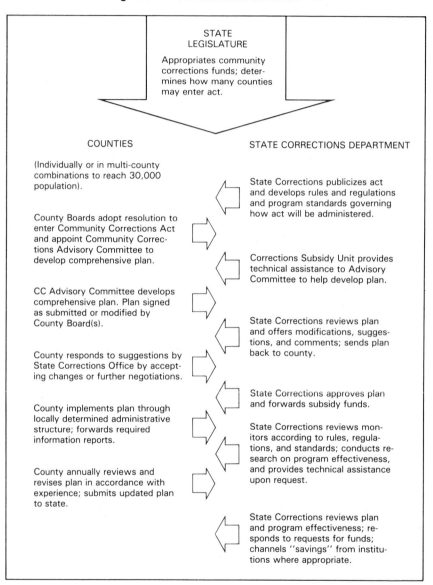

STATE
LEGISLATURE

Appropriates community
corrections funds; deter-
mines how many counties
may enter act.

COUNTIES

(Individually or in multi-county
combinations to reach 30,000
population).

County Boards adopt resolution to
enter Community Corrections Act
and appoint Community Corrections Advisory Committee to
develop comprehensive plan.

CC Advisory Committee develops
comprehensive plan. Plan signed
as submitted or modified by
County Board(s).

County responds to suggestions by
State Corrections Office by accepting changes or further negotiations.

County implements plan through
locally determined administrative
structure; forwards required
information reports.

County annually reviews and
revises plan in accordance with
experience; submits updated plan
to state.

STATE CORRECTIONS DEPARTMENT

State Corrections publicizes act
and develops rules and regulations
and program standards governing
how act will be administered.

Corrections Subsidy Unit provides
technical assistance to Advisory
Committee to help develop plan.

State Corrections reviews plan
and offers modifications, suggestions, and comments; sends plan
back to county.

State Corrections approves plan
and forwards subsidy funds.

State Corrections reviews monitors according to rules, regulations, and standards; conducts research on program effectiveness,
and provides technical assistance
upon request.

State Corrections reviews plan
and program effectiveness; responds to requests for funds;
channels "savings" from institutions where appropriate.

Source: E. Kim Nelson, Howard Ohmart and Nora Harlow. *Promising Strategies in Probation and Parole* (Washington, D.C.: GPO, 1978), p. 61.

overusing the local jails, sometimes in lieu of developing programs. The jails in Minnesota, like those everywhere else, leave a great deal to be desired. The recent passage of a determinate sentencing bill in Minnesota also appears to be reducing the impact of the Community Corrections Act. But overall, Minnesota is still the pacesetter for community-based corrections in the United States.

Evaluation of Community Corrections Acts

States that enact community corrections acts have fewer problems with prison overcrowding than states that do not have them, because the acts encourage participating counties to reduce the number of offenders confined to state prisons and training schools. Yet the rise of determinate sentencing structures will probably reduce the impact of community corrections acts because the locus of control is thereby transferred from county boards to state legislatures.

LOCALLY COORDINATED COMMUNITY-BASED CORRECTIONS PROGRAMS

A few counties have developed an extensive array of coordinated correctional services, so that a comprehensive program that includes several subsystems of the correctional system is administered under local jurisdiction. A model comprehensive program has been developed in Polk County, Iowa.

The Des Moines Project in Polk County, Iowa

The Des Moines Project, designated "exemplary" by the National Institute of Law Enforcement and Criminal Justice, was begun in 1971 and has four components that provide services to defendants and convicted offenders at varying stages of the criminal justice process:

Pretrial Release (ROR)
Supervised Release
Probation/Presentence Investigation
Community Corrections Facility

The pretrial release stage permits release of offenders who qualify for this program on their own recognizance (ROR). The supervised release program enables some who do not qualify for pretrial release to participate in a carefully structured process of supervision, counseling, and treatment. Probation/presentence investigation is the third link in the chain of services. Probation, a county responsibility in Polk County, and supervised release are set up in the same building, since the two programs complement one another. The community corrections facility is a 50-bed residential facility at the edge of the Des Moines city limits. This facility permits work release as well as overnight or weekend furloughs for residents in these reentry programs. If residents prove untrustworthy in this nonsecure environment, then they are placed in the county jail for the duration of their sentences.

A 1974 evaluation of the Des Moines Project found that pretrial release was effective in several ways:

> Community safety: Of the 663 clients released on their own recognizance and later adjudicated, pretrial release clients had a new offense rate slightly lower (7.9 percent) than the rate for persons released on bail (8.8 percent) and significantly lower than those in the supervised release program (16.8 percent).
>
> Appearance in court rate: The failure-to-appear rate was lower for pretrial release clients (1.3 percent) than for those released on bail (6.8 percent) and for those in the supervised release program (16.8 percent).
>
> Conviction rate: The highest conviction rate, which was defined as the percentage of the adjudicated persons convicted of at least one offense, was for pretrial release clients (66.3 percent), but there was no significant difference among the conviction rates for those released on bail (60.9 percent), granted supervised release (58.6 percent), or detained in jail before trial (62.2 percent).
>
> Incarceration rate: The incarceration rate for persons released on their own recognizance and later convicted was only 4.3 percent, significantly lower than the rates for persons released on bail (13.9 percent), granted supervised release (23.6 percent), or detained in jail before trial (60.8 percent).[3]

Attesting to the overall effectiveness of the Des Moines Project are its replication in several other jurisdictions in the United States, its adoption as the model for correctional programs for the entire state of Iowa, and the continuation of its total funding by the Iowa State Legislature after LEAA support ended.

Evaluation of Locally Coordinated Community-Based Programs

Fragmentation of the criminal justice system is reduced and services to offenders are improved in locally coordinated community-based programs. In addition, locally coordinated corrections programs are able to enlist strong support from community volunteers. However, with dwindling fiscal resources, many local correctional systems may not be able to muster support from local policymakers for such a coordinated correctional effort.

PRETRIAL RELEASE AND DIVERSION PROGRAMS

Pretrial intervention programs release eligible offenders from jail before their trials, and pre- and post-trial diversion programs take offenders out of the formal criminal justice process.

---

[3]David Bookman et al., *Community-Based Corrections in Des Moines: An Exemplary Project* (Washington, D.C.: GPO, 1976).

Pretrial Release Programs

The first pretrial release program was established in the United States after Louis Schweitzer, a retired businessman, toured the Brooklyn House of Detention in 1960 and was appalled by the number of youthful defendants being held in jail for lack of small amounts of money. He contacted Herbert Sturz and agreed to put up $25,000 of his own money to do something about it. They set up the Vera Foundation, which was later renamed the Vera Institute of Justice.[4]

Their brainchild, the Manhattan Bail Project, was initiated in 1961 in order to show judges that defendants who appeared to have stable ties in the community could be released without bail. The key aspect of this project of release without bail, or release on one's own recognizance (ROR), was the development of a point scale to determine who would be a good risk to appear for trial.

Of the fourteen types of pretrial alternatives to detention which have developed in the past twenty years, release on recognizance (ROR), percentage bail, and supervised release programs are the most widely used. ROR programs permit defendants to be released without bail or supervision. Other programs allow defendants to deposit a percentage of the bail, usually 10 percent, with the court clerk, and to receive 90 percent of the amount paid as a refund when they appear in court. Supervised release allows a defendant to be released from jail as long as he or she stays in contact with an officer of the program.[5] The Manhattan Court Employment Project in New York City and Project Crossroads in Washington, D.C., are the best known of the 400 pretrial release programs in the United States.

Evaluation of pretrial release programs. These programs spare many defendants weeks or even months of the violence and the notoriously poor living conditions of jail. Pretrial release programs also improve defendants' chances when they do come to trial because sentencing judges seem more likely to sentence to imprisonment defendants who are already in jail than those who stand before them as free persons holding jobs and supporting families. Yet, too many indigent defendants are still held in jail while awaiting trial. Public criticism is reducing the use of pretrial release because it has caused more and more state legislatures to require that community safety be considered a factor in whether or not defendants are released prior to trial.

Pretrial Diversion Programs

Resolution of citizen disputes, deferred prosecution, and Treatment Alternatives to Street Crime are the most widely used pretrial diversion programs.

---

[4]Stephen Gettinger, "Has the Bail Reform Movement Stalled?" *Corrections Magazine* 6 (February 1980): 28.

[5]John L. Galvin et al., in *Alternatives to Pretrial Detention* (Washington, D.C.: GPO, October 1977), p. 2, list pretrial diversions as: field citation, station house citation, own recognizance, unsecured bail, third-party release, conditional release, monitored O R, privately secured bail, percentage bail, fully secured bond, cash bail, supervised release, and pretrial work release.

Resolution of citizen disputes. Resolution of citizen disputes programs try to keep minor conflicts between citizens out of the criminal courts. Most of the fifty such programs across the nation are based on mediation, whereby a third party recommends a solution to the conflict but does not have the authority to make a binding decision. Citizen dispute programs may come under the jurisdictions of city governments, municipal courts, prosecuting attorneys' offices, bar associations, or grass-roots citizens groups within the community.

The citizen dispute settlement program of Columbus, Ohio, an exemplary LEAA project, is the most widely known such program. This project began in 1971 when the Columbus city prosecutor's office developed an alternative system to divert interpersonal disputes from the justice system. In this dispute resolution process, called the Night Prosecutor's Program because hearings are held in the evening, antagonistic parties seek to resolve their disputes in face-to-face confrontations. Although at first the cases involved only interpersonal disputes, they now include bad check complaints, failure to pay support, disorderly conduct, criminal damages, and complaints about animals. The main goals of the program are to avoid the stigma of an arrest record for those involved in minor personal disputes, to expedite the justice process for those involved in minor criminal offenses, to reduce the backlog of the courts, and to ease interpersonal tensions in the community.[6]

The Columbus dispute resolution process begins when the prosecutor's office decides to refer a case to the Night Prosecutor's Program rather than to prepare, sign, and file an affidavit with the clerk of court. An administrative hearing is scheduled about a week later; both the complainant, with his or her witnesses, and the accused are notified to appear at the hearing, which is held privately in the office of the prosecutor. The hearing itself is informal and is conducted without regard to rules of evidence, burdens of proof, or other legalities. After asking questions and permitting the parties to talk with each other in an attempt to resolve the conflict, the hearing officer informs the parties of any applicable laws and of criminal sanctions involved in the case. The case may be referred to the court if either one of the parties refuses to attend the informal hearing or if the case cannot be resolved during the mediation process.

Deferred prosecution programs. Deferred prosecution programs deal with persons for whom conviction is likely, but enable them to avoid the stigma of prosecution and a criminal record. The pilot deferred prosecution programs were the Flint (Michigan) Citizens Probation Authority, the Manhattan Court Employment Project, and the District of Columbia's Project Crossroads. Now about one hundred and fifty programs operate in thirty-seven states, and seven states have authorizing legislation.[7] Deferred prosecution programs operate in one of two ways: An arrested offender is deemed eligible for the program on the basis of preestablished

---

[6]John W. Palmer, "The Night Prosecutor," *Judicature* 59 (June-July 1975): 23.

[7]Colorado, Arkansas, Connecticut, Florida, Massachusetts, Tennessee, and Washington have statewide enabling legislation.

criteria, and the court is asked to defer formal charges because of willing participation in the formal diversionary program; or formal charges are made before defendants are screened for their eligibility, but criminal proceedings are suspended for defendants accepted into the program, pending their successful completion of the deferred prosecution program.

Treatment alternatives to street crime (TASC). The Special Action Office for Drug Abuse Prevention created TASC in 1971 to identify and provide treatment for the greatest possible number of drug abusers entering the criminal justice system.[8] More than fifty cities have established TASC programs. TASC has three main stages: (1) a screening unit offers the program to drug abusers eligible under locally determined criteria; (2) an intake unit diagnoses each drug user referred and recommends the appropriate treatment program; and (3) a tracking unit monitors the progress of TASC clients and returns those who fail the locally determined success-failure criteria to the criminal justice system for appropriate action.

TASC, originally conceived as a pretrial diversion program, now includes services for prearrest and postarrest police diversion, pretrial intervention (conditional release), presentence referral, conditional probation, and conditional parole. Although initially only adult heroin addicts were accepted into TASC, all types of adult and juvenile drug abusers are now treated.

Evaluation of pretrial diversion programs. The outstanding feature of dispute-resolution programs is their success in resolving disputes informally. Defendants may have their records expunged after completing the program, thereby avoiding the stigma of prosecution and conviction. Thus, TASC programs give offenders a chance to deal with their drug problems outside the criminal justice system. An LEAA report evaluating twelve TASC projects concluded that TASC provided a beneficial and cost-effective alternative for drug-abusing offenders and achieved impressive success rates given the previous crime and drug involvement histories of participants.[9]

However, there are some dangers to pretrial diversion programs. The lack of procedural guidelines may result in the violation of clients' civil rights. Also, some of these programs may widen the net of the criminal justice system since they include offenders who otherwise would have merely been fined and released.

Therapeutic Communities for Drug Offenders

Synanon (California), Daytop Village (New York), Phoenix House (New York), Delancey Street (California), and Gateway House (Illinois) are frequently

---

[8]Law Enforcement Assistance Administration, *The National Treatment Alternative to Street Crime Program,* mimeographed (1 July 1977), pp. 2–3.

[9]National Institute of Law Enforcement and Criminal Justice, *Evaluation of Treatment Alternatives to Street Crime: National Evaluation Program, Phase II Report* (Washington, D.C.: GPO, January 1979), p. 5.

called upon both at the pre- and post-trial stages to divert drug addicts from the criminal justice system. Delancey Street and Gateway House can stand as examples of how some therapeutic communities work.

Delancey Street.   John Maher, a former drug addict and member of Synanon for eight years, started Delancey Street in 1970 with a $1,000 gift from an under-world loan shark.[10] Paramount Pictures made a movie about Delancey Street; CBS's "60 Minutes" examined the program; and two books have been written about this impressive therapeutic community.[11]

Delancey Street, which now has about 320 members plus a waiting list, thrives on the work ethic. It operates six businesses: a restaurant, a moving company, a flower shop, a Volkswagen repair shop, a construction and building maintenance company, and a specialty advertising firm. Delancey Street owns several million dollars worth of property all over the San Francisco Bay area, including a posh mansion on Pacific Heights, a residential hotel, and a 35-unit apartment complex with a pool in Sausalito.

John Maher suggests that treatment at Delancey Street begins with the humiliation of newcomers in order to break down any facades and to convince them that they are parasites with the impulses of children. Then, the Delancey Street family tries to convert each individual into a self-respecting, hardworking, constructive member of society. Hard, unpaid work in the family's residences and businesses and "the Games" are the two main treatment methods used in this transformation.

The Games, which are adapted from the "attack therapy" used at Synanon, are designed to force residents to spill out the huge reservoir of guilt they feel for the harm to their families and friends and for the crimes they have committed. In the Games, residents are encouraged to vent their anger and hostility against each other; thus, every Game thunders with shouts and curses. But every Game concludes with a "patch-up" session, in which residents make clear their genuine concern for each other.[12]

Delancey Street has five basic rules:

No "chemicals," including alcohol and drugs.

No physical violence.

Everyone must work or go to school, but no one is permitted to go to school unless he or she also works.

No "promiscuity."

A commitment of two years.[13]

[10]Most of the following materials on Delancey Street are adapted from Michael S. Serrill, "Delancey Street," *Corrections Magazine* 1 (September 1974): 13–28. Copyright 1974, *Corrections Magazine.* All rights reserved.

[11]Charles Hampden-Turner, *Sane Asylums* (San Francisco: San Francisco Book, 1975), and Grover Sales, *John Maher of Delancey* (New York: Norton, 1975).

[12]Michael S. Serrill, review of *Sane Asylums, Corrections Magazine* 2 (December 1976): 54.

[13]Serrill, "Delancey Street," p. 18.

nal health practices and proper diet, family responsibilities, Social Medicare benefits, and human relations.[19]

House in Cincinnati, the Magdala Foundation and Dismas House in Bureau of Rehabilitation of the National Capital Area of Washington, r House in St. Paul, and Nexus House in Minneapolis are some of administered agencies that offer high-quality residential services to he Mahoning County Residential Treatment Center in Youngstown, obationed Offenders Rehabilitation Training (PORT) Center in Roch-sota, and the Montgomery County Work-Release/Prerelease Center oteworthy county-administered residential facilities. The Probationed ehabilitation Training Center in Rochester, Minnesota, and the Mont-nty Work-Release/Prerelease Center are highlighted here as examples l facilities.

RT corrections center, a halfway house for probationers, is a nationally community-based residential facility. The PORT program serves a three-in southeastern Minnesota consisting of Olmsted, Dodge, and Fillmore l provides treatment for offenders who would otherwise be considered obationers or would have to be placed in state correctional facilities. aff includes an executive director, a group home director, three program n office supervisor, a secretary, and twelve live-in volunteer counselors, e part-time services. The PORT advisory committee, a group of about ochester citizens, generates support through employment, social in-education, legislation, finance, prevention, and public awareness. Dr. Tyce, medical director of the Rochester State Hospital, tells about the nt and development of PORT in the interview excerpted in Box 6-2.

terview with Francis A. Tyce, M.D.

anding outside a local hotel one day and talking to one of the district s who was bewailing the fact he saw the same people time after time. em to prison, and they came back to the same neighborhoods and the ems. I told him, "Let me have a look at the next felon you're thinking to prison." He sent me the son of a local police chief. The kid had sight e eye and had been involved in some serious trouble. The most recent was caught with a truck full of TV sets. We got him involved in group sions. After six months, he decided he was ready to do something else. d him in a training institute for radio broadcasting, and he came out at his class. He got a job in a radio station in a neighboring state. In six onths after I heard how well he was doing, I went down to the police

aduated Release," *Contemporary Corrections,* ed. Benjamin Frank (Reston, Va.: Reston, 24–226.

The Delancey Street family is divided into six "tribes," each with fifty to sixty members and headed by a "barber." The barber, a veteran family member, is responsible for the behavior of the members of the tribe. It is his or her responsibility to give misbehaving members of the tribe a "verbal haircut." The barber has almost autocratic control over the personal lives of members of the tribe. He or she decides what job a man or woman will be assigned, whether a family member has progressed far enough to be placed in a more responsible position in the family or business, whether proposed trial or real marriages will be approved, and whether members of the tribe will be permitted to see relatives.[14]

Delancey Street is typical of other therapeutic communities for drug abusers in that about one-third of the newcomers leave within six months. But few of those who stay more than a year drop out of the program. Delancey Street now has a number of "graduates" who have been formally released from the program. Most of them return several evenings a week for the Games and receive some financial backing from the family. Although Delancey Street keeps no statistics, it claims that nearly all of its graduates are doing well.

Delancey Street's striking program has successfully reclaimed hopeless drug addicts. Among the interesting concepts used at Delancey Street are the pooling of money, the emphasis on self-help, and the reliance on the work ethic. Charles Silberman, author of the widely acclaimed *Criminal Violence, Criminal Justice,* claims the major weakness of this program is that it fosters dependence on Maher, its founder, and on the Delancey Street family, but acknowledges that persons who have long histories of drug abuse may need the support of a substitute family to live productively without returning to the use of drugs.[15]

Gateway House. In 1968, Gateway House was opened as Illinois' first therapeutic community for the rehabilitation of drug addicts. There are now three Gateway residences in Illinois—in Chicago, in Lake Villa (northern suburb of Chicago), and in Springfield. Gateway also operates two store-front centers in Chicago called Maze I and Maze II. The three Gateway residences can handle 250 residents.

The Gateway philosophy is contained in the following statement:

We are here because there is no refuge, finally, from ourselves. Until a person confronts himself in the eyes and hearts of others, he is running. Until he suffers them to share his secrets, he has no safety from them. Afraid to be known, he can know neither himself nor any other. He will be alone.

Where else but in our common ground can we find such a mirror? Here, at last a person can appear clearly to himself, not as the giant of his dreams nor the dwarf of his fears, but as a man, part of the whole, with a share of its purpose. In this ground

[14]Ibid., pp. 20–21.

[15]Stephen Gettinger, "A Talk with Author Charles Silberman," *Corrections Magazine* 5 (March 1979): 31.

we can each take root and grow, not alone anymore as in death but alive to ourselves and to others.[16]

Formal treatment at Gateway takes three major forms: encounter groups, support from the family, and development of marketable skills. Each resident goes to three encounter sessions a week, which are designed so the drug abuser sees a mirror image of himself or herself, encounters pressure to change self-defeating attitudes, learns to be honest and to trust others, and uses the group as a safety valve to vent feelings that could not otherwise be released.

The surrogate family is a vital part of Gateway's treatment philosophy. Each Gateway house resembles a large, well-ordered family residence with clearly defined values and specific job responsibilities established. As a resident displays greater self-discipline and responsibility, he or she is rewarded with increased job status, privileges, and peer approval. Negative behavior—such as drug use, criminality, violence, and inappropriate relationships with the opposite sex—is punished through job demotions, loss of privileges, and verbal criticism.[17]

Residents are expected to learn marketable skills while in the program. Those without high school diplomas are encouraged to enter school full-time within their first six months in the program. Gateway offers training for the high school equivalency examination, along with remedial reading, writing, and mathematics and the Illinois Division of Vocational Rehabilitation also provides comprehensive training in a wide range of trades and vocations for the residents.

The three stages of the Gateway program take eighteen months to two years to complete. During the first phase, which usually takes nine to twelve months, the resident lives in the facility and participates in the daily program. During the second phase, the resident continues to live in the facility but goes to work or school outside and returns to the residence each evening to participate in a program especially designed to smooth the transition into the community. In the third phase, the client lives outside the facility but returns on a regular schedule until graduation. Even after a client has formally completed the program, he or she usually retains ties with the Gateway family and often remains involved in many of the Gateway community's activities.

A 1978 evaluation of the Gateway House Foundation program demonstrated the efficacy of the program for those who remained in treatment for a substantial period of time. A random sample of all admissions to the program between 1974 and 1978 (admissions totaled 1,410) was selected for follow-up. Of the variables examined, only time in program affected posttreatment drug use and rates of arrests: Generally, the longer an individual spent in treatment, the lower the rates of arrests and the less likely he or she was to return to the use of drugs.[18]

---

[16]Richard Boveau, "Furthering Man's Awareness of Himself . . ." (Chicago: Gateway House Foundation, Inc., n.d.), p. 23.

[17]Sherry Holland, "Gateway House: Effectiveness of Treatment on Criminal Behavior," *International Journal of the Addictions* 3 (1978): 371.

[18]"Follow-up Evaluation of the Gateway House Foundation's Treatment Program," mimeographed (n.d.), pp. 1–3. Holland's "Gateway House" contains an evaluation of a smaller sample.

Evaluation of therapeutic communities

apeutic community programs stand an exce dependency on drugs and of avoiding furt system. Thus, therapeutic communities some have a life-long history of personal failure and A second strength of TCs rests in their policy for these typically highly committed graduate walk away from drugs. A third strength lies i esteem that graduates ordinarily receive from

However, TCs have certain major limit monitored by some governmental agency to a treatment. For example, such means of humi shaving the heads of males upon arrival, ta dressing misbehaving males in diapers were p Second, the due process rights of residents mu no longer leave their due process rights at the still leave their constitutional rights at the doo family member for weeks or even months is a process rights. Third, because most drug abuse and self-commitment required in a therapeutic grams can only have limited impact on the dru

In short, TCs are lifesavers for the major these graduates have in the community are s treatment works for some offenders. But the 80 o who drop out receive little benefit and perhaps in these programs.

RESIDENTIAL PROGRAMS

Probation centers, work-release centers, restitut halfway houses are the main residential programs are reserved either for those probationers who ar community supervision or for parolees who are condition of their release from prison.

Nearly all of these facilities also provide furloughs, which are also called home visits, t community release, permit offenders to spend tir their families at home.

Most residential facilities offer work-releas leave the facility in the morning, usually with lun portation, and return at the end of the workday. S centers offer information and instruction on such employment aids, the purpose and function of the la and insurance, legal problems and contracts, basic

station and asked the man at the desk about the chief's son. He responded, "I suppose the son-of-a-bitch is in prison." I told him how well he was doing. He went to tell the chief. The chief and his wife drove on weekends to the edge of the state to listen to their son broadcasting. Eventually they got together with him and worked out a good relationship.

Our early cases did so well that the two district court judges and I got together and decided to open the PORT program. We had no information and no idea what we were doing except we were convinced that confining people in prison was often unsuccessful. They always came back worse than when they went in. We thought that there ought to be a better way of doing things, and we were thinking only about our own community. If you looked at the board of directors over the years, you would see we have had the most successful people in the community on it. The community is behind us 100 percent. The program wouldn't last another twenty-four hours if the important people in the community weren't behind it.

Source: Interview conducted in August 1981. Used with permission.

The PORT corrections center has several striking features. The local community strongly supports this residential facility. The facility has a tradition of able staff leadership. A problem-solving model developed by staff members appears effective in helping residents make more responsible decisions for their lives. Residents vote on the accepting of each applicant to the program. Residents also must negotiate a treatment contract with members of their group; by completing the various items on the contract, residents gain release from the facility. Finally, most of the residents interviewed were quite positive about the impact of its program. The following are representative of their reactions:

> This program has helped me to take a look at how serious my crime is. It has helped me to take a look at what will happen if I keep stealing cars or doing dope.

> PORT is helpful to most of us because it teaches you problem solving and how to survive on the streets. It helps you to think of the consequences of your behavior.

> It has given me an understanding of myself. It has given me hope. It has changed a lot of my negative attitudes.[20]

Although follow-up data on the effectiveness of this program are lacking, the PORT corrections center appears to be one of the most promising programs in American corrections.

Montgomery County Work-Release/Prerelease Program

The Montgomery County (Maryland) Work-Release/Prerelease Center, designated an exemplary project in 1978 by LEAA, has an extensive array of services for exoffenders. PRC clients include local residents from federal and state correc-

---

[20]Interviewed in August 1981.

tional institutions as well as inmates of the County Detention Center, which houses individuals sentenced to eighteen months or less.[21]

Components of the treatment program include work and educational release, counseling, community social services, and social awareness instruction. All new residents are expected to be employed within three weeks, and a full-time work release counselor helps new residents find jobs. Residents also meet at least once a week with their counselors. The community social services arranged for residents include mental health services, drug or alcohol counseling, family counseling, pastoral counseling, and group therapy in the community. Social awareness instruction provides prerelease seminars for residents; these twice-weekly seminars are designed to improve residents' skills in problem solving, decision making, and communication.

Accountability of residents' behavior is ensured through a contractual agreement developed jointly by each resident and a staff member; through periodic, unannounced counts and drug/alcohol testing; through frequent checks with employers and personnel of community service agencies to verify residents' continued employment and participation in those agencies' activities; and through a closely supervised furlough/release plan. The Prerelease Center also has adopted a three-phase prerelease plan under which each successive phase affords additional privileges.

A 1978 evaluation found that PRC has several benefits. First, nearly all of the 297 residents who were successfully discharged between August 1972 and August 1975 had jobs, housing, and savings upon release. Second, during the study period, residents paid approximately $73,000 in taxes, over $3,000 in fines, and about $500 for restitution and legal fees; residents also paid more than $100,000 for their families' support during this time. Third, PRC clients had a walk-off rate of less than 5 percent, and only 1 percent were arrested for new crimes committed while in the program—and these were all larcenies. A one-year follow-up study indicated that 80 percent of the successfully released clients had not been rearrested.

The strength of this program rests in its carefully conceived and systematically administered approach. Freedom through responsibility, the underlying philosophy of this program, is one that is worthy of emulation by other community-based residential facilities.

Evaluation of Residential Programs

Nearly all offenders prefer residential facilities to fortress-like prisons. Some offenders use their time in residential programs in very constructive ways. However, while such showplace facilities as PORT and the Montgomery County Work-Release/Prerelease Center are certainly impressive programs, the overall recidivism rate of parolees placed in residential programs is less impressive. Robert Martinson's and Judith Wilks' report "Knowledge in Criminal Planning" found that the mean

---

[21]The material on this program was adapted from Robert Rosenblum and Debra Whitcomb, *Montgomery County Work Release/Pre-Release Program: An Exemplary Project* (Washington, D.C.: GPO, 1978).

recidivism rate for "partial physical custody following imprisonment" was 24.82 percent, a higher rate than that of any other correctional program.[22] The high recidivism rate of halfway-out programs is not surprising when it is remembered that offenders placed in these facilities usually are not considered good risks in the first place and are the losers of the losers—the most marginal of the criminal population. The difficulties of establishing good will among neighborhood residents, a problem which is too often solved by locating residential facilities in the worst types of neighborhoods, probably also contributes to the high recidivism rate for halfway-out programs.

COMMUNITY ASSISTANCE PROGRAMS

Various programs have been established since the early 1970s to find jobs, to furnish services, and to provide support groups for exoffenders. Some are associated with parole departments; some are sponsored by volunteer groups, such as the Volunteers in Probation (VIP) Association; some are run under the auspices of the Salvation Army; some are adjunct programs of a state employment service; others are sponsored by the Comprehensive Employment and Training Act (CETA); and still others are administered by private agencies.

Friends Outside, a private agency with 18 chapters in California, provides a variety of services, including family counseling and support, educational help for prisoners' children, in-prison therapy and reentry preparation, and transportation to state institutions. Seventh Step, another buffering agency, picks up inmates at the prison gates and takes them to the city in which they will live. Founded by William Sands, an exoffender himself, Seventh Step also provides job contacts and a place for an exoffender to come to in those first crucial days after release. The Fortune Society in New York City, which serves the largest number of exoffenders in the United States, has 38,000 names on its mailing list and provides services for between 4,000 and 5,000 exoffenders who come in for help each year. In Ohio, the Cincinnati Comprehensive One-Stop Offender Aid Program (COSOAP) offers social, vocational, and psychological services all in one location. The Alston Wilkes Society in South Carolina is an impressive example of a community assistance program.

The Alston Wilkes Society

South Carolina's Alston Wilkes Society, the "brainchild" of Ellis MacDougall, is a hybrid volunteer/professional agency with 6,000 members and 57 full-time staff members. Although it has a budget of over one million dollars, it considers itself primarily a volunteer human service agency.[23]

---

[22]The Center for Knowledge in Criminal Justice Planning, 38 E. 85th Street, New York, N.Y.

[23]Donald R. Bailey, "Privatization of Justice in South Carolina" (Paper presented at the American Society of Criminology Annual Meeting, Toronto, Canada 3-6 November 1982).

The Alston Wilkes Society works closely with the Department of Corrections and attempts to fill in the gaps in state services to inmates, delinquents, and their families. It operates two halfway houses and provides parole assistance, on-the-job training, prison visitation, inmate grievance arbitration, family services, and, for status offenders, volunteer emergency homes. County chapters are somewhat autonomous. Volunteers are found throughout the population, but the majority are United Methodists and come from a white middle-class background.

As South Carolina's private correctional service, the Wilkes Society is a notable example of the valuable services a community can provide offenders and exoffenders. Both volunteers and staff involved in this organization are highly enthusiastic about the services it is providing. The results of an initial in-house evaluation were positive, and a more extensive external evaluation is being conducted at the present time.

Evaluation of Community Assistance Programs

Programs for persons coming out of prison perform necessary and helpful services, but there are too few such programs and too many exoffenders. The more often that a continuum of services is provided to participants and that community volunteers are involved in these programs, the more likely that community assistance programs will provide the quality of services needed for offenders to make it in the community. The importance of these buffering agencies to exoffenders makes it mandatory that society increase the number and quality of these programs.

SUMMARY

Community-based corrections for adults include an array of diversion, probation and parole, residential and nonresidential, and community assistance programs of which this chapter has described a few. These programs are administered on federal, state, county, and private levels. Community corrections acts encourage participating counties to deal with crime within the community instead of sending so many offenders to state institutions. Coordinated corrections programs in several counties across the nation also offer an excellent way to deal with crime problems locally. Pretrial release permits the release of eligible defendants awaiting trial. Pretrial diversion programs are helpful in giving offenders a chance to deal with their problems outside the criminal justice system. Graduates of therapeutic communities for drug abusers stand an excellent chance of living a drug-free life. Community assistance programs are helpful in providing necessary services for exoffenders.

Many reasons justify the continued reliance on community-based programs over institutional ones. Crime is a community problem, and society must deal with it within the community. Participants in community programs do not suffer the violence and victimization found in long-term correctional institutions. Better relationships exist between residents and staff in community programs, and community-based programs have greater available resources than do institutional programs. Also, community-based programs are generally more economical than institutional programs. In short, community-based corrections provides more humane environments and settings in which treatment programs are more likely to be effective than within the walls of a prison.

Discussion Questions

1. How do community-based corrections tailor programs to fit the individual needs of the offender?
2. What are the drawbacks and the advantages of community-based programs?
3. Do you see more possibilities in community corrections for adults or juveniles? Why?
4. You have committed a crime and the judge permits you to pick a community-based corrections program. Which one will you pick? Why?
5. You have spent five years in prison and will be leaving tomorrow with a bus ticket and $75. What assistance will you need to make a successful return to community life? What programs offer such assistance?

7

Treatment Technologies in Correctional Institutions

Objectives

1. *To examine the use of classification in juvenile and adult correctional institutions.*

2. *To describe and evaluate the most widely used treatment modalities in juvenile and adult correctional institutions.*

3. *To identify the principles underlying the treatment technologies used in juvenile and adult correctional institutions.*

In the past forty years, one method after another has been hailed as the panacea for criminal rehabilitation. Cures are lauded, disregarded, and rediscovered; the wheel turns. No sooner is a reform strategy put into practice than a critic like Martinson emerges to point out its failures. Whether the prison becomes hospital with various treatments, community brokerage service, or safe warehouse where interested prisoners can choose from various self-help courses, the empiricists make the same rejoinder: "The data say that your treatment works no better than one you dismissed as obsolete and ineffectual."

Yet treatment programs continue to be used in correctional institutions throughout the United States. The purpose of this chapter is to examine the more popular treatment modalities. Beginning with a discussion of classification of inmates, it then considers psychotherapy, psychodrama, transactional analysis, reality therapy, behavior modification, guided group interaction, positive peer culture, and therapeutic communities.

CLASSIFICATION

For the past century, classification has been considered as the first step of the medical model. Psychiatric evaluations and psychological workups, especially of youthful offenders, have been administered in both community and institutional settings. A number of reception and diagnostic centers have been built so that inmates' psychological, educational, and vocational needs could be identified and so that they could be assigned to programs compatible with those needs.

Juvenile Corrections

Classification in juvenile corrections has lost much of its popularity since the early 1970s. But in the 1960s, many classification techniques were used in both the community and the institution as part of the rehabilitation process. Classifying youths according to their personality dynamics, world views, and behavior were the three most popular schemes.

Personality dynamics.   Youths can be classified in several ways in terms of personality dynamics. Psychiatric categories include mentally retarded, psychoneurotic, antisocial, passive-aggressive, passive-dependent, adolescent adjustment reaction, group delinquent, and unsocialized. The Jesness Personality Inventory uses seven scales to classify offenders and to evaluate the following personality characteristics: social maladjustment, value orientation, immaturity, autism, alienation, manifest aggression, withdrawal-depression, social anxiety, repression, denial, and asocial index.

I-Level.   The use of the Interpersonal Maturity Level Classification System began in California in the 1960s and spread throughout the country. Developed by a team headed by Marguerite Q. Warren and first tested at the Preston Boys School in California, the I-Level Classification System assumes that personality development follows a normal sequence. This classification system attempts to identify the developmental stage of individual offenders by focusing on their perception of themselves, others, and the world. The I-Level is a measure of adolescents' abilities to identify and involve themselves with others. A seven-point classification scheme ranges from I_1 (infantile in interpersonal maturity) to I_7 (perfect interpersonal maturity). Research has indicated that most youthful offenders are at the I_2, I_3, or I_4 levels, and these levels are further divided into nine delinquent subtypes. The I-Level Classification System also serves as a theory of differential treatment. The system contends that the impact of treatment varies from one youth to another according to developmental stage. Thus what works with one may have no effect, or even a negative impact, on another.[1]

The Quay System. The belief that youthful offenders ought to be evaluated according to practical measures of their behavior rather than their theoretical world views led administrators at the Robert F. Kennedy Youth Center in Morgantown, West Virginia, to adopt the classification system designed by Hubert C. Quay. The Quay System divides delinquent behavior into four types: inadequate-immature, neurotic-conflicted, unsocialized-aggressive, and subcultural. Inadequate-immature offenders behave childishly and irresponsibly. Neurotic-conflicted offenders are anxious, insecure young people whose internal conflicts create problems for themselves and others. Unsocialized offenders adhere to the values of their delinquent peer group. And offenders in the subculture classification are involved in a culture of gang delinquency.[2]

Classification systems under fire. The difficulty with these three classification systems comes in translating broad abstract categories into concrete treatment plans. Critics contend that psychiatric categories are better suited to the needs of psychologists and psychiatrists than to the correction of offenders and the protection of society.

The staff of the Robert F. Kennedy Training School eventually rejected the Quay classification system, questioning whether the behavior of offenders in each of the four categories is actually distinctive. Cottage staff members also agreed that the Quay System created more behavior problems among inmates, especially incorrigibility and escapes, than it solved. Cottage staff members further criticized the lack of specific guidelines by which the four categories classified offenders. Finally, the staff accused the Quay System of resulting in racially homogeneous

---

[1]Marguerite Q. Warren "The Community Treatment Project: History and Prospects," in *Law Enforcement Science and Technology*, ed. S. A. Yefsky (Washington, D.C.: Thompson, 1972), pp. 193–195.

[2]Roy Gerard, "Institutional Innovations in Juvenile Corrections," *Federal Probation*, 34 (December 1970): 38–40.

groups or cottages. Administrators were forced to withdraw the Quay System because of the lack of commitment by staff members.[3]

The I-Level Classification System has several advantages over the other two systems and, therefore, has had a greater impact on juvenile corrections. An instructional manual teaches staff members at institutions that have adopted the program how to work with each type of offender. I-Level tends to reduce institutional management problems and to identify the most suitable placement for offenders. In addition, the process of classification offers some protection for passive youths, because they are usually separated from more aggressive offenders.[4]

But serious criticism has reduced the popularity of the I-Level System. The major criticism is that I-Level also leads to racially homogeneous groups or cottages. Thus an I_4 cottage (made up of four neurotic subtypes) often has only white youths, while an I_3MP cottage (a peer-oriented subtype) may have all black residents. Another criticism concerns the difficulty of matching inmate needs and available services in this age of public unions, for line staff are protected by union agreements from being shifted from cottage to cottage. A further criticism is that institutional problems are caused by a lack of commitment by security staff to this scheme of differential treatment. Even though I-Level is still being used in some parts of the country, California—where the scheme originated and received much of its support—has now dropped its use in juvenile corrections. The system's drawbacks, especially the creation of racial groupings, have reduced its use throughout the country.

Adult Corrections

Classifying adult offenders in community-based corrections has never been popular. For one reason, adults are seen more as dead-end offenders than are juveniles. Nevertheless, classification—based on the reintegration rather than on the medical model—remains alive and well in adult institutions.

The most widely administered psychological test in adult prisons is the Minnesota Multiphasic Personality Inventory (the MMPI). The MMPI, a standardized personality inventory of 556 true-false items, has fourteen commonly scored scales: ten clinical scales which measure different personality dimensions and four validity scales which measure test-taking attitudes that could influence the validity of the scores on the clinical scales. The ten clinical scales measure hypochondriasis, depression, hysteria, psychopathic deviancy, masculinity-femininity, paranoia, psychasthenia, schizophrenia, hypomania, and social introversion.[5]

Edwin I. Megargee and associates have used the MMPI as a basis for developing a typology of criminal offenders. As part of an extensive longitudinal

---

[3]Ibid.

[4]Carl F. Jesness et al., *The Youth Center Research Project* (Sacramento, Calif.: American Justice Institute, 1972), pp. 3–4.

[5]Edwin E. Megargee and Martin J. Bohn, Jr., *Classifying Criminal Offenders: A New System Based on the MMPI* (Beverly Hills: Sage, 1979), pp. 75–76.

research program at the Federal Correctional Institution at Tallahassee, Florida, they identified ten groups of criminal offenders. This MMPI-based typology was found to be helpful in reducing victimization and violence at the Tallahassee Correctional Institution. It is now being tested in a number of adult corrrectional institutions in the South, and it may serve as a valuable management tool in dealing with the complex problems of contemporary prisons.[6]

Most prisons in the United States have in-house reception and classification centers; there are only seventeen adult centers unattached to prisons. In-house classification programs typically are set up in a special cellblock. New inmates are often isolated from the rest of the prison population for the three weeks or so the classification process usually requires. But recent prison overcrowding sometimes means inmates now stay only a few days at the reception center before they are transferred to their assigned prison.

Recently built reception and classification centers in Florida, Nebraska, North Carolina, and Oklahoma are notable exceptions to the more typical half-hearted use of orientation. The Reception and Medical Center at Lake Butler in Florida is a campus-style facility with buildings scattered over fifty-two acres. Morale seems high among both staff and inmates, relationships among staff and inmates appear unrestrained, and a variety of recreational and self-improvement activities are available.[7] The new twelve-story diagnostic and evaluation center in North Carolina, the diagnostic and evaluation center in Nebraska, and the reception center in Oklahoma are also more modern and provide better orientation services to inmates than traditional reception and classification centers.

The Federal Prison System has the most sophisticated classification system of any correctional system in the United States. Its institutions range in security from cocorrections, or coeducational institutions, to maximum security facilities, or penitentiaries. Unit management, or the creation of functional units, is used in nearly every federal correctional institution. Organizational restructuring through unit management divides the prison into smaller units and provides both authority and communication links within each unit. The rationale behind this organizational structure is twofold: (1) decentralizing authority in the institution will assure maximum services to inmates, and (2) dividing the prison into smaller units will assure better control of inmates.[8]

In the late 1970s, administrators of Illinois' Stateville Correctional Center used unit management to regain control of the prison from three violent Chicago-based prisoner gangs. The first step in the reclassification process was to identify three categories of inmates: gang leaders who had been involved in aggressive and assaultive behavior during incarceration; inmates who were making an essentially

[6]Ibid., pp. 235–239.

[7]National Advisory Commission on Criminal Justice Standards and Goals, *Corrections* (Washington, D.C.: GPO, 1973), p. 349.

[8]See Robert B. Levinson and Roy E. Gerard, "Functional Units: A Different Correctional Approach," *Federal Probation* 37 (December 1973): 8–16, for a more extensive explanation of the philosophy and structure of unit management.

normal adjustment to prison; and inmates who required separation from more aggressive inmates. Once all the inmates in the institution were divided into these three categories, inmates in each group were placed in a separate cellhouse, and a unit management system was established throughout the institution.[9]

The classification process has several shortcomings in adult correctional institutions. First, filling up bed space or guaranteeing security are given much higher priorities than placing inmates appropriately. Second, prison administrators cannot afford to hire enough qualified psychologists and psychiatrists to set up adequate classification programs. Third, conflicting correctional goals in most states make it difficult for correctional administrators to determine what they want to achieve from the classification process.[10] Finally, the whole process of classification is currently under attack because the philosophy of differential programming in correctional institutions is being challenged by a rising number of civil rights suits.

However, despite these limiting factors, classification in adult institutions is likely to remain because correctional administrators will continue to insist that incoming inmates be put in appropriate security placements. Classification in juvenile institutions is in a more precarious position because it has more of a rehabilitative focus than does classification in adult prisons.

TREATMENT MODALITIES

In adult corrections, psychotherapy, psychodrama, transactional analysis (TA), reality therapy, behavior modification, and the therapeutic community are the most commonly used treatment modalities. In juvenile institutions, guided group interaction (GGI) and positive peer culture (PPC), both unique to juvenile corrections, are the two most widely used modalities. Transactional analysis and reality therapy are also popular in juvenile corrections.

Psychotherapy

Psychiatrists, clinical psychologists, and psychiatric social workers have treated both juvenile and adult offenders with different variations of Freudian psychotherapy for several decades. The basic technique, whether in a one-on-one relationship with a therapist or in group therapy, is to encourage inmates to talk about past conflicts that are causing them to express their emotional problems in aggressive or antisocial behavior. Ideally, offenders gain insight from individual or group therapeutic relationships that help them resolve the conflicts and unconscious needs that drive them to crime. The basic goal of psychotherapy, then, is for inmates to become responsible for their behavior.

[9]See Clemens Bartollas, *Introduction to Corrections* (New York: Harper & Row, 1981), pp. 275–280, for more information on the procedures involved in the reclassification of inmates and the implementation of unit management at Stateville.

[10]National Advisory Commission, *Corrections*, pp. 349–350.

Richard Jenkins defines some of the other effects of psychotherapy:

1. A sense of emotional security which the patient develops from interaction with the therapist.
2. Respect for the integrity and self-determination of the individual or respect for the patient's identity.
3. The relief of pent-up emotional tension.
4. Reduction or stimulation of the patient's sense of responsibility for his actions.
5. Reduction of the guilt or anxiety of the person.
6. Reduction of feelings of inferiority or inadequacy of patients.[11]

Both individual and group psychotherapy have many limitations in corrections. First, the few available psychotherapists have too many demands on their time. Because they are often swamped with classification and with emergency cases, psychotherapists seldom work with individuals or groups with sufficient frequency or regularity for progress to be made. Second, even if more therapists were available, few inmates would accept their help. Prisoners generally feel that engaging in "mind games" is accepting the opinion of the establishment that they are sick, and typical lower-class offenders have never thought of themselves as sick. Third, violent and overcrowded prisons are hardly the ideal setting for psychotherapy. Fourth, psychological and psychiatric recommendations often ignore the social factors encouraging illegal behavior in delinquent or adult criminals. Finally, many therapists are long on diagnosis but short on recommendations for dealing with offenders' problems.

Despite these drawbacks, some studies found that certain types of offenders seem to benefit from psychotherapy in correctional settings. The most effective programs are led by enthusiastic and involved treatment staff who use a combination of individual and group psychotherapy.[12] Although the few positive evaluations do not cancel out the other studies that show the behavior of treated and untreated offenders released from institutions usually does not differ significantly, the positive results point out that some offenders can profit from psychotherapy in institutional settings.

Psychodrama

Like most of the other therapies at work in corrections today, psychodrama was conceived as a tool for the free society. Jacob Moreno introduced it in the United States in 1925, as a model for bringing social situations into the psychiatrist's office. The premise of psychodrama is that inmates learn through dealing with conflicts openly. Psychodrama appeals to offenders because it turns institutional

---

[11]Donald G. Gibbons, *Society, Crime, and Criminal Careers* (Englewood Cliffs, N.J.: Prentice-Hall, 1968), p. 145.

[12]Douglas Lipton, Robert Martinson, and Judith Wilks, *The Effectiveness of Correctional Treatment: A Survey of Treatment Evaluation Studies* (New York: Praeger, 1975), p. 210.

time into a dress rehearsal for the rest of their lives. Moreno explains the main principles of psychodrama as follows:

(1) Self-presentation. The protagonist presents himself, his own mother, his own father, his brother, his favorite professor, or other significant others. He acts all these roles himself, in complete subjectiveness, as he experiences and perceives them.

(2) Self-realization. The protagonist enacts, with the aid of a few auxiliary egos [persons], the plan of his life, no matter how remote this may be from his present situation. It is his vision of his past, present, and future life.

(3) Direct soliloquy. A monologue in which the protagonist steps outside the scene and speaks his thoughts freely to himself or the group.

(4) Therapeutic soliloquy. The protagonist is able to share hidden feelings and thoughts.

(5) Doubling. An auxiliary ego [person] is asked also to represent the protagonist, to establish identity with him, to move, act, and behave like him.

(6) Multiple doubling. The protagonist is on the stage with several doubles of himself, each portraying another part of his personality.

(7) Mirroring. An auxiliary ego helps the protagonist to see himself as others see him by copying his behavior and trying to express his feelings in word and movement.

(8) Role reversal. The protagonist plays the part of his antagonist in a relevant scene.

(9) Future projection. The protagonist portrays in action how he thinks his future will shape itself.

(10) Life rehearsal. The protagonist practices in advance a situation he expects to encounter.

(11) Psychodramatic hallucination. The protagonist portrays his own hallucinations, by acting them out on the stage.

(12) Psychodramatic dream technique. The protagonist enacts a dream, instead of telling it.[13]

Psychodrama places individuals in role-playing situations which demand they act out their feelings or behaviors. As their spontaneity increases, the individuals can more easily demonstrate their problems to the therapy group and to themselves, with new understanding and openness. Individuals in a psychodrama group can spontaneously create new behaviors and improve their behavioral repertoire, obtain feedback, see themselves as others do, and improve their communication with others. Within the reconstituted society of the group, they can experience, express, and observe feelings and their effects upon others.

Psychodrama in its pure form is rare in U.S. correctional institutions, but sex offender therapy at the Rahway Treatment Unit in New Jersey uses a form of psychodrama. The main purpose of the ROARE program (Reeducation of Attitudes and Repressed Emotions) is to uncover and analyze the psychological wounds and past sexual traumas of the sex offender. The therapy uses an inmate playing the role of therapist to force another offender to relive his sexual assaults. The offender who is the focus of treatment usually undergoes an intense emotional regression during the session; he often relives childhood incidents in which he was sexually abused himself.[14]

[13]J. L. Moreno, *Psychodrama* (Beacon, N.Y.: Beacon House, 1969), pp. 239–242.

[14]"Treating Sex Offenders in New Jersey," *Corrections Magazine* 1 (November-December 1974): 13–24.

Techniques related to psychodrama, such as role playing and improvisational theater, are common in juvenile and adult correctional institutions. For example, in the mid-1970s, Ma Goose, Inc., began a twice-weekly improvisational theater workshop series at the San Francisco Juvenile Court's Hidden Valley Ranch. By using various improvisational structures, youths are able to focus on their relationships, take on new roles, switch roles, and develop desired characteristics.

Psychodrama and other similar techniques are especially useful for offenders who have committed compulsive crimes, but the shortage of individuals trained in these techniques limits their use in correctional institutions.

Transactional Analysis

Transactional analysis, a therapy founded on interpreting and evaluating relationships among people, has generated more interest in corrections than either psychotherapy or psychodrama because offenders, like people in the society, see its immediate value. TA uses catchy language to promise people who feel "not OK" that several easy steps can take them to the other side—feeling "OK."

The TA leader and the offender, whether in a community facility or in an institution, first do a "script analysis," in which they estimate the effect "tapes" of past experiences have on present behavior. According to TA, memory acts like a three-track tape, recording the events of early childhood, the meaning attached to these events, and the emotions felt when they happened. Each person has a strong tendency to play back these tapes when confronted with similar situations later in life. Offenders have become "losers" or "nonwinners" because they play back tapes of self-defeating behaviors. The TA leader then teaches offenders to change their negative scripts, assuring them it is possible to become winners and to succeed in life's goals. These early clarification stages are intended to be motivational. At this point, if the offender decides to negotiate a treatment contract with both short- and long-range goals, treatment begins.[15]

Once offenders become part of a TA group, they are taught that they act according to three roles in dealing with others. The "child" is one-half a dependent, a relic of the past, and one-half a spontaneous, disarming person; the "parent" copies, often unconsciously, the values held by the individual's own parents; and the "adult" is the mature, responsible part of each individual. The therapist and the group are quick to identify these roles in each member. The purpose is to help the offender use the adult ego state more frequently and to turn off the "not OK" feelings buried in the child tape.[16]

Offenders in TA learn that four "life positions" describe the judgments they make about themselves and others:

> "I'm OK—You're OK." The healthy person sees values in people; agrees that both the self and others are well adjusted to life.

[15]Eric Berne, *What Do You Say After You Say Hello?* (New York: Grove Press, 1972).
[16]Ibid.

"I'm not OK—You're OK." The self-deprecating person sees others as emotionally healthy but the self as inept.

"I'm not OK—You're not OK." The malcontent believes that neither the self nor anybody else is healthy.

"I'm OK—You're not OK." The egoist praises the self as adjusted but rejects others.[17]

Offenders also learn that people play games to avoid knowing themselves and growing up. TA therapists claim that games played in institutions serve several special negative purposes. They keep offenders from achieving intimacy with others; they cause them to act in the impulsive, immature child state too much of the time; they keep the therapist at an emotional distance; and they allow the inmate to circumvent rules and procedures. Box 7-1 relates the success of TA with one youthful offender.

Box 7-1 A TA Success Story

Bill, a sixteen-year-old black youth, had spent several years in juvenile institutions before he arrived at the training school. Although his home was intact, he felt a great deal of rejection from his mother. His offenses involved incorrigibility at home and in school and two charges of assault and battery toward peers (fighting in school). He also had had poor relationships with his peers; his average to above-average intelligence was not apparent from his school performance. Psychiatric reports diagnosed him as withdrawn and as having schizoid tendencies.

His first adjustment report stated: "The prognosis is poor. Extremely depressed about his home life, especially his relationship with mother, Bill is experiencing conflict with peers and staff alike. Bill is resistant to his placement and refuses to become involved in any institutional program."

Then, Bill was persuaded by a TA leader to join a group. TA fascinated Bill, who took an active part in the group and never missed a meeting; he also read all he could find on this therapy. More importantly, he used the concepts of TA to change his behavior and his perception of himself. He frequently informed staff, "I came out of the child state on that one, didn't I." Bill decided he would finish his last three years of high school, and he did complete high school at the institutional high school in the next year and a half. He was granted a home visit to resolve his conflict with his mother, but when she blatantly rejected him on the visit, he used TA to work through the pain of rejection. He applied to Ohio State University, was accepted and, upon his release, became a college student. Four years later, the youth given such a poor prognosis received his college diploma.

Source: Case study of a youth with whom the author worked.

Transactional analysis, widely used in juvenile and adult correctional institutions, has several advantages for offenders: (1) it is easy to learn; (2) it is appealing because it offers hope; (3) it serves to reduce disciplinary problems in units where

---

[17]Thomas A. Harris, *I'm OK–You're OK* (New York: Harper & Row, 1965).

it is used; and (4) it provides a future job possibility for offenders who become highly skilled in its use. Although many juveniles and adult inmates find TA a therapy offering a promise of dealing with their present and future problems, it has not proved effective with inmates who lack the motivation to change, who have little or no interest in examining their own problems, and who have ongoing behavior problems. Individuals with immature personalities, borderline intelligence, or sociopathic tendencies also usually do not benefit from this modality.

Reality Therapy

Reality therapy, developed by William Glasser and G. L. Harrington, is based on the assumption that all individuals have basic needs and that they act irresponsibly when they are unable to fulfill those needs. Reality therapy defines relatedness and respect as the basic human needs, which are satisfied by realistic, responsible, and right actions—the three Rs of reality therapy.[18] Significantly, Glasser developed much of the theory and application of reality therapy while he was a psychiatrist at the Ventura Training School for Girls in California.

Richard L. Rauchin outlined fourteen steps that the effective reality therapist takes to become involved with and influence the behavior of clients:

1. Personalizes. The reality therapist becomes emotionally involved. He carefully models responsibility and does not practice something other than what he preaches.
2. Reveals self. He does not need to project an image of being all-knowing or all-powerful.
3. Concentrates on the "here and now." He does not allow the person to use the unfavorable past as a justification of irresponsible action in the present.
4. Emphasizes behavior. The reality therapist is not interested in uncovering underlying motivation or drives; rather, he concentrates on helping the person act in a manner that will help him meet his needs responsibly.
5. Rarely asks why. The reality therapist takes the posture that irresponsible behavior is just that, regardless of the reasons.
6. Helps the person evaluate his behavior. He repeatedly asks the person what his current behavior is accomplishing and whether it is meeting his needs.
7. Helps him develop a better plan for future behavior. If the person cannot develop his own plan, the reality therapist will help him develop one. A contract is drawn up and signed by the person and the reality therapist.
8. Rejects excuses.
9. Offers no tears of sympathy.
10. Praises and approves responsible behavior.
11. Believes people are capable of changing their behavior.
12. Tries to work in groups. People are most responsive to the influence and pressure of their peers. People are also more likely to be open and honest with a peer group.
13. Does not give up.
14. Does not label people. Behavior is simply described as responsible or irresponsible. The therapist does not classify people as sick, disturbed, or emotionally disturbed.[19]

---

[18]William Glasser, *Reality Therapy* (New York: Harper & Row, 1965), p. xii.

[19]Richard L. Rachin, "Reality Therapy: Helping People Help Themselves," *Crime and Delinquency* 20 (January 1974): 51–53.

Glasser, based upon his work with the girls at the Ventura Training School, believes that offenders need both consistent discipline and warm acceptance, but that neither warmth nor discipline should supersede each other. At the same time they are receiving consistent discipline and warm acceptance, offenders should be given increased responsibilities.[20]

More empirical evaluation is necessary before any conclusive statement can be made about the effectiveness of reality therapy. E. Williams found that a fifteen-week reality therapy program in the Glades Correctional Institution (Florida) improved institutional behavior.[21] Glasser estimates that it succeeded with about 80 percent of the girls at the Ventura School, and he says only 43 of 370 graduates of the program returned while he was a therapist there.[22] An in-house study of the reality therapy program for adult and juvenile sex offenders at the Western State Hospital in the state of Washington showed that from 1958 to 1968 only 8.9 percent of these exoffenders were rearrested.[23]

There are several reasons why staff members in juvenile and adult institutions are attracted to reality therapy. They feel that the basic principles of this modality are easily learned. They also like the therapy's present focus and the authority and power it gives them. Further, they like the emphasis reality therapy places on responsibility and discipline. But critics charge that reality therapy oversimplifies human behavior and that it can lead to an authoritarian attitude on the part of the therapist. They also question whether it is always wise to ignore the past.

Behavior Modification

Behavior modification assumes that rewarding a behavior positively, immediately, and systematically increases the occurrence of the behavior. Similarly, if behavior is not reinforced, its frequency should decrease.

The kinds of behavior modification or behavior therapy programs used in correctional institutions most often are the token economy, programmed learning, behavioral contracts, and contingency management. The variety of techniques used to reinforce positive and eradicate negative behaviors include systematic desensitization, training in assertiveness, conditioning against avoidance response, counterconditioning, and tokens. The desired positive reinforcers consist of attention, praise, money, food, and privileges; negative reinforcers, which ordinarily are avoided, include threats, confinement, punishment, and ridicule.[24] Behavior therapists also avoid such terms as *repressed desires, self-concepts, unconscious needs,* and *superego* because these refer to internal psychological characteristics. Instead,

---

[20]Glasser, *Reality Therapy*, p. 70.

[21]E. Williams, "Reality Therapy in a Correctional Institution," *Corrective and Social Psychiatry and Journal of Behavior Technology Methods and Therapy,* 22 (1976): 6–11.

[22]Glasser, *Reality Therapy*, p. 68.

[23]George J. MacDonald et al., "Treatment of the Sex Offender" (Fort Steilbacoon, Wash.: Western State Hospital, 1968).

[24]Jesness, et al., *The Youth Center Research Project.*, p. 7.

behavior therapists try to change behavior by determining the desired result, the stimuli controlling it, and the reinforcers needed to attain the desired response.

Behavior modification therapy depends on consistency in the treatment environment, which means each staff member must consistently provide positive and negative reinforcers. Proponents of this modality usually advise against punishment, unless prisoners are dangerous to themselves or to others, but recommend brief time-out periods during which offenders receive no reinforcement of any kind. Further, if the undesired behavior is eradicated, advocates of this therapy believe, ultimately the negative attitudes prompting the behavior will also disappear.

Behavioral contracts are widely used both in juvenile and adult correctional institutions. For example, the New Mexico Boys Training School in Springer employs a four-step behavioral contract program. In step one, the youth is limited in movement, visiting, and canteen privileges, but as he fulfills his behavioral contracts, he is promoted and receives increasing freedoms in all areas. By the time he reaches step four, he is eligible for a 72-hour home pass and usually begins planning for discharge and parole.[25]

Robert R. Ross and Bryan McKay, in their review of the literature, found twenty-four studies of institutional behavior modification programs. Yet only a small number of these programs presented data on rehabilitation, and of those that did provide such data, little or no difference in outcome was reported between behavior-oriented programs and other comparable treatment programs.[26] But Ross and McKay did find that these twenty-four programs were successful either in reducing negative behavior in the institution or in enhancing inmates' academic achievements or industrial productivity.[27]

Three features make behavior modification therapy ideally suited to the correctional setting. First, its principles are few, easy to understand and to remember, and simple to explain. Second, it can be effective on a short-term basis.[28] Third, it appears to have a greater impact on the sociopathic offender than has any other treatment modality. Bernard and Eiseman reported that sociopathic offenders are easier to condition than normal subjects once the behavior therapist discovers what is rewarding for the offender he or she is treating.[29]

Nevertheless, behavior modification has been widely criticized. The use of aversion therapy in American corrections resulted in the public's belief that all techniques of behavior modification are bizarre means of people-changing. Aversion therapy, which was used primarily with sexual offenders and with alcoholics and drug addicts, consisted of attempting to change a person's behavior by using pun-

---

[25]William Hart, "Profile/New Mexico," *Corrections Magazine,* Volume 2 (March 1976), p. 46.

[26]Robert R. Ross and Bryan McKay, "Behavioral Approaches to Treatment in Corrections: Requiem for a Panacea," in *Effective Correctional Treatment,* ed. Robert R. Ross and Paul Gendreau (Toronto: Butterworths, 1980), p. 47.

[27]Ibid., pp. 47–48.

[28]Ibid., p. 41.

[29]J. L. Bernard and R. Eiseman, "Verbal Conditioning in Sociopaths with Spiral and Monetary Reinforcement," *Journal of Personality and Social Psychology,* 6 (1976): 203–206.

ishment to suppress undesirable behavior. For example, the California Medical Facility at Vacaville and the California Institute for Women at Frontera both used anectine to treat alcoholics in the early 1970s. Patients would then be given a small amount of their favorite alcoholic beverage, but a few seconds after tasting the alcohol, they would feel that they were suffocating and have to be ventilated with a breathing bag.

Critics also claim that treating only the overt symptoms is too superficial and that even if such therapy should be effective on a short-term basis, its effects will not be lasting. Critics further charge that behavior modification therapists sometimes have used inmates as guinea pigs. In addition, critics assert, behavior modification requires considerable consistency and continuity which are atypical of correctional settings. Too, critics question how behavior modification can be used with offenders without overt behavior problems.

Because of the criticisms against behavior modification, formal treatment modalities based on social learning principles are on the decline in juvenile and adult corrections. The Federal Prison System no longer conducts such programs, and the federal government will no longer fund behavior modification programs. Yet, reinforcing inmates for positive behavior is one of the most universally accepted principles in corrections. In correctional institutions throughout the nation, residents receive additional privileges as they accept institutional rules and procedures and as they show more positive attitudes.

Guided Group Interaction

The most widely used means of rehabilitating institutionalized delinquents is some form of group counseling. Forms of group counseling vary from informal and unstructured meetings between cottage staff and residents to sophisticated treatment modalities led by trained or professional staff.[30] Guided group interaction and positive peer culture are the most popular means of group counseling in juvenile corrections at the present time.

Guided group interaction is used in at least eleven states, including New Jersey, South Dakota, Minnesota, West Virginia, Illinois, Georgia, Florida, New Hampshire, Maryland, Michigan, and Kentucky. Children being treated live, study, and play together in campus settings under the direction of adult leaders. Interaction is intensive, but the atmosphere is typically neither hostile nor authoritarian, and group participants are given considerable choice. In institutions, GGI groups often determine when a group member will be released or granted a home furlough, how a group member will be punished, or whether the front door will be locked at night.

Guided group programs typically involve several stages. In the first stage, new members gradually relax their defenses as they are encouraged by group members and the leader. Residents share their life stories and problems during the

---

[30]See Dennis A. Romig, *Justice for Our Children: An Examination of Juvenile Delinquent Rehabilitation Programs* (Lexington, Mass: Heath, 1978), pp. 57–76, for an excellent review of group counseling interventions used in juvenile correctional institutions.

second stage, as they begin to trust their group. In the third stage, offenders frequently examine how they got in trouble and begin to discuss the problems of institutional and street living. By the fourth stage, they may feel sufficiently secure to accept reeducation, and in the fifth stage, participants set up their own plans for change. Guided by both their own and the group's evaluations, participants reach a conscious decision about their futures.

The adult leader makes certain a delinquent subculture does not develop in the group. Delinquent leaders always pose a threat to the emerging prosocial values of the group, and the leader makes certain the threat does not materialize. The adult leader also must refer decision making back to the group. If a group member plans to run away, the rest of the group is responsible for preventing the defection. As one adult leader asked his group, "What do you want me to do? He's your buddy; he's part of your group. You can talk to him, sit on him if you have to; but it's up to all of you to help one another."[31]

Does guided group interaction work? Several studies, as indicated in Chapter 5, found that noninstitutional GGI programs are at least as effective as and much less costly than correctional confinement.[32] But little research has been done on the efficacy of GGI in institutional settings.

The main strength of GGI rests in its ability to involve group participants in alternative, closely knit communities, thus circumventing the values of delinquent-peer subcultures. GGI is a comprehensive rather than a piecemeal strategy, which substitutes a whole new structure of beliefs, values, and behaviors for the old, antisocial structure. Because GGI can be led by trained custodial staff members, more staff members can be involved in the treatment process without significantly increasing costs. GGI also teaches offenders to take responsibility for their own lives and to reduce their dependency on the delinquent peer group.

However, GGI also has several disadvantages. The shortage of trained leaders is a major problem. In addition, the wide variation in GGI programs has prevented the development of clear, consistent, and repeatable treatment designs. Some critics believe that the emphasis on peer group norms leaves too little room for individualism and that the achievements made are not easily transferable to real life.

Guided group interaction began to draw increased criticism in the late 1970s because of these disadvantages, but it continues to be widely used in juvenile correctional institutions.

Positive Peer Culture

Positive peer culture is another group approach for building productive youth subcultures. Like its parent model, guided group interaction, positive peer culture is a total strategy extending to all aspects of daily living. Developed by Harry

---

[31]Joseph W. Scott and Jerry B. Hissong, "Changing the Delinquent Subculture: A Sociological Approach," in *Readings in Juvenile Delinquency*, ed. Ruth Shonle Cavan (Philadelphia: Lippincott, 1975), pp. 486–488.

[32]See Ashley H. Weeks, "The Highfields Project," in *Juvenile Delinquency: A Book of Readings*, ed. Rose Giallombardo (New York: Wiley, 1976), pp. 535–547.

Vorrath and associates, PPC is used in every state juvenile institution in Michigan, Missouri, and West Virginia.

The basic goal of PPC is to "turn around" a negative peer group toward a productive direction. PPC does this by teaching participants to care for one another. Caring is interpreted as wanting what is best for a person. Through this caring context, youths learn to identify problems and to work toward their resolution. Proponents of this modality believe that once caring becomes fashionable and is accepted by the group, "hurting goes out of style."[33]

The stages in PPC follow the pattern of GGI, but PPC places significantly greater emphasis on positive behavior. Participants learn to speak of positive behavior as "great," "intelligent," "independent," "improving," and "winning." In contrast, negative behavior is described as "childish," "unintelligent," "helpless," "destructive," "copping out," and "losing." Caring is presented as a strong, appropriate trait for both sexes.

The positive peer culture approach also recognizes the destructive power of "negative indigenous leaders" (NIL) and has strategies to neutralize their threat. The method undercuts foundations of negative peer support by winning the negative leader's lieutenants away from their earlier allegiance. Table 7-1 shows qualities desirable and undesirable in a PPC staff member.

Jerry D. Mitchell and David L. Cochrum, in the major study that has been conducted on the effectiveness of positive peer culture, found that the use of PPC

TABLE 7-1   Desired Qualities of Positive Peer Culture Staff Members: "More ofs" and "Less ofs" for enhancing and maintaining group effectiveness and maturity levels

Less	More
Failure-oriented activities	Success-oriented activities
Manipulation	Honesty and trust
Emphasizing on staff control	Emphasizing group and individual strength and responsibility
	Viewing each youth as a unique individual
Punishing and abuse confrontation	Modeling caring and supportive behaviors, i.e., more patting and less chewing out
Cold neutrality, aloofness, and superior attitudes	Empathy and understanding (Kids are human too!)
Over-labeling and values dumping	Accurate communication
Certainty and absoluteness	Willingness to learn, grow, and seek new challenge
Fronting	"Being for real" and having no need to play games
Mixing personal issues with work performance	Professionalism: Being able to separate private life from work

Source: Prepared for this volume by R. Johnson, P. Wilson, and C. Oakwood, former youth supervisors for the Arden Shore Home for Boys (Illinois).

[33]Harry H. Vorrath and Larry K. Brendtro, *Positive Peer Culture* (Chicago: Aldine, 1974).

means fewer incidents and a smoother, less traumatic program in an adolescent treatment facility.[34] PPC has the same strengths as guided group interaction. Both programs undermine the values of the delinquent peer culture, depend on comprehensive strategies for treating juvenile offenders, and place responsibility on the shoulders of offenders.

Three limitations on its effectiveness and applicability have been cited. First, some critics claim that Vorrath may have underestimated the ingenuity and resourcefulness of peer subcultures, expressing reservations about PPC's ability to undermine the power of negative inmate leaders. Second, to be successful this model depends on staff members' abilities to remain unpredictable to their groups. Such inscrutability is a trait not usually found in the average person, the critics claim. Finally, critics question whether it is possible to teach caring relationships to young people who have experienced exploitation and deprivation all their lives.

Nevertheless, PPC—which must be more extensively evaluated—remains one of the most promising ways to treat juvenile offenders.

Therapeutic Communities

Self-contained therapeutic communities are more difficult to establish in institutional settings than in community settings. Prison authorities are reluctant to delegate responsibility and authority to the therapeutic community and to modify traditional prison rules to accommodate an atypical social system (i.e., a therapeutic community).[35]

The most widely hailed therapeutic community in adult correctional institutions was developed by Martin Groder at the federal penitentiary at Marion, Illinois; this program has been copied in correctional facilities at Terminal Island, California; Oxford, Wisconsin; Stillwater, Minnesota; and the Fort Grant Training Center, Arizona. Other therapeutic communities are found at Niantic in Connecticut, Patuxent in Maryland, St. Cloud in Minnesota, and throughout the prison systems of California and New York. Therapeutic communities are also found at the Maricopa County Jail in Phoenix, Arizona, and at the Baltimore City Jail, Maryland. Monzanita Lodge, which houses the California Youth Authority's Drug Abuse Program, is the best example of a therapeutic community in a juvenile correctional institution.

Psychiatrist Groder established a TC at the maximum security federal prison at Marion, Illinois, from 1968 to 1974. The community was named Asklepieion, after the temple of the Greek god of healing. Groder, influenced by his contacts with Synanon in California and by transactional analysis, managed to convince institutional administrators to sanction an inmate group of about twenty-five volunteers who would evolve their own treatment program. Inmates initially lived in

---

[34]Jerry D. Mitchell and David L. Cochrum, "Positive Peer Culture and a Legal System: A Comparison in an Adolescent Treatment Facility, *Criminal Justice and Behavior* 7 (December 1980): 399–406.

[35]Maxwell Jones, "Desirable Features of a Therapeutic Community in a Prison," in *Therapeutic Communities in Corrections,* ed. Hans Toch (New York: Praeger, 1980), p. 34.

a separate unit in the prison hospital, attended lectures on TA, and used Synanon-type confrontation groups. Regularly scheduled games, or confrontations, were held twice a week, although the use of these games could be invoked at any time of day or night by any member of the group. Jobs in the unit were allocated according to merit; the newcomer always started at the lowest level. The basic rules, prohibiting physical violence or threats of violence, gambling, drugs, or homosexual behavior, were rigidly enforced, and violation brought automatic expulsion from the group. Gestalt therapy, primal therapy, behavior modification, and other techniques were also used. (See the interview with Groder in Chapter 9 for more information on Asklepieion.)[36]

In 1971, a program called the Just Community was initiated at the Niantic Correctional Institution for Women in East Lyme, Connecticut. Joseph E. Hickey and Peter L. Scharf, with the guidance of Lawrence E. Kohlberg of Harvard, launched the project to create a democratic prison environment that would be perceived as fair by inmates and staff and that would stimulate moral thinking on the part of inmates. Participants in the Just Community make decisions on such matters as all discipline within units and disciplines occurring outside the unit for any problems other than felonies, escapes, riots, and drugs; parole referrals; inmate selection; expulsion of inmates; recreation activities; and furlough nominations. The design for moral reeducation of program participants was guided by the stages of moral development evolved by Lawrence E. Kohlberg.[37]

Empirical studies on the effectiveness of the therapeutic community in a prison context show mixed findings. Examining two prison TCs, researchers concluded that treatment inmates did no better than untreated populations.[38] Yet, Monte MacKenzie and Bill Smith, both graduates of Groder's Marion program who later established TCs in other correctional facilities, are examples of exoffenders who benefited from a therapeutic community in prison.[39]

The most outstanding feature of the therapeutic community is its focus on the entire living unit. This modality also provides more opportunities for individual decision making than do other treatment programs. Furthermore, the conflicts between treatment and custodial staff traditional in other treatment programs are absent in the therapeutic community. The Therapeutic Community Act of 1978, a bill introduced by Senator DeConcini, 95th Congress S. 3227, has encouraged the establishment of TCs in more prisons across the nation. However, prison overcrowding is an inhibiting factor in the establishment of therapeutic communities in adult prisons. Many prison administrators also are reluctant to allow the degree of inmate self-government necessary to create a therapeutic community because they are afraid that they may lose control of that unit. In this regard, administrators frequently raise several questions concerning control in a therapeutic community:

[36]Ibid., pp. 38–39.

[37]Joseph E. Hickey and Peter L. Scharf, *Toward a Just Correctional System* (San Francisco: Jossey-Bass, 1980).

[38]Lipton Martinson, and Wilkes, *Effectiveness of Correctional Treatment*, pp. 225–228.

[39]Toch, ed. *Therapeutic Communities in Corrections*, p. 206.

Is the staff still in charge, or are inmates running the shop? Why do inmates involved in a TC not have to follow the rules like everyone else? How do we know that inmates are not plotting a mass escape or a takeover of the institution?[40]

SUMMARY

This chapter has discussed the classification techniques and the most widely used treatment modalities in juvenile and adult correctional institutions. The aim of psychotherapy is to help inmates gain insight so that they can resolve the conflicts and unconscious needs that drive them to crime. Psychodrama uses role reversal so that inmates can examine attitudes and behaviors within the reconstituted society of the group. The purpose of transactional analysis is to help offenders examine individual problems in a group context and to learn a new approach to interpersonal relationships. Reality therapy, which focuses on present behavior rather than on past emotional conflicts, tries to teach inmates responsible behavior and right from wrong. Behavior modification assumes that rewarding a behavior positively, immediately, and systematically will increase the occurrence of this behavior. Guided group interaction involves juvenile participants in alternative, closely knit, positive communities, in order to circumvent the values of delinquent-peer cultures. Positive peer culture, another group approach for building productive youth cultures, tries to achieve its goal by teaching participants to care for one another. Therapeutic communities, which are more widely used in adult than in juvenile facilities, focus on treatment through changing the total environment. This modality provides more opportunities for individual decision making than do other treatment programs.

Many correctional institutions remain jungles in which only the strong survive. In these violent settings, no one is trusted and residents interpret human warmth and kindness as weakness. However, although treatment programs frequently make promises they cannot deliver, the programs described in this chapter do have an impact on some juvenile and adult inmates. The insights these individuals learn, the responsible behaviors they are taught, and the caring they receive from treatment agents and other inmates are carried over into community life. When one exoffender was asked, "Does rehabilitation work?" he answered, "It worked for me."[41] The challenge is to develop treatment programs that will enable more offenders to make that reply.

DISCUSSION QUESTIONS

1. Why is classification emphasized more in adult than in juvenile institutions?
2. Why is TA popular with many offenders?

---

[40]Robert B. Levinson, "TC or Not TC? That Is the Question," in *Therapeutic Communities in Corrections*, ed. Toch, p. 52.

[41]Interviewed in January 1981.

3. Why do line staff frequently favor reality therapy over other treatment techniques discussed in this chapter?
4. What attitudes and changes do GGI and PPC hope to bring forth in the inmate culture?
5. Which modality do you believe is the most promising for use in correctional institutions? Why?

8

Programs in Correctional Institutions

Objectives

1. To examine various academic programs for prisoners.
2. To evaluate vocational education programs.
3. To survey industrial employment available in prisons.
4. To evaluate religious programs and the roles of chaplains.
5. To discuss the variety of recreational activities.
6. To list and evaluate self-improvement and service programs for inmates.

Educational and vocational programs, religious services and counseling, industrial employment, and self-improvement and service programs are designed both to rehabilitate offenders and to ease the pains of confinement. Some inmates become interested in education while in prison and later graduate from high school or even from college. While in prison and training schools, other inmates learn vocational skills that are later instrumental in their finding community employment. A few inmates become deeply involved in religion, which helps them cope with the present and sometimes provides a philosophy or mission in their lives. Meditation and other self-growth programs help some prisoners deal with the stresses of confinement; other inmates become deeply involved in a service project and feel, perhaps for the first time in their lives, that they are doing something for others.

However, there is abundant evidence that these programs are frequently anything but treatment. The casual visitor to a prison education class is often struck by evidence that little education is taking place: dozing inmates, inmates talking with each other, bored and ineffectual teachers, and outdated and inadequate textbooks. Recreational programs are sometimes not much better: prisoners cheering against the prison team; convicts perceiving the yard as one of the best places to make a hit on an enemy; and inmates seeking to avoid the gym because it is controlled by predators. In industrial employment programs, inmates are often idle or dawdling or working in situations that really require fewer workers. Religious programs in prison often seem even more of a mockery: inept chaplains speaking to sparsely attended worship services; chaplains being regarded only as extensions of the administration; chaplains' offices being used as drug drop-offs; and inmates being sexually victimized in an empty chapel or chaplain's office.

This chapter will describe and evaluate these ancillary programs for inmates in correctional institutions. More attention is given to adult prisons than to juvenile correctional institutions because, except for academic education, programs are usually more fully developed in adult facilities.

ACADEMIC EDUCATION

The task of academic education in correctional institutions is particularly difficult because most offenders come with great educational deficiencies and many are either functionally or totally illiterate. In adult facilities, the average school achievement score of arriving prisoners does not exceed the ninth-grade level in any state and in some states the average scores are at the fifth- or sixth-grade level.[1] The bilingualism of many Hispanic or Chicano inmates, who are illiterate in English and barely more proficient in Spanish, makes the task even more difficult. In juvenile facilities, residents have as many educational deficiencies but show greater resistance because the majority are faced with compulsory educational programs.

[1]John P. Conrad, *Adult Offender Education Programs* (Washington, D.C.: National Institute of Justice, 1981).

In adult institutions, academic education is generally available through adult basic education (ABE) programs, secondary education and general education diploma (GED) studies, postsecondary education programs, and social education programs. In juvenile facilities, the programs are generally the same except postsecondary programs are seldom available.

Minnesota and Texas have been innovative in using advanced educational technology, such as computer-assisted instruction. The PLATO Corrections Project is being used in three Illinois prisons; twenty-three PLATO computer terminals provide inmates access to nearly four hundred programmed lessons in both skills and subject matter areas.[2] Most inmates agree that the most meaningful programs are those that prepare them to pass the General Education Development Test or offer college-level studies.

College education courses are provided through live instruction, correspondence courses, television hookups, and release time allowing prisoners to attend educational institutions outside the prison. Most commonly, a nearby community college offers inmates courses leading to a two-year college degree. But the recent decline in federal educational funding is curtailing these nationwide programs. Some inmates have been able to earn their bachelor's degrees, and a few have been fortunate enough to earn master's and doctoral degrees while serving time in prison.

Most inmates tend to be very committed to the college courses they take in prison. Some do superior academic work, but others have difficulty doing acceptable work, usually because of limited language and reading skills. Prisoners who are permitted to leave the institution during the day and to attend a nearby college express particularly positive attitudes toward their college programs. They know that attending classes in the community rather than in prison allows greater latitude in their selection of courses and teachers, wider choices in areas of concentration and majors, and greater access to libraries and research materials.

Prisoners interested in college work obviously prefer programs that permit them to be transferred to a residential facility in a community so that they can attend classes without returning to the prison at night. The California Department of Corrections has several community-based residential facilities near campuses of the University of California. Project NewGate is a program that begins in prison and also has residential facilities so residents can attend college classes in the community.[3]

It is difficult to appraise the effectiveness of academic education, both since an authoritative evaluation of academic education is unavailable and since the quality and support of academic programs differ widely among various states and throughout

---

[2]PLATO Corrections Staff, "Computer-Based Education Has Been Introduced in Three Illinois Prisons," *American Journal of Corrections* 40 (January-February 1978): 6–7, 34, 37–38.

[3]A study of the Office of Economic Opportunity and the Department of Health, Education and Welfare compared five NewGate programs with three non-NewGate programs and found that while the recidivism was no lower in the NewGate programs, participants in the NewGate programs had greater success in reducing their problems with alcohol and drugs, had higher occupational aspirations, and had greater academic success. See Marjorie J. Seashore et al., *Prisoner Education: Project NewGate and Other College Programs* (New York: Holt, Rinehart, and Winston, 1976), p. 187.

the Federal Prison System. Daniel Glaser's study of 1,051 prisoners released from federal prisons in 1956 concluded that those inmates who had not attended prison school committed fewer crimes after release than those who had.[4] Although Lipton, Martinson, and Wilks found that dynamic and effective instruction can help prisoners to improve their academic skills, their evaluation of educational and vocational training in prison led them to conclude that "education and skill development have not reduced recidivism by rehabilitating criminals."[5] Dennis A. Romig, in reviewing the studies evaluating education in training schools, concluded that the following ingredients were present in those studies reporting positive results:

1. Understanding teachers combined with 3 R's and practical skills
2. Understanding teachers combined with discussion group and academic skills
3. Differential reinforcement
4. Rewarding positive classroom behavior and learning
5. Positive emotional support combined with individualized program
6. Contingent social and material rewards
7. Special GED programs.[6]

These conflicting findings about the effectiveness of academic education show that a comprehensive evaluation of education in connection with correctional facilities must be done. Information is vitally needed on what kinds of educational programs will produce the most positive results for the largest number of inmates.

VOCATIONAL TRAINING

The basic purpose of vocational training is to prepare inmates for jobs in the community. Most inmates are educable and trainable but lack any regular experience of work or any demonstrable skill at a trade. The need for vocational programs has been clear to penologists ever since such training was embodied in the declaration of principles formulated at the first meeting of the National Prison Association in 1870. Indeed, the reformatory movement was based on the notion that academic and vocational education would change offenders.

The variety of vocational programs in prisons and training schools for males across the nation is impressive. Included are such programs as printing, barbering, welding, meat cutting, machine shop work, electronics, baking, plumbing, television and radio repair, bus repair, air conditioning maintenance, automotive body and fender repair, sheet metal work, painting, blueprint reading, and furniture repair

[4]Daniel Glaser, *The Effectiveness of a Prison and Parole System* (Indianapolis: Bobbs-Merrill, 1964).

[5]Robert Martinson, "What Works—Questions and Answers about Prison Reform," *The Public Interest* 35 (Spring 1974): 28.

[6]Dennis A. Romig, *Justice for Our Children: An Examination of Juvenile Rehabilitation Programs* (Lexington, Mass.: Heath, 1978): p. 35.

and upholstering. Federal correctional institutions usually provide a greater variety of vocational programs than do state correctional facilities. State and federal prisons also typically have a greater variety of vocational programs than do training schools, but the smaller inmate populations of training schools make existing vocational programs more likely to be available to interested residents.

There are fewer types of vocational programs for women and girls in correctional institutions. Typically, they include beauty culture, secretarial training, business machine operation, data processing, baking and food preparation, and key punch operation. Thus, the programs in correctional facilities for women and girls still tend to conform to stereotype: i.e., they prepare inmates for food service or work as beauticians. Recently there has been evidence of a movement toward nontraditional vocational programs in women's prisons, and Bedford Hills in New York, for example, offers training in auto mechanics, electronics, and video technology, while the women's prison in Nebraska makes available a course in truck driving.

However, despite their variety and quantity, vocational programs in correctional institutions show an overall quality that is not impressive. For the most part, the instructors are poorly trained, use out-of-date equipment, and teach nonmarketable skills. Several factors deter the development of more effective vocational programs: the equipment necessary for many of the programs is considered too costly in most correctional systems; the inmate's average term of two or three years is too short for the completion of apprenticeship requirements for most trades; overcrowded conditions often result in waiting lists for training programs; and the debilitating conditions of prison life discourage offenders from participating in training until it is too late for them to learn enough to make participation worthwhile.[7] But even with up-to-date equipment and good instructors, inmates often have difficulty gaining admission into labor unions in the free community and difficulty in persuading private industry to hire them.

A number of noteworthy exceptions do exist, especially in the Federal Prison Industries and in Connecticut and Minnesota. Inmates at the Kettle Moraine Correctional Institution in Connecticut receive training in meat cutting, blueprint reading, baking, and food preparation, and private industry then provides them with jobs. Honeywell, Inc., a computer firm, provides volunteers and the equipment to teach Kettle Moraine's inmates to use computers; over one thousand prisoners have completed the course. In another Connecticut institution, inmates are trained to design, sell, and supervise the installation of residential and light commercial solar energy systems.[8] However, studies of vocational training are not encouraging. A survey of vocational training in Ohio correctional institutions found the programs to be ineffective. The investigators concluded, "It is our opinion that education, especially vocational education, does not hold a very high priority in treatment."[9]

---

[7]John Conrad, "Correctional Treatment," *Encyclopedia of Crime & Justice* (New York: Macmillan, 1983).

[8]Roul Tinley, *Baltimore Sun,* 22 April 1979.

[9]Ken Kearle, "Penal Education: United States and Europe," *The Prison Journal* 53 (Autumn-Winter 1973): 18.

But for individuals who have intelligence, good educational preparation, and the motivation to avoid crime upon release, vocational training offers more assurance of making it in the community.

INDUSTRIAL EMPLOYMENT

The efficacy of inmate employment has been one assumption that has met nearly universal agreement in corrections. In the past one hundred years, prison industry has been administered according to six methods:

1. Lease system—prisoner labor is leased to private individuals in the community
2. Contract system—private contractors establish factories in the prison
3. Piece-price system—private companies furnish inmates with the raw materials and receive the finished product at an agreed-upon unit price
4. State-account system—prison industry fulfills orders of other state agencies
5. State-use system—articles produced are used in state institutions and agencies
6. Public works and ways system—inmates are employed in construction and repair of public streets and highways and public works[10]

The financial hardship of the Depression led 33 states to pass laws prohibiting the sale of prison products on the open market. The opposition of the unions, as well as the mistreatment of prisoners, also led to the enactment of two federal laws, the 1929 Hawes-Cooper Act and the 1935 Ashurst-Sumners Act, which for all practical purposes put an end to the interstate transport of prison products.

The resurgence of the work ethic in corrections philosophy in the 1970s resulted in an expansion of prison industry. But inmates are still primarily involved in such tasks as making license plates, road signs, clothing, mattresses, shoes, and soap and detergent. They also repair and refinish wood furniture and do the laundry and dry cleaning in many states. These tasks, most of which are unmarketable in the community, earn inmates a few cents an hour and, not surprisingly, result in a good deal of idleness. The prison industries of the Federal Prison System are typically more challenging and pay inmates more than do those in state correctional systems.

Yet some exceptional prison industries do exist. Stillwater Data Processing Systems, Inc., which operates within the Stillwater maximum security prison in Minnesota, teaches inmates computer programming and starts them at the minimum wage. Some inmates earn as much as $7 per hour. The program at Stillwater is one example of the Free Venture Prison Industries Program, a project funded by the LEAA and administered by the American Institute of Criminal Justice. Free Venture has also helped in Illinois, Connecticut, South Carolina, Iowa, Colorado, and Washington State to establish programs that emulate private industry.[11]

[10]Wayne Morris, "The Attorney General's Survey of Release Procedures," in *Penology: The Evolution of Corrections in America,* ed. George C. Killinger and Paul O. Cromwell, Jr. (St. Paul: West, 1973): 52.

[11]Michael Fedo, "Free Enterprise Goes to Prison," *Corrections Magazine* 7 (April 1981): 6.

These exemplary programs both provide prisoners with training that is marketable in the free community and allow them to earn a much higher rate of pay than is traditional for prison industry. But because neither employers nor organized labor welcome the intrusion of prison industry into the free and competitive market, prison industries in general are unlikely to experience much improvement.

RELIGION

Historically, chaplains were the first treatment agents to enter the prison gates, and up until the twentieth century, religious training was the only rehabilitative program offered in many correctional institutions. Some early chaplains were pioneers who opened libraries, taught classes, ran sports programs, and counseled inmates. But there is some evidence of the fact that prison chaplains traditionally have been those who were failures of the clerical world.[12] Charles Myers, a former chaplain now serving as a counselor in a Texas prison, claims:

> Historically, they couldn't make it anywhere else. They were the failures: the alcoholics, the mentally ill, guys with sexual hang-ups, guys in trouble. They were the chaplains.[13]

At present, the Federal Prison System employs 62 full-time chaplains in 39 facilities, and there are from 600 to 1,000 chaplains in state facilities. Chaplains often are involved in the conservative evangelical movement or are liberal, clinically trained clergy. Myers says: "The chaplain can wield tremendous power because there is no one looking over his shoulder," but adds, "They aren't looking over his shoulder because they think he is incompetent."[14] Prison officials generally agree that no more than 15 percent of prisoners participate in religious programs, and only 5 percent may be committed to a faith.

Yet, several religious groups have had a stirring impact on inmates. Charles Colson's *Born Again* describes some of the religious enthusiasm generated by Protestant fundamentalism and the charismatic movement.[15] Colson himself has formed a group called the Prison Fellowship, which trains volunteers to work with inmates. He and his entourage travel around the country conducting three-day seminars designed to bring volunteers and inmates together and to promote religious vitality in prisons. Cursillos, a short course in the tenets of Christianity, has been received enthusiastically by Roman Catholic inmates in several of this nation's prisons. The Moslem faith of the Black Muslims, as well as its splinter group the Moorish Science Temple of America, has had substantial impact on many black

[12]The following section is adapted from Philip B. Taft, Jr., "Whatever Happened to That Old-Time Prison Chaplain," *Corrections Magazine* 4 (December 1978): 54–55.

[13]Ibid., p. 55.

[14]Ibid.

[15]Charles W. Colson, *Born Again* (Old Tappan, N.J.: Spire, 1977).

prisoners. One avid member of the Moorish Science Temple of America explained his faith:

> I just got off segregation today. I've been [involved] in segregation for three years, and the only way I've made it is through my religion, the Moorish Science Temple of America. It has given me something to live for.[16]

RECREATION

Recreational activities, not surprisingly, are the most popular programs in prisons. Recreation alleviates the monotony of prison life, serves as a safety valve for pent-up emotions, and provides good survival insurance because of the physical conditioning and body building exercises.

Organized sports programs thrive in most prisons and training schools. Cell-blocks or cottages compete against each other, or one correctional facility may even compete against another facility in such sports as touch football, basketball, baseball, softball, and volleyball. Also popular are weight lifting, boxing, and jogging. Television, movies, cards, chess, dominoes, checkers, pool, and ping-pong help many inmates get through seemingly endless days. Listening to music or playing a musical instrument, singing in a choir, painting, and writing engage the attention of many inmates. For example, Theatre Without Bars, a nonprofit organization, offers acting and writing workshops in New Jersey prisons and training schools. Finally, special events are scheduled, especially on major holidays and long weekends, to entertain juvenile and adult prisoners. Picnics, talent shows, track and field days, and musical and variety shows are typical. A more unusual event is the annual rodeo sponsored each year by the Texas Department of Corrections.

It would be farfetched to define a game of dominoes or checkers as treatment; at most these forms of recreation help bored inmates pass the time. Yet, other forms of recreation can have a more permanent effect on some inmates. Ron LeFlore, an outstanding baseball player featured in the television movie, *The Ron LeFlore Story,* learned to play baseball in prison, and, through the intervention of another inmate, he attracted the interest of the Detroit Tigers, who signed him to a contract after his release. James Scott, who is currently serving a 30- to 40-year term for armed robbery at the Rahway State Prison in New Jersey, has fought several nationally televised light heavyweight boxing matches while in prison. He is hoping for a chance at the world title. Murad Muhammed, Scott's promoter, said, "I had to create my own champion, and I got him. 'Cause where he is, nobody can get at him." If Scott does get a chance to fight the champion and beats him, he will have the light heavyweight crown locked up (literally).[17]

Writing has long been a popular activity for prisoners, and a large number

[16]Interviewed in August 1979.

[17]Bill Powers, "James Scott: Fighting His Way Out," *Corrections Magazine* 5 (June 1979): 34–35.

of inmates have published books. In the 1950s and 1960s, widely read books written behind the walls included Robert E. Burns' *I Am a Fugitive from a Georgia Chain Gang*, Caryl Chessman's *Cell 2455, Death Row*, Eldridge Cleaver's *Soul on Ice*, George Jackson's *Soledad Brother*, and Malcolm Braly's *False Starts* and *On the Yard*. Migual Pinero's play *Short Eyes* was later made into a movie. In the 1970s, the best-selling prison books were written by those convicted after the Watergate scandal.

Writing workshops, established in prisons across the nation, develop the writing potential of prisoners.[18] Consequently, an increasing amount of inmate prose and poetry is being published in magazines and anthologies. John Paul Minarik, an exoffender and founder of the Academy of Prison Arts in the Western Penitentiary in Pittsburgh, Pennsylvania, tells what writing has meant to him:

> I had to do some work on my emotions. I needed insight into myself and needed to grow. I had book learning and technical skills but I had never looked at my life. I'd committed a crime and needed to reexamine everything. So you could say that writing has definitely been helpful in my rehabilitation.[19]

However, the case of Jack Henry Abbott proves that success in learning a skill such as writing, painting, or repairing automobiles does not necessarily mean an inmate is "rehabilitated." Norman Mailer heard from Abbott when he was doing research on a book about the execution of Gary Gilmore. Mailer took a personal interest in Abbott, who had spent almost his entire life in institutions, and was instrumental in having him paroled from prison in 1981. Abbott's *In the Belly of the Beast*, a book that contains his letters to Mailer, was published shortly after his release and sold extremely well. But six weeks after his release from prison, Abbott stabbed a waiter to death in a dispute over the use of a restaurant bathroom.[20]

SKILL DEVELOPMENT PROGRAMS

Skill development programs are presently enjoying considerable popularity in juvenile correctional institutions. These programs are concerned with developing communication, daily living and survival, educational advancement and study, and career skills. Dennis A. Romig, in evaluating the efficacy of institutional treatment for delinquents, found that skill development has experienced more success than any other rehabilitative technique.[21] Using skill development as his focus, Romig then designed the following model for rehabilitating institutionalized youth:

1.   Get the youths' attention
2.   Obtain input using staff who have empathy

---

[18]See Greg Mitchell, "Voices from the New Literary Underground," *Corrections Magazine* 8 (February 1982): 43–50.

[19]Ibid., p. 47.

[20]Ibid., p. 44.

[21]Romig, *Justice for Our Children*, p. 109.

3. Objectively diagnose
4. Set behavioral goal
5. Teach youths new behavior using effective teaching methods:

   a. Individualized diagnosis
   b. Specific learning goal
   c. Individualized program based upon personally relevant material
   d. Teach basic academic skills
   e. Multisensory techniques
   f. Sequential presentation, breaking complex skills into simple steps
   g. Initially rewarding youths' attention and persistence
   h. Differential reinforcement of learning performance

6. Teach skills in the following areas:

   a. Communication skills
   b. Daily living and survival skills
   c. Educational advancement and study skills that result in a diploma or certificate that supports career goals
   d. Career skills, such as career decisionmaking and career advancement

7. Practice skills in problem solving
8. Differentially reinforce
9. Family training in communication, problem-solving, and disciplining skills
10. Follow-up skill training and reinforcement.[22]

R. R. Carkhuff and B. G. Berenson have identified a method for effectively teaching youths a skill. This method involves teaching facts and concepts concerning the skill as well as the principles of why a skill works and how it is useful. The skill itself is taught through modeling, didactic presentation, and practice. In addition, youths are to be taught the check steps they can use to determine for themselves whether or not they are doing the skill correctly.[23]

Skill development is one correctional intervention that merits far greater use in juvenile and adult corrections.

SELF-HELP PROGRAMS

Self-help programs are extremely popular in prisons at present. Typically, the programs are operated by the prisoners themselves and focus in one or more of the following areas: ethnic and cultural studies, skill development, personal insight, attitude improvement, or consciousness raising. Most self-help groups are required to have a staff member present at meetings and to establish bylaws and procedures for governing themselves. These groups usually meet in the evenings or on weekends.

[22]Ibid., p. 110.

[23]R. R. Carkhuff and B. G. Berenson, *Teaching as Treatment* (Amherst, Mass.: Humane Resource Development Press, 1976).

Among the most popular self-help programs are Jaycees, Lifers, Dale Carnegie, Checks Anonymous, Native American Spiritual and Cultural Awareness Group, Yoga, Y'ai Chi Ch'uan, Transcendental Meditation (*TM*), Erhards Seminars Training (est), Insight Incorporated, Positive Mental Attitude (P.M.A.), assertiveness training, anger management, moral development, and Emotional Maturity Instruction.

The drug abuse unit at the federal correctional institution at Lompoc, California, offers nine different self-help programs from which prisoners can select. To graduate from the program, an inmate completes four of the nine self-improvement programs, each of which lasts 12 weeks. Current programs include the following:

> The Relaxation Program, which teaches a series of physical and mental exercises to help inmates relax;
>
> General Semantics, which tries to help inmates avoid "self-defeating language traps";
>
> Self-Charting, which requires inmates to look "objectively" at their lives and quantitatively rate their behavior. This program is mandatory for all participants;
>
> Assertive Training, which teaches shy inmates to be more aggressive and aggressive offenders to get what they want without threatening others;
>
> Anger Management, which is a stress control program;
>
> Bible Study, which exposes inmates to the religious teachings of the Bible;
>
> Guides for Better Living (Positive Mental Attitudes), which is designed to motivate inmates to pursue success goals;
>
> Pre-Release Program, which provides for reentry into the community; and
>
> Vocational Guidance, which emphasizes helping inmates plan for future careers.[24]

Jaycees, Guides for Better Living and other similar motivational programs, Transcendental Meditation, and Erhards Seminars Training (est) are four widely used self-help programs in American prisons.

Jaycees

A national service organization, Jaycees has 16,000 inmate members in 420 chapters in state and federal prisons.[25] The first Jaycee chapter in a prison was established in the Moundsville (West Virginia) State Penitentiary in 1962. Sponsored by Jaycee chapters in the community, Jaycee groups in prisons raise money for charities, refurbish visiting rooms, donate toys to children's hospitals, sponsor entertainment and sport events for prisoners, and operate radio stations. Women cannot belong officially to Jaycees, but they have formed "Jayceettes" chapters in about 75 prisons that follow the same programs as those in men's prisons.

[24]John Blackmore, "More and More Inmates Are Subjecting Themselves to a Variety of Physical and Mental Rigors as Chic Self-Help Therapies Expand in Prison," *Corrections Magazine* 4 (December 1978): 35. Copyright 1978 *Corrections Magazine*. All rights reserved.

[25]This section is adapted from Joan Potter, "The Jaycees: Tapping Inmate Initiative," *Corrections Magazine* 8 (February 1982): 35–42. Copyright 1982 *Corrections Magazine*. All rights reserved.

The effectiveness of Jaycee programs varies from institution to institution, depending on the acceptance of prison officials, the amount of involvement from the outside, and the dedication of the inmates within each chapter. However, many inmates claim that the Jaycee program of personal development and leadership training has taught them self-respect, motivation, initiative, and the gratification of helping others. DeWitt Lee, an exoffender and a charter member of the Jaycee chapter at Auburn Prison in New York State, tells of the impact this organization had upon him:

> I am someone who was convicted of murder, but I am considered an equal by those who know me because of the amount of respect I have in the community. It's all because the Jaycees turned my life around. They took a person, myself, who really had no direction, no idea what I was going to do while in prison or after I got out, and gave me their specialized programs. If it hadn't been for that, there's no doubt in my mind that I'd still be in prison.[26]

Teaching Motivation to Offenders

Zoom, Winners, Insight Incorporated, Guides for Better Living, and Feminine Development Programs are the most popular motivational courses taught in training schools and prisons. Fifteen thousand offenders at 175 institutional sites have completed the Guides for Better Living course, which is based on the philosophy of businessman and millionaire W. Clement Stone. The aim of these self-motivational courses is to help students put their lives in order by teaching them the principles of success.[27]

Beginning with the basic assumption that juvenile delinquents and adult criminals do want to change their lives, these motivational programs teach inmates the success patterns other people have used to accomplish their goals. The courses use such books as *I Dare You,* by William Danforth; *Think and Grow Rich,* by Napoleon Hill and W. Clement Stone; and *The Success System That Never Fails,* by W. Clement Stone, as well as records, films, and the magazine *Success Unlimited.*

The primary strength of these self-motivational courses is that they teach positive attitudes. They assure residents that they have the power to change their lives and to become winners, rather than losers. There is considerable question of how helpful these middle-class, success-oriented programs are to lower-class offenders when they are released into the community, but there is no question that many offenders gain hope and inspiration from these courses.

Transcendental Meditation (TM)

Maharishi Mahesh Yogi introduced TM into the United States two decades ago; to date, inmates in more than 25 correctional institutions have been taught

[26]Ibid., p. 36.

[27]See Harry W. Woodward, Jr., and Frederick M. Chievers, "Teaching Motivation to Inmates," *Federal Probation* 40 (March 1976): 41–48, for a description of Guides for Better Living and Feminine Development Programs.

TM. This meditation technique involves sitting in a relaxed position and repeating a mantra for twenty minutes. A profound state of relaxation is usually the result of meditation. TM proponents claim that it promotes clearer thinking and lessens stress and that it is particularly useful in prisons because it reduces aggressiveness, hostility, and other negative behaviors.[28]

Some prisoners claim that its effects are sufficiently pervasive and long-lasting to be considered rehabilitative. Dr. C. Scott Moss, chief psychologist at the federal prison at Lompoc, California, reported favorable results from a two-year experiment on the use of meditation. He wanted to expand the program, but inadequate funds and some "fantastic claims, such as TM enabled people to levitate" alarmed the prison administration. Moss noted that "the warden was alarmed that prisoners might learn to fly over the walls."[29]

Preliminary research findings on the use of TM in corrections have been positive. The 115 inmates studied at the California State Prison at Folsom reported significant reductions in anxiety, neurosis, hostility, insomnia, and the incidence of behavioral infractions. Twelve drug abusers at the federal correctional institution at La Tuna, Texas were found to have less tension and obsessive-compulsive behavior. Furthermore, 48 inmates at the federal correctional institution at Lompoc also had less nervousness, irritability, and depression.[30] A. I. Abrams and Larry M. Siegel also found lower preliminary rates of recidivism among discharged participants in a TM program at Folsom State Prison.[31]

It would appear that TM is a program that merits greater availability in American prisons. Whether or not it reduces recidivism, TM is able to reduce tension and to promote relaxation, thereby promoting better physical and emotional health among prisoners.

Erhards Seminars Training (est)

The first prison "est" session was conducted by "est" founder Werner Erhard at the federal correctional institution at Lompoc in 1971. "Est," a 60-hour experience, claims to help participants to examine some of their fundamental beliefs about life. "Getting it" is the hoped for result of looking at the belief systems that govern one's life and accepting that these belief systems have put individuals into a "machine state," in which they fail to act in their own best interest.

"Est" training encourages participants to experience fully those belief systems that cause their actions to be automatic and habitual. Self-examination should enable an inmate to become the source, rather than merely the agent, of his or her be-

---

[28]Blackmore, "More and More Inmates," pp. 29–30.

[29]Ibid.

[30]Ibid., p. 29.

[31]A. I. Abrams and Larry M. Siegel, "The Transcendental Meditation Program at Folsom State Prison: A Cross Validation Study, *Criminal Justice and Behavior* 5 (1978): 3–19; and A. I. Abrams and Larry M. Siegel, "Transcendental Meditation at Folsom Prison: Response to a Critique," *Criminal Justice and Behavior* 6 (March 1979): 13–21.

havior.[32] "Est" training has been conducted at the federal prisons at Lompoc; Leavenworth, Kansas; and Anderson, West Virginia; as well as the California State Prison at San Quentin.

Preliminary research by Moss and Hosford at Lompoc indicates that neurosis and anxiety were reduced among prisoners who completed "est" training.[33] However, because some evidence exists that "est" may be dangerous, this self-help program needs additional evaluation before it is more extensively used in American correctional institutions.

SERVICE PROJECTS

Many inmates want to become involved in projects involving service. These projects may have both self-help and service aspects or may focus on a needed institutional or community service. Although service projects are usually ongoing, some arise because of a disaster or emergency in the community. Service projects include providing child care for prison visitors, adopting war orphans, fighting forest fires and floods, doing peer counseling, scaring juveniles out of crime, recording books for the blind, donating blood, participating as paramedics and in other lifesaving roles, and umpiring Little League baseball games in the community.

A number of correctional facilities use inmate volunteers to help educate and entertain visiting children: Federal facilities with child-care programs include Fort Worth (Texas), Seagoville (Texas), Lompoc (California), Butner (North Carolina), Oxford (Wisconsin), Lexington (Kentucky), and Anderson (West Virginia); state facilities with such programs include Bedford Hills (New York), Green Haven (New York), Kirkland (South Carolina), and Joliet (Illinois). The Children's Television Workshop, creator of the "Sesame Street" television series, contributed its technical expertise to establish a version of "Sesame Street" for visiting children at the Bedford Hills and Fort Worth institutions. The program at Bedford Hills features a puppet show entitled "The Cookie Monster Goes to Prison"; the program at Fort Worth, the most structured and elaborate of these child-care programs, is divided into five sections: reading, arts and crafts, music, homemaking, and play.[34] Inmate volunteers at Bedford say the program has probably done more for them than it has for the visiting children. Some of the inmate participants made the following observations about their involvement:

> I'm doing quite a bit of time. I have two children of my own and working with children is important to me. It is a way of benefiting myself and the visiting children as well.

[32]Blackmore, "More and More Inmates," p. 30.

[33]Ibid.

[34]Peter Haley, "Sesame Street: The Cookie Monster Goes to Prison," *Corrections Magazine* 4 (December 1978): 27. Copyright 1978 *Corrections Magazine*. All rights reserved.

Being around children takes away some of the loneliness you feel inside. It relieves the frustration because being with someone's child you can transfer some love and affection.

I don't intend to come back here, and this child care is an indication to me that there can be more that I can do outside.[35]

Programs to scare juveniles out of crime have been popular in a dozen or more prisons. These programs have usually been conducted by Lifers, an organization made up of inmates who have been sentenced to spend the rest of their lives in prison. "Scared Straight," a television documentary portraying the Lifers' delinquency prevention program at the Rahway State Prison in New Jersey, showed the methods used to warn juveniles about the violence and victimization of prison life. Although the general public, which has always sought simple answers to the problem of youth crime, reacted extremely favorably to this documentary, researchers studying the project questioned its effectiveness in preventing or controlling law-violating behavior in juveniles.[36] Consequently, the number of such programs sponsored in prisons has declined in the last several years.

Inmates at the Vienna (Illinois) Correctional Institution offer a variety of service programs to citizens of the local community. They provide around-the-clock emergency paramedical care, teach cardiopulmonary resuscitation (CPR), umpire Little League games on a baseball field they built and maintain, and assist firefighters in nearby communities by providing labor and volunteers for a fire truck. In Box 8-2, a former resident of Vienna describes how much his involvement in the cardiopulmonary resuscitation (CPR) program meant to him.

Box 8-2   *Letter from a Former Resident of the Vienna Correctional Facility*

The Vienna Correctional Facility in Vienna, Illinois, has the most unique program in the history of prisons. Cardiopulmonary resuscitation (CPR) is the program which typifies what can be done with the proper positive atmosphere in a prison. Vienna's warden Vernon G. Housewright created the atmosphere for residents to give vent to their desperation through self-expression; thereby an organization was formed by residents called Help Individual Progress (HIP) and the three founders, of which one was female, founded the CPR program, which continues to this day.

Vienna's CPR project was developed, implemented, and controlled by residents, and the HIP organization was organized by the same residents, which made it possible for the state to receive something meaningful in return for their tax dollars. I am extremely proud of the leadership role I have played in making this a successful program.

We have trained hundreds of people in the prison system and also in local communities, schools, and church organizations. We received an award from the

[35]Ibid.

[36]See James Finckenauer, *Scared Straight* (Englewood Cliffs, N.J.: Prentice-Hall, 1981).

Illinois Heart Association, and we have earned credibility and respectability from governmental agencies and the current Governor of Illinois.

Residents found their lives changed from the austere severity of incarceration and each day was filled with goals to achieve.

CPR offered the resident instructors not only a valuable lifesaving skill to save lives but also gave them a chance to teach others how to save lives—rather than taking them.

Through CPR the gap in so-called rehabilitation was bridged. Each resident has achieved a rare desire to save a life. Some residents were so bent on saving lives through CPR that they searched daily for someone to save; within the confines of prison! [This attitude is] a far cry from what armchair criminologists depict as [that of the] hardened animals. . . .

Source: Letter received from Walter Danner on 12 March 1979. Used with permission.

Some of the prisoners in a Wisconsin prison are paramedics. Inmates in a number of prisons record books for the blind, and many inmates have donated blood. During the 1977 Johnstown flood in Pennsylvania, fifty inmates helped in rescuing people and another five hundred baked bread and helped prepare clothing and canned goods.

Service projects for inmates have not been empirically evaluated, but they appear to be one of the most positive experiences an inmate can have in a correctional institution.

SUMMARY

Academic and vocational education, prison employment, recreational activities, religious services, skill development, self-help and service programs are used in correctional settings with varying benefits. Many programs are inadequately staffed and equipped to meet inmates' needs, especially education and vocational training. But at a time in which indeterminate sentencing is being replaced by determinate sentencing in state after state, an amazing proliferation of self-help and service programs is an indication that a sizable number of inmates want to do more with their months and years in prison than serve time. Although many inmates become involved in a program merely to overcome the boredom of prison life, there are others whose involvement in a program affects their attitudes and values in such a way that they make a conscious decision to avoid returning to crime.

In short, the programs discussed in this chapter make the cage-like experience of correctional institutions more humane. They relieve some of the boredom of institutional life and bring hope to what might otherwise be a dead-end and dreary experience. The programs may not have lasting effects on a majority of participants, but they still are a necessary part of humane confinement in a free and democratic society.

DISCUSSION QUESTIONS

1. Explain why educational programs in prisons have received strong criticism. Name some noteworthy programs.

2. Give three reasons why vocational training programs generally do not have a lasting effect on prisoners.

3. Explain why chaplains' programs in prison are criticized.

4. Why are recreational programs considered survival insurance? Explain the benefits of recreational programs for prisoners.

5. Why would service programs, such as Jaycees, aid prisoners in changing their attitudes or behavior?

6. The judge says, "Go to prison and participate in a self-help or service program." Which program or programs would you select? Why?

9

Ingredients of Effective Programs

Objectives

1. *To examine the Asklepieion therapeutic community as an example of an effective program, in an interview with Dr. Martin Groder.*

2. *To discuss the common elements in effective programs.*

3. *To describe the roles of theory and research in developing more effective programs.*

4. *To design a strategy for developing more effective programs.*

The basic task of this chapter is to set out a plan for a better future for correctional treatment. In the process of describing and evaluating treatment modalities, skill development programs, residential and nonresidential interventions, and self-help and service-oriented programs highlighted in the past four chapters, it has become apparent that model programs are very impressive. They are usually varied in their approaches and sophisticated in their technologies. They also have some common elements. But because the overall quality of correctional treatment still leaves much to be desired, it is necessary for proponents to develop a strategy in which they can better discover what works for which group of offenders and in what context.

This chapter begins with an interview with Dr. Martin Groder, founder of the Asklepieion therapeutic community at the Marion Federal Penitentiary. Then, the chapter discusses several important characteristics effective programs have in common and identifies steps needed to make programs more effective in juvenile and adult corrections.

Interview with Martin Groder

QUESTION: Why have you been so strongly committed to therapeutic communities?

GRODER: The traditional prison community is a closed culture that tends to maintain a fixed role structure through its various members, especially the caste division between staff and inmates. The efficacy of the therapeutic community is that it provides an alternative culture which does not of necessity have the exact characteristics either of the general culture that rejected inmates and placed them in prison nor of the prison culture which maintains their prison status. In addition, as a true alternative to the prison culture, the therapeutic community provides hope for the application, participation, and cooperative implementation of whatever therapeutic modalities are being applied. The therapeutic community provides a defined population for testing, recording, and observing and providing morale, momentum, and role modeling, independent of specific modalities. Furthermore, the therapeutic community results in less staff burnout than is found in traditional prison programs. The typical prison structure usually results in staff burnout within at least eighteen months, whereas the therapeutic community seems to take from three to seven years before staff burnout becomes an active issue.

QUESTION: What do you feel are the most important ingredients of the effective therapeutic community?

GRODER: The first ingredient of the effective therapeutic community is legitimacy. A therapeutic community, especially one that is sponsored by outside agencies, provides a legitimacy to individuals in the program as a whole and provides an entry point upon graduation from the therapeutic community to an alternative culture outside the prison.

A second important ingredient is commitment. Because of the missionary arduousness of setting up, running, maintaining, fostering, keeping clean, and legitimizing a therapeutic community, it requires a tremendous level of commitment, not only by the staff but also by at least a percentage of the members participating at any time. Ritualization, or doing it by the book, that is typically true of prison operations eliminates the issue of commitment and tends to mean that the inventive and shrewd energies that go into committed social action go into corruption. So a program that is not run by people committed to it tends to be corrupted. The corollary of this is that you cannot expect a model program without a commitment to it.

A third crucial component is competence. This, of course, is measured within the context, the concept, and the processes of the specific technologies used within the therapeutic community. Inmates tend to be very refractory to ordinary methods and require the highest level of technological competence in the particular methodologies used. But because of the nature of the prison environment, recruitment policies, salaries, and career patterns, the most competent persons are not available at all or only are available in a transitory fashion. Therefore, the crucial ingredient of competence in terms of the technologies employed is often absent and precludes a testable model.

A fourth ingredient has to do with the nature of the acculturation that is taking place within the prison. Inmates typically are very alienated. They see themselves as permanently outside the mainstream culture. But the therapeutic community has an alternative culture that provides internal and external identity. As the alcoholic involved in Alcoholics Anonymous is still wrapped up in being an alcoholic but is no longer drinking, the inmate member of the therapeutic community in the same way is vastly wrapped up in the whole nature of being a prisoner and a criminal and whatever concept there is of his problem, but he is now affiliated with an outside-the-mainstream culture which does not include violence, robbery, rape, theft, or mayhem. That affiliation may be an end state or provide a bridge to the main culture at a later time.

A fifth ingredient is that the therapeutic communities that were most successful over longer periods of time tended to be highly innovative and to be constantly shifting and changing as they presented new methods and processes to inmates. Because of the enormous ability of inmates to subvert, to get bored, or to find ways to corrupt the program, I have found that stable, progressive models are deterred from effectiveness—even when they are implemented in a legitimate, committed, and competent way. The efficacy decreased after time as inmates learned the games and system, and they began to find successful means of corrupting it. This decline was easily observed in the behavior modification models. The therapeutic community is corruptible to a much lesser degree because it is a moving target.

The last crucial component is a philosophy, which is based on an individual internalizing some degree of role modeling and a great deal of the peer group culture. When an individual is removed from the influence of the peer group, from the program, and from the role models, we have found that the internalized structure has the stability, with varying degrees of efficacy, to maintain the behavioral, characterological, and attitudinal changes experienced within the therapeutic community.

QUESTION: Do you have any data to indicate how effective the Asklepieion therapeutic community was at Marion?

GRODER: We found in those studies that we were able to perform with multiple retesting models and simplistic follow-up that the individuals who were exposed to longer periods in the programs were more likely to be in the successful group than individuals who had six months or less in the program—even though there were some benefits to the six-month group compared to the dropouts who attended for days or weeks. Conversely, attendance and involvement past the two-year mark did not appear to have a significant effect upon community adjustment.

Nonrecidivism was defined as someone who had been out for two years and had not been arrested for a new crime, committed to the system for a new crime, or had his parole revoked due to a violation. In the various studies, the recidivism rate of the two-year follow-up varied between 9 and 13 percent.

In my own informal follow-ups, which now extend over as long as twelve years in some individual cases, those who had passed the first year without being reincarcerated have attained some position in the community. They have not had criminal problems, but they have not been without significant characterological problems. The characterological problems observed had much to do with the fact that we worked with long-term offenders who had, in spite of a great deal of instruction on our part, a feeling that they wanted to catch up. So frequently in the first year or two, there would be an episode of bankruptcy, though one that did not involve fraud, and an inappropriate marriage with divorce. However, none of these involved criminal behavior or abuse. They primarily involved immature judgment within the context of the larger society. Often the lessons learned from this first year or two of insolvency and of marital strife were integrated through the same methodologies that they had used in the program, and these errors were not repeated. No cases to my knowledge involved bankruptcy or divorce a second time.

A number of graduates, all individuals who had over two years in the program, went on either to help set up or to take over and run programs in other prisons or to be employed subsequent to release in community-based or institutional programs. Thus, they have persisted in useful careers in corrections and in the criminal justice system. As a whole, few have reached high levels, but there have been one warden, a chief of classification and parole, a number of program directors, and a number of consultants to correctional agencies. These individuals have reached middle-class levels of accomplishments, monetary remuneration, and respect and dignity in the community, which was not predictable by their educational, social, and cultural backgrounds. Others who had more solid careers prior to incarceration tended to return to them. For example, one lawyer we had in the program was able to gain work as a law clerk due to the California legal system and later retook the bar examination and is a practicing attorney.

QUESTION: What are the advantages of therapeutic communities to correctional systems?

GRODER: The primary advantages of a therapeutic community for correctional systems on a day-by-day basis are as follows. First, therapeutic communities are an inexpensive modality for control. Since they uniformly nearly eliminate any violence, major theft, escape attempts, or other kinds of custodial issues, they represent a net savings even though they require a higher degree of program personnel, salaries, and mild-to-moderate increases in equipment, such as typewriters, educational recording devices, and a printing press. But therapeutic communities per man per year still require a significantly lower operating cost, and, if they were a generally accepted modality, they would require an even lower capital cost because they could operate in security conditions much lower than usual in the correctional environment. As an anecdote, one of my minimum security units at Marion had in it at one time two of the three men who had successfully escaped from Atlanta Penitentiary. These were the first successful escapes ever in the history of that institution. This scared the hell out of fellows in the front office, but there were never any problems or escape attempts.

Second, the personnel in a therapeutic community have a much longer longevity as effective personnel, with greater degrees of both therapeutic and administrative skills. They also have the ability to replicate their training and experience in other settings.

Third, the therapeutic community is such a positive environment that it develops close relationships with community-based organizations and individuals and provides a means of positive communication to the community. It also provides a means of raising funds in community projects and of involvement with community educational and business institutions that are not available through the rigid, caste-oriented, and paranoid-oriented culture of the prison.

Fourth, because there are many different kinds of technological models for therapeutic communities, this variety provides a great degree of choice. Parallel programs can exist providing choice for both inmates and staff as they find that one program suits them more than another.

QUESTION: Why, then, have not therapeutic communities been more widely used in corrections?

GRODER: It primarily has to do with the prison culture which finds the effective therapeutic community an alien body that represents a presence antagonistic to all the basic assumptions and methods of the standard prison environment. This is even true for the so-called rehabilitative or liberal prison reform movements, which really tend to see the inmate as an individual to be acted upon and fixed. In a real sense, prison reform movements actually maintain a caste culture although more humanely.

QUESTION: What effect does bureaucratic repression have on therapeutic communities?

GRODER: Two issues are involved in bureaucratic repression. One, since the bureaucracy is hired to maintain an integral part of the caste system prison culture, it is, of course, antithetical to the alternative culture modality of the therapeutic community. Second, bureaucracy tends to be antithetical even if it has the same values as the therapeutic community because the nature of bureaucracy is to ritualize, rationalize, and compartmentalize, and all of these go against the functioning, evolving, growing, constantly shifting and changing, and unpredictable therapeutic community. So even if the bureaucracy were changed to a sympathetic mode, it would have to be dramatically decentralized and broken up in ways that are not typical anywhere yet. There have been some experiments with team management and unit management, but the overriding fact is that bureaucracy independent of its ideology tends to interfere with the necessary innovativeness that is required.

QUESTION: What is the most desirable model for the expansion of the therapeutic community concept?

GRODER: In terms of feasible models, I would see a contractual model, which has been used in community-based halfway houses and drug therapeutic communities, in which inmates can choose to be members of therapeutic communities. I would then organize institutional structures totally on the concept of the therapeutic community. These institutions, or pseudo- or dispersed institutions, would have the responsibility of providing standardized levels of care, custody, and control, which would be checked periodically by a central body, much as the Federal Drug Administration checks pharmaceutical houses and the Department of Agriculture checks meat or butter, to make certain that the quality is being maintained and that the care-custody-control are being provided. The contractees who would run these institutions would have to go through the same kind of procedures as lawyers, doctors, and other high-level professionals go through to be licensed and certified as competent, proficient practitioners. Although there would still be a lot of incompetence by people who were at one time committed or competent, the general level of competence would be higher, and there would be more positive programs for inmates to choose.

Given the cost of crime and the cost of dealing with those who have committed criminal activity, I believe this model would be feasible, since the costs are at least commensurate with the costs of medical care, legal action, political action, and military action—all of which require high levels of standards and long periods of training until people are certified and competent in their work.

QUESTION: Let me raise one more question: What are the dynamics of correctional change?

GRODER: First, I see the dynamics of correctional change as providing an environment in which change can occur. Second, it is necessary to provide a technology through which the change can be implemented. Third, a method must be utilized to reinforce and protect those changes against the corrupting environment of the prison. Fourth, an exit procedure is needed that allows for continuity, enhancement, and follow-up of these changes subsequent to the termination or release from the program.

In effective correctional change, an individual seems to go from an alienated outsider who is basically a loser to a person who at least has the goal of being able to be reintegrated in the mainstream and to see himself or herself as a competent individual. This person is capable of standing on his or her own feet in the community, both in terms of technical or occupational skills and in terms of being a person. Once these goals are achieved, they turn a prisoner into a person—sometimes a citizen with difficult characterological problems but nonetheless a nondangerous taxpaying citizen.

I believe, as I have said throughout this interview, that the therapeutic community provides the most effective means of correctional change. The therapeutic community provides high levels of human caring for the inmates entrusted to it, provides a higher and more reliable level of control than traditional correctional environments, involves all members of the community as responsible participants, and uses an alternative peer group culture and staff role modeling as key steps in the change process. I believe that the involved member of a therapeutic community leaves with enhanced competence, legitimacy, commitment, maturity, and ability to make it in the free world.

Dr. Martin Groder became involved with the U.S. Bureau of Prisons in July 1968, after completing his residency in psychiatry. During the next four years, he established the Asklepieion therapeutic community at the Marion Federal Penitentiary (Illinois), which has since become the model of other therapeutic communities in both community-based and institutional settings. He now has a psychiatric practice in Chapel Hill, North Carolina.
Source: Interview conducted in June 1982. Used with permission.

In this interview, Groder questions the effectiveness of most treatment technologies in correctional institutions as he makes the following observations: (1) that the traditional prison environment is not compatible with treatment; (2) that most treatment technologies are not effective in circumventing the negative aspects of the prison environment; (3) that most interventions lack the technological sophistication to make an enduring impact upon prisoners; (4) that inmates can make responsible decisions for themselves; and (5) that the technology is available in the Asklepieion therapeutic communities to effect rehabilitation with inmates who are committed to and graduate from these programs.

Although not everyone shares Groder's enthusiasm for the Asklepieion therapeutic communities, these communities are among the model programs discussed in the past five chapters that clearly stand head and shoulders above other interventions in juvenile and adult corrections. In addition to being based upon more highly developed theoretical constructs with more sophisticated delivery of intervention services, all these model programs appear to have several common elements.

COMMON ELEMENTS IN EFFECTIVE PROGRAMS

Effective programs usually are set up by an inspired individual or group of individuals, have unified teamwork on the part of the staff, have a transmittable philosophy of life, trust offenders with decision-making responsibilities, help offenders develop needed skills, are regarded as unique and different by offenders, avoid conflict with formal decision makers, avoid isolation from social institutions (such as the family and the school), and provide a support network following release or graduation.[1]

The Inspired Leader Who Means Business

That effective programs are set up by an inspired individual or group of individuals who mean business has been stressed throughout these chapters. The PORT program was conceived on the streets of Rochester when a judge and a psychiatrist decided that there must be a better way of dealing with offenders than sending them to institutions. Kurt Hahn—an inspired and charismatic leader—was able to generate enthusiasm and support for Outward Bound among all who came in contact with him. The Umoja House in Philadelphia is also the work of an inspired woman and her husband who were seeking to do something about the gang problem in their community. The inspiration of Clifford Shaw continues to live on in the Chicago Area Projects long after his death. Most offenders who participated in their programs would also agree that John Maher, Joe Ricci, and Martin Groder are inspired and mean business. Ken Windes, a graduate of the Marion program who now works in Alabama as a consultant in Asklepieion and TA methods, had this to say about Groder:

> I'm thirty-two now. When I was at Marion, I had spent fifteen of my years behind bars. When I entered there [for two counts of assault with a deadly weapon, plus an escape charge], I was a scared little boy acting tough. I was convinced that nobody wanted me, so I cut myself off from other people, and was actively working to get myself killed.
> Now I'm happily married. I have a lot of people I love, and a lot of people who love me. I'm paid top consultant fees.
> Dr. Groder's program? It saved my life, turned me completely around. It did that with most of the other guys in the program.[2]

The importance of the relationship between the person giving the treatment and the treated person must not be minimized. The fact is that this relationship is probably far more important to model programs than the particular technology used. In other words, some treatment staff, because of their personal characteristics, are able to involve offenders much more so than others in the relationship needed for self-improvement and personal growth to take place.

However, the components of model treatment programs cannot be oversimplified to fit a psychological reductionism that equates effective treatment with

---

[1]These elements of effective programs are suggested by Martin Groder and by Alden D. Miller, Lloyd E. Ohlin, and Robert B. Coates. See "Dr. Martin Groder: An Angry Resignation," *Corrections Magazine* 1 (July-August 1975): 3; and Alden D. Miller, Lloyd E. Ohlin, and Robert B. Coates, *A Theory of Social Reform: Correctional Change Processes in Two States* Cambridge, Mass.: Ballinger, 1977).

[2]Quoted in "Dr. Martin Groder," p. 33.

persuasive charismatic individuals. The inspired leader may be the first step in developing effective treatment programs, but the other ingredients discussed in this section also are crucial in the implementation of these model programs.

Unified Treatment Team

Effective programs are also usually characterized by a unified treatment team. All staff members take responsibility for designing the program, for developing its short- and long-range goals, and for involving themselves with offenders in the execution of the program. All staff members, then, become treatment agents.

In settings merging custodial and treatment roles, such as therapeutic communities, unified treatment teams are more likely to develop than in those that divide job responsibilities between custody and treatment. In settings containing both custody and treatment staff, custody staff members often see their roles as the "dirty work" of guarding usually resistant, sometimes unpredictable, and frequently dangerous residents and, consequently, these staff members question why they should become involved in the treatment process.

Philosophy of Life That is Transmittable

Effective programs commonly are able to transmit a philosophy of life that generates a sense of mission or purpose among offenders. As Martin Groder has said, "It's not that the guy has got to adopt the philosophy of the program, but he's got to learn it well enough to integrate it with his own life experience and come out with his own version."[3] Bartollas, Stuart Miller, and Simon Dinitz found that having a sense of a mission or purpose in life was one characteristic of hard-core offenders who make it in the community.[4]

Delancey Street, Daytop, Synanon, the Gateway House Foundation, the House of Umoja, Outward Bound, TM, "est," the Fortune Society, and the Black Muslims are examples of the many programs that offer a mission or purpose in life for offenders. A wall poster at the Fortune Society (reproduced in Box 9-2) outlines the philosophy needed for an offender to walk away from crime.

*Box 9-2 **The Philosophy of the Fortune Society***

I THINK, THEREFORE I AM . . .

As a thinking person, I believe that I am worthy of being loved and accepted. I believe that my ability to accept myself is a part of my real freedom. It is vital that I develop a foundation of belief about myself—for freedom and love and respect

---

[3]Ibid., p. 35.

[4]Clemens Bartollas, Stuart J. Miller, and Simon Dinitz, "Boys Who Profit: The Limits of Institutional Success," in *Reform in Corrections: Problems and Issues,* ed. Harry E. Allen and Nancy J. Beran (New York: Praeger, 1977), pp. 18–19.

are not an "end result" but, rather, a process which changes, refines and grows. My ability to offer love and respect and my acceptance of freedom is a reflection of my view of myself.

SUGGESTED STEPS

Facing the truth about ourselves, we decided to change. Realizing that there is a power from which we can gain strength, we decided to use that power. Evaluating ourselves by taking an honest self-appraisal, we examined both our strengths and weaknesses. [We] admitted to God (as we understand Him), to ourselves, and to another human being the exact nature of our weaknesses. Endeavoring to help ourselves overcome our weaknesses, we enlisted the aid of that power to help us concentrate on our strengths. Deciding that our freedom is worth more than our resentments, we are using that power to help free us from those resentments. [So we] made a list of all persons we had harmed and become willing to make amends to them all. [And] made direct amends to such people wherever possible, except when to do so would injure them or others. Observing that daily progress is necessary, we set an attainable goal toward which we can work each day. [We] continued to take personal inventory, and when we were wrong promptly admitted it. Maintaining our own freedom, we pledge ourselves to help.

Source: A wall poster at the Fortune Society.

Involvement of Offenders in the Decision-Making Process

It is not surprising that the correctional process breeds resentment among offenders. In correctional institutions, inmates are told when to get up, what to do during the day, and when to go to bed. They are treated as helpless children who are incapable of making responsible decisions for themselves.

Effective programs commonly provide decision-making opportunities for offenders. Therapeutic communities permit the greatest degree of decision making by offenders. Residents of a therapeutic community typically decide who will be admitted to the program, what discipline will be administered for violations of the rules, when residents will be promoted to the next step or stage of the treatment process, and how adequately they are fulfilling their own treatment contracts. Some therapeutic communities permit residents to have input into when others are ready to graduate from the program. Positive peer culture and guided group interaction groups permit juvenile offenders to share widely in the decision-making process.

Skill Development

Effective programs also usually help offenders develop skills that will improve their behavior in the community. Communication, interpersonal, daily living and survival, educational advancement and study, and career skills make offenders feel they can do something positive or have mastered some important insight about themselves or life. For example, TA teaches offenders how to develop more effective interpersonal relations. TM teaches a technique that helps offenders relax and feel more in control of their lives. Assertiveness training and anger management teach the appropriate use of aggression and self-control. PORT teaches offenders the process of responsible decision making. Outward Bound programs teach juveniles survival skills in the wilderness, desert, mountains, or at sea. The marine programs in Florida teach youths how to become scuba divers. Vocational programs teach offenders welding, printing, barbering, and many other occupational skills.

Uniqueness of Effective Interventions

The very uniqueness of effective programs is sometimes their most distinguishing characteristic. For example, Dr. Kenneth Lebow and colleagues conducted an experiment at the Lompoc's Drug Abuse Treatment Center by which they set out to do the following:

> [We sought] to isolate all elements popularly conceived to be part of a successful program, and do just the opposite. Whenever something was thought to be absolutely essential [to a good program], we added an activity that was just its reverse. So when everyone said you needed a lot of personal interaction, we came up with something that was outrageously intrapsychic and impersonal. Despite our efforts, we got extremely positive results. We weren't really prepared for that.[5]

This program, which used biofeedback exercises and the martial art of T'ai Chi Ch'uan, no doubt attracted the interest of inmates because it was different from other programs that they had known. Juvenile and adult offenders have usually been exposed to many treatment programs, but each program usually seems much the same as previous ones. When they are exposed to an intervention that is different and unique, they usually struggle to put this program in a box in order to fit it into familiar categories, but sometimes the very uniqueness of the program overcomes their initial resistance. Some residents then proceed to become deeply involved in the program's format and philosophy, to be stimulated by the challenges it offers them, and to benefit from the potential it has for their lives.

Avoidance of Conflict with Formal Decision Makers

Those responsible for effective community-based and institutional programs must be careful not to alienate formal decision makers, because their approval is a critical factor for the survival and growth of such programs. Community-based

---

[5]John Blackmore, "More and More Inmates Are Subjecting Themselves to a Variety of Physical and Mental Rigors as Chic Self-Help Therapies Expand in Prison," *Corrections Magazine* 4 (December 1978): 31.

and institutional treatment staff members often feel oppressed by bureaucratic rules and regulations. They feel that they are always fighting red tape, excessive paperwork, and reactionary administrators. However, if treatment staff members become resistant or hostile toward the administration, they are likely to jeopardize the support of or even the continuation of the program.

Grass-roots programs in the community are in many ways more fortunate than programs within community-based or institutional facilities. These grass-roots programs usually arise because of a recognition of need at the community level, and they tend to thrive because they are not stifled by bureaucratic rules and restraints. But even these programs must be careful not to alienate formal decision makers. PORT is an excellent example of a program that thrives because of enthusiastic community support; many other good programs have been forced to close down because poor public relations have resulted in the loss of their funding base.

Adequate Community Support Networks

Finally, model programs must develop effective community support networks. Juvenile offenders often need advocates to help them deal with their parents, school authorities, and officials of the justice system, so effective juvenile programs must work with families and school authorities rather than isolating themselves. Community-based and institutional programs also need community follow-up in order for offenders to sustain the positive change in their lives. For example, the impact of Outward Bound unfortunately diminishes over time because of the lack of community follow-up. One of the reasons for the success of therapeutic drug communities is that they continue to involve members after their graduation. Alcoholics Anonymous groups encourage members who have maintained sobriety for years to continue attending their meetings. Exoffenders also need a variety of community assistance programs, and if these programs are not available, their chances of returning to crime are dramatically increased.

STRATEGY FOR IMPROVING THE EFFECTIVENESS OF CORRECTIONAL TREATMENT

Proponents of treatment have known for more than a decade that in order to improve the overall quality of correctional interventions, it is necessary to discover what works for which offenders in what context. In other words, correctional treatment could work if *amenable* offenders were offered *appropriate* treatments by *matched* workers in environments *conducive* to producing maximal effects.[6]

Ted Palmer defines what must be done:

---

[6]Reproduced from Lee Sechrest, Susan O. White, and Elizabeth D. Brown, eds., *The Rehabilitation of Criminal Offenders: Problems and Prospects* (Washington, D.C.: National Academy of Sciences Press, 1979), p. 45.

To determine what works for which offenders, we must engage in what I call differentiated research. Basically, this involves a study of interactions, and the variables involved seem numerous. The interactions in question center on four broad categories of variables or factors: (1) program operations, (2) program setting, (3) program staff, and (4) offenders.

In the coming years, correctional researchers should give heavy emphasis to studying offenders, treatment control/personnel, and treatment/control settings. They should focus on offenders and staff not merely separately but in mutual interaction; possibly their research should be done largely in the contexts of programs that try to take account of the needs, interests, abilities, and limitations of offenders as individuals. In studying the interaction of offenders and staff, researchers should try to match these groups on the one hand and to examine the effects of the treatment/control setting on the other.[7]

For correctional interventions to identify what works for which offenders, the Panel on Research on Rehabilitative Techniques adds, programs must be based on sound theoretical constructs, must have quality intervention services, and must be evaluated with much better techniques than those typically used.[8] The panel adds that research on offender rehabilitation is the key to developing programs based on sound theory, quality of intervention, and adequate methods:

The strongest recommendation that the Panel can make at this time is that the research on offender rehabilitation should be pursued more vigorously, more systematically, more imaginatively, and more rigorously. Specifically, treatment should be based upon strong theoretical rationales, perhaps involving total programs rather than weak or piecemeal treatments. In addition, the strength and integrity of all treatments should be monitored and fully documented, along with documentation of the costs of operation of the treatment. To implement this recommendation it is essential that researchers become more involved in developing appropriate methodologies for evaluation of interventions and that appropriate funding agencies support research on criminal rehabilitation, while making the criteria for funding more rigorous with respect to experimental design, theoretical rationale, and monitoring of integrity and strength of treatment.[9]

This section discusses the important steps of program design, program intervention, and program evaluation in developing more effective correctional interventions.

Program Design

The theoretical premises, or constructs, of most correctional interventions have been largely unexamined.[10] These implicit theoretical premises sometimes are

---

[7]Interviewed in December 1982.

[8]Sechrest, White, and Brown, *Rehabilitation of Criminal Offenders,* p. 5.

[9]Ibid., p. 10.

[10]This material on program design is adapted from Sechrest, White, and Brown, *Rehabilitation of Criminal Offenders,* pp. 35–37.

derived from conventional wisdom, with little consideration of the task to be accomplished and without any carefully thought-out analysis of what the program as it is designed can realistically expect to accomplish with a particular group of offenders. Accordingly, Greenberg has described the theoretical assumptions of many interventions as "bordering on the preposterous."[11]

Failure to base interventions on sound theoretical constructs has resulted in several problems with program designs. First, it is frequently assumed that an intervention can "cure" offenders of the tendency to commit criminal behavior, in much the same way as a patient suffering from bacterial pneumonia can be cured by a dose of antibiotics. This simplistic and misguided notion of cure overlooks the circumstances precipitating the crime, the offender's characteristics and predilections, the social conditions affecting the offender, and the environment in which treatment is to take place. This notion of cure has also led to the assumption that minimal treatments can produce major effects and, consequently, to the implication that a little nudge can put offenders back on the right track, where they will stay. Furthermore, the notion of cure has resulted in a limitation on the number of interventions being used at one time, so that few programs employ a variety of intervention efforts.

Second, treatment personnel frequently fail to consider whether the theoretical constructs of the interventions are appropriate for a particular group of offenders. An examination of theoretical premises may show in fact that the theory of criminal behavior on which the treatment is based is inappropriate for that group of offenders. Or examination might show that the theoretical premises of a certain treatment do not mesh with the interests or needs of offenders at the time it is given or that the effectiveness of the intervention would be enhanced if offenders were divided into homogeneous groups. Box 9-3 describes the intended outcome of each theory of treatment and the presumed cause of criminality on which each is based.

Box 9-3 Theories of Treatment and Presumed Causes of Criminality

Although many correctional interventions offer a multidimensional approach to dealing with criminal behavior, twelve strategies differentiate specific problem areas that frequently appear, and the strategies offer a system for discussing theories of treatment. These strategies are: biological/physiological, psychological, social network development, criminal influence, power enhancement, role development, activities/recreation, skill development, clear and consistent social expectations, economic resource, deterrence, and abandonment of legal control, and social tolerance.

[11]D. F. Greenberg, "The Correctional Effects of Corrections: A Survey of Evaluations," in *Corrections and Punishment,* ed. D. F. Greenberg (Beverly Hills: Sage, 1977), pp. 111–148.

BIOLOGICAL/PHYSIOLOGICAL STRATEGIES

These strategies seek to remove, diminish, or control the biological/physiological limitations of offenders. They include health promotion, nutrition, and aid with genetic defects. Biological/physiological strategies assume that criminal behavior derives from underlying physiological, biological, or biopsychiatric conditions.

PSYCHOLOGICAL STRATEGIES

The purpose of psychological strategies is to alter psychological states of individuals so that they are no longer controlled by past emotional deprivations or by their maladaptive behavior. Such strategies include epidemiological, psychotherapeutic, and behavior approaches. Psychological strategies assume that criminality originates in internal maladaptive or pathological psychological states.

SOCIAL NETWORK DEVELOPMENT STRATEGIES

These strategies seek to help offenders develop a social network by increasing motivation, attachment, and involvement between offenders and nondeviant others. Such programs include linkages in the community and positive influence strategies. These strategies assume that criminality or delinquency is caused by weak attachment to prosocial others.

CRIMINAL INFLUENCE REDUCTION STRATEGIES

These strategies seek to reduce the influence of antisocial norms and contact with those who hold such norms. Programs consist of disengagement and redirection strategies. Strategies based on reducing criminal influences assume that crime stems from the influence of others who directly or indirectly encourage offenders to commit antisocial acts.

POWER ENHANCEMENT STRATEGIES

Some strategies seek to increase the power of offenders to control their environment either directly by participation or indirectly by increasing the influence of individuals in the communities in which they live. Strategies designed to enhance an individual's power assume that crime stems from a lack of power or control over impinging environmental factors.

ROLE DEVELOPMENT/ROLE ENHANCEMENT STRATEGIES

Strategies involving role development attempt to create opportunities for involvement in legitimate roles or activities that individuals perceive as personally gratifying. Such strategies include development of offenders in service roles, production roles, and/or student roles. These strategies based on role enhancement assume that delinquency or criminality stems from a lack of opportunity to be involved in legitimate roles or activities that are personally gratifying.

ACTIVITIES/RECREATION STRATEGIES

These strategies seek to provide nondeviant activities as alternatives to criminal or delinquent activities. Although activities/recreation strategies are not well grounded in theories of delinquency or criminality, they assume that delinquency or criminality arises from unoccupied time.

SKILL DEVELOPMENT STRATEGIES

Skill strategies provide individuals with personal skills and patterns of behavior to prepare them for lives free from criminal activities. Cognitive, affective, moral, and informational strategies are subsumed under skill development theories of treatment. Cognitive education strategies focus on acquisition of knowledge and intellectual skills. Affective education strategies seek to increase emotional skills for competent functioning in a complex social world. Identity clarification skills (values clarification and self-awareness), communication skills (including conflict resolution), and decision-making skills are included under the affective education category. Moral education strategies seek to instill norms for conforming participation in the social order. Informational strategies attempt to increase individuals' knowledge about specific topics related to crime and delinquency. Skills strategies assume that delinquency or criminality arises from a lack of the skills necessary to live in society without violating its laws.

CLEAR AND CONSISTENT SOCIAL EXPECTATIONS STRATEGIES

Some strategies seek to provide clear and consistent social expectations for offenders rather than competing or conflicting demands and expectations from legitimate organizations and institutions, such as the media, families, schools, and communities. Inconsistent expectations or norms place offenders in situations in which conformity to a given set of norms or expectations results in an infraction of another set of norms or expectations. These strategies assume that criminality arises from conflicting environmental demands.

ECONOMIC RESOURCE STRATEGIES

Economic strategies seek to provide basic resources to preclude the need for delinquency or crime. Such strategies include resource-maintenance and resource-attainment programs. Strategies to enhance economic resources assume that crime or delinquency occurs when individuals do not have adequate economic resources.

DETERRENCE STRATEGIES

Strategies concerned with deterrence attempt to change the presumed low degree or risk or difficulty associated with committing criminal or delinquent acts. These programs seek to change the cost-benefit ratio of participation in crime by increasing its cost and decreasing its benefit. These strategies assume that crime or delinquency results when there is a low degree of risk or difficulty associated with committing criminal acts.

ABANDONMENT OF LEGAL CONTROL/SOCIAL TOLERANCE STRATEGIES

These strategies seek to remove the label "delinquent" or "criminal" from certain behaviors. The abandonment of legal controls removes certain behaviors from the control of the justice system. Explicit jurisdictional strategies seek to remove certain behaviors from the jurisdiction of the justice system through legal or administrative action. Implicit jurisdictional abandonment strategies remove jurisdiction from the justice system on a case-by-case basis. Covert jurisdictional abandonment strategies involve informal agreements, and social tolerance strategies seek to increase the levels of community tolerance for certain behaviors which have been viewed as delinquent or troublesome in the past. These strategies assume that society creates deviance by the labels it gives those who become involved in currently socially unacceptable behavior.

Source: Adapted from J. David Hawkins et al., *Reports of the National Juvenile Justice Assessment Centers: A Typology of Cause-Focused Strategies of Delinquency Prevention* (Washington, D.C.: GPO, 1980), pp. 11–25.

Third, to develop more effective programs it is necessary to conceptualize clearly the purpose, the process, and the end result of intervention. The processes by which any set of interventions will change criminal behavior are often left unexamined. The timing of treatment, as well as the dynamics of what takes place within the program, are critical concerns. The treatment must have sufficient strength to make it likely to produce the desired behavior or attitudinal change. Finally, program planners must consider which treatment personnel are equipped to deliver the services specified in the interventions.

Fourth, the theoretical constructions of the interventions are frequently not meshed with the setting in which treatment will take place, and programs are sometimes implemented in inappropriate settings. In designing interventions for correctional environments, planners must raise questions such as: What can be done to ensure cooperation from administrators? What can be done to neutralize the negative values and norms of the inmate culture? What can be done to minimize the resistance inmate gangs will demonstrate against the treatment process? What positive networks or persons are available to supplement the treatment process?

Program Implementation

Effective implementation of treatment ultimately depends on research to provide the information on who should get what treatment, when treatment is best given, and what frequency and intensity of treatment is necessary.

Who gets what treatment: the template-matching strategy. To link up individual offenders with the interventions most likely to benefit them, the Panel of Rehabilitative Techniques recommends the use of the "template-matching technique."[12] This technique creates a set of descriptors, or a "template," of the kinds of people who, according to the theory or basic assumptions underlying each particular treatment, are most likely to benefit from it.[13] Obviously, with the scarcity of treatment resources, using programs with those individuals who are most likely to profit from the specific technique is only sensible.

The panel has illustrated this matching technique as applied to job training. That is, the offender most likely to gain from job training is the one who does not have marketable skills, who does have the cognitive and motor capacities to acquire the job skills offered, who does have the motivation to learn and to seek out employment, and who will be able to use the job skills relatively soon after learning them. The panel warns that for most programs, the template will be relatively imprecise.[14]

Templates can also be devised for units rather than for individuals. For example, a family treatment program might require that the family have sufficient economic resources to allow one parent to be at home whenever the children are at home, that the wage earner be employed in a legitimate job, and that no adult member of the household be a drug abuser or alcoholic. Also, template matching may be useful at the community level. An intervention designed to utilize com-

---

[12]The template-matching technique was proposed by D. Bem and D. Funder in "Predicting More of the People More of the Time: Assessing the Personality of Situations," *Psychological Review*, 85 (1978): 485–501.

[13]Reproduced from Susan Martin, Lee Sechrest, and Robin Redner, eds. *The Rehabilitation of Criminal Offenders: New Directions for Research* (Washington, D.C.: National Academy of Sciences Press, 1981), p. 82.

[14]Ibid., pp. 81–82.

munity, or grass-roots, organizations may begin by screening communities for existing types of community structures. The community might be deemed suitable if it has a certain percentage of permanent residents, a certain proportion of such private organizations as clubs and churches, and particular patterns of crime.[15]

However, the panel warns that the template-matching technique may have deficiencies:

> If the template has too many facets, very few cases will fit its demands, and it will prove uneconomical and unfeasible. On the other hand, if a template is too coarse [with too few factors], it will not accomplish its aim of yielding a reasonably homogeneous group of persons suitable for a program.
>
> Templates always fit somewhat imperfectly, and tolerances will have to be guessed at, but the template notion does not demand that everyone fitting a given template be forced into the same program. Template matching is aimed at selecting persons for whom a particular program is best designed; that need not preclude offering additional services or highly individualized treatment programs as needed. Obviously, some, perhaps many, offenders may not fit very well into any program. If so, it is useful to discover these failures, for they point clearly toward the problem of which new items [templates] are needed.[16]

The template-matching technique is one of the most useful concepts in improving the overall quality of correctional treatment because it has the potential of identifying what works for whom in what situations. This concept also has the potential of conserving scarce resources, because it shows that a program is not suited for a particular population and does not need to be tried with that population.

The timing of treatment.   Once template matching or some other technique has established what works for which group of offenders, the next step is deciding when treatment is most helpful to a particular offender. An offender may be indifferent or even hostile to a program that might have had considerable impact if offered at a different point in his or her criminal career. Preventing a person from becoming involved in crime is clearly more desirable than rehabilitating one who is committed to a criminal career. But there is some evidence that correctional interventions started too early can have boomerang effects.[17] In addition, early interventions incur the risk of widening the net of social control, with the negative result of labeling those who should not be labeled and of needlessly spending limited financial resources.

In order to determine the best time to intervene in the lives of juvenile and adult offenders, the research panel stresses that further knowledge is needed about such matters as "criminal career patterns, including the variables related to and the situational antecedents of crime; patterns of entry into criminal activities; offend-

[15]Ibid., p. 82.
[16]Ibid., p. 83.
[17]Ibid., pp. 89–90

ers' responses to various and differently timed interventions; and factors related to desistance" from crime.[18] The panel adds that "research now focuses on the failures, measured by recidivism, rather than on understanding the factors leading to termination of criminal activities and on ways to accelerate or produce desistance."[19]

Program integrity. If offenders are placed in the right program at the optimal time for them to benefit from treatment, then program integrity becomes a matter of major importance. Program integrity has four key aspects. First, the plan of what is supposed to take place, of how it will take place, and of what are the hoped-for outcomes must be clearly conceptualized. Generally, the clearer and more thought-out the plan, the greater the ease of implementation. Second, effective interventions should deliver the services that they claim to deliver to offenders with sufficient strength to accomplish the goals of treatment. For example, if psychotherapy is the treatment selected, the therapy sessions should be held regularly and the content of the sessions should constitute therapy as specified by the particular model of psychotherapy. The therapy should also have sufficient strength to accomplish the goals of psychotherapy. Third, the program personnel should be equipped to deliver the specified services. In addition to being honest, sensitive, and caring persons, treatment personnel should have some degree of expertise in what they are doing, sufficient training to do it, and adequate supervision. Fourth, the treatment not only should be matched to the interests and needs of offenders, but also should have the flexibility to be modified according to the changing interests and needs of offenders.[20]

Not surprisingly, the vast majority of correctional interventions lack several of these elements of program integrity. A group counseling program in a California prison studied by Kassebaum and others is a good example of the lack of program integrity. With respect to the conceptualization of the program, Kassebaum and others reported that the theoretical base of the group counseling sessions was not clearly spelled out nor were the aims of group counseling described in terms that lent themselves to the precise analysis of group structure or process. The researchers also indicated that the services delivered tended to be superficial and to permit talkative members to monopolize the discussion. Furthermore, Kassebaum and colleagues found that the groups were poorly run by insufficiently trained counselors. Finally, prisoners questioned the value of this group counseling and took part in it merely because their participation looked good to the parole board.[21]

---

[18]Martin, Sechrest, and Redner, *Rehabilitation of Criminal Offenders*, p. 99.

[19]Ibid.

[20]Herbert C. Quay, "The Three Faces of Evaluation: What Can Be Expected to Work?" *Criminal Justice and Behavior* 4 (December 1977): 341–353.

[21]G. Kassebaum, D. Ward, and D. Wilners, *Prison Treatment and Parole Survival: An Empirical Assessment* (New York: Wiley, 1971).

Program Evaluation

The Panel on Research on Rehabilitative Techniques concluded after nearly two years of examining the effectiveness of offender rehabilitation:

> The current state of knowledge about rehabilitation of criminal offenders is cause of grave concern, particularly in view of the obvious importance of the problem. After 40 years of research and literally hundreds of studies, almost all of the conclusions that can be reached have to be formulated in terms of what we do not know. The one positive conclusion is discouraging; the research methodology that has been brought to bear on the problem of finding ways to rehabilitate criminal offenders has been generally so inadequate that only a relatively few studies warrant any unequivocal interpretations. . . .[22]

The panel suggests that studies on rehabilitative techniques generally have weak methodologies, with many projects and reports almost totally lacking in considerations of research design. Also, sample sizes are often too small for subtle effects, such as interaction, to be detected. The panel recommends true randomized experiments be done whenever feasible for evaluating rehabilitative programs, because such forms of design allow some certainty to be inferred about causal relationships. Less exact designs, according to the panel, allow mistaken conclusions so that a workable program may be discontinued or an ineffective one retained.

As soon as better research designs are used to evaluate correctional interventions, researchers should find it possible to develop template-matching techniques, to ascertain the best time for treatment, and to identify the program integrity needed for particular groups of offenders. More empirical work also must be done on the outcomes of correctional treatment. In addition to providing more empirical work to standardize measures of recidivism and to determine the suitability of multiple measures in reducing recidivism, researchers need to examine the ability of treatment to provide growth, insight, skills, or happiness for offenders.[23] Researchers further need to identify the common elements of effective programs and to determine how these elements affect success with various groups of offenders. They also need to discover why model programs appear to taper off and what can be done about it. Finally, researchers need to discover how effective programs can be replicated in other settings.

SUMMARY

This chapter began with an interview with Martin Groder, in which he discusses the ingredients, the advantages, and the effectiveness of therapeutic communities. The chapter continued by defining some common elements in effective correctional interventions; namely, the inspired leader who means business; the unified treatment

---

[22]Sechrest, White, and Brown, *Rehabilitation of Criminal Offenders*, pp. 3–4.
[23]Martin, Sechrest, and Redner, *Rehabilitation of Criminal Offenders*, p. 6.

team; a philosophy of life that is transmittable; involvement of offenders in the decision-making process; skill development; uniqueness of effective interventions; avoidance of conflict with formal decision makers; and adequate community support networks. The steps that are needed to develop effective interventions then were delineated. These consist of basing program designs on sound theoretical under-pinnings, improving the quality of programs, and evaluating programs with much improved techniques. The template-matching technique is one of the most promising methods discussed in this chapter; this technique creates a set of descriptors to fit the kinds of people most likely to benefit from a particular program.

Obviously, considerable distance exists between our elementary knowledge about correctional treatment and our ability to design template-matching techniques to determine when treatment is most appropriate for a particular group of offenders, to ascertain the program integrity needed by a group of offenders, and to evaluate common elements present in effective programs. Once theory and research help us design, implement, and evaluate effective interventions, our task will be to replicate these programs in other settings.

DISCUSSION QUESTIONS

1. What, according to Martin Groder, are the most important ingredients of therapeutic communities?
2. What is the basic technology of therapeutic communities?
3. What are the basic steps in developing more effective correctional interventions? Explain what is involved in each step.
4. What are the most important elements of effective programs?
5. Why do each of the common elements tend to have an impact upon offenders?

10

Correctional Treatment Agents in the Community

Objectives

1. *To indicate the role expectations for the Outward Bound instructor.*

2. *To describe the pressures on the Outward Bound instructor.*

3. *To indicate the role expectations for the teacher in an alternative school.*

4. *To describe the pressures on the teacher in an alternative school.*

5. *To indicate the role expectations for the staff member in a therapeutic community.*

6. *To describe the pressures on the staff member in a therapeutic community.*

7. *To compare the treatment processes in an Outward Bound program, in an alternative school, and in a therapeutic community.*

8. *To express the shared characteristics of the sensitive and dedicated treatment agent who works with offenders in the community.*

When an exoffender thinks back to the turning point in his or her life, it may be associated with a treatment agent he or she knew in the community. The exoffender's memory may be of contact with an effective juvenile officer, love given by a caring foster parent, challenge from an Outward Bound staff member, or acceptance by a staff member in a therapeutic community or in a youth service bureau.

As examples of many agents who deal with offenders in the community, this chapter examines in detail the work of Outward Bound staff members, teachers in an alternative school, and staff members in a therapeutic community. Each program has specific role expectations for the treatment agent. Similarly, each program has specialized treatment responsibilities and exerts special pressures upon the treatment agent.

THE OUTWARD BOUND INSTRUCTOR

Outward Bound, as previously mentioned, offers one of the most exciting and promising programs in youth services. First established in the United States in 1961 at the Colorado Outward Bound School, the program now has six other Outward Bound Schools throughout the nation. In the interview in Box 10-1, Rick Weider, project director of the Youth-At-Risk programs of the Colorado Outward Bound School, talks about the philosophy of Outward Bound and about the application of this program to juvenile delinquents.

Box 10-1 Interview with Rick Weider

QUESTION: What is the basic philosophy of Outward Bound?

WEIDER: The man who founded Outward Bound was Kurt Hahn, a British educator. He didn't sit down and put his thoughts on paper, but he put his thoughts in action. This left the door open for people to follow his lead and make interpretations of what Outward Bound is all about. Although the basic format is the same for all Outward Bound schools, there are significant differences among the schools in the environments they utilize and the adaptive programs they promote.

Outward Bound focuses on working with people through shared experiences or shared adventure, with the idea that through that experience you'll stretch your limits and do more than you ever thought possible. You'll learn to draw upon the inner strength you discovered in Outward Bound in making decisions for the future. In making future decisions, you'll also take into consideration a lot of things besides the impulsive feelings you might have when you're first confronted with those decisions. In other words, you'll take into consideration how these decisions affect other people because you have seen how your actions affected others in a high-stress setting. We believe that Outward Bound will make you a better person, a more successful person, and a more sensitive person to others.

The Outward Bound program is different from a traditional wilderness experience in which you take people to the mountains for three days. Our approach is not oriented toward teaching mountaineering skills so that you'll become a better mountaineer; it is toward teaching mountaineering skills and learning through those skills. That is not to say we dilute the experience in the mountains; we have on our staff some of the most experienced mountaineers in the country.

QUESTION: So how does Outward Bound relate to the delinquent kid?

WEIDER: Delinquent kids have often had rough value experiences in the past. They know what rejection is all about from being rejected by their parents. But they don't know what inner control is all about. They don't often make a distinction between their actions or what they did and what the consequences are. They have not established much of a value system. They're pretty immature for their ages. Their inability to deal with authority and to understand the consequences of their actions continually gets them in trouble.

Our objectives in working with delinquent kids are to help them develop greater self-esteem from experiencing success, to help them acquire a sense of responsibility, to help them establish some inner controls as they realize the consequences of their actions very concretely, to help them let their defenses down because they recognize that, after you've been out there with a group of folks for a while, you can establish some trust re-

lationships. Some adult modeling also goes on. The instructor doesn't tell them what pattern to follow, but he lays out a series of challenges so that the youth can challenge himself or herself in a way that the chances of success increase.

An Outward Bound course is an excellent arena for delinquent kids to learn some of their own strengths and weaknesses and to learn how to develop good relations with people. Certainly, delinquent kids are going to test limits, and this opportunity to test and expand one's limits is what Outward Bound is all about.

Before I got involved in Outward Bound, I was working as a VISTA worker in a youthful offender camp in North Carolina's department of corrections. I saw how seventeen- to twenty-one-year olds were making real messes out of their lives and getting nowhere. These characters were basically "nice guys" who made mistakes. Had they confronted some real challenges and real risks and had they been able to sort out their values and make some responsible decisions for themselves, they probably wouldn't have been where they were.

Source: Interview conducted in April 1982. Used with permission.

Role Expectations for the Outward Bound Instructor

Outward Bound is an experiential learning situation that encourages participants to explore new or unusual areas. Because its goal is to place students in situations—usually in wilderness environments—that encourage them to learn from their experiences, Outward Bound instructors are expected to foster

1. Personal Development. To extend the individual's self-awareness by identifying personal limits, by clarifying personal needs and goals and by helping the student to recognize his or her role in society and to acknowledge a responsibility to himself and others. To have fun.
2. Interpersonal Effectiveness. To expand the student's capacity for responding to others, to encourage open and effective communications, and to construct cooperative relationships around common projects, involvements, and commitments.
3. Environmental Awareness. To enhance students' understanding of the fragile nature of wild areas and to increase the sense of responsibility for their care and preservation.

4. Learning. To create and maintain an environment and an attitude in which the emphasis is on experimentation and participation in experimental learning. To provide training in the skills essential to living and traveling in the mountains.
5. Philosophy and Values. To provide situations and experiences in which students can test and refine their personal values and which will stimulate them to examine and articulate their basic beliefs.[1]

To accomplish these objectives, each of which often would take months or years to achieve in more traditional correctional settings, the instructor is expected to be a guide, a resource person, a teacher, a counselor, and a friend. Weider describes the qualities of leadership that the instructor is supposed to demonstrate:

When we hire staff, we look for people who are confident, intelligent, and flexible. They need to relate well to student populations, to understand students' behavior and why they do what they do, to have good common sense, to have a good sense of humor, and to have personal charisma. They also need to know when students are accomplishing something, even if it may or may not seem as if they are accomplishing very much compared to a higher achiever, but they need to be reinforced for what they are achieving.[2]

Pressures on the Outward Bound Instructor

The personal and physical demands of the job and the high-risk nature of the experiential learning situation itself cause pressures with which the Outward Bound instructor must be ready to deal.

Demands of the job. It requires great commitment and intensive involvement for instructors to fulfill the high expectations of Outward Bound, especially with a delinquent population. Delinquents often test limits, are resistant to authority, and lack self-control. They find it difficult to trust adults and are unpredictable under stress. In addition to the difficulty of working with delinquents in this experiential learning situation is the traditional Outward Bound requirement that instructors maintain excellent physical conditioning. Outward Bound programs also require instructors to be separated from spouses and families, often for days or even weeks at a time. Thus, it is not surprising that the personally demanding and emotionally draining aspects of the job can result in job burnout and high turnover among staff. Outward Bound currently structures its special programs with this issue in mind.

Safety factors. The Outward Bound course does pose some physical risk to both students and instructors. Although the organization's long-established safety policies and procedures have evolved over the years from the 1960s and are highly respected, there have been student deaths on Outward Bound courses. In 1978, added emphasis was placed on risk management and since then instructors have

[1]Outward Bound, "Instructor's Manual" (n.d.), p. 4.
[2]Interviewed in April 1982.

stressed safety even more. But safety is not easy to accomplish with high-risk delinquents in the potentially dangerous situation posed by an Outward Bound course. Rick Weider tells how the schools' instructors work to ensure that delinquents are not reckless during an Outward Bound course:

> You have to take a lot of safety factors into consideration so that these kids will be prepared to make the right decisions. On a standard course across the United States, you often have groups of highly motivated and well-adjusted people who are there to affirm their strengths. They have a high probability of making the right decision under stress.
> It is not easy to put a delinquent in this setting and develop a program that has all the risks and challenges of the standard program. These kids are highly unpredictable under stress. If you get kids with character disorders and put them in the mountains, they often do not trust you or their peers. They are anxious about their perceived lack of control over the situation. We have to prepare them for that setting. We put a lot of energy into trying to anticipate how they will respond to the program. We then structure the course in such a way that they can develop strong relationships and can trust us and do so through a safe, manageable adventure experience.[3]

Correctional Treatment and Outward Bound

Outward Bound uses the same basic process in its working with delinquents as it does with other students. Using a social setting in a highly stressful environment, it helps participants master a series of challenges and problem-solving tasks, so they will develop greater self-awareness, self-esteem, and acceptance of others.

The treatment process begins with the learner who is motivated and committed to the program. The learner is given increasingly difficult challenges and problem-solving tasks, which are intended to be concrete and manageable and to draw upon his or her mental, emotional, and physical resources. These tasks and challenges usually create stress and anxiety. Although individual response to these stresses may be positive (mastery) or negative (defeat or withdrawal), the Outward Bound process is designed to permit the learner a high probability of mastering those tasks. As its goals, Outward Bound attempts through the experience of solving new, reasonable, and worthwhile problems within a supportive group and in a stimulating environment to make students feel good about themselves and those who have assisted them. This change process is also based upon the assumption that the ability to master the challenges of the course will provide participants with new awareness, attitudes, and values and, thereby, make them better equipped and ready to tackle future problems. Figure 10-1 presents a diagrammatic form of this change process.

Arthur Conquest, a former delinquent who is now an Outward Bound instructor, tells why he thinks this learning experience works for delinquents:

> If I don't know anything else, I know poor kids and delinquent kids. I believe in them. Because that's where I came from—and if I could do it, they can do it. Believing in the kids is all it boils down to. These kids will take you to great lengths to test if

---

[3]Interviewed in April 1982.

Figure 10-1   The Outward Bound Process

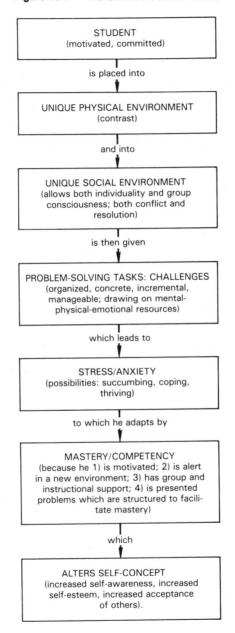

Source: "Colorado Outward Bound School Instructor's Manual" (n.d.), p. 7.

you really believe in them. They make you give second, third, fourth, and final effort. I made the course a little tougher, and people didn't think the kids would do it. But they did. Sure, they were leaner, and they had been through a hard experience. But I think in the end, and I don't just mean the end of the course, but when the kids have to deal with life—they'll have whatever it takes to go to the wall. That's what an Outward Bound course for these kids is for—when things get tough, you've got to really believe in yourself, persevere, go to that wall, and do all the things you're capable of doing.[4]

As Chapter 5 indicated, there is evidence that the change process gained from Outward Bound has a positive impact upon delinquent youth.

THE TEACHER IN AN ALTERNATIVE SCHOOL

Although the classroom situation of an alternative school is a setting much different from the outdoor environment where Outward Bound takes place, the disruptive student who is sent to the alternative school and the youth who is referred to an Outward Bound program usually are very similar. Darrell Dierks, the principal of Van Eaton Alternative School in Waterloo, Iowa, describes the philosophy of the school and the role expectations for teachers in the interview in Box 10-2.

Box 10-2 *Interview with Darrell Dierks*

QUESTION: Why are alternative schools needed?

DIERKS: Too many kids fail in the public school system. Some youths can't buy into the system because they don't trust it very much. You need to make them feel they're cared about and are important. You need to give them high feedback on desirable behavior. However, you need to use a different approach with the unsocialized, strongly aggressive youths. These students would interpret the supportive approach alone as weakness. It would increase their defiance.

QUESTION: How is the school different from the public school?

DIERKS: We have to deal with the kids when they're angry. Most of the time in the public school system when the students get upset, that's when officials send the student home. They say that we'll talk about this when you're calm. Well, when they're calm, they don't have a problem. The principal says, "I've suspended this kid fifteen times this semester and the little devil is still having problems. In fact, he is getting worse."

We measure, we calculate the amount of affect [emotional involvement] and the amount of structure we put on the kids. You have to blend treatment to meet where the kid is. He changes. He'll show you different adjustment levels at different times. The students are never clearly in one category or another. The most unsocialized kid is probably socialized at least 90 percent of the time.

Positive reinforcement is given in reverse proportions to the way it ought to be given in the public schools. The clean-cut, bright-eyed, sharp kid always gets a 100. They are always receiving nice com-

---

[4]Quoted in Joshua L. Miner and Joe Boldt, *Outward Bound USA: Learning through Experience in Adventure-Based Education* (New York: Morrow, 1981), pp. 327–328.

ments—"My, I like your paper." They already know they're good. The kid that gets only five out of twenty right week after week needs to hear: "That wasn't a bad try. That's a tough list. You got five of those words. That isn't bad." You've got to reach out to that kind of a kid. What we do here from the start is try to look at strengths the kid has to build on. We talk about all the problems a kid has, but that's really not how we treat kids. We treat them through their strengths. If we sit down with a kid and start in on all the things wrong with them—first of all, they aren't going to want to talk very long. But if we go with the positives, they're receptive and they'll hear you. Sometimes, you have to hunt like hell, "So, you're a roller skater, huh?" "Yes, I like to skate." "Well, where do you go?" The kid will probably be thinking, "Well, I'll be damned; maybe, this person is different." In finding positives about kids, you build, encourage, and give them strength. They'll play the macho role and tell you that they're strong, but it's a veneer.

QUESTION: What part does support staff play in making your program work?

DIERKS: We've a hell of a lot of support staff. One staff member is always on the phone calling parents saying, "Your kid got fifty points today [the highest number possible]. Just wanted you to know." He or she is also constantly contacting case workers. It takes this type of communication to make this milieu work. There just isn't any way a teacher in an ordinary situation has the time to do that.

We also have the advantage here of escapism. If you're getting so uptight that you're about ready to scream at a kid,

then you signal your aide (or the aide signals the teacher), and you tell him or her, "I'm going to fill my coffee cup." You have to get the hell out of there before you undignify yourself. Most teachers in public schools have twenty-five or thirty kids in class and can't leave the room. If they have a disaster, they have a disaster. A teacher can give more in our system because they know they can escape. They can risk more. That's why we get more mileage from our staff than most schools do. The teachers also know the support staff will be there when they need us.

Part of developing a relationship with these kids is a trick of communicating with them when they're not in conflict. Support staff can do that. We catch the kids in the hall; we meet them when they get off the bus. We heard they were going fishing and so we say, "Did you catch any fish last night?" Or we say, "Did you get your bike fixed?" Just little things. I had a kid that was sent to the office this morning; he came in and sat down and said, "I'll tell you what the problem is. I wasn't working. I was just tired. I've so many assignments. You tell me to go back and work, and I'll go back and work, but I want to tell you something." I said, "Okay, what do you want to tell me?" He whispered, "I think I got a girlfriend." I said, "Tommy, you have a girlfriend?" He said, "I've never had a girlfriend, but she's gonna tell me tonight." I said, "Where did you meet her?" He talked on and said, "I told my mother and she said, 'You better not get her pregnant.'" He said, "God! Get her pregnant! You know, I only just got a girlfriend."

Source: Interview conducted in July 1981. Used with permission.

Role Expectations of the Teacher in an Alternative School

The teacher in an alternative school is expected to know the characteristics of emotionally disturbed (ED) and chronically disruptive (CD) students. Table 10-1 shows the ways ED and CD students differ in terms of behavior and attitudes.

TABLE 10-1   Differential Diagnosis of Severe Behavioral Problems: A Dichotomous
Approach by Symptoms

Rationale—Numerous methods exist for classifying behaviors. Few approaches use
instructional needs as a basis of categorization. The treatment programs at the school level
for students with severe behavior problems depend on proper classification for behavior
management techniques. The method below separates students according to behavior
management strategy of high structure (emotionally disabled) and low structure (chronically
disruptive).

EMOTIONALLY DISABLED	CHRONICALLY DISRUPTIVE
High anxiety level	Low anxiety level
Reactive behaviors to stress	Habitual behavioral patterns
Worried about what happens	Not worried about what happens
Insight to behavior problems	Does not have insight to own behaviors
Sudden onset of problems	Gradual onset of problem
Little antisocial behavior (things)	Lots of antisocial behavior (things)
Wants to reduce anxiety	Wants to be left alone
Wants to change self	Wants others to change
Sees conflict in desire and defenses	Sees no fault in self
Aware of problems	Little or no awareness of problems
Doesn't read environment well	Reads environment well
Personality deficits (poor self-concept, social withdrawal)	Conduct problems (expresses impulses against society)
Frightened—upset	Calm—not threatened
Inappropriate learning (poor model of behavior to copy)	Conflict learning (work for pleasure at expense of disapproval)
Doesn't shift behaviors well from setting to setting	Controls environment

Source: Darrell Dierks. Used with permission.

Teachers are expected to be objective and to anticipate ("read") these behaviors so
that they can respond to each student's treatment plan. Situations arise continually
in which the teacher's ability to "read" his or her students affects whether the
student's behavior escalates out of control or returns to acceptable limits.[5]

Second, although verbal abuse and explosive behaviors are dealt with on a
daily basis, teachers are expected to be highly committed to their jobs. Caring is
a necessary extension of such commitment. The treatment plans for some students
require high nurturance, while the plans for other students emphasize high structure,
but neither plan can be carried out except through the development of a caring
relationship between the teacher and the student.

Third, because ED and CD students come from varied backgrounds and
socioeconomic classes, teachers are expected to be insightful about their pathology
and values. As a teacher develops a trusting relationship with a student, it is
important for the teacher to seek out information on their values and expectations.
Once teachers see things through their students' eyes, they have a much better
chance of getting students to feel they can change their lives for the better.

[5]Linda Bartollas developed this section on the role expectations of the teacher in an alternative
school.

Fourth, the teacher in an alternative school is expected to reinforce students for positive behavior. The rule of thumb is frequently five positive statements to every one negative statement. Students are given point cards for every class period with positive and negative points recorded upon them. (See Figure 10-2.) A card is filled out each day by the classroom teachers in the Chronically Disruptive program at Van Eaton Alternative School in Waterloo, Iowa, and in the Emotionally Disturbed program at Area 7-Bremwood Alternative School in Waverly, Iowa. In these two programs, students can earn up to fifty possible positive points daily—with forty-five or more positive points and ten or fewer negative points indicating a very good day.

Fifth, because few alternative students have experienced classroom success, teachers are expected to help students achieve positive and successful experiences. With students whose backgrounds frequently include expulsion from Head Start, numerous suspensions from public school, assaults on both teachers and fellow students, and treatment in mental health clinics and commitment to psychiatric wards, success appears unreachable. The teacher must begin slowly by continually

Figure 10-2   Positive Point Card

INITIATIVE
____Okay/Late_____
        /Slow start_____
        /Clues_____
VERBAL ACTIONS
____Okay/Not coop_____
        /Rude_____
        /Profane_____
CLASSROOM WORK
____Okay/Not_____
        /Some effort_____
        /Refused_____
INTERACTIONS
____Okay/Provoking_____
        /Physical_____
        /Interferes_____
EQUIPMENT USAGE
____Okay/Not_____
        /Misuse_____
        /Damage_____

_____POINTS_____STAFF

Source: Van Eaton Alternative School. Used with permission.

giving positive experiences which will lead to small successes in behavioral areas. Academic success becomes possible only after some success is experienced in behavioral areas.

Sixth, the teacher in an alternative school is expected to maintain control and to enforce the limits in the classroom without being rigid or unyielding. Although the teacher must establish that he or she is in control, it is imperative to communicate the attitude that students' opinions are important and that they have input into what happens in the classroom. Such inappropriate behavior as leaving supervision, use of profanity, failure to respond to staff, or abuse of school equipment may cause a teacher to turn a student over to the office. Upon the "turnover," the office staff accepts supervision of the student. The student is usually counseled in the office by a psychologist, a social worker, or the principal, who will work to get the negative behavior under control and then return the student to the classroom. A psychologist at the Van Eaton Alternative School emphasized the importance of control:

> The kid has to realize that there are certain limits, and you'll enforce them. When we tell them to leave the room, they're going to go. It is not a debatable kind of thing. If a child isn't returned to his regular classroom, he or she may spend much time in the office as a time out.
>
> If the kid becomes physically assaultive, we'll usually have him arrested, and then we'll go to court. You almost have to use a punishment type of model. The message you give is: If you don't behave, punishment will be swiftly administered.[6]

Pressures on the Teacher in an Alternative School

The task of working with difficult students and the problem of managing the resulting stress are two pressures faced by alternative school teachers.

The daily challenge of working with disruptive students. The teacher in an alternative school is working with the failures of the public school system. They have been troublemakers in every school situation they have ever encountered; many have been in special education programs since kindergarten. Gaining control of the classroom requires that the teacher develop rapport with the students, but the majority of these students have had problems with developing trusting relationships and, therefore, repeatedly test the teacher to see whether or not he or she can be trusted. The teacher must give and give to the students to show them that he or she cares, understands, and accepts them, while receiving little positive response or appreciation in return. Two teachers comment on the lack of appreciation from students:

> You've got to give an awful lot in this business. There are no thanks or appreciation for what you've done. The best you can do is to break even.

[6]Interviewed in May 1981.

The lack of positive strokes from the kids is hard to take. There isn't much there to receive back. It is a combative type of situation. They're always testing the limits. They incite such emotional reactions from people that you can easily let your emotions be hooked and want a sense of revenge.[7]

The challenge of working with disruptive and emotionally disturbed students requires that teachers always be "on top of their game" and that they maintain a balance between classroom structure and nurturant support. However, teachers themselves have their good and bad days: They may not feel well, may have problems at home, or may be upset because of conflicts with other staff members. Then students typically become more demanding and difficult to control. Another problem with maintaining a balance between structure and nurture is that a teacher who is high in either nurturant skills or high in structure skills frequently is low in the other area.

The Management of Stress

Teachers in alternative schools typically go home emotionally exhausted because they have dealt with a high-stress environment the entire day. Rarely does a teacher fail to receive some verbal abuse from students during a day. One teacher in an alternative school speaks about the verbal abuse she endures from students:

It's hard to sit there all day and be called a f———ing bitch and whore and keep a stone face. When you leave here, you have to have good ways to relax.[8]

It is also stressful to deal constantly with acting-out behavior from students, who are frequently involved in verbal conflict and physical altercations, sometimes attempt to destroy school property or the property of other students, or may even try to assault the teacher physically. A psychologist in an alternative school, after describing the acting-out behavior of students, adds: "We have kids who have been involved in some heavy acts. They've pulled knives on people and are physically assaultive."[9]

To handle this constant message that they are no good and are merely harassing the students, classroom teachers must find adequate support systems and positive stress reduction techniques when they are away from the work environment. Otherwise, the inevitable result will be job burnout and a debilitating load of stress.

Treatment in an Alternative School

The basic program of the alternative school, which represents a second chance for disruptive students in the public school system, is focused on behavioral treatment rather than on academic pursuits. As one of the few options that deal with

[7]Interviewed in May 1981.
[8]Interviewed in June 1981.
[9]Interviewed in May 1981.

both treatment and education, these programs clearly cannot help every youth referred to them, but they do serve a very valuable purpose for those students who can be helped. A majority of alternative school students would drop out of public school entirely without this option. Some of these students would be committed to group homes or juvenile institutions if these schools were unavailable.

The key task of teachers in alternative schools is to set students up for success rather than for failure. They do this by showing a great deal of caring and by using a positive reinforcement system, which rewards students with points for positive behavior, possibly through a point card system. The card system also assists the staff in evaluating the progress of students' classroom behavior and performance.

The ability of the alternative school to deal effectively with students depends largely on the teamwork of the entire staff. As Darrell Dierks noted in his interview, support staff is a key element which enables teachers to respond appropriately to their students. Sometimes daily in-service training sessions help teachers unwind from the conflicts of the day and share problems and accomplishments with other staff members.

In alternative schools, as Chapter 5 indicated, some students do make real progress. The caring of the teachers, the controlled classroom setting, the positive reinforcement model used, and the help given by support staff all contribute to the effectiveness of the alternative school as a treatment model with these students.

THE STAFF MEMBER IN A COMMUNITY-BASED THERAPEUTIC COMMUNITY

Therapeutic communities, which are described in Chapters 6 and 7, have been widely praised and sharply criticized. These communities differ in several respects from other treatment programs, but one of the most significant differences is that exoffenders or former drug abusers make up the majority of staff members. Box 10-3 is taken from an interview with John Stepniewski, director of the Gateway House in Springfield, Illinois. In this interview, Stepniewski tells why Gateway works and identifies the role expectations for staff members.

Box 10-3   Interview with John Stepniewski

QUESTION: Does Gateway work? Is it effective with drug abusers?

STEPNIEWSKI: It worked for me. I spent years of my life shooting heroin, committing burglaries, and serving time in a variety of correctional facilities, including penitentiaries, before Gateway turned me around. But I was here three times before it worked for me. The first two times I took off, but the third time I came

to stay. Gateway worked for me because of the sincere and honest relationships I had with people here. I was also impressed by the role models here. I had grown up with several staff members, and they had been as hooked on drugs as I was. They had made it, and so it gave me hope that I could make it.

A TC [therapeutic community] is not easy. You have to learn to believe in yourself to be able to live a drug-free life. You have to share with others. You have to reveal your weaknesses, your inhibitions, and your anxieties. The involvement with others and the structure of the program puts a lot of stress on you. The hardest thing about a TC is that it makes you look at yourself for what you are. It forces you to admit the kind of person you are. Everyone here is angry on the outside, but hurt on the inside. Even those who split eventually look at themselves.

Gateway is like a religion. People have to buy into it—believe in it. It's a mystical kind of thing. It's a way of life. People have to make a great commitment to this program. For those who are willing to make this commitment it works.

QUESTION: What roles are staff members expected to play in Gateway?

STEPNIEWSKI: A person isn't born to abuse chemicals. I believe your family relationships are where abuse starts, and those have a lot to do with your putting heroin and PPC in your veins. Whether you've grown up in a ghetto or in a middle-class home, you have a basic need to feel love, to feel you're accepted, and to feel you're okay. If you have a person who has abused chemicals for five or ten years, abusing mother, father, and everybody, he has a lot of guilt and needs to be told he's okay. So, first, our job is to provide the family and the acceptance that the residents didn't receive as a child.

Second, staff members also have to be aggressive and forceful because residents are slick and have learned to manipulate to get a bag of dope. If they're doing something wrong, we have to tell them. Almost all residents say at graduation, "Thanks for putting that sign around my neck. Thanks for verbally kicking me in the ass."

Third, staff members have got to know residents' moods and where they are. We need to know who's sincere and who is not. Residents can fool you at times, but we've been there and somebody will know who's putting on a "front."

Fourth, staff members must make sure residents are getting the right services. We've a lot of services we offer these people. We give them a lot of support; we have an AA program, a parents program, a GED program, and a college program.

Fifth, we have to do our best to talk residents into staying. We have a waiting list of eighty now; some are waiting in jail and some are in out-patient clinics. But we have to do our best to encourage those who are in the program to stay. This is a hard program, and most residents want to take off at one time or the other. If they do leave, we go after them for two weeks. We want to bring them back to protect them; no travel agency is going to give them $20 to get home. If they are determined to leave, we give them a bus ticket.

Source: Interview conducted in January 1982. Used with permission.

Another role expectation of staff in most therapeutic communities is that they expose residents to Synanon-type confrontation games. In such therapy groups, which range from verbally violent to more supportive, analytic, nurturing types of interaction, staff members must be certain that the group avoids being too harsh or too brutal. Yet, it is commonly accepted that these games are needed to strip residents of their denial and rationalization behaviors and to make them uncomfortable with their self-destructive habits.[10]

[10]For an evaluation of confrontation models in therapeutic communities, see Hans Toch, *Therapeutic Communities in Corrections* (New York: Praeger, 1980), pp. 110–114.

Pressures on Staff in a Therapeutic Community

The temptation to return to chemicals and to abuse authority with residents are two pressures facing staff in therapeutic communities.

Return to addiction.   Staff members in therapeutic communities, most of whom are graduates of such a similar program, have usually spent years abusing drugs. As they deal with job stress, marital difficulties, financial responsibility, and personal insecurity and inadequacies, they may think occasionally that it would be nice to get high again. A small percentage of staff members do return to drugs, but more commonly, staff members switch their dependency from chemicals to alcohol. Because of the danger of staff members' developing new addictions or returning to old ones, it is an unwritten rule in therapeutic communities that staff members keep an eye on each other and give mutual support in the stressful work situation.

Abuse of authority.   Staff members in a therapeutic community have tremendous power over residents. They decide whether and when a resident will have visitors, whether a resident will be accepted into the house, when a resident will be promoted to the next level, and when a resident will be released. They also decide on the type of punishment to be administered for inappropriate behavior. For example, they can require that a resident wear a derogatory sign around his or her neck, that a male resident be subjected to the humiliating experience of having his head shaved, that a resident be required to participate in an attack group, or that a resident return to the entry-level position or even be dismissed from the program. It is not surprising that some staff members begin to abuse their authority. Charles Dietrich, the founder and director of Synanon, is an extreme example of a leader who has abused his power. When he wanted to shave his head, all the males in the house were required to shave their heads. When he decided to quit smoking, everyone in the house was required to quit smoking. When he made the decision to divorce his wife, all the marriages in the house were dissolved.

Treatment in a Therapeutic Community

The treatment methods in a therapeutic community are clearly based on the rehabilitation model. As indicated in Chapter 6 residents are generally viewed as immature people who must be forced to face themselves through the vehicle of self-degradation and heavy peer pressure. Confrontation, or "attack" therapy, is usually one of the group techniques the family uses to force residents to face their emotional conflicts and their guilt over past histories of drug abuse. As individuals become more responsible for their behavior, they are promoted through the various treatment levels until they are ready to graduate from the program. In some therapeutic communities, residents are expected to maintain contact with the family after graduation, and graduates of some TCs are given financial resources to get started in the community. Therapeutic communities do not work for everyone, but they show impressive results with some offenders.

THE SENSITIVE AND DEDICATED
TREATMENT AGENT
IN THE COMMUNITY

Effective treatment agents in community-based corrections share a number of similar characteristics. First, they are very loving and caring persons who have the capacity and willingness to involve themselves in the lives of other human beings. Second, they are extremely dedicated to working with offenders; this means that they are willing to invest considerable time and energy in helping offenders straighten out their lives and realize their goals. Third, they are street-wise; they either have grown up on the streets or have learned how to recognize the games and fronts that residents try to use on them. Fourth, they are persistent and do not quickly give up on offenders. Fifth, they know how to expose repeatedly offenders to experiences of success. They communicate to offenders that they have the capacity to change, and when an offender has a successful experience, they are quick to recognize or reinforce that positive experience. Sixth, they are trusted by offenders, who are typically good at reading people. Juvenile and adult offenders often know instinctively that these treatment persons care and can be trusted. Seventh, they generally put considerable energy into helping offenders plan for the future, which is important because many offenders are completely unrealistic about the future. Eighth, they have learned how to cope with the strain and overload of their jobs so that they can avoid burnout. Finally, effective treatment agents know how to deal with failure both in others and in themselves. They tend to know the right words to say when an offender has failed so that the youth or adult will not be overwhelmed by that failure.

SUMMARY

This chapter has examined three of the many treatment agents who work with offenders in the community. The Outward Bound staff member is expected to deal with students in a short-term experiential situation. The Outward Bound program was originally designed for nondelinquent populations, but there has been an increased tendency to adapt the learning situation in the program to delinquent populations. The hoped-for outcome of this change process is that the ability to master the challenges of the course will provide students with new awareness, attitudes, and values and, thereby, make them better equipped to solve future problems in a positive manner.

The teacher in an alternative school deals with students who cannot succeed in the regular public school situation. Because of the students' histories of disruptive behavior or emotional disturbance, alternative school teachers are expected to gain control of the classroom while simultaneously dealing with the students' emotional deprivations and needs. The goals of this treatment process are that students either will return to the public school and do acceptable work or will use their positive experiences in the alternative school setting to avoid further contact with the justice system.

The staff member in a therapeutic community is frequently a person who has abused drugs in the past and who has spent time in correctional institutions. Treatment in a TC usually takes two or three years and demands much of both residents and staff. The goal of TC treatment is to enable residents to give up drugs and avoid further involvement with the correctional system.

All of the actors discussed in this chapter have draining jobs. The difficult professional expectations, as well as the ongoing pressures, can easily lead to burnout and high job turnover. Fortunately, in spite of the demands of these jobs, sensitive and dedicated treatment agents abound in the community.

DISCUSSION QUESTIONS

1. What community agent do you believe you would respond to as a role model if you needed to change your behavior? Why? What effect did setting—outdoors, school, substitute family—have on your choice?

2. What qualities fostered in Outward Bound programs do you think help an individual refrain from criminal behavior? Explain the reasons for your choice.

3. What are the role expectations for and the pressures on an Outward Bound instructor? Why would these qualifications make the instructor an effective worker with juvenile offenders?

4. Why would an alternative school teacher be an effective agent of change? What problems have you seen in regular school settings that might lead some students to exhibit disruptive or emotionally disturbed behavior?

5. Why would an alternative school teacher need support services and be liable to burnout?

6. Why do you think the structured environment and confrontation model of therapeutic communities works for substance abusers? Discuss how rules indicate either caring or punishment and result in either change or rebellion.

7. You have been offered a job for a year in your choice of one of the types of programs described in this chapter. You have the necessary qualifications. Your goal is to help as many young people as possible. Which job would you choose? Why?

8. Each of these treatment agents is working in an environment that is somewhat unusual. Why would the situations be stressful for the agent but promote change for the participant?

9. How do the qualities of an effective treatment agent overlap those of an effective parent? How do the qualities differ?

11

The Probation Officer and the Parole Officer

Objectives

1. To list the role expectations of probation and parole officers.

2. To examine the changing treatment roles of probation and parole officers.

3. To describe the pressures these officers face.

4. To indicate the treatment strategies being used with probationers and parolees.

5. To define the characteristics of effective probation and parole officers.

Probation means a court sentence by which the defendant's freedom in the community is continued or only briefly interrupted, but under which the person is subject to supervision by a probation officer and to the conditions imposed by the court. The sentencing court retains the authority to modify the conditions of the sentence or to resentence the offender if he or she violates the conditions of probation.[1] Parole is designed to supervise exoffenders who have served a portion of their sentences in a correctional institution and who are under the continued custody of the state. Parolees who violate the law usually are returned to prison to complete their sentences or are given new sentences by the courts. In 1981, of the 1,445, 800 offenders on probation and parole supervision, more than 1,200,000 adults and juveniles were on probation.[2]

The mounting criticism of correctional treatment during the 1970s caused probation and parole officers to respond in four basic ways. Some probation and parole officers who had already given up on the treatment model were relieved that the model was being buried. Others, disillusioned by the empirical evidence that nothing could be done to reform the criminal offender, sought out more effective models for dealing with criminal offenders. Still others refused to dismiss correctional treatment, contending that, while treatment may not work for every offender, a humane justice system demands that correctional treatment services and programs be provided for those offenders who want them and can benefit from them and need them. Finally, some officers continued to support correctional treatment with the claim that the only problem with the model is that practitioners have not tried hard enough; this last group has explored a number of ways in the past decade to provide improved treatment services to probationers and parolees.

Beginning with the role expectations of the probation officer and the parole officer, this chapter also considers probation and parole officers' changing response toward treatment, the pressures on these agents, and the specific treatment interventions they use, concluding with a profile of effective treatment agents in probation and parole.

ROLE EXPECTATIONS FOR THE PROBATION AND PAROLE OFFICER

The formal and informal role expectations of probation and parole officers influence their interaction and treatment intervention with clients.

Formal Role Expectations

The probation officer is expected by the court to provide presentence reports or conduct other investigative activities requested by the judge, to supervise persons

---

[1]Harry E. Allen et al., *Critical Issues in Adult Probation: Summary* (Washington, D.C.: GPO, September 1979), pp. 12–13.

[2]Stephen Gettinger, "The Prison Population," *Corrections Magazine* 9 (June 1983), p. 8.

placed on probation, to maintain case files and other evaluative information needed to determine probationers' progress and needs, to advise probationers on the conditions of their sentences, to inform the court when persons on probation have violated the terms of that probation, and to perform any other probationary services that a judge may request. The probation officer is also expected to handle complaints dealing with probationers and to utilize the community and its resources to aid the person on probation.[3]

The parole officer is responsible to the parole board and is expected to gather information to aid the parole board in deciding whether or not to grant parole, to supervise the conduct of parolees assigned to him or her, to advise clients on the conditions of parole, to recommend when necessary that the board issue warrants for parolees' return to prison, and to issue such warrants after being delegated to do so by the parole board. The parole officer also is expected to assist clients in locating services needed to achieve their successful reintegration to the community, to handle complaints dealing with parolees, to make certain that clients receive their due process rights during the revocation process, to make investigations and supervise inmates released in accordance with the mandatory release laws, and to investigate and report to the governor of the state on persons applying for pardon, commutation of sentence, or clemency.[4]

Departmental Role Expectations

Directors and supervisors of probation and parole departments require that departmental responsibilities, such as reports to the courts, must be given precedence, even over the needs of the clients. Nearly all parole departments, and an increasing number of probation departments, also emphasize that the safety of the community is the most important goal of their officers. Thus, probation and parole officers are under pressure to avoid any unfavorable publicity for their departments through too lenient handling of probationers or parolees. A probation officer in an adult probation office in the Midwest describes this job expectation:

> Our principal departmental role is that of ensuring the safety of the community. In so performing that service, we are not expected to run interference for our clients. We are expected to make appropriate referrals to ensure law-abiding behavior. I suppose we are police officers more than we used to be, but we still go a step further and attempt to change behavior.[5]

Societal Role Expectations

The current atmosphere means society expects both probation and parole officers to "get tough with the criminal." Probation is one subsystem of the justice systems to which the various sectors of the public have a common reaction, believing

---

[3]*Annotated Code of Maryland,* Article 41, Section 115–131A (1974).
[4]Ibid.
[5]Interviewed in September 1982.

that probation is too soft and permissive. Even practitioners of the justice system are quick to criticize probation. A staff member in a youth shelter said:

> I'm not very impressed with probation. When a kid gets picked up for shoplifting, it's a joke. I think probation is like a slap on the hand. Many kids simply disregard it. The kids will say that they know they [probation officers] are not going to do a damn thing to them. It's just an empty threat. They'll say, "Oh, I *just* got probation."[6]

THE CHANGING TREATMENT ROLES OF PROBATION AND PAROLE OFFICERS

Rehabilitative philosophy, as indicated in Chapter 2, was widely accepted in probation and parole until the mid-1970s; then the justice model, the logical consequences model, and the punishment model began to receive support from more and more probation and parole officers.

Rehabilitative Philosophy

The medical model received early acceptance in probation departments because graduates of clinically-oriented professional social work programs were attracted to positions as juvenile probation officers. Acceptance of the model spread as juvenile courts and juvenile probation departments and professional social work programs developed throughout the nation. The medical model also surfaced in adult probation during the 1920s as professional social workers took jobs as adult probation officers.

By the late 1960s, however, the basic assumption of the medical model that offenders are sick and therefore not responsible for their behavior was questioned by most probation and parole officers. These advocates of rehabilitative philosophy continued to hold that offenders could be rehabilitated through individual counseling or group therapy, but they emphasized present behavior over the continuing effect of past emotional problems and stressed that offenders could make responsible and law-abiding decisions. Accordingly, these advocates turned to humanistic and behavioral psychology for treatment modalities that would challenge offenders to deal more effectively with their behaviors and with the world in which they lived. Reality therapy, transactional analysis, behavior modification, gestalt therapy, guided group interaction, and positive peer culture were the modalities most widely accepted by these probation and parole officers.

The role expectations of the probation officer changed once again in 1973 when the National Advisory Commission on Criminal Justice Standards and Goals recommended that the community resource manager role could meet the goals of probation and parole more effectively than the caseworker role. The community

---

[6]Interviewed in May 1981.

resource manager, or broker, role meant that probation officers were to refer clients to the community resources needed for their rehabilitation. The first step was for the probation officer to assess the needs of the probationer. The second step involved assessing the service delivery options appropriate for each client, contacting the appropriate resources, and assisting the client in obtaining these services. The final step was to monitor the offender's progress in these programs.[7]

A juvenile probation officer tells how helpful these services sometimes are:

I remember working with a seventeen-year-old black girl who had been arrested on first degree robbery and prostitution. She had never been referred before. What it came down to was two juvenile girls, spurred on by their two adult boyfriends, were in a bar trying to shake down this white guy. The girls got him up to their apartment, and they were going to get it on with him. Then their boyfriends came up, and pretended to be really mad because he was with their women. The white guy said, "Take anything," and they took some money he had in his car. The robbery charge was dropped, but there was a finding of fact on the prostitution charge, and she was placed on supervision until her eighteenth birthday. When she was assigned to my caseload, the first thing we did was to go together to the hospital's family practice center to have her checked out and placed on birth control. But she was already pregnant. The majority of time we spent together was concentrated on getting a job, obtaining an education, getting ready for the baby, and promoting independent living skills. We spent a lot of time together getting ready for the future. Her mother was dead and her father was in the Mental Health Institute. She didn't have anyone else, and so I felt like I was the one she counted on. I took her to the hospital when she had her baby and was with her during delivery. It was a neat experience. She asked me to be godmother for her baby. She's now motivated to make something of herself. She is now nineteen, has her own car, and keeps an apartment fairly well. She has either gone to school or worked since before she had the baby. I think she has done very well.[8]

More commonly, probation officers refer probationers to resources in the community. For example, an offender with mental health problems will be referred to either in- or out-patient therapy in a mental health facility. An offender with a drug problem will be referred to a substance abuse program or to a therapeutic community for drug offenders. Similarly, an offender with a history of alcohol abuse will be referred to Alcoholic Anonymous.

In the mid-1970s, as the reintegration model came under increasing attack, a number of probation administrators adopted the concept of the Community Resource Management Team (CRMT). Under this approach to probation services, officers are divided into teams, and each team takes responsibility for a caseload and makes decisions on what community resources are needed by clients. New probationers are interviewed by one member of the team, and their needs are plotted on a needs-assessment scale. The members of the teams are usually specialists in "needs subsystems," dealing with such problems as drug abuse, alcoholism, mental illness, or unemployment, and the specialist links the probationer with whatever

[7]National Advisory Commission on Criminal Justice Standards and Goals, *Corrections* (Washington, D.C.: GPO, 1973), pp. 313–316.

[8]Interviewed in April 1981.

services in the community are necessary.[9] Figure 11-1 shows the reintegrative services that the Monterey County Probation Department's Community Resource Management Team delivers to probationers.

Allen and colleagues aptly summarize the reintegrative tasks of a probation department:

Figure 11-1 Monterey County Probation Department, Community Resource Management Team Delivery System

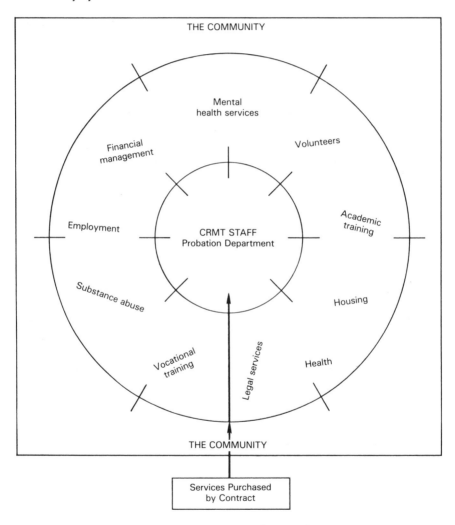

Source: E. Kim Nelson, Howard Ohmart, and Nora Harlow. *Promising Strategies in Probation and Parole* (Washington, D.C.: GPO, 1978), p. 56.

[9]Rob Wilson, "Probation/Parole Officers as 'Resource Brokers,'" *Corrections Magazine* 5 (June 1978): 48.

1. Assess the personal and social conditions of persons referred for probation services with emphasis on needs which must be satisfied or controlled to achieve successful reintegration into the community.
2. Provide information and recommendations to the courts which will assist in achieving dispositions favorable to the individual offender's reintegration.
3. Design and delineate a plan of action for each probationer referred which includes goals leading to law-abiding and socially acceptable behavior, and appropriate methods for achieving those goals.
4. Provide a level of supervision appropriate to reintegrate goals.
5. While carrying out the supervisory plan, continually reassess and modify it as necessary to achieve the reintegrative goals.
6. Encourage and conduct research designed to develop and improve reintegrative techniques for offenders placed on probation.[10]

Similarly, in parole departments as well many officers were attracted to the reintegration model during the 1970s. As part of their basic objective of helping exoffenders return to community life, they provided parolees with or referred them to the community resources to effect changed behavior or to support the change process that had taken place in institutional settings. Thus, they sometimes visited inmates in prisons or training schools before release, found community placements for them if no home placement was available, helped them find jobs or obtain mental health or substance abuse counseling, and occasionally provided financial assistance until parolees completed the transition into the community. These officers also became advocates of parolees at work, at school, and in their home situations.

The Logical Consequences Model

An emerging model in juvenile probation, the logical consequences model is having an increasing impact nationally on how juvenile probationers are treated. Advocates of this model believe that antisocial behavior should exact a cost and that youthful offenders should be made aware of the consequences of socially unacceptable behavior. Three probation officers explain why they are now using the logical consequences model:

> I basically believe in the logical consequence model. If they do such and such which is unacceptable, then they have to pay the consequences.

> I try to give them a consequence. For example, we give them work projects. We used to be too easy, but we've found that the work is much harder than seeing a probation officer once a week. I had a kid tell me, "I'll never come back to see you because I'll never do another work project. You guys made me go out and shovel ice and snow." He looked upon work as the worst thing in the world. I think the work had a positive effect on him.

> I think probation is frequently too soft. I try to set myself up in a power position and show them that there is a cost to their behavior. Then, I let up and am more flexible. If kids are doing well, I take them bowling, canoeing, or on fun trips.[11]

[10]Allen et al., *Critical Issues in Adult Probation,* p. 25.
[11]Interviewed in May through July 1981.

The logical consequences model is based on at least five major assumptions. One is that juvenile offenders have free will and, therefore, should be held responsible for what they do. Another is that juvenile offenders know the justice system so well that they are able to take advantage of the permissiveness of the system; for example, offenders often know that another burglary charge will bring only a lecture from the juvenile judge and a continuation of probation. A third assumption is that youthful offenders will only modify their behavior when the cost of their behavior becomes too high. A fourth is that it is necessary to put penalties in probation supervision because juveniles do not take seriously regular supervision of probation (i.e., reporting on a regular basis to the probation officer). A final assumption is that it is possible to develop effective relationships with probationers once they decide to take probation seriously.

The ineffectiveness of regular juvenile probation has led many officers to accept this model. As a probation officer said, "One of the frustrating things about this job is that we never see any real results."[12] Another juvenile probation officer added:

A boy and his brother went into a house to burglarize it and found an old man laying on a couch downstairs. They tried to take his wallet, and the old man resisted. They beat him to death. At the age of eleven, the older youth was first referred to us for burglary. We never did anything. At age thirteen, after twenty-four burglaries and thefts, we finally decided to do something, and what we did was to put him in training school. He came out, committed another crime, and was put back in training school. Each time he came out he was a little smarter, and it was harder to prove he was committing the crime he was accused of. He would laugh at the probation officer and tell him that he was too slick to get caught. I feel he was an indictment of the system. He was an example of the system being too soft, and we paid for it in the end.[13]

The design of the logical consequences model was adapted from an approach to disciplining children that became popular in American society in the late 1970s and early 1980s, whereby the parent or primary caretaker gives the child a choice, while informing him or her of the specific consequences of negative behavior. Its advocates believe that this approach puts the responsibility for behavior on the child rather than on the parent and, therefore, the negative consequences are what the child has chosen rather than punishment the parent has chosen to administer.

Finally, proponents of the logical consequences model in juvenile probation believe that clients become receptive to treatment once they realize that there is a cost to negative behavior. Advocates also claim that putting a cost on behavior when juveniles first come into the justice system reduces the number of offenders who must later be sent to training school.

The Justice Model

The acceptance of the justice model is beginning to affect probation and parole in a number of ways. Advocates of the justice model propose that determinate

[12]Interviewed in April 1981.
[13]Interviewed in May 1981.

sentencing replace indeterminate sentencing and the parole board. As David Fogel indicated in his interview in Chapter 3, according to the justice model probation officers should respond to probationers as responsible, volitional human beings. Treatment should be voluntary and compliance with treatment should not be related to revocation of probation. Fogel does not believe that probation officers should be responsible for providing specialized, intensive services, even when probationers need these services. Proponents of the justice model want to reduce the discretionary authority of all actors in the justice system, including probation officers, and, therefore, would require that the standard of proof for the revocation of probation be as strong as the original finding which resulted in the sentence of probation; that is, beyond a reasonable doubt. The presentence investigation report should be regarded as a legal document, and defendants should know the contents of this report to the court. Probation officers should make quasijudicial decisions concerning probationers only within the legal authority granted by the criminal justice system. Supporters of the justice model discourage the use of informal juvenile probation, because they see this means of handling youthful offenders as one that has allowed much abuse in the past. Proponents further recommend increasing restitution programs, believing that it is only just for offenders to pay for the social harm they have inflicted. Fogel goes so far as to say that probation should be as concerned with the victim of the crime as it is with the offender. Advocates of the justice model foresee wide acceptance of its principles by probation agencies, and it appears that the mission and structure of adult probation especially will be shaped by the justice model in the years to come.

The Utilitarian Punishment Model

Parole traditionally has had a more punishment-oriented emphasis than probation. Its "trail 'em, nail 'em, and jail 'em" orientation has made parole officers regard exoffenders as culprits who would continue to commit serious criminal acts if they were not watched. The punishment model became even more popular during the 1970s as parole officers saw their jobs jeopardized by the growing acceptance of determinate sentencing and reacted by trying to prove that they were taking a tougher stance toward parolees. The popularity of the punishment model was further enhanced during the 1970s by parole officers' growing fear of their clients. Parole officers increasingly began to carry firearms, obtain unlisted phone numbers, and advise new parole officers to take a strong stand with clients. One adult parole officer discusses his acceptance of a punishment-oriented attitude:

Parolees try to threaten me all the time. But if they give me any bullshit, I'll put them in jail. We don't let them get away with what we used to. If we can prove they're doing anything out of line, then we send them back to prison.[14]

Although the punishment model has had a greater impact on parole than on probation, the current emphasis on the protection of the community is leading more

---

[14]Interviewed in February 1976.

probation agencies to adopt a punishment model. To achieve the objective of community protection, probation agencies are expected to perform the following tasks:

1. Assess the nature and degree of dangerousness of persons referred for investigation or supervision.
2. Assess the probability that persons assigned for investigation or supervision will recidivate.
3. For persons under investigation, recommend dispositions to courts which are most likely to protect the community.
4. For persons under supervision, exercise the degree of supervision and control necessary to protect the community, by taking preventive or corrective action where necessary.
5. Encourage and conduct research designed to improve prediction and control technique in relation to community protection.[15]

Probation officers who have a background in law enforcement are frequently attracted to the punishment model. These officers are determined to comply with court orders and are reluctant to deviate from the authorization given them by the court. They also do not want to permit dangerous offenders to remain on the streets. One probation officer put it this way, "What it simmers down to is police work. We're the policemen back of the agencies."[16]

PRESSURES ON PROBATION AND PAROLE OFFICERS

Three pressures affect probation and parole officers and interfere with their becoming effective treatment agents: lack of time for individualized treatment, inadequate community resources, and job stress.

Lack of Time for Individualized Treatment

Probation and parole officers simply lack the time to provide individualized treatment of clients. First, caseloads are typically too large. The average caseload is usually eighty or more for federal probation and parole officers, one hundred or more for state officers, and even larger for county probation officers. Such large caseloads make it difficult enough for officers to know the names of their clients, much less to develop rapport and a working relationship with them.

Second, probation and parole officers lack the time for individualized treatment because they have too many other duties. A frequent complaint of these officers is that they are inundated with paperwork and administrative duties. A 1973 survey of federal probation and parole officers by the Federal Judicial Center revealed that one third of the average officer's work time was spent on investigation

---

[15]Allen et al., *Critical Issues in Adult Probation,* p. 24.

[16]Diana Lewis, "What Is Probation?" *Journal of Criminal Law, Criminology and Police Science* 51 (1960): 199.

and reports and more than a third on office work not related to cases. Only 28.7 percent of the officer's time was left for supervision of clients. These figures mean that each probationer or parolee could expect to receive only 6.4 hours of supervision in the course of a year, 32 minutes a month, or 7 minutes a week.[17]

Inadequate Community Resources

Jim Bergum, director of juvenile court services in Hennepin County, Minnesota (Minneapolis), is pleased with the resources that probation is given in his county:

> We're well funded. We have support from the court because it values our support services. We have a community that is rich in resources and the administrative capacity to engineer and deliver services.[18]

Their varied resources include a county institution, hospital and outpatient facilities for the chemically dependent, residential facilities, day treatment programs, short- and long-term restitution programs, and safe houses for runaways.[19] But Hennepin County, with a history of strong juvenile court services, is not typical by any means.

More commonly, probation, the most widely used judicial sentence, receives the smallest share of the correctional dollar. Consequently, too few probation officers are hired, resulting in large caseloads and overworked officers. Inadequate funding also means officers are both underpaid and inadequately trained. Insufficient funding results further to lessened community resources. State parole officers may be better paid and receive more training than most, but, as discussed earlier, community assistance programs are far too few to deal with the reintegration needs of parolees.

Inadequate community resources make it difficult for probation and parole officers to do their jobs by providing sufficient services for clients. Officers always have the option of developing community resources, but few have the time or energy to do this. Officers, of course, can provide the services themselves, but still the lack of time makes it difficult for them to provide individual services for many clients. Probation and parole officers do the best they can with limited community resources but they know clients may find it difficult to resist a return to crime when needed services are unavailable.

Job Stress

A major source of stress for probation and parole officers is the pressure of working with individuals who are constantly involved in crisis and failure. One probation officer noted that "a PO never gets a client very far away from the crisis

---

[17]Federal Judicial Center, "Probation Time Study," processed (26 February 1973); and Susi Megathalim, "Probation Parole Caseload Review," processed (Georgia Department of Offender Rehabilitation, November 1973).

[18]Interviewed in August 1981.

[19]Ibid.

line."[20] The consequence of working with so many offenders who are "losers" makes it easy to generalize and to look upon all clients as "losers." Their situation also leads to officers' withdrawal from clients and to job burnout.

Probation and parole officers encounter stress because clients are commonly resistant and sometimes hostile to them. One juvenile probationer demonstrates this resistance in his evaluation of his probation officer:

> The PO is all right, but I don't go along with all her ideas. I filter out what I want to hear and do as I please. She's always hassling me about having quit school.[21]

The hostility of some parolees results in even more stress. It is not uncommon for a parole officer to have his or her life threatened or to face a potentially assaultive situation. Many parolees have committed violent crimes, so the possibility of their acting out such behavior is one the parole officer can not ignore.

The criticism that parole has been bombarded with in recent years also causes stress for parole officers. In the late 1970s and early 1980s, a number of states turned away from indeterminate sentencing and the parole board and adopted some variation of determinate sentencing structures. Parole was widely viewed as an endangered system, for it was predicted that the majority of states would abandon indeterminate sentencing and the parole board during the 1980s. Although this pessimistic view of the future of parole has probably been overstated, parole officers understandably are defensive and feel that they must prove the validity of parole supervision for those recently released from correctional institutions.

CORRECTIONAL TREATMENT IN ACTION IN PROBATION AND PAROLE

Probation and parole officers are now using a number of intervention strategies to deal with criminal behavior. These strategies fall into the following categories: nutritional counseling, diversionary programs, classification systems, therapeutic modalities, community assistance programs, restitution programs, survival experiences, intensive supervision, secure supervision, weekends in jail, and assistance of volunteers and paraprofessional staff.

Nutritional Counseling

Providing nutritional counseling to improve the diets of probationers is a recent innovation in treatment by probation services. Barbara Reed, chief probation officer of the Cuyahoga Falls Municipal Probation Department (Ohio), is the best

---

[20]Interviewed in October 1980.
[21]Interviewed in May 1981.

known proponent of nutritional counseling with probationers. In 1977, she reported to the U.S. Senate Committee on Nutrition and Human Needs that 252 out of 318 probationers she had worked with had deficient diets. She then noted, "We have not had one single person back in court for trouble who has maintained and stayed on the nutritional diet."[22]

Nutritional counseling is also used by several California departments of juvenile probation. In 1979, Herb Goldsmith, food service manager for the Alameda County Probation Department, reduced the consumption of granulated sugar and sweetened foods by juveniles in his dining rooms at two youth camps, a dependent child care facility, and the county juvenile detention centers. Staff found that the improved diets had a positive impact upon the behavior of the 350 juveniles in these facilities.[23] In 1977, Robert G. Lucas, chief probation officer of the Tehama County Probation Department, found that using the Feingold Diet in the county juvenile hall reduced hyperactivity and misbehavior and resulted in longer attention spans in the classrooms.[24]

Diversionary Programs

Both probation and parole officers use a variety of diversionary programs for correctional clients. They may refer offenders who abuse drugs to a substance abuse program or to a therapeutic community for drug offenders, those who abuse alcohol to Alcoholics Anonymous, or those who habitually gamble to Gamblers Anonymous. A probationer who has sexually abused a son or a daughter may be referred to a child abuse program. A probation officer who is an intake worker in the juvenile court is likely to refer minor offenders to the youth service bureau or to place them on informal probation. Juvenile probation departments also now are referring shoplifters to diversionary programs designed for first-time offenders.

The Black Hawk County Juvenile Probation Department (Iowa) has developed a community shoplifting program to deal with first-time offenders. When a young person picked up for shoplifting has no prior police record, the arresting officer has the option of referring him or her to the community shoplifting program. The youth and at least one parent must attend one session of the two-hour program. Beginning with a short introduction, the program consists of a brief film on shoplifting; fifteen-minute presentations by a local merchant, a police officer, and a juvenile probation officer; and a sixty-minute open-ended discussion on parent-child relationships directed by a school psychologist from the area. The program concludes with a client evaluation. If the youth and parent attend the program, the charge against the child is dismissed by the police department, but if they fail to attend, the charge is referred to the juvenile probation officer.

---

[22]U.S. Senate, Select Committee on Nutrition and Human Needs, Hearing, 22 June 1977.

[23]Alexander Schauss, *Diet, Crime, and Delinquency* (Berkeley, Calif.: Parker House, 1981), p. 11.

[24]Ibid., p. 12.

Classification Systems

Generally, probation officers divide their caseloads into different categories in order to make them manageable. The Santa Clara County (California) Probation Department conducted an adult probationer needs survey to determine the percentages of the department's caseload that were at different levels of risk, to determine the need for treatment and services of probationers, and to determine who should deliver the needed services.[25] The probation office of the District of Columbia initiated a probation caseload classification study to accomplish three objectives: to classify the entire population under supervision by using a multifactor testing instrument designed to predict the success or failure of supervision, to validate the predictive ability of the instrument by comparing all cases closed successfully with those closed unsuccessfully, and to devise from the obtained data a model of caseload management that would place probationers into caseloads according to high or low potential for success.[26] The Wisconsin Classification System is designed to place probationers and parolees in appropriate treatment groups. A structured interview is used to assign clients to one of four case-management treatment strategies: (1) a selective intervention group (35 percent) required minimal supervision; (2) a casework/control group (30 percent) required a great deal of time, direction, and support; (3) an environment structure group (20 percent) required structure, support, and guidance; and (4) a limit-setting group (15 percent) required strict rules and regulations.[27]

Therapeutic Modalities

Despite the shift away from the rehabilitative philosophy, some probation officers and a smaller number of parole officers continue to practice such modalities as transactional analysis (TA), reality therapy, behavior modification, and group therapy with clients. Most probation and parole officers intervene when clients become involved in crisis situations. Most probation officers also refer youths and adults who appear to have emotional problems to mental health agencies and initiate family therapy for certain probationers.

Probation and parole departments also have experimented with a number of individual and group treatment modalities. The Special Offenders Clinic, an outpatient treatment facility for sexual offenders and assaultive offenders in Maryland, used group therapy to resolve the relationship between emotional problems and antisocial behavior.[28] Group counseling was also used as part of the treatment plan

[25]John W. Pearson and Gary G. Taylor, *Adult Probationer Needs Survey* (Santa Clara, Calif.: Santa Clara County Probation Department, Criminal Justice Pilot Program, 1973).

[26]Ronald I. Weinger, *Probation Caseload Classification Study in the United States District Court for the District of Columbia* (Washington, D.C.: American University Press, n.d.), pp. 11–35.

[27]Wisconsin Division of Corrections, *Client-Management Classification Progress: Report No. 7* (Madison, Wis.: Division of Corrections, 1976).

[28]James Olsson, *Final Evaluation Report: An Outpatient Treatment Clinic for Special Offenders* (Hunt Valley, Md.: Maryland Division of Parole and Probation, 1973).

in the Multiphasic Diagnostic and Treatment Program in Florida.[29] The Santa Clara Probation Department (California) compared the effect of Zzoommm, a short-term motivational program, with traditional counseling in its regular probation division.[30]

Community Assistance Programs

Parole and probation officers commonly refer clients to community assistance programs for vocational counseling and employment, housing placement, financial assistance, and marriage counseling. As indicated in Chapter 6, these community assistance programs—which are experiencing severe financial cuts at the present time—provide critical support services for probationers and exoffenders.

Restitution Programs

Monetary restitution and community service projects, as previously noted, are widely used with juvenile and adult probationers. There are one hundred community service projects for adults in the United States and at least one to two hundred formal community service programs for juveniles.[31] Examples are the Alternative Community Service Program (ACSP) in Multomay County, Oregon, and the Court Referral (CR) Program in Alameda County, California, which both use community service in place of, or in addition to, traditional court sentences. More and more probation departments have restitution officers, and a few juvenile probation departments even have work squads to which juveniles are assigned for a specific number of hours as a condition of probation. The state of Georgia also requires parolees to participate in symbolic restitution, or community service, while they are residing at a restitution center.

Survival Experiences

Juvenile probation officers frequently recommend to the juvenile judge that a problem probationer be given a choice: either commitment to a state or private training school or participation in a survival experience. Outward Bound and variations of this program are found throughout the nation. These programs take place in the mountains, in the desert, in the woods, and at sea.

Intensive Supervision

The "tracker" and "proctor/advocacy" programs in Massachusetts and Utah are examples of intensive supervision programs sometimes used with juvenile pro-

---

[29]Sunil B. Nath, *Evaluation: Multiphasic Diagnostic and Treatment Program* (Tampa/Miami, Fla.: Florida Parole and Probation Commission, 1975).

[30]Santa Clara County Adult Probation Department, *A Two-Track Demonstration Project to Reduce Probationer Recidivism* (Santa Clara County: Adult Probation Department, 1973).

[31]Kevin Krajick, "The Work Ethic Approach to Punishment," *Corrections Magazine* 8 (October 1982): 8.

bationers. New York, Texas, Washington, New Jersey, and Georgia also have programs of intensive supervision for adult offenders. In Georgia, the Georgia Intensive Probation Supervision (IPS) Program uses team probation to supervise offenders who would go to prison if the program did not exist. Thirteen teams are scattered across the state; each team supervises no more than twenty-five probationers.

Secure Supervision

More commonly, probation and parole officers use a variety of residential programs for difficult correctional clients: probation centers, restitution centers, work-release centers, halfway houses, pre-release centers, and community service centers. Some of these facilities provide treatment modalities, such as group therapy, but more typically such centers have work release and more secure supervision than traditional probation and parole services would provide as the basic treatment components of their interventions.

Weekend Sentence in Jail

Some probation officers believe that a weekend or more in jail will persuade a recalcitrant client to comply more readily with the conditions of probation. Thus, they frequently recommend to the court that probationers spend a certain number of weekends in jail. Some parole officers also freely use jail confinement to convince parolees that they mean business.

Assistance of Volunteers

Volunteers, as previously mentioned, are widely used in juvenile and adult probation and used to a lesser degree in juvenile and adult parole. Although probation was established by volunteers, they were replaced by paid probation officers at the turn of the century. However, the volunteer movement made a resurgence in the late 1950s when Judge Keith J. Leenhouts of Royal Oak, Michigan, initiated a court-sponsored program. Only four courts were using volunteers in 1961; today, over two thousand court-sponsored volunteer programs are in operation. Volunteers may serve as

> advisory council members
> arts and crafts teachers
> home skills teachers
> recreation leaders
> employment counselors
> information officers
> office workers
> one-to-one assignment with probationers

professional skill volunteers
public relations workers
record keepers
tutors

The establishment of a volunteer program requires that probation and parole officers define how to determine the need for volunteers, how to solicit the best resources for the need, how to train volunteers, and how to monitor their work with correctional clients.[32]

Volunteers are necessary because of the limitations facing probation and parole programs today. Probation or parole officers do not have the time to provide adequate personal contact with clients. Office staff often lack the time to perform all the necessary administrative services. The probation department frequently does not have the resources to obtain needed professional services for clients or to improve community relations.

The means by which volunteers are solicited is a critical part of providing effective volunteer services. What is the best way to find the right person to lead a substance abuse group for clients or to locate a psychiatrist, a psychologist, a physician, or a dentist who will donate his or her services? The preferred way is through personal contacts with nearby colleges, faculties, professionals, and agencies. Newspaper advertising may attract individuals interested in becoming volunteers, but some of these individuals may lack the proper motivation or mental well-being necessary to provide effective volunteer services.

Volunteers in most probation departments, especially those who will work on one-to-one assignments with clients, go through a period of training. Although every probation department has its own method of matching volunteer and client, a coordinator usually informs probation officers of the availability of a volunteer. Officers search the files for a client who might be suitable, and the coordinator and the probation officer meet to discuss the suitability of the match. Once a match has been established, the coordinator provides the probation officer with the address and phone number of the volunteer, and the volunteer meets with the probation officer to review the match and to set goals and expectations for the client. If the volunteer accepts the case, a time is arranged for the volunteer and client to meet.

Nearly all volunteer programs monitor the contacts between the volunteer and the correctional client. Usually they require that the volunteers document all contacts with their clients in a log, which is then submitted to the supervising probation officer at least once a month for a review of progress or of potential problem areas. Some volunteer programs provide monthly training sessions to keep volunteers abreast of new ideas, trends, and techniques in the field. Opportunities are also generally given to volunteers to participate in other areas of the program. Box 12-

---

[32]Penny Rinehart, Diane Ducett, and Steve Smith were all helpful in designing this section on volunteers.

1 lists helpful hints provided for volunteers by the Black Hawk County (Iowa) Juvenile Services.

Box 11-1   Considerations When Working with Juveniles

1. *Keep in contact with the child.* We recommend one visit a week, as a minimum.
2. *Patience.* Don't expect overnight success. When things have been going wrong for years, they don't get corrected in a few weeks, or months, or even years.
3. *Be ready for setbacks.* Although we all like to achieve success with a child, remember he does not owe it to us, he owes it only to himself.
4. *Give attention and affection.* The child you are working with may never have known really sustained attention and affection and (at least at first) may not know how to handle it in a normal way.
5. *Be prepared to listen and to understand what your child says.* Too much talking on your part is more likely to break communication than enhance it.
6. *Be a discerning listener.* But listening does not mean you have to believe everything you hear.
7. *Don't prejudge.* Avoid forming fixed and premature opinions, until you have gathered all the background information you can.
8. *Know your youngster.* Get all the information you can on him.
9. *Respect confidentiality, utterly and completely.* Whatever you know about a youngster is under no circumstances to be divulged to or discussed with anyone but a person fully authorized by the Court to receive this information.
10. *Report violations.* Confidentiality does not include keeping known violations a secret from the probation officer in charge of the youngster.
11. *Be supportive, encouraging, friendly, but also firm.* Whatever role and obligation you have to report infractions, you can still be supportive, encouraging, friendly, to the limit possible.
12. *Present your ideas clearly, firmly, and simply.* Always mean what you say, be consistent, and keep your promises.
13. *Be a good role model.* Before accepting Court volunteer work, you must decide to live up to this special condition.
14. *Avoid being caught in the middle.* Be careful not to get caught between the child and his parents, the child and his teachers, or the child and the Court.
15. *Be yourself and care sincerely about the child.* The more you are yourself, the easier it will be to communicate with the child. And the more you care about the child, the more impact on him you will have.

Source: "Manual for Volunteer Probation Officer Aides" (Waterloo, Iowa: Black Hawk County Juvenile Court Services, 1981), pp. 35–39.

Assistance of Paraprofessional Staff

To assist the parole officer, sixteen states use exoffenders as parole officer aides. In an Ohio study of exoffenders as parole aides, Joseph E. Scott found that both professional parole officers and parolees supervised by these exoffenders were positive about the program.[33] Paraprofessional staff members are more frequently used in parole than in probation, but the Community Outreach Probation Experiment (C.O.P.E.) in Denver, Colorado, and the Bakery in Minneapolis, Minnesota, are two probation programs using paraprofessional staff.[34] According to Gary M. Meitz, the director of the Minneapolis program, "Probation in the inner city is crisis-oriented. We have found that people from the neighborhood can provide very effective and very supportive probation services to our clients."[35]

EFFECTIVENESS IN PROBATION AND PAROLE

The effectiveness of probation, which is the most widely used disposition of the juvenile and adult court, is widely debated. David Rothman calls the probation officer a "gun-carrying psychiatrist. . . . The probation officer is the ultimate reflection of the failure of the idea in American corrections that you can guard and treat at the same time. . . . It's a patently absurd notion."[36] Yet several studies have demonstrated the effectiveness of probation.[37] For example, a comprehensive nine-volume study compiled by the Ohio State University Program for the Study of Crime and Delinquency shows that probation is effective for first offenders, that it is probably less costly than incarceration, and that unsupervised probation may be just as effective for misdemeanants as is supervised probation.[38]

The effectiveness of parole has been more problematic, primarily because parolees have usually had more extensive involvements with a criminal career than is true of probationers. But Robert Martinson and Judith Wilks found that parole supervision was more effective in reducing recidivism than was releasing offenders without parole. They summarize their findings as follows:

> Those who propose the abolition of parole supervision in this country often speak of "fairness to the offender." It is difficult to detect [in our findings] evidence of such fairness. On the contrary. The evidence seems to indicate that the abolition of parole supervision would result in substantial increases in arrest, conviction, and return to prison. . . .[39]

[33]Joseph E. Scott, *Ex-Offenders as Parole Officers* (Lexington, Mass.: Heath, 1975), pp. 88–95.

[34]Refer to Gary M. Meitz, "The Bakery: Probation Reaches the Inner City," *Federal Probation* 42 (March 1978): 50–52, for more information about the Bakery.

[35]Interviewed in August 1981.

[36]Kevin Krajick, "Probation: The Original Community Program," *Corrections Magazine* 6 (December 1980): 11.

[37]Frank F. Scarpitti and Richard M. Stephenson, "A Study of Probation Effectiveness," *Journal of Criminal Law, Criminology and Police Science* 59 (1968): 361–369; Douglas Lipton, Robert Martinson, and Judith Wilks, *Effectiveness of Correctional Treatment: A Survey of Evaluation Studies* (New York: Praeger, 1975), pp. 59–61; and Robert Martinson and Judith Wilks, "Knowledge in Criminal Justice Planning" (New York: Center for Knowledge in Criminal Justice Planning, September 1977).

[38]Allen et al., *Critical Issues in Adult Probation*.

[39]Robert Martinson and Judith Wilks, "Save Parole Supervision," *Federal Probation* 41 (September 1977): 26–27.

The effectiveness of probation and parole may ultimately depend upon the quality of services provided by probation and parole officers. High-quality services require that these officers demonstrate skills in several areas. First, they must be able to predict offenders' future behavior with reasonable accuracy. Prediction takes place at two stages of the justice process: during the presentence investigation before an offender is placed on probation, and immediately after the offender has been placed on probation or parole. This basically intuitive predictive process is important because it enables probation officers to make recommendations to the court that will enhance the probability of clients' success, thereby ensuring better protection of the community. Predictive skills are also needed to classify correctional clients so that they will receive appropriate levels of supervision and needed services.

Second, high-quality probation and parole services require that officers understand and accept their correctional clients. Because effective officers know what life on the streets is like, they are neither gullible nor easily hoodwinked by clients. They also are able to avoid the judgmental and moralistic attitudes characteristic of some probation and parole officers who respond to lower-class offenders with middle-class values. Further, they are able to avoid either placing unreal expectations of correctional clients or becoming inflexible in interpreting the terms of probation or parole. They understand that it is unwise to do things for clients that they are capable of doing for themselves because clients can develop an unhealthy dependency.

Third, high-quality services require that officers are able to develop trusting relationships with offenders on their caseloads. A warm response to a client as a human being is an important initial step in developing a trusting relationship. An experienced probation officer put it this way:

> One of the most essential skills is a person's ability to cut through everything in that human being and actually see him as a human being. I don't know how you attain this or how you measure it, but when somebody relates to me, I can tell whether he sees me as a human being and understands where I'm at. I can tell it. And so can kids.[40]

As part of building a trusting relationship with clients, officers must have the capacity to listen and reach out to other people. Officers must also keep their word, because offenders will not trust those who do not. Furthermore, officers who offer high-quality services are committed to their jobs of helping offenders and are willing sometimes to go beyond the call of duty.

Finally, high-quality services require that officers are able to create support networks for offenders. These officers know that clients' histories of failure make it difficult to "go straight" without such support networks in the community. In addition to making themselves available as part of a support network, especially during times of crisis for clients, officers often find it necessary to generate other means of support in the community.

---

[40]Interviewed in October 1981.

SUMMARY

The probation officer does not have an easy job; overwhelming caseloads and too much paperwork leave probation officers with little time and energy for correctional treatment. Although rehabilitative philosophy, especially the reintegration model, is still widely used in probation services, increasing numbers of probation officers are turning to the logical consequences and justice models. Some probation officers choose to use the punishment model in dealing with offenders because they have given up on the effectiveness of treatment.

The widespread criticism of parole makes it even more difficult for a parole officer than for a probation officer to be an effective treatment agent. Consequently, parole officers are more likely to accept the justice and punishment models in dealing with clients. While some parole officers, especially in juvenile corrections, still advocate the rehabilitative philosophy, the punishment model is becoming the dominant model used with juvenile and adult parolees.

Effective treatment agents in probation and parole have some skill in predicting offenders' future behavior. They also understand the backgrounds, attitudes, and behaviors of correctional clients. In addition, they are not easily manipulated, they are honest with clients, they avoid placing unreal expectations on clients, and they seek to avoid doing for offenders what they can do for themselves. Furthermore, effective treatment agents are able to develop trusting relationships with offenders. They respond warmly to clients as human beings, are genuine in relationships with their clients, are able to listen and to reach out to other persons, and are so committed to helping offenders that they are willing to go beyond the call of duty when necessary. Finally, effective treatment agents must be able to develop support networks for offenders.

DISCUSSION QUESTIONS

1. What are the differences between the role requirements of probation officers and parole officers?
2. Is the probation officer or the parole officer more subject to pressures to protect public safety? Why?
3. How do probation or parole officers differ in their uses of community services? Explain some different purposes for the use of community services.
4. If your personal goal were to treat and rehabilitate offenders, would you take a job as a probation officer or as a parole officer? Why?
5. What are the built-in conflicts in the jobs of probation and parole officers? What changes in regulations and procedures could make the officer's task of relating to the offender easier?
6. Could you be an effective probation or parole officer? Why or why not? What status would you have in the general community if you took such a job?

12

Institutional Treatment Agents

Chapter Objectives

1. To describe the duties of the social worker in juvenile training schools.

2. To indicate the pressures facing social workers in training schools.

3. To describe the duties of the youth supervisor in juvenile training schools.

4. To indicate the pressures facing youth supervisors in juvenile training schools.

5. To describe the duties of the correctional counselor in adult prisons.

6. To survey the pressures facing correctional counselors in adult prisons.

7. To discuss the opportunities and challenges of a career in correctional treatment.

The social worker in a juvenile correctional facility and the correctional counselor in an adult prison are the chief treatment agents in these correctional facilities. Although clinical psychologists and psychiatrists also provide treatment services in correctional institutions, they do not have the day-by-day contact with inmates that social workers and correctional counselors do. The twenty-four hour custodial care of inmates is the responsibility of youth supervisors in training schools and of correctional officers in adult prisons. However, in juvenile corrections during the late 1970s and early 1980s, the philosophy of treatment in training schools changed, and more and more private and state juvenile institutions have combined the treatment and custodial roles of the institutional staff. In adult corrections, correctional counselors, who started work in prisons in the late 1960s and early 1970s, also began to redefine their treatment roles.

This chapter examines the model of treatment emerging in training schools; describes the duties of social workers and youth supervisors in this model; presents the duties of correctional counselors in adult prisons; indicates the pressures facing social workers, youth supervisors, and correctional counselors in correctional institutions; and discusses the opportunities and challenges of a career in correctional treatment.

THE TRADITIONAL AND EMERGING MODELS OF TREATMENT

In the traditional model of treatment, which is still used in many training schools throughout the nation, the social worker is the chief treatment agent, but the social worker provides varying interventions.[1] In minimum-security institutions, such as work camps, farms, and ranches, social workers generally use the reintegration model. The social worker, who becomes a community resource manager in this model, often has the authority to arrange home furloughs, to enroll residents in community schools, to find community jobs and supervise work release, and to maintain regular contact with parents. The smallness of these facilities, which generally house fifty or fewer residents, allows social workers to give their clients individualized attention. Social workers are also usually part of a cottage team that has the additional authority to return residents to their families or to group homes. Much of the traditional conflict with the custodial staff is eliminated in minimum-security facilities, and some well-liked social workers are given considerable informal power by the security staff.[2]

In medium-security training schools, social workers commonly are expected

---

[1] Persons occupying the position of social worker are often trained in sociology, corrections, or criminal justice.

[2] See Clemens Bartollas, Stuart J. Miller, and Paul B. Wice, *Participants in American Criminal Justice: The Promise and the Performance* (Englewood Cliffs, N.J.: Prentice-Hall, 1983), pp. 282–315, for an expansion of the traditional roles of social workers and youth supervisors in juvenile correctional facilities.

to use social casework methods in their interactions with residents. They collect background information on families and the criminal histories of clients and construct psychological profiles. They then delve into residents' feelings, attitudes, and goals. When serious emotional conflicts appear to be present, social workers help residents to gain insight into their problems and to resolve them in socially acceptable ways. Social workers in medium-security training schools have much less involvement with community resources than do those in minimum-security facilities, although well-adjusted youths are occasionally permitted home visits and off-campus privileges. Unless a social worker is the director or supervisor of a cottage, he or she usually has no authority, formal or informal, over the nontreatment staff.

In some maximum-security juvenile institutions, social workers are expected to use the rehabilitation model with the hard-core inmates. Yet, because the concern for security greatly overshadows the interest in treatment, social workers have neither formal authority nor informal power in these training schools. Social workers are supposed to be treatment specialists who gain important insights about inmates that they will share with the custodial staff, but the conflict between treatment and security staff members is often so great that neither group is receptive to what the other might contribute to improving institutional life.

In other maximum-security training schools, social workers utilize a time management philosophy, in which they enter into contracts with inmates that assure residents of such specifics as the date of release, providing they behave acceptably in the institution. These end-of-the-line institutions actually institute a form of determinate sentencing because they see residents as unreceptive to rehabilitation programs. Social workers in these training schools sometimes have considerable informal power with the staff because they help control the dangerous and difficult-to-manage inmates.

Youth supervisors, who are also called youth leaders, cottage supervisors, group supervisors, child-care workers, or group-care workers, replaced cottage parents in most juvenile correctional systems during the 1960s. Youth supervisors' jobs vary less among maximum-, medium-, and minimum-security institutions than do social workers' jobs. These custodial staff are responsible for waking residents in the morning, seeing that they wash and dress, supervising breakfast in the cottage or in a central dining room, and conducting room inspections. Youth supervisors also see that the youths go to academic and vocational programs or to their jobs on the grounds, in the kitchen, or in the community. Although residents in medium- and maximum-security institutions are usually escorted to their assignments, those in minimum-security institutions are frequently permitted to move about without staff supervision.

While residents are working or in school, youth supervisors monitor the academic and vocational areas, conduct inspections of the rooms of inmates on restriction, and patrol the recreation field until lunch. They usually meet residents at assigned areas and take them to the cottage for lunch, after which they return them to school or other duties. The afternoon shift of youth supervisors picks up the residents at the end of school and returns them to the cottage.

In some institutions, inmates have a free period from the end of school or work until the evening meal. In other institutions, youth supervisors may hold group programs during this time. After the evening meal, especially during warm weather, residents are escorted to outside recreational activities. The custodial staff must be particularly alert when residents are involved in outdoor recreational activities because runaways frequently occur during this time. Following showers and a little time to watch television, inmates are sent to their rooms, with lights out about 9:30 or 10:00 p.m.

One staff member is usually in charge during the night shift. The night supervisor makes certain no residents escape from the cottage and is available if residents become ill. The night supervisor usually sits at a desk in the staff office for most of the eight-hour shift and responds to periodic checks on cottage security by telephone.

In this traditional model, open conflict between the custodially oriented youth supervisor and the treatment-oriented social worker often occurs. Youth supervisors typically resent having treatment responsibilities. As one youth supervisor said, "Why should I do treatment? I don't get paid for it."[3] Security is usually the dominant goal of the institution in the traditional model and, therefore, the custodially oriented staff members fight the social worker over every step in treatment decisions, especially if the decisions might jeopardize institutional security. Social workers are expected to make treatment recommendations to the institutional staff but lack the formal authority to implement the decisions.

However, within the traditional model, some private and public juvenile correctional facilities do require youth supervisors to provide treatment programs for residents. In these facilities, youth supervisors may conduct guided group interaction or positive peer culture groups, may make some of the arrangements for inmates' home visits, and may even find jobs for residents approved for work in the community. Youth supervisors may also talk with parents who visit when the social worker is not on duty. They may be asked to give oral or written evaluations of residents being interviewed, and they often have voting rights in the review process.

A treatment model currently emerging in juvenile institutions is based on the examples of these progressive institutions. This treatment model attempts to resolve the dichotomy of aims between custody and treatment by synthesizing them. The cottage team becomes the cement that holds the model together. The social worker, sometimes called the youth counselor or counselor in this treatment model, serves as the cottage director and supervises both treatment and security staff. The youth supervisor is required to be part of a treatment team and also to provide custodial care for his or her charges. Custodial staff members, then, are evaluated in terms of both their abilities in delivering treatment services and their skills in providing custodial care. Treatment staff members are also evaluated according to their involvements in institutional security. Hence, in the emerging treatment model, the

[3]Interviewed in April 1972.

conflict between treatment and custody typically found in the traditional model is resolved largely by combining the two roles and by requiring that all cottage staff members become proficient in both roles.[4]

This treatment model is being used in more and more private and state juvenile facilities in the United States. The duties of and the pressures on social workers and supervisors in this emerging model are examined in the next two sections.

ROLE EXPECTATIONS
OF THE SOCIAL WORKER

The social worker, who is usually required to be a graduate of an accredited four-year college or university, should have the following knowledge, abilities, skills, and personal characteristics:

> Knowledge of human growth and behavior especially as it relates to juvenile delinquency.
>
> Knowledge of social factors relating to juvenile delinquency and their relationships to treatment plans.
>
> Knowledge of the means of group supervision and disciplines.
>
> Ability to develop a treatment plan for delinquent youth.
>
> Ability to develop techniques and acquire skills in interviewing, counseling, and casework.
>
> Ability to recognize and report behavior patterns, and to incorporate this information into treatment goals and plans.
>
> Ability to establish and maintain satisfactory working relationships with residents, staff, and the public.
>
> Ability to interpret and apply laws, rules and regulations, policies, and procedures governing the institution.
>
> Ability to communicate effectively both orally and in writing.[5]

Social workers participate in planning and reviewing treatment programs for the cottage units. They provide counseling for residents both individually and in groups. They interview families of residents and prepare social histories, progress notes, prerelease summaries, and various other reports. They participate in staff meetings and diagnostic case evaluations and pursue the treatment plans developed. They assist in coordinating cottage activities with institutional goals and objectives. Then, they outline to youth supervisors the proper procedures for handling individual youths and explain the technical treatment plans to youth supervisors. Social workers participate in establishing and maintaining standards of sanitation, security, discipline, and order. They visit prospective employers or public school officials to facilitate home placements of youth. They sometimes must transport youths to the

---

[4]David Renaud, clinical director of the Eldora Training School (Iowa), was helpful in identifying the components of this emerging model.

[5]Iowa Merit Employment Department "Youth Counselor 2," mimeographed (n.d.), p. 1.

hospital, job interviews, and home. Finally, social workers participate in the supervision of cottage recreational activities.[6]

PRESSURES ON THE SOCIAL WORKER

The danger in working with delinquents, the challenge of gaining credibility with staff, and the task of providing effective treatment services to residents are three major pressures facing social workers in the emerging model of juvenile corrections.

Danger in Institutional Environments

Most social workers enter the juvenile correctional institution with some misgivings. They are aware that some residents have committed violent crimes in the community. But it usually does not take them long to work through this initial anxiety about working with delinquents. One institutional social worker explains this initial anxiety:

> When you first walk into a place which has delinquent kids, you can't help but feel scared. You think that they're going to jump out with a knife. You fear the worst. But they're just kids. You have to deal with the real person, not with their histories or what they have done in the past. Often the kids with the worst records turn out to be the best kids and are a real joy to work with.[7]

Yet, a social worker cannot forget that some danger does exist in working with youngsters who have committed serious or violent offenses. Social workers are frequently verbally threatened and occasionally even physically or sexually assaulted. One social worker was choked by an angry youth; only the quick action of the youth supervisors in the cottage prevented this attack from being fatal.[8] Another social worker tells of an experience she had:

> I worked with a fifteen-year-old who was there for sexual offenses. We couldn't get him to say the word "sex" or deal with his sexual feelings. He eventually started acting-out on staff. I had night duty, and he turned his radio on real loud. I told him to turn it off. He was masturbating and pulled me on top of him when I reached for the radio. I finally got away from him, and he followed me to the door masturbating. I had him removed to a security cottage. There were other attacks on the staff. He spent a lot of time sitting down and watching the staff; I think he was undressing us in his mind. I feel that he is dangerous and will eventually use a weapon to get what he wants.[9]

---

[6]From the State of Iowa Confidential Performance Review/Evaluations of the Eldora Training School.

[7]Interviewed in April 1981.

[8]This incident took place in an institution in which the author was employed.

[9]Interviewed in May 1981.

The Challenge of Gaining Credibility with Youth Supervisors

The success of the emerging model of treatment depends upon the social worker serving as the catalyst of the cottage team. Youth supervisors, some of whom have worked under the traditional model of separation between security and treatment, watch the social worker carefully. They want to see whether the social worker is easily manipulated or naïve about cottage youth. They know that many social workers come from middle-class backgrounds and have had little or no contact with delinquents before working at the institution. If youth supervisors find that the social worker is unrealistic or inexperienced, they are reluctant to accept his or her insights or judgments about youth and to become committed to the treatment milieu of the cottage.

Conflicts may also arise between social workers and youth supervisors because the social worker is given higher status and more formal authority in the institution. Social workers, who are regarded as professionals, are paid better than the nonprofessional youth supervisors and have better working hours, with less evening and weekend duty. In addition, under the emerging model the social worker supervises youth supervisors, which sets up one more area of potential conflict among the cottage staff.

Social workers are aware that the more they demonstrate competence to youth supervisors, the less jealousy youth supervisors will feel toward them and the more receptive they will be to committing themselves to the concept of a unified treatment team. In short, social workers know that the effectiveness of treatment within a cottage milieu depends largely on their own ability to gain the credibility of the youth supervisors. New social workers experience much pressure and stress while they are trying to prove themselves to other cottage staff members.

The Task of Providing Treatment in a Training School

Juvenile correctional institutions are not as violent, inhumane, and criminogenic as they were a generation ago, but there are still many reasons why training schools are not ideal settings for treatment.[10] Some youths in training schools do not feel safe from predatory peers, and, indeed, they are not safe.[11] As long as

[10]See Clemens Bartollas and Christopher M. Sieverdes, "Juvenile Correctional Institutions: A Policy Statement," *Federal Probation* 46 (September 1982):22–26, for an evaluation of the present status of training schools.

[11]For an examination of victimization in a private training school, refer to Howard W. Polsky, *Cottage Six: The Social System of Delinquent Boys in Residential Treatment* (New York: Russell Sage Foundation, 1962); for an examination of victimization in training schools for girls, see Alice Propper, *Prison Homosexuality: Myth and Reality* (Lexington, Mass.: Heath, 1981); for an examination of victimization in coeducational training schools, see Christopher M. Sieverdes and Clemens Bartollas, "Race, Sex, and Juvenile Inmate Roles," *Deviant Behavior: An Indisciplinary Journal,* 3 (1982):203–218; and for an examination of victimization in a maximum-security training school, refer to Clemens Bartollas, Stuart J. Miller, and Simon Dinitz, *Juvenile Victimization: The Institutional Paradox* (New York: Halsted, 1976).

safety remains a primary consideration, it is unlikely that residents will be receptive to treatment. The inmate subculture often discourages residents from becoming involved in the treatment process, and inmates are aware that involvement may result in loss of prestige with peers. In addition, most residents have participated in treatment for some time and have lost any confidence they originally had in the treatment process. Furthermore, residents may simulate involvement in treatment because it will expedite their release, but they have little commitment to treatment. Finally, many residents have become committed to juvenile crime and are not ready to exit from that life.

To attempt to provide treatment in such a setting places considerable pressure on the social worker. He or she must ensure that all cottage residents are safe from predatory peers. He or she must intervene before any youths become so desperate they try to injure themselves. The social worker also is ultimately responsible for creating a cottage milieu that will foster the treatment process; this means that the influence of negative inmate leaders must be neutralized. While many residents will continue to be unreceptive to treatment, the social worker must identify those who are ready to experience growth and change in their lives.

ROLE EXPECTATIONS
OF THE YOUTH SUPERVISOR

The youth supervisor is expected to have the following knowledge, abilities, skills, and personal characteristics:

> Knowledge of the organization, physical layout, functions, rules, and regulations of the employing institution.
> Ability to secure the confidence, respect, and cooperation of youths and exercise tact, initiative, and good judgment in dealing with them.
> Ability to anticipate disciplinary problems and to cope quickly and decisively with unexpected situations and behavior.
> Good perception, powers of observation, and mental alertness.
> Ability to report accurately on conditions noted during hours on duty.[12]

Thus youth supervisors must provide security for and direct supervision of residents, must communicate with all appropriate staff members in such a manner that the unit operates cohesively; must be integral parts of a cottage team; must become involved in the execution of the treatment plan; must serve as surrogate parents in order to effect relationship therapy with residents; must ensure that the living unit and grounds are clean and that defective or damaged equipment is replaced, repaired, or removed; and must provide miscellaneous services to the

---

[12]Youth Services Worker 2, Iowa Merit Employment Department, 1–2.

living unit and the entire institution in order to facilitate smooth overall functioning of both the unit and the institution.[13]

These many role expectations can be divided into four categories: custodian, role model, facilitator, and disciplinarian.[14] The custodial role requires that youth supervisors prevent runaways from the institution, but preventing runaways is no easy task. Juvenile facilities often have no perimeter security (i.e., fences or walls), and many confined juveniles have strong tendencies toward runaway behavior, both from home and from institutional settings. The custodian must deal with desperate youths who are ready to injure or to kill themselves. Furthermore, because sexual victimization occurs in nearly all training schools, the youth supervisor must identify potential victims and give them the protection they need against predatory peers.[15]

Youth supervisors are expected to be good role models. Many have grown up in working-class environments themselves and can often communicate more easily with delinquent youths than those social workers who have grown up in middle-class environments. Youth supervisors have the additional advantage that they can approach the youth as a "friend" rather than as a therapist, as institutionalized youths often resist the formalized therapeutic relationship. Consequently, in every institution, some youth supervisors are looked on as "significant others" by residents, and even after the residents leave the institution, they continue to correspond with and to visit these positive role models.

The youth supervisor is a key facilitator in the institution. This line staff person is responsible for maintaining good communication with those in other areas affecting the inmate's life. Residents frequently have problems in the academic area, and the youth supervisor must either mediate the conflict between the resident and the school administrators and teachers or help the resident work through resistance to the school. Also, recreational, maintenance, and medical staff personnel sometimes have problems with particular cottage residents and the youth supervisor must help resolve these conflicts before they jeopardize the treatment plans for residents. Equally important, the youth supervisor talks daily with residents and may conduct group sessions for them. The supervisor, thus, must be an ongoing source of information and insights for the cottage team about how residents are progressing in their treatment plans.

The disciplinarian role of the youth supervisor requires that he or she deal with the acting-out behavior of residents in the cottage and in other areas of the institution. As a member of the cottage team, the youth supervisor must help decide what is the most appropriate action when a resident takes pills in order to get high, tries to escape from the institution, becomes involved in a physical altercation with another resident, sexually assaults a peer, or verbally threatens or physically assaults a staff member.

---

[13]From the State of Iowa Confidential Performance Review/Evaluations of the Eldora Training School.

[14]Jack Farnum, a youth supervisor in an institution for emotionally disturbed and chronically disruptive residents, was helpful in conceptualizing these four categories.

[15]See Bartollas, Miller, and Dinitz, *Juvenile Victimization*.

PRESSURES ON THE YOUTH SUPERVISOR

Preventing acting-out behavior in the cottage, accepting the responsibilities of treatment, and avoiding personal burnout are the three main sources of pressure on youth supervisors in the emerging model of treatment.

Preventing Acting-Out Behavior

Runaways continue to be a problem in both the traditional and the emerging models of treatment. Even if a facility has fences and locked doors, these barriers usually offer little challenge to the resident who is determined to escape into the woods or the nearby streets. The hard-line mood of society requires administrators of juvenile facilities to focus on reducing the number of runaways as much as possible. To a great extent, the administrators' jobs depend upon controlling the runaway problem. In juvenile facilities across the nation, the superintendent is usually replaced when the number of runaways for the year equals the number of runaways in the last year of his or her predecessor's administration.

Administrators, not surprisingly, put pressure on youth supervisors to control the runaway problem. To minimize runaways, youth supervisors are responsible for keeping constantly alert. They must not leave keys on the desk or permit residents to bring cutters or other contraband useful for escapes into the cottage. If a resident escapes from a door left unlocked, the responsible staff member may receive several days of suspension. In cases of mass escapes, a negligent youth supervisor may be suspended for thirty days or may even be fired.

Youth supervisors are also responsible for preventing mass disturbances or riots, altercations among residents, victimization of weaker residents, and suicides. Residents sometimes riot or try to take control of the cottage, and it is up to youth supervisors to prevent this. Many residents have a history of fighting and are quick to "fly off the handle," and administrators usually look upon frequent physical altercations in the cottage as a sign of poor supervision. Many residents have commonly exploited weaker persons in the community, and youth supervisors must constantly be on guard to avoid victimization in the cottage milieu. Suicides are infrequent occurrences in training schools, but when one occurs, youth supervisors must prove that adequate supervision was provided.

Accepting the Responsibility of Treatment

The treatment orientation of the new model places pressure on each youth supervisor at several points. First, youth supervisors who want to be effective treatment agents are sometimes held back by the indifference and low morale of fellow youth supervisors. Those supervisors with negative attitudes may have worked under the traditional model or simply may have little interest in treatment. Second, the union to which the youth supervisors belong may challenge the acceptability of treatment responsibilities, questioning the inequity of custodial staff doing the same jobs as professional treatment staff members and yet making much lower salaries. Third, youth supervisors may question the viability of treatment within an institutional context or may challenge the way treatment is conducted in a cottage milieu. For example, reality therapy may make sense to them as a treatment method for delinquent boys, but they may feel strongly that the treatment modality used in the cottage has little application to the present or future behavior of residents. One youth supervisor was feeling such pressure when he said, "You don't last if you don't fit in with what the social worker wants to do."[16] Fourth, keeping the twin responsibilities of treatment and security in balance is not always easy. Youth supervisors may question the assignment of certain youths to an off-campus program because runaways from the institution will result in pressures on them.

Avoiding Personal Burnout

Youth supervisors are constantly on the firing line of institutional life. They must deal directly with the acting-out behavior of residents. They may have disagreements or ongoing conflicts with the cottage social worker. They are expected to commit themselves to the constant demands of providing a therapeutic relationship in the cottage. In addition, they may have conflicts with fellow youth supervisors over treatment or over custodial matters in the cottage. They may feel alienated from the administration or may feel they are receiving little support from it. Consequently, burnout, or job fatigue, is not surprising as an ongoing problem with these line staff members. Burnout may cause a youth supervisor to withdraw emotionally or even to quit the job. One youth supervisor tells how he avoids burnout, "You develop support systems with others to survive. You also avoid burnout by developing space for yourself. If you don't have this space for yourself, the kids will never leave you alone."[17]

ADULT INSTITUTIONS: THE CORRECTIONAL COUNSELOR

In adult correctional institutions, the correctional counselor remains the primary treatment agent. The correctional counselor, who must serve the functions of the social worker, sociologist, and psychologist in the prison setting, plays one of the most difficult treatment roles in corrections. As college-educated individuals were brought into the prison during the late 1960s and early 1970s, correctional counselors generally agreed that they would function as: (1) a change agent who is involved with opening up a closed and coercive system; (2) a resource developer who provides the link between community and institutional services; (3) a therapist who helps

---

[16]Interviewed in March 1981.
[17]Interviewed in September 1982.

inmates relate successfully to the community; and (4) an advocate who ensures to the greatest possible extent that prisoners are not deprived of their rights.[18] Because the counselor's role was developed during the rise of reintegration philosophy in corrections, the lessening acceptance of this model, especially in maximum-security institutions, has meant that counselors have been forced to redefine their roles.

The Role Expectations for the Correctional Counselor

Although the role expectations for correctional counselors vary from state to state and even within states depending upon the security level of the institution, the 1975 National Manpower Survey of the Criminal Justice System found that the counselor in adult correctional institutions performs the following basic tasks:

Interviews clients and administers tests to identify and classify client's skills, abilities, and interests.

Establishes a periodic verbal or personal contact schedule with clients and interviews clients on conformance to conditions of incarceration.

Establishes and posts case files and evaluates information to determine client's progress and needs.

Receives and takes action on complaints against clients.

Negotiates and develops individual treatment program for corrections client and assists client in implementing the program.

Advises and counsels clients, individually or in groups, concerning conditions of incarceration, employment, housing, education, community services, and management of personal affairs to establish realistic and socially acceptable behavior patterns.

Advises and counsels client's family, or complainants, on problems in dealing with clients.

Prepares recommendations, reports, and dispositional plans on clients for court, parole board, or classification board.

Testifies at judicial proceedings, parole boards, or committees as expert witness to evaluate client progress, and assists in decision making.

Establishes and develops contact with potential employers of clients.

Contacts and consults with community agencies, individuals, and commercial firms to evaluate and establish resources for client treatment and assistance.

Promotes and explains correctional programs to improve public understanding and support of programs.

Coordinates use of citizen volunteers in correctional activities.

Attends meetings, hearings, and legal proceedings to gather and exchange information and provide input to decisions regarding clients.

Coordinates information and plans concerning clients among law enforcement/criminal justice agencies, client's family, community agencies, and commercial firms.[19]

[18]Allen E. Ivey, "Adapting Systems to People," *Personnel and Guidance Journal* 53 (October 1974):37–38.

[19]National Institute of Law Enforcement and Criminal Justice, *National Manpower Survey of the Criminal Justice System,* vol. 3, *Corrections* (Washington, D.C.: GPO, 1978), p. 78.

Role variations in adult correctional institutions. In the minimum-security prison, the counselor is usually committed to reintegration philosophy, as his or her mission is to get the offender back into the community. Thus, a great deal of the counselor's time involves processing home furloughs or work release applications, making family contacts and arranging emergency visits when necessary, helping make parole arrangements, coordinating the regular trips that residents make into town, approving outside phone calls, and seeking information from the community that inmates need for successful reentry into society. Counselors in minimum-security facilities usually feel secure in their jobs and fairly satisfied with them. They also tend to have better relationships with both inmates and guards than do counselors in medium- and maximum-security prisons.

In contrast, the counselor in a maximum-security prison generally finds it overwhelming to be part of a Big House prison that is full of violence, fear, and oppression. The counselor, who is essentially reduced to a paper pusher, finds the job of keeping up with the paperwork necessary to process the vast numbers of inmates on his or her caseload a staggering undertaking. Custody is clearly the primary organizational goal in such an environment, and counselors typically are made to feel like outsiders. Relationships with inmates are frequently impersonal or conflict-oriented. Not surprisingly, poor job morale and rapid turnover are inevitable responses to the counselor's role in these megaprisons.

In the intermediate situation of a medium-security prison, the counselor works with custodial restrictions, but usually is spared the atmosphere of violence, fear, and oppression of a maximum-security prison. At least part of the counselor's time is spent on reintegrative functions, such as arranging transfers to minimum-security prisons and preparing inmates to return to the community. Much of the remainder of the counselor's time is spent in delivering services to inmates on his or her caseload and in doing the paperwork necessary to process inmates through the institution. Casework duties range from providing crisis counseling to helping inmates prepare civil suits for the federal courts. In some medium-security institutions, counselors have developed a cohesive group culture, are often satisfied with their jobs, and may even plan to pursue a lifetime career in corrections.[20]

Pressures on the Correctional Counselor

The pressures on counselors, of course, vary in minimum-, medium-, and maximum-security prisons. Many counselors, however, especially those in maximum-security institutions, face the pressures of working in a violent and punishment-oriented setting, of experiencing impersonal and mostly unsatisfying relationships with prisoners, and of receiving little support and cooperation from security staff.

Institutional violence. Like other line staff members in maximum-security prisons, counselors must deal with the stresses of working in a violent atmosphere.

---

[20]Refer to Bartollas, Miller, and Wice, *Participants in American Criminal Justice,* pp. 263–281 for a more extensive discussion of the duties of correctional counselors.

Rapes and stabbings frequently occur. Although inmates are unlikely to attack professional staff, counselors who have their offices in the cellhouses or spend most of their work time in the cellhouses feel vulnerable. A female counselor describes a riot that occurred at the Pontiac Correctional Center (Illinois) in 1978:

> I was scheduled to be in the cellhouse when the riot broke out, but I had some other duties to take care of down front. If I had been in the cellhouse, I would have been injured or killed like the other three were [two male correctional officers were killed and a female correctional officer was stabbed repeatedly].[21]

Lack of satisfying relationships with clients.   Counselors usually find relationships with clients unsatisfying for several reasons. First, counselors must try to deal with unmanageably large caseloads—up to one hundred or more on the average. The sheer volume of paperwork required to process inmates through the institution makes it nearly impossible for the counselor to deal with inmates on a meaningful level.

Second, inmates frequently distrust the counselor. They know that there is considerable risk in confiding in their counselor. A prisoner who tells his or her counselor that he smoked a joint last night is likely to find that the counselor has informed security staff about the incident. Inmates also tend to resent the power counselors have over them. Yet, because inmates do need their counselor's assistance in obtaining transfer to a minimum-security facility, in processing a home furlough or work release application, or in gaining permission to call home, they usually try to con their counselors.

Third, counselors have few success stories even about those inmates willing to develop meaningful relationships with them. A female counselor in a maximum-security institution was particularly pleased with the progress one inmate on her caseload was making. She recounted his progress to a visiting newspaper reporter, who then decided to write a feature story about the prisoner. Not long after that, it was discovered that the inmate was operating one of the largest drug rings in the institution. Afterwards the counselor said, "All we do is work with failures. I'm getting fed up with it."[22]

Lack of support from security staff.   Correctional counselors in adult prisons are hindered in delivering treatment services because they do not have the support that social workers do in the emerging treatment model in juvenile corrections. Although there have been efforts from time to time to bring correctional officers into the treatment process, the danger of the prison environment has made the contemporary correctional officer much more interested in personal survival than in the treatment of prisoners.[23] Robert Johnson and Susan Price propose that some

---

[21]Interviewed in October 1981.

[22]Interviewed in September 1981.

[23]See Norman Fenton, *An Introduction to Group Counseling in State Correctional Service* (New York: American Correctional Association, 1958); and R. R. Carkhuff, *Helping and Human Relations,* vol. 1, *Selection and Training,* and vol. 2, *Practice and Research* (New York: Holt, Rinehart, and Winston, 1969).

correctional officers be trained to become human service officers. Their particular role would be to shepherd inmates through periods of serious and potentially disabling stress.[24] Unquestionably, the involvement of the correctional officer in the treatment process would ease the pressure on the counselor to provide all treatment services.

Correctional officers, especially in maximum-security prisons, often question the value of the counselor's role. They tend to look upon counselors as outsiders who interfere with the prison operation, and their negative feelings often lead to open conflict with counselors. Counselors' lack of authority and informal power makes it difficult for them to deal with recalcitrant correctional officers. Counselors frequently find themselves in the predicament of being able only to make inquiries of or recommendations to those in custodial positions. For example, if an inmate has no sheets, the counselor cannot order the appropriate correctional officer to distribute them.

A CAREER IN CORRECTIONAL TREATMENT

Job possibilities, strategies for finding a job, and strategies for maintaining a meaningful career are important concerns for the individual considering a career in correctional treatment.

Job Possibilities

In community-based and institutional corrections, persons may become involved in correctional treatment in the following positions:

Juvenile police officer
Juvenile and adult probation officer
Juvenile and adult parole officer
Social worker or counselor in a residential facility for probationers or parolees
Social worker in a youth shelter
Residential counselor in a drug abuse diversion program
Counselor in a youth service bureau
Social worker with abused and neglected youth in a department of social service
Alternative teacher in a public school system
Staff member in a prevention program
Social worker or counselor in a training school or adult prison
Staff member in a work release or prerelease program
Counselor in a detention facility or jail
Social worker or psychologist in a diagnostic center

[24]Robert Johnson and Susan Price, "The Complete Correctional Officer—Human Service and Human Environment of Prison," *Criminal Justice and Behavior* 8 (1981):343–373.

Strategies for Finding a Job

How does one find a job in a tight job market? These suggestions can be helpful:

1. Be certain to have the necessary educational credentials and job experience for the position which interests you. Most correctional treatment positions require a B.A. degree, with a major in criminal justice, sociology, social work, or psychology.
2. Attain some work experience in the juvenile or adult justice system before graduation. If you have not worked in the justice system, it would probably be wise to seek opportunities to do volunteer work, either during the school year or during summer vacation. The more prior experience a student has with the juvenile or criminal justice system, the easier it will be to find a job.
3. Prepare a good job résumé. It may be helpful to have an instructor look at it before you begin to mail it out.
4. Develop contacts in the particular area of the justice system which interests you. An instructor may be helpful in recommending persons and agencies to write.
5. Be flexible and mobile. You may find it necessary to move to a different part of the nation for a desired job. You also may find it necessary to take a position not involved in treatment to gain the experience that will enable you to land the job you want when it becomes available.

Strategies for Maintaining a Meaningful Correctional Career

Most people want to find jobs that are challenging and meaningful. Jobs in corrections may offer these characteristics, but those interested in such work should be realistic about the personal demands they will face. Because of such demands, the following attitudes and strategies are recommended for those pursuing a career in corrections:

1. Be realistic about what can and cannot be achieved in the job. Unrealistic expectations set a person up for disappointment and disillusionment.
2. Make a constant effort to create ongoing learning experiences for yourself. This can be done by participating in training opportunities as they arise, reading helpful books in the field, and gaining new skills.
3. Participate in local, statewide, and national associations. Involvement with others doing similar jobs can give a fresh and renewed perspective.
4. Do not underestimate what you can contribute to offenders. They are never easy to deal with, but over a lifetime, an effective treatment agent will have significant impact on the lives of many offenders.
5. Be as certain as possible that the promotions you accept will be constructive ones. The person who is not interested in administration may find that the few extra dollars each week do not make up for the frustrations of the new position or for the absence of contact with clients.

In short, careers in juvenile and adult corrections offer many opportunities for students of the social sciences to work at a professional level.

SUMMARY

This chapter has discussed the role expectations, pressures, and treatment respon-sibilities of the social worker and the youth supervisor in juvenile institutions and of the correctional counselor in adult prisons. A traditional model that subordinates treatment to custody and an emerging model that combines treatment and custody are both currently found in juvenile correctional institutions. In the emerging model, which attempts to resolve the dichotomy between the aims of custody and treatment by synthesizing them, the cottage team is the cement that holds the treatment concept together. The social worker becomes the cottage director and supervises both treat-ment and custodial staff members. Youth supervisors are required to be an integral part of the treatment team as well as to provide custodial care for residents. The traditional model seems to result in open conflict between the custodially oriented youth supervisor and the treatment-oriented social worker. Since the dominant organizational goal is security, youth supervisors typically resist treatment respon-sibilities in the traditional model. Social workers also feel demoralized by their lack of formal authority and informal power in the traditional model.

Youth supervisors, whose position was developed from the role of the cottage parent, have strong impact on residents in the emerging model of treatment in juvenile correctional facilities. Residents commonly turn to the concerned youth supervisor when they have serious problems. The perceptive youth supervisor is often responsible for protecting potential victims against sexual predators and for preventing despairing youths from hurting themselves. Social workers and other treatment personnel also count on youth supervisors to persuade residents to accept their interventions.

In adult institutions, correctional counselors are usually looked on as outsiders, but their roles still differ dramatically in minimum-, medium-, and maximum-security institutions. The counselor in the minimum-security prison is usually com-mitted to reintegration philosophy, as his or her goal is to get the offender back into the community. The services he or she provides range from finding out whether an inmate is eligible for a work release or a home furlough program to processing the necessary paperwork for a prisoner's release to the community. Counselors in minimum-security prisons commonly feel overwhelmed in these violent and over-crowded facilities. They are reminded daily of their marginal status in these Big House prisons and spend much of their time in shuffling papers. Not surprisingly, the counselors respond to their jobs in these facilities with poor morale and rapid job turnover. Counselors in medium-security facilities divide their time among reintegrative functions, casework responsibilities, and the paperwork required to process prisoners through the institution. While counselors in medium-security facilities may not be as satisfied with their jobs as those in minimum-security institutions are, they are far more content than those in maximum-security prisons.

Correctional counselors in adult prisons are hindered in delivering treatment services because they do not have the support from security staff that social workers in the emerging treatment model in juvenile corrections do. Indeed, correctional counselors are often in open conflict with custodial staff. Yet, correctional counselors have had an impact upon the prison environment because their presence in prisons as a symbol of the college-educated civilian has contributed to a reduction of some of the flagrant abuses of the past. They literally have become "watchdogs against brutality."[25] The counselor's presence, then, has meant decreased brutality against prisoners, especially in maximum-security prisons. The counselors have also provided hope for those prisoners who are seeking growth and change in their lives.

DISCUSSION QUESTIONS

1. How do the traditional and emerging models of treatment in juvenile facilities differ? What importance does this have for the future of treatment given in these settings?
2. Why are formal authority and informal power important to the social worker?
3. Why are youth supervisors more committed to the treatment process in the emerging model than in the traditional model?
4. Why are youth supervisors often more effective treatment agents than social workers?
5. What are the basic role expectations of the correctional counselor? How does the counselor role differ in minimum-, medium-, and maximum-security institutions?
6. Why are counselors in medium- and minimum-security institutions usually more satisfied with their jobs than those in maximum-security prisons?
7. What are the attributes of effective treatment agents in correctional institutions? Is it more difficult to be an effective treatment agent in a juvenile or an adult correctional institution? Why?

[25]James B. Jacobs, "Notes on Policy and Practice," *Social Service Review* 50 (March 1976):138–147.

13

Correctional Environments and Receptivity Toward Treatment

Objectives

1. To examine the problems that John Conrad sees with individual and group psychotherapy in prison.

2. To present Conrad's viewpoints concerning some key questions about correctional treatment.

3. To define the quality of life necessary for treatment to take place in correctional environments.

4. To examine the responses that offenders make to correctional environments.

The context in which a program takes place greatly influences the impact of correctional treatment. It is unrealistic to believe effective programs can occur in violent and inhumane correctional facilities, because these settings force offenders to be preoccupied with daily survival. It is equally unrealistic to believe effective treatment can take place when offenders are treated as slaves who left all their rights behind when they entered the prison gates. Depriving inmates of their constitutional rights only generates rancor and bitterness toward those who supervise them. In addition, it is unrealistic to expect that many offenders will respond in a positive way to treatment they must undergo as a condition of their releases. In other words, the quality of life within correctional environments very much affects the receptivity offenders have toward treatment. Offenders, not surprisingly, are much more receptive to treatment in humane environments than they are to treatment in settings that breed despair.

This chapter examines the environments of correctional institutions because they are typically more inhumane, more violent, and more criminogenic than the environments of community-based programs. However, while environments in community-based programs may be more compatible with treatment, they still have debilitating features. They frequently are located in undesirable neighborhoods and surrounded by bars and pawn shops. Prostitution and drugs are commonly available within sight of the facility. Residents often live in cramped quarters and have little space to call their own. Due process rights of offenders, especially in diversionary programs, may be ignored. Finally, idleness is sometimes a problem during these economically tough times because residents have difficulty finding jobs and, therefore, may sit around all day with even fewer programs offered than are available to inmates in federal and state correctional institutions.

The offender, the recipient of treatment, is the focus of this chapter and the next. The specific ingredients needed to make the correctional environment more compatible with treatment are examined in this chapter. Chapter 14 extends the discussion by giving the reasons why offenders succeed and fail and the types of programs that are needed for specific offenders.

This chapter begins with an interview with John P. Conrad, noted corrections author and researcher, who provides a historical review of the decline of rehabilitative philosophy, analyzes its shortcomings, and describes the environments needed for correctional treatment to take place. Following Conrad's interview, this chapter explains the necessary elements of humane correctional environments and examines why the setting is such an important factor in determining the receptivity of offenders to correctional treatment.

Box 13-1 Interview with John P. Conrad

QUESTION: When you went into correctional service, what was your attitude toward treatment? Did it change?

CONRAD: You ask me to reconstruct the optimism of simpler times. I started out in corrections in 1946, when America was a nation of victors. We had just won the war, the Depression was over, crime rates were not a prime national concern, and there was a general conviction that all problems could be solved by the application of science. It was the prevailing belief that psychiatry was the science that applied to the problem of criminal offenders. Guided by psychiatrists, preferably those with a psychoanalytic orientation, psychologists and psychiatric social workers would apply their treatment disciplines to offenders. Obviously, we all had much to learn; we knew that most psychiatrists were dubious about the prospect of successfully treating psychopaths. The doubts of the establishment were only to be expected by those who worked on the frontiers of science. We were sure that experimentation and the further development of theory would result in a firmly based discipline of correctional treatment.

None of us had much luck with individual psychotherapy with offenders. We all became interested in group therapy; we thought that in group situations our clients would see their own behavior patterns reflected by men with similar personalities and problems. I think that group treatment helped some people, but the longer I stayed with it, the more uneasy I became. We weren't doing any harm, but I couldn't convince myself that we were not just wasting our time. Two events led me to the conclusion that our prospects for success were less rosy than we had expected.

During my years at San Quentin, I had conducted several therapy groups. One of the best group members I had had, a real star in the interactions that I had tried to stimulate, was a young Portuguese-American burglar named Angelo. I was sure that he was getting real help from the group; after a meeting of that group I was often euphoric about the success of my technique. Well, three or four years after I had been promoted out of San Quentin, I met him by accident one winter evening in Fresno. He had been paroled a few months before, and he was making it, just barely, on odd jobs and hustling. He lived in a single men's hotel that was a half-step better than a skid-row flophouse. The weather was cold and rainy; agricultural labor was not in demand. He had no clothes suitable for outdoor work and no money with which to buy any. He had some experience as a rough carpenter, but there were no steady jobs to be had—maybe he could get on to a payroll in the spring. He was discouraged, but he insisted that he could make it. A few weeks later I heard that he had been killed in an automobile accident.

Maybe I helped him a little in that group at San Quentin, but I could not drive from my mind the reflection that what I could offer as a therapist, even if it had been much more than I thought it was, was trivial when set against the immense obstacles that confronted Angelo. He faced unemployment, lack of money, lack of prospects, and an environment populated by men who were as bad off as he or worse. I wondered how long I—or any of my friends, all of us immeasurably better equipped to emerge from adversity—could have survived on Fresno's skid row that winter. Not much longer, I thought.

The second incident took place in London, some years later, when I was a participant in a panel discussion on correctional treatment offered under the auspices of the Institute for the Study and Treatment of Delinquency. I shared the platform with a psychiatric social worker from the women's prison at Holloway. After our presentations, there was a lively question-and-answer period from an earnest and sympathetic audience. Someone asked the psychiatric social worker if she thought that criminals could be successfully treated in psychotherapy. She replied that, although she had once thought this was possible, she had had to conclude that it really wasn't. Patients who succeeded in psychotherapy were people who felt so bad that they turned to professional help in the hope that they could feel better. Most of the criminals she knew didn't feel at all bad. They usually felt that most of their problems could be solved if they could be let out of prison, if they could have some money, or if they could just have a chance to punch someone in the nose. I had to agree that her observation was consistent with my experience with American criminals. The evening ended on a downbeat.

It takes more than two such experiences to change an attitude, but the accumulation of similar experiences and observations has led me to a much different view of correctional treatment than the one I brought into correctional service. I now see treatment as one of the many opportunities that should be available to those convicted of crime, whether they are to be "corrected" in the community or in prison. Some offenders can use this kind of help when they feel bad enough to seek it. It can't be administered successfully when it is compulsory.

QUESTION: What contributed to the decline of the rehabilitation model?

CONRAD: Intellectual honesty. As the years went on, a lot of people like myself concluded that there really wasn't a rehabilitation model, that public statements to the effect that the object of corrections was rehabilitation simply couldn't hold water. We watched men and women appear before parole boards, reciting the changes that they thought they had made in their attitudes and behavior as a result of rehabilitation programs. It was clear that at best some were offering wishful thought, but in most cases it was a necessary charade which nobody present believed. One of my ruthless friends said that the rehabilitation ideal was nothing more than a convenient way for correctional personnel to feel better about the dirty work they were doing. Nobody, he said, could be proud of a career that consisted of locking people into cages, but anyone who could persuade himself and others that he was really rehabilitating these miserable wretches could then think of himself as a benefactor of suffering humanity.

I am not as cynical as my friend; I still think I've been helpful to some pris-

oners. On the whole, however, I fear that he's more nearly right than wrong. A lot of folks think that the decline you mention started with the articles and speeches of the late Bob Martinson and the book he wrote in collaboration with Douglas Lipton and Judith Wilks.[1] I don't agree. Three years before that book appeared, I wrote that faith in rehabilitation had all but disappeared by 1970.[2] What was killing it was not the statistics of recidivism but the lack of clear-cut successes on which a rehabilitative model—or models—could be projected. Our claims had worn too thin to be made any longer.

QUESTION: What is the proper role of treatment in correctional institutions? In community-based corrections?

CONRAD: To begin with, I think that correctional institutions should simulate so far as possible the conditions of the real world. That means, if a prisoner wants to go to school after work or learn a trade, those opportunities should be open to him. If he thinks he needs counseling—as everyone does from time to time—there should be competent counselors to whom he can turn. But if he doesn't want any of these things, that should be his business. He's got his own life to live, and if he expects that he'll go back to crime, there isn't any specific prison program—outside of continued incarceration—that will stop him. What I would hope for in the prison of the future is an environment in which it would be considered odd not to be doing something to improve oneself. There should be a demand from prisoners for a greater diversity of educational, vocational, and other treatment programs.

If I were running a correctional system, I would insist that every prisoner had to work, and those who would not would find that there were serious disadvantages to their choice of idleness: no pay, cells on the fifth tier, and a program of institutionalized ennui. The idle pris-

[1]Douglas Lipton, Robert Martinson, and Judith Wilks, *The Effectiveness of Correctional Treatment* (New York: Praeger, 1974).

[2]John P. Conrad, "Corrections and Simple Justice," *Journal of Criminal Law and Criminology* 64 (1973): 208–217.

oner would not be allowed to doze on the bunk. Working prisoners would get a reasonable wage, and in addition they would get good time for every full work week. When not working or when in isolation or segregation, they would get nothing. Productive work *is* treatment, and I would insist on it. The great obstacle, of course, is the difficulty of creating a full-employment industry in prison. It can be done, as we can see in the federal prisons, but it takes more determination than we see in most state correctional departments.

As for community-based corrections, that activity takes place in the real world. There isn't any role at all for treatment by the correctional staff. There's no conceivable reason why correctional clients should have an independent set of treatment resources in the community. The correctional agency has a responsibility to open the doors so that probationers and parolees can have the benefit of all the kinds of community services available. Any effort by a correctional agency to set up parallel services will assure that its clients will not have access to the better services available to the general public.

That is not to say that devices like halfway houses, probation hostels, work-release programs, study-release programs, and so forth should not be encouraged. They should not be referred to as "treatment," because that is not what they are. They facilitate treatment in the community, and they should be managed accordingly.

QUESTION: Should recidivism be the only yardstick used to evaluate correctional treatment?

CONRAD: No, I'm surprised you ask. I've said it before, and I'll say it again: This obsession with recidivism is largely attributable to the ease of counting raps on a rapsheet—and to the difficulty of measuring success.[3]

The problem that an evaluator of anything has before he starts his evaluation is to settle on the criterion by which

the usefulness of a program can be measured. I know you don't want me to go on and on about correctional evaluation, but what I want to emphasize is the lesson that any evaluation should impart. We should learn from any evaluation how the program evaluated can be improved. If it's hopeless, and some of them are in our field, we should know *why* it's not worth saving, and perhaps what should be put in its place. But most programs aren't really hopeless—they're just not for everybody.

The kinds of questions we need to have answered by an evaluation begin with the number of people who complete the program, who they are, and what happens to them after they've completed it. Who are the people who drop out—why do they drop out, what happens to them after dropping out? Can we generalize about the dropouts so that others like them can be channeled to other programs? These are the answers that will enable the administrator to decide whether the program is useful enough to continue or whether it needs modification. You won't learn much about any program by counting the enrollees who branch into a box labeled "Recidivism."

QUESTION: What is the most important question to be dealt with in terms of correctional treatment?

CONRAD: The absolutely transcendent question is this: How can the correctional administrator normalize prison life to the greatest extent possible?

We ought to be preoccupied with the immense difficulties in arriving at the numerous changes that have to be made in the way we manage prisons so that prison life is as normal as possible. Both prisons and community-based corrections require by definition a lot of restrictions of choice and autonomy. We have to reduce these restrictions to the absolute minimum necessary, and I claim that we have hardly started to think about how this might be done.

[3]John P. Conrad, "A Lost Ideal, A New Hope: The Way to Effective Correctional Treatment," *Journal of Criminal Law and Criminology* 72 (1981): 1699–1734.

I look for a prison system that offers a fairly wide range of work opportunities to prisoners, with reasonable pay, an assortment of interesting and competently taught school programs, and optional but helpful psychological services. The question that leads to this kind of answer is the question I just stated: How can prison life be normalized? There are those who say that normalization is impossible. It certainly can't be done without making the effort and without a belief that some freedom of choice, some autonomy, can be allowed.

QUESTION: What kinds of programs are most conducive to the self-improvement of prisoners?

CONRAD: The easy answer is the answer that applies to all of us. Any program that enables a person to do something he has not previously been able to do is conducive to self-improvement. That's usually some kind of educational program, and it may well be that the enabling feature of the program is more important than what the program is intended to enable. I suspect that one of the great attractions to weight lifting that keeps so many prisoners grunting and sweating out in the yard is that a man can see himself doing something today that he couldn't do a month ago. It makes him feel good about himself. The same goes for reading, writing, and arithmetic—or learning a foreign language or the basics of accounting.

QUESTION: What appear to be the ingredients of the most effective programs?

CONRAD: I am sure that the personality of the person who administers the program is even more important than his technical competence. A teacher who can convey to the prisoner that he wants him to succeed, that he *can* succeed, and that the effort will be really worthwhile will make the critical difference in the program.

QUESTION: What appear to be the characteristics of those correctional clients who benefit most from treatment?

CONRAD: The short and easy answer is that those clients who want treatment will benefit the most. For conventional therapies this will include the men and women with some ego strength, confidence in the idea of therapy, and the will to persist in it in spite of the emotional turmoil it requires. That excludes most of the people who come to prison and, I think, most of those who are assigned to community correctional programs. It also assumes that treatment programs are mainly some form of psychotherapy. I think I have indicated already as clearly as I can the minimal relevance of psychotherapeutic approaches to the correctional client.

I argue that for most of these people an active program of work and education, probably emphasizing the work, is the most helpful framework for treatment—nothing new in the concept, but a great lack in the application. What we have to learn how to do is to create an environment in which this framework can dominate the correctional process. At present we waste a lot of money going through elaborate diagnostic processes aimed at deciding what kind of therapy, if any, should be offered to our clients. For those who seem to be psychotic or verging on psychosis, I want to know as much as I can about their mental conditions. But for the vast majority of offenders, there's nothing wrong that the therapist can mend. We should be investing money and ingenuity in devising effective correctional and work activities and organizing the correctional process around them. Once we do that, I think we will find a lot more clients will benefit from realistic treatment than we had ever before thought possible.

I want to conclude with a few words about the desperate conditions of corrections today. We have been chatting about correctional treatment in this interview as though such a thing were really possible in the prevailing conditions in prisons and youth facilities and community-based corrections. Various opportunities have come my way during the last ten years to see a lot of correctional institutions and agencies all over the country. I think the one generalization that comes to my mind as I think back over what I have seen is that correctional treatment in these times is virtually an impossibility. I am sure that some readers are going to get out their red pencils and make a marginal note that they know of a *very* effective program right in their own neighborhood, and maybe they are right. But in most correctional institutions today the problem for both staff and inmates is survival. Overcrowding, unmanageable caseloads, understaffing, undertraining, administrative preoccupation with bottom lines and system outputs all combine to leave no time, energy, resources, or interest in serious attempts to do treatment.

There are two deadly consequences to this state of affairs. The first is that the perceived dangers of the institution and the perceived impossibility of community-based programs dominate planning and day-to-day routines. The dangers may not be as great as perceived; after all the homicide rates in prison are still generally less than the homicide rates in the neighborhoods from which the convicts came. But people act on their perceptions of reality, however inaccurate, rather than the realities themselves. Right now a prison is either a dangerous place to work or a lousy place to work, and usually both. Prisons have to be organized to achieve the basic requirements of lawfulness, safety, industriousness, and hopefulness. If this field had leadership capable of keeping its mind on these obligations,

correctional treatment might be possible.

The second deadly consequence of the desperate state of contemporary corrections is that prisons produce hopeless men and women who are dangerous because they have no alternatives to crime. A lot of visionaries insist that with a moratorium on prison construction, alternatives to incarceration will spring into being, and soon we will have most offenders constructively engaged in the wholesome activities of restoration, community service, depth counseling, vocational rehabilitation, and so on. I do not foresee any such outcome of the miserable problem of punishing offenders. Instead I see more and more people being jammed into the same old prisons and left with no alternative to crime if they ever get out alive. There are plenty of pound-foolish legislators and administrators who are ready to take such advice as "nothing works" and "don't build" and not nearly enough people trying to make sense out of an increasingly foul condition in American corrections.

In short, there is no reasonable alternative to correctional treatment. Although the horror of our seemingly unsafe prisons is no place for treatment to take place, we are also faced with the horror of what desperate men and women will do in the streets once they are released from prison.

John P. Conrad is presently a Fellow at the National Institute of Justice, Washington, D.C. He was codirector of the Dangerous Offender Project of the Academy for Contemporary Problems. Conrad has written many books and numerous papers, and, as a career criminologist, he spent twenty years in administration in the California Department of Corrections.
Source: Interview conducted in May 1982. Used with permission.

ELEMENTS OF HUMANE
CORRECTIONAL ENVIRONMENTS

In assessing the role of treatment in corrections, Conrad stresses that treatment is possible only in humane correctional environments that simulate as much as possible the conditions of the real world. He adds that this simulation of the conditions of the real world can be accomplished only when correctional environments are lawful, safe, industrious, and hopeful.[4]

The Lawful Correctional Environment

The purpose of the lawful correctional environment is to prevent proscribed actions and conduct and to provide offenders with all the rights granted by case law. Unlawful behavior is much more difficult to prevent in correctional institutions than in community-based facilities. Violations within the prison must be punished appropriately under conditions in which due process procedures prevail. If administrators tolerate unlawful conduct by staff or prisoners, such as the existence of predatory gangs, freely flowing drugs, thriving rackets, or prostitution rings, nothing else that it attempts will succeed. In too many prisons, the turf belongs to the inmates, and staff have lost control over the prison.[5]

The goal of a lawful prison was easier to achieve in the past. Autocratic wardens were endowed with unlimited powers and authority over all persons in their fiefdoms—guards and prisoners. These autocratic wardens refused to accept either staff or inmate resistance; prisoners, like slaves, were denied nearly every human right beyond mere survival. Wardens mixed terror, incentives, and favoritism in order to keep their subjects "fearful but not desperate, hopeful but always uncertain." Correctional officers were subject to the absolute power of the warden and dependent on his favor for security and promotion.[6]

The post–World War II centralization of power in state prison system bureaucracies reduced the position of the warden to that of a field manager and forced him to be accountable to a director of corrections in the state capital and, through the director, to the governor and the legislature. Although positive changes have resulted from this shift in authority, there have also been negative consequences. Violence has increased, contraband comes in freely, and correctional administrators often feel impotent to do anything about it. In the old days, prison administrators used unlawful means to achieve control.

Today, the courts will no longer allow the use of unlawful means to control

[4]For more on these elements of humane confinement, refer to John P. Conrad and Simon Dinitz, "The State's Strongest Medicine," in *Justice and Consequences,* ed. John P. Conrad (Lexington, Mass.: Heath, 1981), pp. 51–70. Refer to R. Moos and E. Wenk, "Social Climates in Prison: An Attempt to Conceptualize and Measure Environmental Factors in Total Institutions," *Journal of Research in Crime and Delinquency* 9 (1972): 134–138, for another method for measuring the quality of correctional environments.

[5]Simon Dinitz, "Are Safe and Humane Prisons Possible?" *Australia and New Zealand Journal of Criminology* 14 (March 1981): 11.

[6]John Conrad and Simon Dinitz, "Position Paper for the Seminar on the Isolated Prisoner" (Paper presented at the Academy for Contemporary Problems, National Institute of Corrections, Columbus, Ohio, 8–9 December 1977), pp. 4–11.

the prison. No longer can inmates be given corporal punishment, thrown in a dark cell and fed a starvation diet for days on end, denied adequate medical care, or chained in their cells. In 1977, the American Bar Criminal Justice Section published its recommended standards on the legal status of prisoners; the foundation of these standards is this general principle:

> . . . [P]risoners retain all the rights of free citizens except those on which restriction is necessary to assure their orderly confinement or to provide reasonable protection for the rights and physical safety of all members of the prison community.

The rights of offenders.   Correctional law—the accumulated body of constitutional case law; federal, state, and local regulatory law; and standards and legal opinions—defines what rights prisoners have during confinement. The rights of offenders have been litigated and upheld concerning the following areas: conditions of confinement, First Amendment religious rights, mail and access to the media, due process in prison, and rights of access to the courts.[7] Correctional law has evolved through three stages: the "Hands Off" doctrine phase (1789–1966), the "Involved Hands" doctrine phase (1966–1976), and the "Restrained Hands" doctrine phase (1976–Present.)[8] Box 13-2 shows the progression of correctional law.

Box 13-2   *Stages of Correctional Law*

HANDS-OFF DOCTRINE PHASE

The inmate has been a slave of the state for most of the history of corrections in the United States. The 1871 case Ruffin v. the Commonwealth of Virginia expressed it this way:

> [The prisoner] has, as a consequence of his crime, not only forfeited his liberty, but all his personal rights except those which the law in its humanity accords to him. He is for the time being the slave of the state.[9]

Up until the mid-1960s, the courts maintained a hands-off doctrine for at least three reasons: (1) Judges wished to maintain the separation of powers because they felt that the administration of prisons is an executive function; (2) judges acknowl-

---

[7]The outline for these areas is taken from David Fogel, "*. . . We Are the Living Proof": The Justice Model for Corrections* (Cincinnati: Anderson, 1975), pp. 128–168.

[8]William G. Archambeault and Betty J. Archambeault, *Correctional Supervisory Management: Principles of Organization, Policy, and Law* (Englewood Cliffs, N.J.: Prentice-Hall 1982), p. 196.

[9]62 Va (21 Gratt.) 790, 796 (1971).

[10]John W. Palmer, *Constitutional Rights of Prisoners,* 2d ed. (Cincinnati: Anderson, 1977), p. 174.

edged their lack of expertise in penology; and (3) judges feared judicial intervention would subvert prison discipline.[10]

INVOLVED-HANDS DOCTRINE PHASE

From 1966 to 1976, judges did a 180-degree reversal from the previous era and became extensively involved in ruling on offenders' rights within correctional institutions.[11] The U.S. Supreme Court ruled in the Coleman v. Peyton and the Johnson v. Avery cases that access to the courts is a fundamental right which may not be "denied or obstructed" by correctional officials.[12]

These decisions, as well as many later ones, were significant for at least three reasons: (1) They clearly demonstrated that the offender was no longer viewed as a slave of the state; (2) they opened a floodgate of offender litigation as more than twenty thousand petitions came to be filed in federal and state courts each year; and (3) they gave offenders newly gained rights to physical security and the minimum conditions necessary to sustain life, the right to receive their constitutionally guaranteed safeguards, the right to challenge the legality of their convictions through the courts, and the right to receive the benefit of reasonable standards and procedural safeguards.[13]

The balance-of-interest doctrine, a new legal standard that the courts imposed on correctional decision making during the involved stage, required correctional administrators to justify decisions by taking into account both offenders' rights and institutional interests. Correctional administrators frequently complained that the "balance" was unfairly tilted in the favor of inmate rights during the involved-hands phase.

RESTRAINED-HANDS DOCTRINE PHASE

By 1976, court opinions had shifted toward a better balance between inmate rights and legitimate institutional interests. The restrained-hands doctrine of the U.S. Supreme Court was expressed in four decisions during the spring of 1976: Baxter v. Palmigiano,[14] Enomoto v. Clutchette,[15] Meachum v. Fano,[16] and Mon-

---

[11]Archambeault and Archambeault, *Correctional Supervisory Management,* p. 204.

[12]Coleman v. Peyton, 302 2nd (4th Cir. 1966) and Johnson v. Avery, 89 S. Ct. 747 (1969).

[13]Ronald L. Goldfarb and Linda R. Singer, *After Conviction* (New York: Simon & Schuster, 1973), p. 370.

[14]96 S. Ct. 1551 (1976).

[15]96 S. Ct. 1551 (1976).

[16]96 S. Ct. 2543 (1976).

tanye v. Haymes.[17] The restrained-hands doctrine was most clearly expressed in Meachum v. Fano:

> Given a valid conviction, the criminal defendant has been constitutionally deprived of his liberty to the extent that the state may confine him and subject him to the rules of its prison system so long as the conditions of confinement do not otherwise violate the constitution.[18]

These four cases, as well as in other decisions since 1976, have made it clear that, although inmates are not "slaves of the state," neither are they "fully enfranchised citizens." Inmates retain basic human rights, but they are not entitled to the same degree of protection that they enjoyed before conviction.

Source: Adapted from William G. Archambeault and Betty J. Archambeault, *Correctional Supervisory Management: Principles of Organization, Policy, and Law* (Englewood Cliffs, N.J.: Prentice-Hall, 1982), pp. 202–208.

The conditions of confinement have been widely litigated in the courts. Two Arkansas cases, Talley v. Stephens and Jackson v. Bishop, examined the constitutionality of whipping as punishment within the prison, and the decision in Jackson v. Bishop established that whipping as punishment inflicts cruel and unusual punishment upon prisoners.[19] Flogging as a means of disciplining prisoners has now been outlawed in nearly every state.

Prisoners have frequently invoked the Eighth Amendment to challenge solitary confinement. But the courts have generally supported the solitary confinement of troublesome inmates, unless the conditions are clearly "shocking" or "debasing." One decision held that subhuman conditions which constitute cruel and unusual punishment exist when the inmate is denuded, exposed to winter cold, and deprived of such basic elements of hygiene as soap and toilet paper.[20] Yet the intervention of the courts has resulted in making solitary confinement a much different experience from the past when physically beaten prisoners were thrown into dark and damp cells and given a bread-and-water diet for prolonged periods of time. Prisoners in solitary confinement today must be fed the same diet as the other prisoners, must be adequately fed, must be placed in a cell that has sufficient light and warmth, and, of course, must not be physically harmed.

Numerous inmates have sought damages from the prison administration for physical attacks and sexual assaults inflicted by predatory inmates. An inmate seeking redress for failure to provide protection from attack may sue the individual responsible in a civil tort suit for negligence, may use the Federal Tort Claims Act

[17]96 S. Ct. 2543 (1976).

[18]96 S. Ct. 2543 (1976).

[19]Talley v. Stephens, 247 F. Supp. 683 (E.D. Ark, 1965) and Jackson v. Bishop, 404 F. 2d 571 (8th Cir. 1968).

[20]387 F. 2d 519 (2d Cir. 1967).

if the staff member responsible is employed by the federal government, or, in a proper case, may bring an action for violation of civil rights under section 1983 of the Federal Civil Rights Act.[21] The courts have generally agreed that inmates deserve some protection against predatory prisoners and in a few cases have imposed liability on prison officials for failing to protect prisoners from physical attack and sexual assaults by other inmates. But unless a prisoner can prove that repeated attempts were made to warn officials of an impending assault, officials are not likely to be held responsible.

The courts have been reluctant to apply constitutional safeguards to individual allegations of medical malpractice or negligence, but once it has been established that inadequate medical services exist throughout a correctional system, the courts have been quick to order states to upgrade their standards.

The courts have also ruled that the overall conditions of confinement of all the major prisons of Alabama, Arkansas, Florida, Louisiana, Mississippi, Nevada, New Hampshire, Wyoming, and Rhode Island, and individual prisons in Arizona, Minnesota, New Jersey, Ohio, Oklahoma, Delaware, the District of Columbia, Puerto Rico, and Virgin Islands inflict cruel and unusual punishment upon prisoners. In Pugh v. Loche, Judge Frank Johnson ordered that the state of Alabama use forty-four special standards to overhaul its prison system, and this federal judge gave specific deadlines for completing the reforms.[22]

Under the First Amendment, the federal courts have consistently held that the religious rights granted to one religious group must be given to all such groups within correctional institutions. The courts have also held that prisoners have the right to receive religious literature and to correspond with a spiritual advisor.[23] However, the courts have been reluctant to require correctional administrators to provide special diets on religious grounds or to allow the free exercise of religion to a degree that might jeopardize institutional security.

The censorship of personal correspondence has probably attracted more litigation than any other area of correctional procedure. The U.S. Supreme Court ruled in the Procunier v. Martinez case that "censorship of prison mail works a consequential restriction on the First and Fourteenth Amendment rights of those who are not prisoners."[24] Although the decision was disappointing for those who wanted greater procedural restrictions on the censorship of inmate correspondence, this and other cases have essentially eliminated the censorship of outgoing correspondence. Incoming correspondence is still checked for contraband but no longer receives the censorship it did in the past.

The censorship of publications and manuscripts has long been a critical concern of prisoners. Although the courts have cautiously advised a broadening of the right of prisoners to publish articles and books, they have reserved discretionary

---

[21]Fogel, ". . . *We Are the Living Proof,*" p. 135.

[22]406 F. Supp. 318 (M.D. Alb. 1976).

[23]Cooper v. Pate, 382 F. 2d 518 (7th Cir. 1967).

[24]416 U.S. 396 (1974).

responsibility for correctional administrators. In the federal prison system, confidential access to the media is assured via a prisoner mailbox, through which correspondence to media personnel is transmitted unopened.[25] However, judges have usually ruled that treatment of correspondence to the media and interviews with the press in state correctional systems is left to the discretion of correctional administrators.

Intraprison disciplinary meetings have represented the major area of litigation concerning due process rights in prison. Wolff v. McDonnell, a landmark case, defines the due process rights of offenders in disciplinary meetings.[26] In this case, the U.S. Supreme Court specified certain minimum requirements for disciplinary proceedings:

1. The inmate must receive advance written notice of the alleged rules infraction;
2. The prisoner must be allowed sufficient time to present a defense against the charges;
3. The prisoner must be allowed to present disciplinary evidence on his or her behalf and therefore may call witnesses, as long as the security of the institution is not jeopardized;
4. The prisoner is permitted to seek counsel from another inmate or a staff member when the circumstances of the disciplinary infraction are complex or the prisoner is illiterate;
5. The prisoner is to be provided with a written statement of the findings of the committee, the evidence relied upon, and the rationale for the action. A written record of the proceedings must also be maintained.[27]

This case was significant because it standardized certain rights and freedoms in correctional facilities. Inmates received some procedural safeguards to protect them against the flagrant abuses of disciplinary meetings, but they did not receive all the due process rights of a criminal trial. Nor did the U.S. Supreme Court question the right of corrections officials to revoke the good time (whereby the acceptable behavior of inmates during confinement results in the reduction of the length of imprisonment) of inmates.

In addition, the courts have ruled in recent years that inmates have a number of legal rights. First, prisoners have the right of access to the courts to complain about the conditions under which they are confined. The U.S. Supreme Court ruled in Johnson v. Avery that "it is fundamental that access of prisoners to the courts may not be denied or obstructed."[28] Second, the Johnson v. Avery decision further made it clear that a prisoner can receive legal assistance from another prisoner and that officials can not prevent this aid unless alternative legal counsel is provided. Third, the courts have provided inmates the right of privileged communication

---

[25]Washington Post Company v. Kleindienst, 494 F. 2d 994, 997 (D.C. Cir. 1974).

[26]418 U.S. 539 (1974).

[27]Prisoner Law Reporter, "Prison Discipline Must Include Notice," hearing, Commission on Correctional Facilities and Services of the American Bar Association, vol. 3 (July 1975): 51–53.

[28]89 S. Ct. 747 (1969).

within the attorney-client relationship, which includes confidentiality not only in face-to-face communication but in written communication as well.[29] Fourth, the U.S. Supreme Court in Younger v. Gilmore ruled that the failure of institutions to provide an adequate law library is a denial of the equal protection guarantee of the Fourteenth Amendment.[30]

In summary, prisoners have made the greatest gains in their rights to send and receive letters, as the courts have put the burden on correctional officials to justify certain restrictive practices and policies. Great strides have also been made by prisoners regarding their right to correspond with lawyers and the courts. The courts have also helped prisoners in the exercise of religious freedom. Medical care is another area in which courts have generally ruled in favor of prisoners. In addition, courts have been willing to rule on the totality of conditions in a prison setting when prisoners are apparently undergoing severe dehumanization and deterioration of their mental and physical well-being.[31]

However, while the law no longer leaves a prisoner at the prison gate, the changes do not mean prisoners are satisfied with the rights and due process safeguards given them by the courts. The courts have not altered the violent and dehumanizing conditions typical of prisons in the United States. Nor have the courts taken away the vast discretionary authority officials have over inmates' lives; indeed, the restrained-hand doctrine phase of the past few years has increased rather than decreased such discretionary authority. Furthermore, decisions usually are applicable only to conditions within one institution or correctional system and do not extend to similar conditions in other correctional systems.

A lawful prison requires that there be a reasonable set of institutional rules and standards and adequate patrol and inspection to enforce these rules and standards. Prisoners who are responsible for major infractions must be prosecuted and sentenced. If necessary, additional time must be added to the sentences of prisoners convicted of major offenses. Genuine complaints must be heard under a credible grievance system, and rule infractions must be heard by an independent officer whose decisions are subject to appellate review.[32] A lawful prison also requires that prisoners be granted all the rights and due process safeguards given them by the courts.

The Safe Correctional Environment

Offenders must be assured of their safety in both community-based facilities and correctional institutions. Although physical attacks and sexual assaults do take place in community facilities and in minimum-security prisons, medium- and maximum-security institutions are the most common settings for physical and sexual

[29]*In Re: Ferguson*, 55 Cal. 2d 663 (1961).

[30]Younger v. Gilmore, 404 U.S. 15 (1971).

[31]Conclusions of Nan Aron, contained in Clemens Bartollas, *Introduction to Corrections* (New York: Harper & Row, 1981), p. 349.

[32]Dinitz, "Are Safe and Humane Prisons Possible?" p. 12.

victimizations, stabbings, and homicides. A veteran correctional officer in a maximum-security prison explains why many prisons are no longer safe: "[Once] convicts wouldn't lay a hand on you. They didn't dare. They knew that if they did they'd be taken to a quiet place and beaten half to death. That's why we were safe then; we can't do those things any more and that's why conditions are so dangerous now.[33] Guards across the nation express a common complaint—that they have neither the control nor the respect they used to have. They know that life is cheap in the contemporary Big House prisons, and they feel they are at the mercy of the inmates.

Nor do inmates feel any safer. The new breed of inmates brings with them the criminal expertise of the street gang organization, the mechanics of narcotics distribution, and a toleration for mayhem at a level hitherto unknown in American prisons. One prudent exoffender describes how he survived in the violent setting of a maximum security prison:

> When I got to prison, I knew I had to get a weapon to survive. As soon as I got out of orientation, this dude I knew from outside got in my face and hit on me about sex. He said, "Man, you look like you have gained some weight back there." I knew I couldn't let that pass, and I said, "You look like you have too." He said, "Man, I don't go for that sex stuff." We had some more words together and from that point on we had some bad feelings.
> I made sure he didn't get behind me in the bathroom or shower. I also knew I had to get a weapon right away. I approached this con in the metal shop, and he got me a pipe for three cartons of cigarettes. I made sure that I could get strapped down [hide the pipe] pretty quick. Finally, he said something to me one day in the gym. I left the gym, got my pipe, and put a mask on. I knew it was either him or me. The prison is a mean place. If you aren't willing to go all the way [kill somebody] to protect yourself, you're not going to make it.[34]

To insure inmate safety, changes are needed in the design and administration of prisons. Small prisons that will hold no more than four hundred inmates must be built. The physical design of the prison and its operations must be such that adequately trained guards are in close contact with inmates in living quarters and at work assignments. Guards can best service the interests of order and safety when they are competent in human relations, so that information between prisoner and guard can flow freely without fear that it will be misused, without expectation of special favor, and under conditions of respect and responsibility.[35]

The Industrious Correctional Environment

Idleness is much more prevalent in prisons than in residential programs in the community. Because of overcrowded prisons, the work to be done is often spread so thin that it is no longer work. The yards and cellblocks are full throughout

[33]Ibid., p. 13.

[34]Interviewed in March 1981.

[35] Dinitz, "Are Safe and Humane Prisons Possible?" p. 13.

the day with inmates trying to cope with their boredom. Some inmates engage in constructive activities, such as lifting weights, but the day has to be filled somehow, and so too many inmates resort to scheming about drug drop-offs, prostitution rings, or about "hitting" (stabbing) inmates of competing gangs.

As a step toward ending this idleness, inmates must be provided with more work and must have the work they do valued. Inmates must be paid for their work. It is foolish to expect prisoners to gain satisfaction from their labors when they are not paid (as in Texas). Workers in prison are denied the value of their labor when they are paid at the low rates allowed in most correctional systems ($10 to $24 per month). Although to pay inmates free market rates may be unrealistic, progress toward higher pay will produce benefits more than commensurate with the increased cost. Work that is more constructive must be found. The menial work characteristic of most prison industry is useless because it fails to equip inmates for employment in the free community.[36]

The Hopeful Correctional Environment

Finally, correctional environments should provide renewed hope. The point can be made that the loss of hope is one of the consequences of a criminal career. John Conrad put it this way:

> A criminal career is a desperate career, a career in which hope must be satisfied by transient "scores," ultimately and inescapably terminated by the successive disasters of apprehension, prosecution, conviction, and incarceration. Anyone experiencing this sequence may well abandon hope of rejoining the conventional society, if he ever had any aspiration.[37]

To provide renewed hope, correctional environments should offer effective voluntary programs, should permit residents to have some say over what happens to them, and should help residents to feel they have an accepted place in the outside community. It is not surprising that residential facilities are more hopeful settings than correctional institutions.

Leslie Wilkins defined the ingredients of a hopeful prison. He said incarcerated offenders should be taught vocational skills, provided with socially useful activities, paid adequately for work done, provided with individual or group therapy if they desire it, and given the same personal protection as citizens on the outside. The fact that offenders are incarcerated for punishment does not negate their rights to be treated with respect.[38]

To create a hopeful correctional environment, the facility must offer offenders such programs as remedial elementary education, vocational training, individual

[36]Ibid., p. 14.

[37]Conrad and Dinitz, "State's Strongest Medicine," p. 64.

[38]Gordon Hawkins, *The Prison: Policy and Practice* (Chicago: University of Chicago Press, 1976), pp. 52–53.

and group therapy, and self-help techniques. These programs should be provided by competent staff and should be available at the option of the offender. These programs should be based on sound theory, should deliver the services they are supposed to deliver, and should be frequently evaluated. No penalty should be levied against an offender for failure to participate in a program, but there must be some incentive to engage in treatment. Although the inducement of good time granted for program completion would encourage many to enroll in a program who would not otherwise take the initiative, the real incentive should be demonstrably increased employability.[39]

In a hopeful correctional environment, offenders feel that they have some say in their own lives. Although not much is known about the process by which self-improvement begins and proceeds, the degree of involvement in the improvement process appears directly related to the amount of decision-making authority an offender has in a particular setting. It appears that the freedom to make some decisions as an individual is needed to build responsibility and that the absence of this freedom tends to result in impotence and hopelessness.

In a hopeful correctional environment, offenders also feel they have acceptance in the outside community. Residential facilities usually provide daily contact with the community for offenders. Residents participate in work-release programs, have frequent home visits, shop in the community, and attend community recreational and social events. In correctional institutions, acceptance from the community comes in the form of visits from home, the attendance of community members at religious and social events in the prison, the involvement of community volunteers with prisoners, and the participation of community leaders in advisory committees in the prison. Without such contacts with the community, the only reality for the inmate is the cellblock, the yard, and the prison industrial plant.[40]

RESPONSE OF OFFENDERS TO CORRECTIONAL ENVIRONMENTS

Offenders make five basic responses to correctional environments: aggressive reaction, self-satisfying reaction, legalistic reaction, withdrawal reaction, and positive reaction.[41]

Aggressive Reaction

Offenders who demonstrate an aggressive reaction are usually angry because they feel the correctional environment has nothing but a negative impact on them.

---

[39]Dinitz, "Are Safe and Humane Prisons Possible?" p. 15.

[40]For another dimension of hope in prison, John P. Conrad says that the prison should be a school of citizenship. See Conrad, "Where There's Hope There's Life," in *Justice as Fairness*, ed. David Fogel and Joe Hudson (Cincinnati: Anderson, 1981), pp. 16–19.

[41]Bartollas, *Introduction to Corrections*, pp. 392–396.

They may feel brutalized, degraded, and dehumanized, or they may feel oppressed by an authoritarian and an unjust system they believe is punishing them for their race or economic status, rather than for the crime they committed. Such offenders may fight the system individually by disobeying the rules or confronting staff members, or they may fight it collectively through rebellion and protest. Jack Henry Abbott tells in his best-selling book, *In the Belly of the Beast,* how correctional environments brutalized and degraded him for some of his life as a juvenile and most of his life as an adult. He describes one incident in this way:

> I was taken by about twenty guards and other employees into a special psychological observation cell. . . .
> I was stripped nude. I was forced to lie on the steel slab. Each of my ankles was chained in a corner of the bed-structure, and my wrists were chained over my head to the other two corners, so I was chained down in a complete spread-eagle position. . . .
> In order to urinate I had to twist my torso so that my penis would hang in a general direction over the side of the bed-structure, and the urine would cross the floor and go down the drain. . . .
> I was hand-fed at each meal.
> The day after I was chained down, several guards entered the cell and beat me with their fists all over my face, chest, and stomach. I was choked manually and brought to the point—almost—of strangulation, and then they would remove their hands. My throat was blue with bruises caused this way.
> I was chained—now I mean *iron* chains, not "leather restraints"—in this manner for ten days, and I was attacked three times in this period.
> Finally, the "medical technician" observed that the nerves in my arms were dying— the areas between my wrists and elbows.
> So about twenty guards came again. They unchained me and dressed me in nylon coveralls. As I was dressing I glanced in the window at my reflection and my face was black and both eyes [were] swollen. I was covered with bruises.[42]

The offender who fights the correctional environment usually spends considerable time in solitary confinement and a prolonged time in prison, especially when the determinate sentencing system is used. Obviously, these offenders have little interest in the treatment process offered by their captives.

Self-Satisfying Reaction

Instead of fighting their environments, some offenders try to make the best of confinement. In other words, they seek to make the stay in prison as easy as possible. In prison, they may make up for the sexual deprivation by seducing a kid. They may steal food from the dining hall to have food in their cells when they want a snack. They may have prisoners who work in the laundry press their prison clothes. They may find ways to make prison hooch, to provide themselves with an intoxicant. Or they may have drugs brought in from the outside or be part of a drug ring within the institution.

---

[42]Jack Henry Abbott, *In the Belly of the Beast: Letters from Prison* (New York: Random House, 1981), pp. 38–39.

These offenders, who make the best of confinement by satisfying themselves in every way possible, sometimes respond to programs because these enable them to do easier time or, especially under indeterminate sentencing, enable them to get out more quickly. Consequently, they lift weights, participate in individual or team athletic events, read, paint, or write. If they see any advantages for themselves, they may join groups or participate in self-growth programs such as the Jaycees.

Legalistic Reaction

More and more offenders, particularly in prisons, use much of their energies studying criminal law, preparing civil suits, and writing legal briefs to appeal their cases or to ask for new trials. These offenders are using the legal process to resist the conditions or the reality of their confinements. They usually are no more receptive to correctional environments than are those who make an aggressive reaction to confinement. David Fogel claims that offenders now regard themselves as plaintiffs, and this role constitutes their basic response to prison life.[43] The popularity of the legalistic reaction rests on at least three factors: First, the majority of incarcerated offenders have seen the futility of an aggressive reaction to correctional environments. Second, offenders in general have achieved enough success from the courts, as indicated earlier in this chapter, to see an incentive to continue filing legal briefs. Third, a legalistic reaction makes offenders feel that they are doing something concrete about their situation and, thereby, relieves some of the feelings of impotence and rage generated by imprisonment.

The stronger this reaction, the less likely these offenders are to be receptive to programs, because they usually view a receptivity toward programs as "buying into" the very system they are fighting. Yet, some offenders whose basic response is legalistic still avail themselves of programs to make their time pass more easily and quickly.

Withdrawal Reaction

Some offenders find the correctional environment so painful that they withdraw. This reaction varies from staying high on drugs to invoking protective custody to becoming mentally ill or attempting suicide. Although drug use is common in prisons and in community-based facilities, some offenders use drugs to withdraw totally from institutional life. One institutionalized juvenile inhaled so much glue prior to and during confinement that he eventually died; despite the precautions taken, this youth managed to obtain some form of intoxicating inhalant so that he could stay high. Protective custody is the choice of more and more prisoners in maximum security prisons. These inmates choose protective custody, which segregates them from the prison population for twenty-four hours a day, so they can avoid the dangers and hassles of institutional life. Other inmates react to their

[43]Fogel, ". . . *We Are the Living Proof,*" p. 63.

environments with depression or other forms of illness; they simply withdraw psychologically into worlds of their own. Finally, suicide is chosen by some prisoners.

Offenders who withdraw from their correctional environments obviously are unreceptive to programs and other treatment technologies. However, staff members are frequently called on to treat these offenders, especially if one has attempted suicide, and staff members sometimes are able to persuade an offender to choose some other adaptation to institutional life.

Positive Reaction

Some offenders use the correctional environments to pursue self-growth and to develop new skills so they will have a better chance to make it in the community when they are released. These offenders are more likely to be found in community-based facilities or programs than to be in institutional settings. Obviously, this group is the most receptive to the treatment process. Offenders who appear to be making a positive reaction have made statements such as these:

> I believe in rehabilitation. I believe it is helping people. In prison, you get mental scars; in here [PORT], you heal them.[44]

> The most important concept here [Gateway] is the family. Some people care more than others, but they really do care.[45]

> [Outward Bound is] the greatest experience I ever had. For the first time, I realize what a horse's ass I've been all my life.[46]

SUMMARY

Correctional treatment does not take place in a vacuum, but in community-based and institutional settings. To give programs a better chance of success within correctional environments, these environments must become more humane; that is, provide a lawful, a safe, an industrious, and a hopeful setting for offenders. Prisoners' rights are particularly important within the context of correctional institutions. Inmates are unlikely to be receptive to programs when they are treated as slaves with no rights. Offenders further must have the right to participate voluntarily in treatment. The present limitations of offender rehabilitation, both in theory and in practice, make it inhumane to require rehabilitation as a condition of release.

The reality of correctional institutions today, however, is that these desirable conditions are a long way from being achieved. Daily, prisoners experience filth, lack of services, and violence in prisons throughout the United States. Prison gangs

[44]Interviewed in August 1981.

[45]Interviewed in January 1982.

[46]Joshua L. Miner and Joe Boldt, *Outward Bound USA: Learning through Experience in Adventure-Based Education* (New York: Morrow, 1981).

frequently control the turf, and neither staff nor inmates feel safe within these lawless environments. Nor are many inmates content with the rights granted them by the courts. The courts have not taken away the vast discretionary authority that prison officials have over prisoners' lives, and the courts cannot prevent the daily injustices that many prisoners experience in the prison. Even if prisoners are fortunate enough to have these injustices addressed in the various courts, leading all the way to the U.S. Supreme Court, years may be required for the courts to make changes. Moreover, the majority of states still have indeterminate sentencing structures, so more than half of the nearly four hundred thousand incarcerated men and women in state and federal correctional institutions must undergo treatment as a condition of parole.

In short, although the correctional environments in which treatment is given may be more desirable than in the past, prisons are still a long way from being likely places for individuals to experience growth and positive changes in their lives. Correctional environments will become more viable contexts for treatment as they become more humane placements for society's felons.

DISCUSSION QUESTIONS

1. What made John Conrad change his mind about the rehabilitative philosophy?
2. What role does Conrad see for treatment in correctional institutions? What roles does he see for it in community-based corrections?
3. What are the necessary elements of humane correctional environments? Why are these so important?
4. List some rights that the courts have given to inmates during the past twenty years. Are the courts currently as willing to grant inmates due process and procedural safeguards as they were in the past?
5. Why is voluntary participation a better correctional policy than forced participation in treatment?
6. Why is it important for offenders to have some say in their own lives?

The Correctional Client

14

Objectives

1. To examine the three interrelated processes of exiting from crime.

2. To illustrate by statements from offenders and by a case study this process.

3. To explain why offenders who intend to go straight return to crime.

4. To examine how age, sex, social class, personality makeup, and commitment to crime influence receptivity to treatment.

Exoffenders can be divided into three major groups: those who will ultimately fail, those who will make marginal adjustment to society, and those who will be successful. The failures who are returned to prison can be further divided into those who intended to go straight but were unable to and those who had no intention of going straight. Exoffenders making a marginal adjustment have minor skirmishes with the law, and perhaps even do a little more jail time. The successes are able to avoid further involvement with the criminal justice system. A much smaller group of the successful exoffenders even makes a significant contribution to the community. Of the three major groups of exoffenders, the largest group appears to be the marginal ones; the groups of failures and of successes are probably about equal in size.

This chapter first examines why some exoffenders are successful in going straight, then explains the reasons for failure, and concludes by considering how age, sex, social class, personality makeup, and commitment to crime influence involvement in treatment.

EXITING FROM CRIME

The act of exiting from crime appears to depend on three interrelated processes: maturing out of crime, developing internal resources, and having successful experiences in the community.

Maturing Out of Crime

Criminologists say that offenders typically mature out of crime at two points in their criminal careers: late in their teens, as they reach an age group where the crime rate drops as much as 50 percent, and during their mid-30s, when the rate drops sharply again. Don Erickson, former director of the Idaho Bureau of Corrections, has this to say about the crime dropout rate:

> One of the strongest tools we have [with offenders] is chronological age. Regardless of what we do, they're going to grow older and reach a maturity. That has a lot of bearing [on] whether they continue to get involved in crime.[1]

Lloyd Ohlin, Harvard criminologist, adds that for adults the process may involve "burning out" rather than "maturing out." He notes, "Crime is, after all, a young man's game. Offenders do eventually get tired or feel they can't make it any more." Ohlin verbalizes what many corrections officials believe: "You almost have to wait until the person himself is willing to turn around; then almost anything works, any kind of help and assistance."[2] He then sums up a major problem for penologists:

---

[1]Michael S. Serrill, "Is Rehabilitation Dead?" *Corrections Magazine* 1 (May/June 1975): 26.
[2]Ibid., p. 27.

One must remember that lives of crime in many respects have paid off for a lot of these guys. So they've done a little jail time. They've alternatively been rich and broke. They haven't been able to lead any kind of settled life, but they've wanted excitement. The lifestyle has appealed to them. When that no longer seems either feasible or attractive, then they begin to search for some other things. Maybe some prison time is essential to get that to set in. The problem is sorting out those for whom that is the only answer from others who are maybe ready to turn around. We don't do well at predicting each other's behavior.[3]

Individual offenders have explained this process of maturing out of crime by saying that it takes place when one or more of the following events take place: offenders feel that they have personally "hit the bottom," they no longer want the system interfering with their lives, or they simply want to live a normal life.

Life on the bottom.   Many offenders come to grips with their personal failures when they realize that they have slipped to the bottom. Their desire to change, then, arises because they are fed up with being "on the bottom." Similarly, Alcoholics Anonymous theorizes that an alcoholic will not quit drinking until he or she hits bottom. One offender remembers, "I made up my mind that I was sick of what I had done, and then I was ready to change."[4] Another said, "Man, I felt I was on the bottom. I was fed up with my life. I felt I had to change."[5] A drug offender tells what made him realize that it was time to turn his life around:

I had been in the state penitentiary on two different occasions. I came out and made the decision to break my lifelong heroin habit. I got a good job and was making $17 an hour, got married, and we had a baby boy. I was bringing all kinds of money in, working a lot of overtime. Then, when my boy was five, I came home one day and my wife had killed herself and my little boy. I was devastated. I started drinking pretty heavy, started to smoke pot, and then went back to heroin. I went through a hundred thousand dollars of drugs in one year. Then, one morning I woke up in a garbage can, and I knew it had gone far enough. I am forty-one years old, I have spent enough of my life in the penitentiary and so I signed myself in here [a therapeutic community for drug offenders].[6]

The threat of future punishments.   Thomas Meisenhelder, a sociologist at California State College (San Bernardino), found that the primary motive for exiting from crime among the twenty inmates he interviewed was the deterrent impact of additional criminal sanctions; that is, inmates did not want to spend more time in prison.[7] One inmate put this well:

---

[3]Ibid.

[4]Interviewed in August 1981.

[5]Interviewed in August 1981.

[6]Interviewed in January 1982.

[7]Thomas Meisenhelder, "An Exploratory Study of Exiting from Criminal Careers," *Criminology* 15 (November 1977): 319–334.

My point of view changed about things; you don't want to end up like some of these oldtimers who have been cons all their life. They showed me what would happen if I didn't straighten out; you see what you will miss. Wow! I could spend the rest of my life in prison if I don't straighten up. There are some guys here doing life on the installment plan, and I could be one of them. Not me, this is my last time.[8]

The desire to live a normal life.   Thomas Meisenhelder found that another reason offenders go straight is the desire to lead a normal life. The life of crime no longer offers the thrills it once did. This desire to live a normal life is often expressed when an offender has met a "straight" person who would find unacceptable the offender's continued involvement with crime, but with whom the offender wants to settle down. One of Meisenhelder's interviewees expressed it this way:

I just decided I wanted to be like any other person, settle down, have me an old lady, a place to stay at, a good job. I was just tired of it. I really wanted a chance to live a normal, straight life.[9]

Developing Internal Resources

The number of prison inmates who seem intent on experiencing growth so that they can change the direction of their lives is impressive. These inmates may use such expressions as "the strong mind," "get your head together," and "be cool and be a man" in referring to the fact that they must develop maturity and strength so that they can deal with their environment more effectively.[10] One prisoner, a former leader of a Chicago gang, defines "strong mind" in this way:

When we have a "strong mind," we have a feeling of self, a continuity to life, and an enhanced faculty of reasoning. Having a "strong mind" doesn't imply that one strives to be a paragon of information. It has more to do with one not having any feelings of inferiority and worthlessness. A strong mind will help us know who we are, what we are; it will help us to accept and respect who and what we are, and know that virtually everything and every situation we encounter in life offers us a valuable lesson, which if fully understood, makes us wiser.[11]

This prisoner went on to say that he had used his strong mind to endure three years of segregation. He had disciplined his mind through meditation and the spiritual exercises of the Moslem faith of the Moorish Science Temple of America. He contended that the debilitating environment of the prison had been a testing ground and had been helpful to him in developing the "strong mind."[12]

As defined by this prisoner and as conceived by many others, the "strong

[8]Ibid., p. 324.

[9]Ibid.

[10]Clemens Bartollas and Stuart J. Miller, *Correctional Administration: Theory and Practice* (New York: McGraw-Hill, 1978), p. 213.

[11]Ibid.

[12]Interviewed in July 1977.

mind" has at least three components: faith in self, sense of purpose in life, and willingness to grow. Instead of looking on oneself as weak and being caught up in feelings of inferiority and worthlessness, the individual who develops the "strong mind" moves toward self-acceptance and a disciplined approach to the environment. But an individual must develop inner resources. Muslims, for example, develop self-discipline through fasting; abstaining from alcohol, tobacco, or drugs; and depriving themselves of certain creature comforts. A sense of purpose provides a "continuity" to life and a mission and a direction for one's life. Those with the "strong mind" know who they are and where they are going. A willingness to grow requires them to open themselves to life and thereby learn to profit from and learn from the situations and experiences they face each day.

Judge Robert Young represents a dramatic success story of an exoffender who developed the three components of a "strong mind." Young had been jailed three times; his longest time in prison was twenty-two months on a six-year term for mail theft. But after his third release from prison, Young decided to go straight and to get an education. He earned a bachelor's degree and decided to attend law school. Although he was turned down at eleven schools because he was an exoffender, he refused to give up and was finally accepted at McGeorge School of Law in Sacramento. He spent three years in private practice after graduation, served three more as an assistant district attorney, and was elected to the justice court of Auburn, California, in 1977.[13] He now hears minor criminal and civil cases.

Young sums up his philosophy with the statement "I didn't take no for an answer." He refused to accept it when he was informed that he could not be admitted to law school, that he could not be admitted to the bar, and that he could not be elected to a judgeship. Because he believes that "you set your own limits in life," he has little tolerance for exoffenders who claim that their careers are blocked by disciplinary laws. He says:

> I really didn't expect legislature to change laws for exoffenders, because there's no lobby for prisoners. When I'm asked by prisoners, I tell them if you want to make something of your life, go do it.[14]

Young was able to go straight because he set his mind on something, developed his internal resources, and refused to be deterred from his purpose.

Having Successful Experiences in the Community

Exoffenders also need to have successful experiences in the community if they intend to walk away permanently from a criminal way of life. Meisenhelder noted that success in leaving crime is contingent upon the offender's acquiring a

[13]Andrew D. Gilman, "Legal Barriers to Jobs Are Slowly Disappearing," *Corrections Magazine,* 5 (December 1979): 71–72.

[14]Ibid., p. 72.

meaningful bond to the conventional social order.[15] The first condition for acquiring this meaningful bond is the acceptance of the irreversibility of time; that is, the offender can not try to "catch up" or "make up" for prison life, but has to accept starting over:

> You can't go back. You got to start at the beginning. And that is what I think happened to me; I realized that it's now that you have to do it, that you can't start over from where you left off five years ago; you gotta go out there, [and] make a new life for yourself.[16]

This ability to start over, according to Meisenhelder, is very much related to the ability of the exoffender to find what he or she perceives to be a good job. The exoffender must find a place from which to begin constructing a noncriminal social identity. As one exoffender said, "I was working, leading a good life. There was no reason to steal."[17]

Meisenhelder also adds that positive interpersonal relationships with socialized individuals are necessary for a successful exit from crime. These, of course, involve exoffenders further in the conventional world. Some of the dynamics of this process of settling down involve the acquisition, or reacquisition, of a wife, of other familial ties, or of relationships with "straight" peers. The family, especially, is seen as a strong reason for exiting from crime because the offender has someone to care about and to care about him or her:

> Being with my wife and son, doing things that normal people do, actually, seriously, has been the most important months of my life. . . . I settled down, went to work. I played with my kid.[18]

A case study of a delinquent who turned away from crime also indicates the importance of achieving success in the community. When the youth returned home from training school, he developed new friends who were academic achievers. He had completed the eleventh grade before leaving the institution, and he graduated the next year from the public school. In addition, he received a great deal of support and encouragement from family and "significant others" in the community. Finally, he was able to find a good job after his graduation from high school.[19]

The three interrelated processes of exiting from crime—maturing out of crime, developing internal resources, and having successful experiences in the community—are illustrated by twelve eighteen- and nineteen-year-old hard-core offenders. All were serving their second and third commitments to the youth commission. These youthful offenders wanted to exit from crime because they were "fed up"

---

[15]Meisenhelder, "Exploratory Study of Exiting from Criminal Careers." p. 326.

[16]Ibid., p. 327.

[17]Ibid., p. 328.

[18]Ibid.

[19]W. K. Brown, "A Case Study of Delinquency Prevention," *Criminal Justice and Behavior* 8 (December 1981): 425–438.

with the system "messing over them" and they also knew that the next step was the adult reformatory. In the end-of-the-line training school, they developed positive goals they wanted to realize in the community. Once they made the decision to change, they spent considerable time and energy developing their internal resources. They often turned to a treatment modality to help them in this growth process. They also sought and were able to develop positive outlooks and positive responses to life. As they developed more prosocial attitudes and behaviors, their interpersonal cues prompted more favorable responses from the staff and peers. The staff began to treat them like winners rather than losers, and, as a result, these youths left the institution feeling much better about themselves than they had when they arrived. Most of these individuals made excellent adjustments to the community after release, indicating that they were not "conning" their way through the institution. The two who failed were unable to find jobs. After six or seven weeks of disappointing and frustrating job hunting, they rejoined the gang which had been tempting them with promises of easy jobs and big money. The careers in the community of the other ten showed clearly that their positive attitudes and behavior won them the support and assistance that they needed to make it.[20]

EXPLANATIONS OF FAILURE

One of the major frustrations of working with offenders comes from dealing with the failures. Some offenders never intend to walk away from crime; they cannot wait to get back on the streets again. Some offenders intend to stay clean, but when they encounter bad breaks, they return to crime simply to survive. Some go back to crime because they cannot handle the pressures of life without drugs and they resort to criminal behavior to support their drug habit. Offenders who intend to succeed but fail do so for three basic reasons: failure of will, lack of satisfaction from the straight life, and inability to make it in the free world.

The Failure of Will

Changing one's criminal behavior can be regarded in the same way as changing undesirable habits, lifestyles, or poor performance in school for the general population. Many people say that they want to change, and some seriously intend to change, but only a few actually do change. Some people change their behaviors permanently, but others soon go back to the habits or behaviors they were seeking to alter. Significantly, the percentage of those who successfully give up smoking or overeating may well be probably smaller than the percentage of offenders who intend to go straight and who then never return to crime. Thus, failure of will must be seen in a human, as well as a criminal, perspective.

[20]Clemens Bartollas, Stuart J. Miller, and Simon Dinitz, "Boys Who Profit: The Limits of Institutional Success," in *Reform in Corrections: Problems and Issues,* ed. Harry E. Allen and Nancy J. Beran (New York: Praeger, 1977), pp. 8–16.

Criminals who intend to change commonly fail because their will to change was not strong enough to overcome the daily pressures they faced. The initial adjustment from prison is difficult for many exoffenders. Exoffenders leave prison with certain expectations, and they often find that these expectations are unrealistic. The world has progressed without them, and they often find the pace of life staggering compared to life within the walls. Furthermore, they must find a job, a place to live, and a way to buy food until their first paycheck. They must also develop social relationships, which are frequently difficult for exoffenders; indeed, the failure to develop adequate social relationships is commonly a reason why they ended up in prison in the first place. Throughout the process of adjusting to the free community, the exoffender must deal with a parole agent who may or may not be understanding and with a parole system that many exoffenders feel is designed to make them fail.[21] The combination of these pressures, along with the frustrations and disappointments any individual encounters daily, may be too much for the exoffender, resulting in a return to the familiarity of crime or drugs.

The Dissatisfaction with the Straight Life

Exoffenders living in the community sometimes revert to crime because they find that the straight life is not sufficiently exciting, fulfilling, or satisfying. A former drug addict had given speeches in the community about how close she had been to being sentenced to the penitentiary, about the numerous burglaries she had committed, and about the damage that chemicals had done to her body, to her relationship with her parents, and to her reputation. Yet she returned to chemicals, and she gave the following explanation of why she failed:

> I found that living without drugs wasn't that good. All my friends do drugs; you have no social life without drugs. My boyfriend even went back to drugs. The night I saw him shoot up coke, I was devastated. I had to do something. I went to a friend's house and smoked some grass. I decided then that I was going to smoke pot, but I wasn't going back to chemicals. But it wasn't long before I went back to chemicals. It is really a good high, but I'm hooked on them now. I couldn't wait all day yesterday until we broke some crystal [took speed] last night.[22]

The Inability to Make It in the Free World

Some offenders go back to crime simply because they are unable to succeed in the free society. They may not be able to find jobs—a major problem today since the depressed economy does not provide many jobs for exoffenders with limited marketable skills. Or they may find a job that does not pay the bills. Or their pay may not be sufficient to meet unexpected expenses, such as medical care for children or surgery for a spouse, so they resort to crime to raise the necessary money.

---

[21]John Irwin's *The Felon* (Englewood Cliffs, N.J.: Prentice-Hall, 1970) deals with the problems parolees face when they leave prison.

[22]Interviewed in July 1979.

Other offenders fail in the free society because they are involved in some form of compulsive behavior. This author worked with an institutionalized rapist who clearly understood that certain reactions from women triggered in him the compulsion to commit a violent sex act. He was aware that another assault would result in a long sentence in the penitentiary, and, therefore, he spent considerable time plotting with the treatment staff about avoiding those situations that would lead him to sexual assault. But he committed another rape three months after his release and is now serving a long sentence in a penitentiary.

CHARACTERISTICS OF OFFENDERS AND RECEPTIVITY TOWARD TREATMENT

Offenders make various responses to the treatment process. Some are indifferent or even antagonistic toward treatment. Career, or chronic, offenders generally fall into this group. They usually plan to return to crime as soon as they can, and they regard correctional treatment as a waste of time. Interestingly enough, there are some offenders who will go straight after returning to the community in this first group, but they still see correctional treatment as having no relevance to their lives.

A second group consists of offenders who pretend to be involved in the treatment process. These offenders may have been sentenced under the indeterminate sentencing system and, therefore, choose to make an outward display of involvement in treatment to impress the parole board and to shorten their stays. Offenders sentenced to community-based corrections may comply with correctional interventions in order to satisfy their probation or parole officers.

A third group of offenders is interested in treatment as a means to an end, but their motives and depth of involvement may vary considerably. They may become involved in treatment simply to occupy their time in prison. To them, a stint in prison without yoga, TA, or TM would be much harder time. They may become involved in educational or vocational programs in prison because they think a high school diploma or a vocational skill will help them in finding a job when they are released. Or, they may become involved in a treatment modality because they want to manage their lives better.

This section will examine how the characteristics of age, sex, social class, personality makeup, and commitment to crime influence offenders' amenability to the treatment process.

Age

It is frequently assumed that it is easier to rehabilitate juveniles than adults. This belief is based upon several dubious assumptions: first, that juveniles are more malleable than adults because they are still in the process of forming their values and attitudes toward life; second, that juveniles are less committed to a life of crime than adults because they have had less time to become committed to criminal activities; third, that much of juvenile crime is related to family problems; and fourth, that fewer juveniles will be involved in drug addiction, alcoholism, and mental illness because these social problems tend to increase with age.

However, the data currently available indicate that rates of involvement in criminal activity subsequent to adjudication appear to be at least as high for juveniles as for adults with similar offense histories.[23] Moreover, when the treatment methods employed are examined, no startling differences in the effectiveness of treatment for juveniles and for adults are apparent.

Age does appear to make some difference in offenders' amenability to the treatment process.[24] Juveniles may form caring relationships with correctional staff more easily than adults and may regard these staff members more frequently as "significant others" in their lives. Juveniles also may be more receptive to activity- or adventure-oriented programs, such as Outward Bound, than are adults. But it also can be argued that juveniles have not had time to mature out of crime and, even if juveniles are "fed up" with a life of crime, their ability to develop their internal resources is probably less than that of adults. Adults also appear to be more receptive to self-improvement possibilities, such as TM, est; and Jaycees, than are juveniles.

However, much research is needed before any definitive conclusions can be drawn about the relationship between age and the treatment process. The development of template-matching techniques, mentioned earlier, may help determine how to mesh the characteristics and attitudes of specific age groups more effectively with particular treatment technologies.

Sex

The importance of sex has been largely ignored as a factor influencing offenders' receptivity toward treatment. Research has indicated a number of preliminary findings on women involved in crime:

> Women are committing more crimes than they have in the past. The major rise is in arrests for larceny; the rate for women committing this offense has increased three to four times as fast as the rate for men.[25]
> Women do not appear to be committing more violent crimes than they have in the past.[26]

---

[23]Lee Sechrest, Susan O. White, and Elizabeth D. Brown, ed., *The Rehabilitation of Criminal Offenders: Problems and Prospects* (Washington, D.C.: National Academy of Sciences, 1979), p. 51.

[24]See Douglas Lipton, Robert Martinson, and Judith Wilks, *The Effectiveness of Correctional Treatment* (New York: Praeger, 1975) for the variations between the effectiveness of correctional treatment with juveniles and adults.

[25]Rita James Simon, *Women and Crime* (Lexington, Mass.: Heath, 1975), pp. 36–42.

[26]Laura Crites, ed., *The Female Offender* (Lexington, Mass.: Heath, 1976); and Simon, *Women and Crime*.

The women's liberation movement has had little or no effect on the increased criminality among women.[27]

The old norms of chivalry still protect women criminals, but white women benefit more than minority women from this chivalry factor.[28]

Women are not as likely as men to have contact with the criminal justice system early in adolescence, do not view the police as being as harsh and harassing as men do, are more likely to be released on bail than men, and are more likely to go to trial than men.[29]

The incarcerated woman tends to be poor, young, and black. Fewer than one-fifth live with their husbands, but nearly three-quarters have had children.[30]

Confined women are less likely to display aggressive and legalistic responses to imprisonment than men, and a greater percentage of women in prison consent willingly to homosexuality.[31]

In terms of treatment, there are fewer programs for confined women than for confined men. Although women's prisons in New York and Nebraska are beginning to offer nontraditional programs in auto mechanics, electronics, video technology, and truck driving, vocational programs offered women prisoners are typically less helpful than those provided for men in terms of securing postincarceration employment. Women usually receive less preparation for the parole process than do men. Fewer prerelease programs are offered women prisoners, and fewer women are placed in work release than are men prisoners. In addition, women on parole are offered fewer community assistance programs than are men.[32]

Because most of the research has focused either on the crimes that women commit or on their adjustments to prison life, researchers have contributed little information on how to treat women offenders. But women clearly need to have more extensive programming available to them in prison. They need educational and vocational programs to help them find jobs upon their release. This is particularly important because the majority of women must support themselves upon release, and about half of women exoffenders must provide for their children as well.[33] Women also need more programs in prison to help reestablish or improve rela-

---

[27]Laura Crites, "Women Offenders," in *Female Offender,* pp. 36–49.

[28]John R. Faine and Edward Bohlander, Jr., "Sentencing the Female Offender: The Impact of Legal and Extra-Legal Considerations" (Paper presented at the Annual Meeting of the American Society of Criminology, Tucson, Arizona, 4–7 November 1976), pp. 41.

[29]P. C. Kratcoski and K. Scheuerman, "Incarcerated Male and Female Offenders: Perceptions of Their Experiences in the Criminal Justice System," *Journal of Criminal Justice* 2 (Spring 1974): 73–78.

[30]Rugh M. Glick and Virginia V. Neto, *National Study of Women's Correctional Programs* (Washington, D.C.: GPO, 1977), pp. xvii–xx.

[31]See Rose Giallombardo, *Society of Women* (New York: Wiley, 1966); Esther Heffernan, *The Square, The Cool, and the Life* (New York: Wiley-Interscience, 1972); and David H. Ward and Gene S. Kassebaum, *Women's Prisons* (Chicago: Aldine, 1955).

[32]Deborah Levensen drew this conclusion based on the data she collected on women parolees in Illinois.

[33]Glick and Neto, *National Study of Women's Correctional Programs,* pp. xvii–xx.

tionships with their children. Furthermore, women need more preparation for the parole process and greater assistance while they are readjusting to community life.

Social Class

Social class of course is an important variable in understanding criminal behavior. Our society is particularly afraid of lower-class offenders because the street crimes they commit may violate our persons or our property. Crimes against the person, especially homicide, forcible rape, robbery, and aggravated assault, are traditionally those that most alarm society. Larceny-theft, burglary, motor vehicle theft, and fraud are the property crimes most frequently committed by street offenders. Nearly two-thirds of the burglaries, over half of which occur during the day, involve residences.[34]

There are at least four major problems in providing treatment for street offenders. First, most street offenders see no need for rehabilitation. They do not regard themselves as sick, as the medical model contends; nor do they look upon themselves as maladjusted, as the adjustment model suggests. Second, street offenders frequently have been involved in drug and alcohol abuse. This means that in addition to their involvement in criminal activities, they must be treated for their drug and alcohol dependencies. Third, incarcerated street offenders frequently belong to prison gangs or are part of an inmate subculture that disapproves of participation in programs. Fourth, street offenders come from environments plagued by enormous social problems, and they will return to these debilitating environments following their release from confinement. As long as they must deal with an environment pervaded by poverty, unemployment, drug abuse, violence, and crime, it is unrealistic to anticipate that correctional treatment can have much impact on their behavior.

It appears that past interventions with street offenders have been oriented too much toward insight therapies, such as psychotherapy, psychodrama, and transactional analysis. Behavior therapies will probably continue to be more effective in modifying the behaviors of these usually repeat offenders than other techniques, but the most helpful means of intervention with street offenders is likely to be skill development, self-help, and service-oriented programs. With the growing acceptance of determinate sentencing systems, treatment will become voluntary for this group of offenders. This may mean that fewer street offenders will elect treatment, but research must discover the most effective interventions for those who do choose to become involved in the treatment process.

White-collar crime is viewed as the crime of "respectable people." Although white-collar crime is far more costly to society than street crime, the public has little fear of it. Edwin Sutherland, who coined the phrase *white-collar crime,* defined it as "crime committed by a person of respectability and high social status in the course of his occupation."[35] Herbert Edelherz expanded the definition of white-

---

[34]U.S. Department of Justice, *Uniform Crime Reports* (Washington, D.C.: GPO, 1982).

[35]Edwin H. Sutherland, *White Collar Crime* (New York: Holt, 1948), p. 9.

collar crime by describing it as "an illegal act or series of illegal acts committed by nonphysical means and by concealment or guile, to obtain money or property, to avoid the payment of money or property, or to obtain business or personal advantage."[36]

Little is known about the effects of criminal sanctions on white-collar criminals. The debate about the proper handling of white-collar criminals has not progressed much beyond the question of whether or not a prison sentence is "just deserts" for those who commit a white-collar crime. Although some persons feel that a prison sentence may be too severe in relation to the harm inflicted upon society, others believe that imprisonment is necessary and desirable for equity as well as for the purpose of deterrence.[37]

One of the major problems of treating white-collar criminals is that these persons typically are neither receptive to counseling nor in need of job training. White-collar criminals usually do not perceive themselves as criminals, because what they did was merely "good business practices" or normative behavior for those in their business situation. Box 14-1 provides an example of the attitudes frequently expressed by white-collar criminals toward the treatment process.

Box 14-1 The Resistance to Treatment of a White-Collar Criminal

PROBATION OFFICER: You look somewhat pale. Are you ill?

WHITE-COLLAR PROBATIONER: Who, me? No, I'm all right. Well, maybe a slight stomachache.

OFFICER: Sorry to hear about it. Is it something you ate?

PROBATIONER: (sighing) I don't think so. I always get it when I come here.

OFFICER: Coming here gives you a pain in the stomach?

PROBATIONER: (nodding vigorously) Yeah. And a pain in the neck. Why in the hell do I have to be treated like a criminal? I'm a businessman. All I did was really good business.

OFFICER: You broke the law.

PROBATIONER: (indignantly) What kind of law? I went into business to make money. What was wrong with getting together with other business and the union to get a good price for my work?

OFFICER: Nothing wrong in getting a good price. But you fixed the price so your customers couldn't go out and get a lower price from a competitor.

PROBATIONER: But that's good business! Making customers pay the same price to all plasterers.

OFFICER: Your customers paid money to you which they could have saved or used for their own needs. You took away money those people could have used for themselves and their families. You elevated the price of the houses you were working on.

PROBATIONER: (frowning) So what? Isn't this a dog-eat-dog system? Everybody is supposed to look out for number one.

Source: Alexander B. Smith and Louis Berlin, *Treating the Criminal Offender*, 2d ed. (Englewood Cliffs, N.J.: Prentice-Hall, 1981), p. 316.

[36]Herbert Edelhertz, *The Nature, Impact and Prosecution of White Collar Crime* (Washington, D.C.: GPO, 1970), p. 3.

[37]Sechrest, White, and Brown, *Rehabilitation of Criminal Offenders*, pp. 48–49.

Treating the white-collar criminal probably demands nontraditional approaches. Some possibilities include the following: The white-collar criminal could be forced to admit his or her guilt and to explain the offense publicly; the white-collar criminal could be required to document the cost of the crime; the white-collar criminal could be barred from further activity in certain professions or industries by an action such as an injunction, a divestiture order, or suspension of the right to practice a particular occupation; or the white-collar criminal could be required to pay a fine or supply community service proportionate to the social harm caused by the crime. Although ordinarily imprisonment may be inappropriate for the white-collar criminal, the sanctions applied to this offender may result in more lenient treatment of white-collar criminals than of other types of offenders.[38]

Personality Makeup

Some experts speculate that criminals have specific personality characteristics in common. Criminals, especially those with a history of violent behavior, are sometimes labeled as sociopathic or psychopathic.[39] Hervey Cleckley, who is responsible for the most widely accepted work on psychopathic criminals, asserts that these offenders build an emotional wall around themselves at an early age— perhaps as young as one or two years—and, thus, are able to ward off any feelings for others. Although these individuals may mimic such emotions as love, friendship, and loyalty, they are incapable of actually feeling them. They are extremely egocentric and will do anything to get their way. They also feel strongly that the world is a hostile place, which leads to a low tolerance of frustration, to impulsiveness, and to fear of change. Cleckley also notes that their failure to learn from experience does not make these offenders good candidates for traditional treatment methods.[40]

S. Yochelson and S. E. Samenow, therapists who worked in the forensic unit of St. Elizabeth Hospital in Washington, D.C., also see criminals as having certain personality characteristics. They define criminality in terms of irresponsibility and of thinking patterns that are conducive to breaking the law, with the extreme criminal at the far pole of irresponsibility. From their clinical examinations of offenders, these therapists conclude that extreme criminals are irresponsible in the sense that they avoid obligations, are inconsiderate of people, avoid work, and break the law. Yochelson and Samenow's theory of "the structure of the criminal mind" points to fifty-two erroneous thinking patterns that are characteristic of extreme criminals, and these thinking patterns combine with their irresponsibility to influence all their behavior. Some of these "automatic errors of thinking" of extreme criminals include: perception of self as a victim, concrete and compartmentalized thinking, pervasive

---

[38]Ibid.

[39]Over two hundred technical terms describe psychopathic or sociopathic criminals.

[40]Hervey Cleckley, *The Mask of Sanity: An Attempt to Clarify Some Issues about the So-Called Psychopathic Personality,* 3d ed. (St. Louis, Miss.: Mosby, 1955).

lying, failure to consider the injury of others, impulsiveness, and excitement seeking.[41]

However, several criminologists challenge the existence of a clear link between criminality and specific personality traits. Karl F. Schuessler and Donald R. Cressy, in reviewing 113 studies conducted prior to 1950, concluded that these studies did not demonstrate a direct link between delinquency and specific personality traits.[42] Gordon P. Waldo and Simon Dinitz, as well as David J. Tannenbaum, examined more recent studies of adult criminality and drew the same conclusion.[43]

The claim can still be made that some offenders are emotionally disturbed, while others commit crimes that are directly related to obsessive-compulsive traits in their personalities. The percentage of mental illness among offenders has been a subject of wide disagreement. On one hand, Abrahamsen claims that in all his work with offenders, he has been unable to find one without symptoms of mental pathology.[44] On the other hand, Bromberg—who examined the records of sixty thousand convicted felons who passed through the courts of New York County during a period of twenty-five years—found that fewer than 20 percent of this population were diagnosed as either psychotic, neurotic, or psychopathic.[45] It would appear from the evidence of the various studies, as well as from this author's experience in working with offenders, that Bromberg is correct in his view that only a small percentage of offenders are mentally ill.

The following are examples of offenders who are severely disturbed:

> A ten-year-old boy brought home a little frog. His mother picked up a butcher knife and killed it. That night the boy killed his mother and father while they slept. The police found him under the kitchen table saying, "I still love you," to the decapitated frog.
>
> A sixteen-year-old boy was looked upon as a model student in school, was active in church and Boy Scouts, and was acknowledged as one of the finest young men in the community. One night he came home from school, killed his parents, and proceeded to quarter them. He then ate the supper his mother had prepared. Upon being questioned about this, he answered, "I didn't kill my parents. What kind of person do you think I am?"
>
> A fifteen-year-old, who had been abused in his home, was placed in a private residential facility. He sporadically urinated on the floor, rubbed his feces on the walls of his room, and masturbated before peers. Upon being challenged for his inappropriate

---

[41]S. Yochelson and S. E. Samenow, *The Criminal Personality, Vol. 1, A Profile for Change* (New York: Aronson, 1976); and S. Yochelson and S. E. Samenow, *The Criminal Personality, Vol. 2, The Change Process* (1977).

[42]Karl F. Schuessler and Donald R. Cressey, "Personality Characteristics of Criminals," *American Journal of Sociology* (March 1950): 476–484.

[43]Gordon P. Waldo and Simon Dinitz, "Personality Attributes of the Criminal: An Analysis of Research Studies," *Journal of Research in Crime and Delinquency* 4 (July 1967): 185–191; and David J. Tannenbaum, "Personality and Criminality: A Summary and Implications of the Literature," *Journal of Criminal Justice* 5 (1977): 225–235.

[44]David Abrahamsen, *Who Are the Guilty?* (New York: Rinehart, 1952).

[45]W. Bromberg, *The Mold of Murder* (New York: Grune and Stratton, 1961).

behavior, he would simply respond in a weird voice, "Piss on the floor, piss on the floor, piss on the floor."[46]

One of the burning questions today is the issue of sanity and responsibility. Criminal law states that an individual is responsible for his or her behavior only if *mens rea* is present; that is, if the person has both the intent to commit a crime and the capacity to know right from wrong. The 1843 *McNaghten* decision, which is still widely held as the standard of sanity, states that "at the time of the committing of the act, the party accused [must be] labouring under such a defect of reason, from disease of the mind, as not to know the nature and quality of the act he was doing; or if he did know it, that he did not know he was doing what was wrong."[47] But since the successful use of the insanity plea following the assassination attempt against President Reagan, a movement has gathered momentum to reduce the use of this plea in U.S. courtrooms.

A larger percentage of offenders commit obsessive-compulsive crimes. These neurotic individuals appear to be unable to stop themselves from performing certain irrational actions. Kleptomania (compulsive stealing) or pyromania (compulsive fire-setting) are examples of compulsive behavior over which an individual appears to have little control.[48] Some sexual crimes, such as exhibitionism and voyeurism, are also examples of obsessive-compulsive behavior.

Proponents of treatment rightfully claim that the emotionally disturbed and obsessive-compulsive offenders need treatment; otherwise, they will continue to engage in their self-defeating and antisocial behavior. Significantly, the courts have also agreed that mentally ill offenders, especially, have a right to treatment; the Rouse v. Cameron decision, for example, held that mentally ill individuals are entitled to treatment.[49]

Commitment to Crime

Researchers generally conclude that the majority of juveniles and adults in American society have been involved in criminal activities at one time or another.[50] David Matza found that many juveniles drift in and out of delinquent activity during their adolescence, but that they are not committed to delinquency as a way of life.[51]

---

[46]The author has worked with these offenders or has personal knowledge of their situations.

[47]McNaghten case, House of Lords, 8 Eng. Rep. (1843).

[48]Michael J. Lillyquist, *Understanding and Changing Criminal Behavior* (Englewood Cliffs, N.J.: Prentice-Hall 1980), p. 23.

[49]373 G. 2d 451 (D.C. Cir. 1966).

[50]LaMar T. Empey, *Studies in Delinquency: Alternatives to Incarceration* (Washington, D.C.: GPO, 1967), pp. 27–32; Maynard L. Erickson and LaMar T. Empey, "Court Records, Undetected Delinquency and Decision-Making," *Journal of Criminal Law, Criminology and Police Science* 54 (December 1963): 456–469.

[51]David Matza, *Delinquency and Drift* (New York: Wiley, 1964), pp. 184–190.

Nevertheless, a small number of criminals and delinquents appear to regard crime as a way of life. Their commitment to crime may be long-standing, perhaps having been established when they were young children, or it may be more recent.

The evidence indicates that these career, or repeat, offenders commit many of the violent crimes and serious property crimes in the United States. A number of studies have shown that a few juvenile chronic offenders—most of whom are black and lower-class—commit half or more of the violent and serious crimes by youths in this nation.[52] For example, in *Delinquency in a Birth Cohort,* Wolfgang, Figlio, and Sellin state that 627 chronic offenders—who each committed five or more known offenses—were responsible for over half of all offenses and two-thirds of the serious offenses committed in Philadelphia.[53]

Some evidence also exists to show that these career offenders—also known as habitual criminals, repeat criminals, multiple offenders, chronic offenders, or professional criminals—are nonspecialists in terms of the crimes they commit. Most criminals today hustle as a major activity and use fences and loan sharks to get money for what they have stolen. They also are caught in a perpetuating cycle of criminal activity because of increases in the cost of daily living.[54] However, as career offenders formerly specialized in cracking safes, in writing bad checks, or in hoodwinking victims in fraudulent flim-flam setups, nonspecialization is a recent change.[55]

The argument can be made that career offenders are the group most in need of rehabilitation. Morris speaks of the need for complete renovation in these offenders:

> Career offenders have a lifestyle in which the patterns of noncriminal behavior which occupy most of their time are different in many important ways from those of citizens who are normally law-abiding. To the extent that offenders are committed to a lifestyle associated with crime, the correction of their law-violating behavior has to be a process analogous to completely remodeling a house or even a neighborhood rather than to that of repairing a leaky roof or replacing a defective heating system. In other words, correcting the criminal behavior of the career offender involves the virtual destruction and remodeling of a personality. . . . In other words, the career offender must become a new man.[56]

However, as noted throughout this book, career or repeat offenders usually have little interest in rehabilitation. In the early 1970s, some support was given to

[52]Paul S. Strasburg, *Violent Delinquents* (New York: Vera Institute of Justice, 1977); Donna Martin Hamparian et al., *The Violent Few: A Study of Dangerous Juvenile Offenders* (Lexington, Mass.: Heath, 1978); and Marvin E. Wolfgang et al., *Delinquency in a Birth Cohort* (Chicago: University of Chicago Press, 1972).

[53]Wolfgang et al., *Delinquency in a Birth Cohort.*

[54]Gregory R. Staats, "Changing Conceptualizations of Professional Criminals," *Criminology* 15 (May 1977): 57.

[55]Edwin H. Sutherland, *The Professional Thief* (Chicago: University of Chicago Press, 1937).

[56]A. Morris, "Correctional Reform: Illusion and Reality," *Correctional Research* 22 (1972): 2.

the use of various means of aversive conditioning with these offenders, but such bizarre means of personality change are no longer acceptable with the public. The best strategy at this time is to make programs available to these offenders while they are doing "time," and those who are ready to exit from crime will respond to these programs.

Nigel Walker, realizing that interventions work differently for particular types of offenders, has developed a progressive scale which predicts probability of continued involvement in crime:

1. Females are less likely to recidivate after a sentence has been carried out;
2. Older offenders are less likely to repeat after a sentence;
3. The more "priors" an offender has the more he will be reconvicted;
4. The more time he has spent in prison the likelier he is to be reconvicted; and
5. Reconviction rates are higher for certain types of crimes (burglary) than others (sexual offenders).[57]

Walker then goes on to summarize the hundreds of studies which have been reported:

1. In general, *fines* are followed by fewer reconvictions than other measures.
2. *Heavy fines* are followed by fewer reconvictions than light fines.
3. In general, next to fines, the measures followed by fewer reconvictions seemed to be *discharged* (absolute or conditional). The exceptions were the older "first offenders" aged thirty or more who received a discharge; these tended to have an abnormally *high* reconviction rate.
4. *Imprisonment* was followed by more reconvictions than fines or discharges.
5. *Probation* was followed by more reconvictions than imprisonment.
6. *Probation* compared rather better with the other measures when it was applied not to "first offenders" but to offenders with previous convictions (but was still the least often effective).
7. For some reason, however, "first offenders" convicted of house-breaking showed lower recidivism rates than any kind of probationer when placed on probation.[58]

Although Martinson and other researchers differ somewhat in the conclusion they draw about the various studies, especially in terms of the efficacy of imprisonment over probation, it seems clear that the least restrictive sanctions are still the most appropriate for the majority of first-time and occasional offenders. But for those who commit one serious crime after another, it appears that some form of confinement is more appropriate. The task of research is to ascertain the relationship between offenses committed and the type of interventions needed.

---

[57]Nigel Walker, "The Interchangeability of Criminal Sanctions," cited in Leonard Orland, *Justice, Punishment, Treatment: The Correctional Process* (New York: Free Press, 1972), pp. 5–6.

[58]Ibid., p. 6.

SUMMARY

This chapter began with an explanation of the three major groups into which exoffenders fall: those who will ultimately fail, those who will make marginal adjustments to society, and those who will be successful. Exoffenders who go straight generally do so because they have matured out of crime, because they have developed internal resources, and because they have successful experiences in the community. Offenders who fail usually do so because of failure of will, lack of satisfaction from the "straight life," or inability to make it in the free world.

Offenders also appear to make three responses to the treatment process. One group is indifferent or even antagonistic to treatment. A second group pretends to be involved in treatment, but these offenders actually are concerned only about making an impression on the parole board or on criminal justice actors in community-based corrections. A third group is genuinely interested in treatment as a means to an end, and although these offenders' motives and depth of involvement may vary considerably, they still look to treatment in order to satisfy some short- or long-term purpose in their lives. They may involve themselves in a program only to make the time go easier in prison, or they may be genuinely concerned about learning a skill, achieving some educational credential, or gaining some insight into themselves.

To match the most appropriate interventions with particular groups of offenders by the use of the template-matching technique or some other approach, it is important to ascertain how age, sex, social class, personality characteristics, and commitment to crime influence offender's amenability to treatment. Very little is presently known about how these personal and criminal characteristics affect the amenability to treatment and the success of interventions in correctional settings, but such information is critical in developing more effective programs in community-based and institutional corrections.

DISCUSSION QUESTIONS

1. Explain the dynamics involved in exiting from crime.
2. What does it mean for an inmate to develop "a strong mind?"
3. Why do so many offenders fail or make only marginal adjustments to community living?
4. How can society help more offenders make it in the community?
5. How do age, sex, social class, personality characteristics, and commitment to crime influence offenders' amenability to treatment?

15

Summary, Future, and Recommendations

Objectives

1. To present an overview of this book.
2. To answer several pertinent questions about correctional treatment.
3. To examine the future of correctional treatment.
4. To present recommendations to improve the effectiveness of correctional treatment.

This book has examined the role of correctional treatment in dealing with the crime problem in the United States. Correctional treatment is a subject that stirs strong emotions among both supporters and critics. Even with the general public, the popularity of correctional treatment waxes and wanes from one generation to the next. Correctional treatment is certainly easily criticized, for in the past two hundred and fifty years every conceivable method has been tried to reform criminal behavior. The panaceas of one generation too frequently turn out to be the disasters of the next.

With the emergence of rehabilitation philosophy in the early twentieth century, advocates believed that science at last had provided a means by which crime could be cured. However, rehabilitative philosophy came under heavy attack during the 1960s, and Robert Martinson's "nothing works" thesis of the mid-1970s was widely regarded as the requiem for a well-meant but futile experiment in corrections. Rehabilitative philosophy, like many previous methods to change adult and juvenile offenders was to be set aside and forgotten.

Yet rehabilitative programs continue to be conducted in community-based and institutional settings; treatment staff members understandably were defensive and somewhat disillusioned about the task of effecting correctional change. In the late 1970s and early 1980s, correctional treatment became more varied in its approach and promised to become more sophisticated in its application. Proponents of correctional treatment began to argue that the new approaches had a chance to become much better than the old ones.

This final chapter first presents a broad review of the book, answers questions about the role of correctional treatment, considers the future of correctional treatment, and presents recommendations to improve the effectiveness of correctional treatment.

SUMMARY OF THE BOOK

The dominant theme of Chapters 1 and 2 is the decline of the rehabilitative ideal. No longer is rehabilitation acknowledged as the exclusive justification for penal sanctions or the sole objective of the correctional system. Many factors have contributed to the loss of confidence in rehabilitative philosophy. The euphemisms often used—"constructive meditation" for solitary confinement, "the quiet room" for a cell for such confinement—demonstrates the vagueness and ambiguity of the basic assumptions of rehabilitative philosophy. Critics persuasively argue that rehabilitative philosophy, especially the medical model, makes erroneous assumptions about human nature and overstates the ability of the scientific expert. The rehabilitative ideal, coupled with indeterminate sentencing and parole boards, has even been accused of being a disaster. A fair assessment, then, of the future of rehabilitative philosophy is that it is likely to be peripheral rather than central to the administration of the justice system.[1]

[1]Francis A. Allen, *The Decline of the Rehabilitative Ideal* (New Haven: Yale University Press, 1981), pp. 32–59.

The decline of the rehabilitative ideal has led to the growing acceptance of two other correctional philosophies for dealing with juvenile and adult offenders: the justice model and the utilitarian punishment model. The justice model, developed by David Fogel in the early 1970s, is intended to result in a just and fair approach for dealing with criminal offenders. This model is based upon the doctrine of "just punishment" or "just deserts"; that is, that criminals deserve punishment proportionate to the harm they have inflicted on society. Determinate sentencing replaces indeterminate sentencing and parole in this model; the use of discretion in the justice system is also discouraged because of its potential for abuse. Proponents of the justice model hold that treatment programs should be available for those offenders who want them. Advocates are also concerned that victims and practitioners in the criminal justice system, as well as offenders, receive justice.

The growing acceptance of the justice model has come about in part because it deals with some of the basic concerns of today's citizens. The theories of "just deserts" and "just punishment" reaffirm the reality of moral values at a time when the current decay of values is breeding feelings of loss and normlessness and when dwindling confidence about the future is seen as clearly related to the erosion of the moral values of the past. In addition, there is concern that the powers of the state be contained, and the justice model does set limits, by making penal sanctions definite and limited, abolishing the indeterminate sentence, and eliminating or curtailing sentencing discretion. However, the idea of "just deserts" has been around for centuries and has never totally dominated the penal policy of any advanced society, so whether this theory will determine the correctional policy of this nation at any time in the future is questionable.[2]

Advocates of utilitarian punishment philosophy, which was proposed by James Q. Wilson, Ernest Van den Haag, and others, insist on repressive measures against juvenile and adult offenders because these measures will presumably result in deterring crime and protecting society. Proponents support the increased use of incapacitation, the binding over of serious juvenile offenders to the adult court, increased police surveillance and prosecution of serious crimes, the replacement of indeterminate sentencing with determinate and mandatory sentencing, the replacement of "country-club" prisons with more repressive correctional facilities, and the return of the death penalty. In short, proponents of the punishment model wish to deal with the serious crime problem in this society by declaring war on the criminal.

Advocates have turned to this model because they resent losses in the quality of life caused by widespread crime. They long for a return to an earlier era, when values were clearer and the future seemed inviting and predictable.[3] The utilitarian punishment model has also become popular because the public is convinced other models failed to reduce recidivism. An increased policy of confinement gets more offenders out of sight and out of mind, and policymakers are capitalizing on the law-and-order backlash.

---

[2]Ibid., p. 69.

[3]Francis Allen, *The Crimes of Politics* (Cambridge: Harvard University Press, 1974), pp. 33–35.

However, there is little evidence that the punishment model, which is as old as corrections itself, has ever successfully reduced the amount of antisocial behavior in society. A repressive approach seems particularly impractical at the present time. To revert to the old repression would result in violent reactions from inmates, from correctional administrators, and eventually even from the public. As Gordon Hawkins states, "The clock cannot be set back to a simple, rigidly disciplined, punitive routine."[4]

Chapters 5 and 6 focus on programs, first describing and evaluating the interventions used in community-based corrections for juveniles and adults. Such community-based programs as the Chicago Area Projects, Outward Bound, Project New Pride, Delancey Street, Gateway House, and PORT are all exemplary programs. Unfortunately, model programs are sometimes nothing more than window dressing, because too many community programs lack adequate resources, are made up of overworked and inadequately trained staff, and have little program integrity. The growing public resistance to community-based corrections, along with declining federal funds, also makes it more difficult to set up or operate community-based programs than in the past.

Chapters 7 and 8 discuss and evaluate institutional treatment modalities and programs. On a positive note, the number of treatment technologies is impressive and they have been successful in reclaiming some criminals from a life of crime. The expansion of programs in correctional institutions, including skill development, self-growth, and service involvement, is also encouraging. Yet, at present, the best hope for institutional treatment is to provide safe prisons which conform to minimal standards of human dignity and in which residents are free to choose to change, and programs through which to change. Small institutions, voluntary programs, well-trained treatment agents, increased interaction with the community, and options for treatment outside prison walls are all necessary to improve the present treatment system.

Chapter 9 considers how correctional treatment can become more effective and discusses several common elements of effective programs. Improving correctional treatment involves a three-stage process. The first stage requires that planners design programs with sound theoretical premises for the lack of well-thought-out theoretical underpinnings reduces the probability of positive outcomes in correctional treatment. Relating treatment strategies to the presumed causes of crime is an important aspect of this first stage. The second stage requires implementing programs with proper timing, necessary strength, and real integrity. The third stage requires that programs use experimental designs and good evaluation methods so that researchers can: (1) identify which programs work and which do not work; (2) identify which programs work with which groups of offenders; (3) identify the proper timing of treatment for a particular group of offenders; (4) identify the necessary strength of treatment for a particular group of offenders; and (5) identify

[4]Gordon Hawkins, *The Prison: Policy and Practice* (Chicago: University of Chicago Press, 1976), p. 15.

the program integrity needed for a particular group of offenders. Needless to say, little real progress will be made in correctional treatment until these three stages are realized in both juvenile and adult corrections.

Chapters 10 through 12 describe the role expectations, pressures, and treatment responsibilities of eight treatment agents in juvenile and adult corrections. Chapter 10 focuses on the Outward Bound staff member, the alternative school teacher, and the residential staff member in a therapeutic community, all of whom strongly endorse rehabilitation philosophy, although the setting and methods used are different for each of these treatment actors. Chapter 11 focuses on the various correctional models and interventions used in probation and parole. While the reintegration model continues to be widely used in probation, the logical-consequences and justice models are gaining greater acceptance in this subsystem. Those working in parole continue to give lip service to reintegration, but, in reality, parole officers are becoming more punishment-oriented in their responses to parolees. Chapter 12 in this unit considers social workers and youth supervisors in juvenile institutions and correctional counselors in adult prisons. In more and more training schools the traditional model, which separates treatment and custody, is being replaced by a model merging treatment and custody. Juvenile institutions that use this new model are more treatment-oriented and do not have the conflict between treatment and custody staff members typical under the traditional model. Correctional counselors in minimum-security institutions for adults generally use reintegration philosophy and derive much more satisfaction from their work than their peers in more security-oriented facilities.

Chapters 13 and 14 discuss the correctional client. For treatment to have any chance of success in correctional environments, offenders must be placed in facilities that are safe, lawful, industrious, and hopeful. In terms of humane imprisonment, offenders are also entitled to all the due process rights guaranteed in the U.S. Constitution. Beginning with the basic reasons offenders exit from crime, this unit also examines the reasons offenders fail and the interventions that appear to be most helpful to various categories of juvenile and adult offenders.

PERTINENT QUESTIONS ABOUT CORRECTIONAL TREATMENT

The following section summarizes the answers to questions raised throughout this book:

Why Are Criminal Offenders Incapable of Learning or Acquiring New and Positive Behaviors?

The assumption that criminal and juvenile offenders are incapable of changing or acquiring more positive behaviors is at the base of the argument that correctional treatment is futile. Significantly, the rise of a new psychological emphasis in society has occurred at the same time as the loss of confidence in the rehabilitation ideal. This psychological emphasis is evidenced by the millions of persons who are now or have recently been involved in traditional and nontraditional therapeutic programs. Indeed, the "therapeutic person" is inescapable in modern America: psychological literature engulfs the book stands, psychological discussions pervade television talk shows, and psychology shows up in advertising, pop music, and other popular arts.[5]

However, while this psychological emphasis has become increasingly pervasive, the probability of criminal offenders learning new and positive behaviors has been increasingly questioned. First, it is rightly claimed that correctional clients are usually unlikely candidates for treatment. Offenders generally reject the notion that they need treatment, because they do not believe they are sick. They also usually have little patience with the treatment process. Furthermore, offenders commonly react in a negative way to the coerciveness of the state that requires rehabilitation before release from community-based or institutional settings.

Second, even for those offenders who are receptive to change, correctional treatment is hampered by the lack of community and institutional resources. Nearly all practitioners in the juvenile justice and criminal justice systems have case overloads, so they have scant time for supervision of clients, and too few institutional treatment staff members must deal with too many inmates in overcrowded prisons and training schools.

Third, prisons and training schools are unlikely settings for treatment. Violence, victimization, and the rackets occupy the attention of prisoners in Big House prisons. Many juvenile correctional institutions are also characterized by a "survival-of-the-fittest" inmate social system. In addition, treatment staff members may be forced to join other staff members in chasing escapees or to don riot gear and take their places fighting rioting prisoners; they may have their programs cancelled because of inmate disturbances; or they may be locked out of a particular cellhouse or not allowed to enter the prison yard. They do not need to be informed of the insignificance of the treatment role in prisons.

Yet, there are countless success stories in institutionally and community-based corrections. John Irwin, a former San Quentin inmate, is one of the most widely renowned criminologists in the United States. Irwin's book on parole and his writings on prison life are highly respected and used in classrooms across the nation.[6] William Sands, another San Quentin inmate, established Seventh Step, which has helped hundreds of exoffenders readjust to community life. Johnny Cash knows prison life well because he served time in Folsom Prison in California. John Maher, the founder and president of Delancey Street, spent time in New York City jails and correctional institutions. Joe Ricci, the cofounder of Élan, was a dope addict who served time before he was rehabilitated by Daytop, the drug therapeutic community in New York City. Indeed, nearly all the staff in drug therapeutic communities and many of the residential staff in community-based corrections are

---

[5]Allen, *Decline of the Rehabilitative Ideal,* p. 26.
[6]John Irwin, *The Felon* (Englewood Cliffs, N.J.: Prentice-Hall, 1970).

exoffenders. Judge Robert Young, who was elected to the justice court in Auburn, California, represents another dramatic success story of an exoffender going straight. The late Malcolm Braly, who wrote several successful novels about prison, spent much of his life behind bars. Ron LeFlore learned to play baseball while doing time at the state prison in southern Michigan. In nearly every community, there are exoffenders now living productive and crime-free lives.

What Kinds of People Respond Favorably to What Types of Treatment?

Clearly, we still lack much knowledge about this question. But we do know that drug offenders are more likely to be rehabilitated in a therapeutic community than in a correctional institution. Sex offenders generally require the type of intensive group interaction and psychotherapy conducted at ROARE (Rahway) and at the Western State Hospital Unit for Sex Offenders.[7] Researchers have also found that eight of the nine subtypes of the Interpersonal Maturity Level, or I-Level, profit more from a community placement than from an institutional placement.[8] Juveniles who have committed minor crimes or status offenses usually benefit far more from a diversionary program, such as a youth service bureau or a runaway house, than from a more secure placement. Offenders who are motivated to change or to examine their own problems are likely candidates for transactional analysis and reality therapy. Finally, sociopathic offenders—who are typically unreceptive to change—are the most unlikely candidates for treatment; only behavior modification techniques appear to have any impact upon these offenders.

The Panel on Research on Rehabilitative Techniques has recommended the template-matching technique as a means of identifying what works for what groups of offenders. The template-matching technique involves creating a set of descriptors, or a template, of those offenders who could be expected to do best in a program. The panel speculates that offender templates would have to be developed by examining certain assumptions or expected outcomes of programs and that such templates might vary in inclusiveness or specificity.[9]

Improving our elementary level of knowledge concerning what works for particular groups of offenders requires considerable commitment from policymakers. First, extensive research must be done, using the template-matching technique or some other concept to determine which treatment efforts are most effective with which group of offenders. Second, increased resources must be provided for institutional and community-based corrections so that these treatment plans can be

---

[7]"Treating Sex Offenders in New Jersey," *Corrections Magazine* 1 (November -December 1974): 13–24.

[8]Marguerite Q. Warren, "The Community Treatment Project: History and Prospects," in *Law Enforcement Science and Technology,* ed. S. A. Yefsky (Washington, D.C.: Thompson, 1972), pp. 193–195.

[9]Susan Martin, Lee Sechrest, and Robin Redner, eds., *Rehabilitation of Criminal Offenders: New Directions for Research* (Washington D.C.: National Academy of Sciences, 1981), p. 81.

implemented with sufficient strength and integrity. Third, correctional environments that are more compatible with the process of social restoration must be created.

Why Rely on a Single Cure for a Variety of Complex Problems?

As Daniel Glaser indicated in his 1960s examination of the correctional institutions of the U.S. Bureau of Prisons, the pre-1970s treatment agents often used only one technique in working with offenders.[10] Indeed, the "nothing works" findings of Martinson and others were largely based on programs that used a single method. But such reliance on a single method at any one time is much less likely now, as most effective treatment programs in community and institutional settings use a variety of treatment approaches. Therapeutic communities illustrate well the multiple treatment approach. They commonly provide the support network of a cohesive family group, require that family members earn privileges and responsibilities, use some means of confrontation or "attack" group therapy, reinforce positive behavior in a number of ways, require members to work, and reintegrate members gradually into the community. Some programs, such as Delancey Street, even provide financial assistance to ease the community adjustment of graduates. The best examples of the multiple approach in an institutional setting were the Asklepieion therapeutic community at the federal penitentiary at Marion, Illinois, and the drug abuse unit at the federal correctional institution at Lompoc, California. To graduate from the drug abuse unit at Lompoc, participants were required to complete four of nine self-improvement programs, each of which ran for twelve weeks. These programs consisted of a relaxation program, general semantics, self-charting, assertiveness training, anger management, Bible study, Guides for Better Living, prerelease instruction, and vocational guidance.

Should Recidivism Be the Only Dimension Used to Evaluate Correctional Treatment?

Rehabilitation has been defined "as any measure taken to change an offender's character, habits, or behavior patterns so as to dismiss his criminal propensities."[11] The primary goal of rehabilitation, then, is to alter the offender so he or she is less inclined to commit crime again. Given this definition of rehabilitation, it is not surprising that measuring the rates on recidivism has commonly been the sole means used to evaluate offender rehabilitation.

Proponents of rehabilitation argue that equating treatment effectiveness with lower recidivism rates causes several problems. First, recidivism rates tend to be crude measures that vary in definition and in methodological sophistication from

---

[10]Daniel Glaser, "Achieving Better Questions: A Half-Century Progress in Correctional Research," *Federal Probation* 39 (1975): 3–9.

[11]Andrew von Hirsh, ed., *Doing Justice: The Choice of Punishments* (New York: Hill and Wang, 1976), p. 11.

one study to the next. As Paul Gendreau and Robert Ross have noted, "Recidivism measurement can be arbitrary, imprecise, and biased."[12] Second, lack of follow-up in the community causes another problem when treatment is evaluated solely through recidivism. Outward Bound is an example of an intervention which has shown remarkable success during the first year a youth graduates from the program, but lack of community follow-up eventually results in a failure rate that is no better than it would have been had the youth been sent to training school.[13] Third, regardless of the effectiveness of treatment in a correctional setting, offenders face social conditions, such as unemployment, that greatly influence whether or not they return to crime. Finally, treatment should be evaluated in terms of whether it achieves its immediate goals as well as the long-term goal of eliminating recidivism. The immediate goals of treatment include such benefits as personal growth, insight, happiness, or satisfaction. Some programs intended only to make prison time pass more easily must be defined as successful treatment because of their salutary effects on offenders.

Although policymakers probably will not give up measuring the effectiveness of treatment by recidivism rates, proponents of rehabilitation make a good point that both the immediate and the long-range goals should be considered in evaluating the efficacy of treatment. Emphasizing the immediate goals of treatment can be advantageous because policymakers, corrections officials, and treatment personnel are forced to consider the changes necessary in correctional environments to make them more compatible with the immediate goals of treatment.

How Competent Are Treatment Personnel?

A number of remarkable treatment agents are described in this book. Highly dedicated to working with correctional clients, they go beyond the call of duty in countless ways. They are sensitive and understanding, able to perceive the problems and needs of clients, and highly skillful in persuading both staff and clients to become involved in treatment programs.

But how typical are the exemplary treatment agents? Unfortunately, for several reasons, the average treatment agent in county, state, federal, and private correctional agencies typically falls far short of the high standards demonstrated by outstanding treatment personnel.

First, the debilitating environments in which treatment takes place reduce the quality of services most treatment agents deliver to offenders. Both treatment and custody staff members in Big House prisons feel oppressed by the environment and often feel they are doing time just like the prisoners. Although the old inmate code which warned against talking with a staff member has broken down, the increased

---

[12]Paul Gendreau and Robert R. Ross, "Effective Correctional Treatment: Bibliotherapy for Cynics," *Crime and Delinquency* 25 (1979): 463–489.

[13]Joseph Nold and Mary Wilpers, "Wilderness Training as an Alternative to the Institutionalization of Adjudicated Juvenile Offenders," in George C. Killinger and Paul F. Cromwell, Jr., eds., *Alternatives to Imprisonment: Corrections in the Community* (St. Paul, Minn.: West, 1974), pp. 157–158.

dangers in prison settings has discouraged much genuine exchange between the "keepers" and the "kept."

Second, probation and parole officers, along with residential staff in community and institutional corrections, tend to be overwhelmed by the sheer volume of casework, by lack of appreciation from offenders, by low rates of success, and by the lack of positive reinforcement they receive from administrators. Treatment staff members usually follow a process of socialization during which they start the job highly involved, then, confronted with a variety of pressures on the job, they begin to develop negative feelings toward clients. Some treatment staff members do not move off this plateau; they take every shortcut they can and keep clients at arm's length. Yet most treatment staff members move up to another plateau where they keep trying to do their jobs competently, but with a dramatic decline in commitment to their jobs and in the quality of services they provide.

Third, custodial staff members are more directly affected by the debilitating correctional environments than are treatment staff members. Treatment staff members often have some privacy from offenders, but institutional line staff members must deal with them twenty-four hours a day. Custody staff are also deeply affected by an informal code or conduct norms that discourage them from becoming involved in treatment. Such norms are unfortunate because some evidence exists that non-professional staff can often have greater treatment impact on offenders than can professional staff. The nonprofessional staff member frequently has better rapport with and is trusted more by correctional clients because he or she has grown up on the streets and so understands the experiences offenders have had.

In short, probation officers, parole officers, residential staff, and institutional staff are generally educationally competent and sufficiently trained to do their jobs, but the quality of services they provide clients is reduced greatly by debilitating environments and bureaucratic rules, by the lack of appreciation from offenders and the low rate of success in dealing with them, and by the socialization process they go through. Some staff members clearly rise above the obstacles and do exceptional jobs as treatment agents, but the average staff member tends to withdraw from the commitment needed to provide first-rate treatment services.

Why Do Some Offenders Walk Away from Crime?

Offenders who mature out of crime usually do so because of one or more of the following experiences: They decided to go straight because they feel they have hit bottom, and it is time to turn their lives around. Or they may conclude that they have spent too much of their lives in prison. Female offenders may decide to walk away from drugs because they have dependent children and want to provide an adequate home for them. Or offenders may be fed up with living a life of crime; in other words, the life of crime is no longer as satisfying as it once was.[14]

[14]See Thomas Meisenhelder, "An Exploratory Study of Exiting from Criminal Careers," *Criminology* 15 (November 1977): 318–334.

Offenders who make more than marginal adjustments to community life usually are successful because they have developed their internal resources: they have acquired faith in themselves, a sense of purpose in life, and a willingness to grow. Exoffenders also need to have support networks and successful experiences in the community to live a crime-free life. They must be able to locate adequate employment and to involve themselves in satisfying social relationships with citizens in the noncriminal community.

What Are the Common Elements of Effective Programs?

The most effective treatment programs appear to have a number of common elements. First, many of these programs are set up by inspired leaders who mean business. Second, they commonly transmit a philosophy of life that generates a sense of mission or purpose among offenders. Third, they usually have a unified treatment team. Fourth, they generally trust offenders with some decision-making responsibilities. Fifth, they usually help offenders develop skills that make them feel they can do something or that they have mastered some important insights about themselves or life. Sixth, the most effective programs often are unique. Seventh, successful community-based and institutional programs avoid alienating formal decision makers. Resistance to administrators is usually costly to institutional programs, and good public relations is a critical factor in the survival and development of community-based programs. Finally, effective programs have adequate community-support networks.

Sometimes the basic element in an effective program is thought to be the charismatic and inspired leader who can persuade others to accept whatever he or she has to offer, regardless of the program structure. This viewpoint reflects a psychological reductionism which claims that effective programs are established and sustained only through the initiative and commitment of such inspired persons. However, as this book has indicated, effective programs depend upon a variety of interrelated factors in addition to effective leaders, such as receptive clients, adequate funding, compliant organizational-environmental structures, and acceptance within the larger political and correctional community.

The task of correctional research today is to determine the effect of the interrelationship between leadership and program structure in various types of settings, to ascertain whether different styles of leadership are needed to implement and conduct effective programs in community-based and institutional settings, to identify the components that are intrinsic to effective programs, and to weigh the effect of the interrelationships among the common elements of effective programs.

How Can Effective Programs Be Replicated in Other Settings?

Donald Cressey, a widely respected criminologist, contends that the reason drug treatment and other rehabilitation programs run by exoffenders are so much more successful than official programs is that "they're not readily replicable." That is, the fact that they are "amateurish, creative and innovative means that you cannot duplicate them; in fact, the easiest way to destroy such a program would be to make it official and 'bureaucratize' it."[15]

However, the example of Outward Bound challenges Cressey's statement about replicating effective programs. Beginning with the Colorado Outward Bound program in 1962, Outward Bound programs or variations conducted in the United States have now expanded to one thousand. Bureaucracy has not destroyed the quality of Outward Bound programs; rather, it can be argued that bureaucracy has been one of the keys to the success of this experiential learning program.

The role of research is to determine the most effective way to replicate effective programs. Because effective correctional interventions are not cellophane-wrapped packages of transportable programs, corrections researchers must discover which elements of successful programs can be adapted to other settings and what new elements are needed for the program to do well in other correctional environments.

How Important Is the Organizational-Environment Setting in Which Treatment Takes Place?

The organizational goals of an agency appear to make a difference in the quality of life for both offenders and staff members. In correctional institutions, the more emphasis there is on custody and control, the more likely it is that there will be conflict between treatment and custody staff, that there will be alienation between staff members and inmates, and that inmates will be negative about their confinement. Research done in Massachusetts has indicated that residents of community-based residential facilities feel better about their placement, and are more receptive to the staff, in treatment-oriented than in custodially oriented programs.[16] David Street, Robert Vinter, and Charles Perrow, in a study of juvenile correctional institutions in Michigan, also found that residents in treatment-oriented institutions were more receptive to staff than were residents in custodially oriented training schools.[17]

However, unless an environment is humane and safe, not much treatment is likely to take place. The lack of a safe and lawful environment presents a major problem in conducting programs in Big House prisons. Inmates who may otherwise be predisposed to treatment will have little interest in anything but survival when they feel unsafe or victimized. As one inmate said, "Some treatment program here if I get my throat cut."[18]

[15]Quoted in "From 'Bums' to Businessmen: The Delancey Street Foundation," *Corrections Magazine* 1 (September 1974): 28.

[16]Robert B. Coates et al., "Exploratory Analysis of Recidivism and Cohort Data on the Massachusetts Youth Correctional System" (Cambridge: Center for Criminal Justice, Harvard Law School, July 1975), pp. 40–45.

[17]David Street, Robert D. Vinter, and Charles Perrow, *Organization for Treatment: A Comparative Study of Institutions for Delinquents* (New York: Free Press, 1966).

[18]Interviewed in August 1981.

Similarly, it is doubtful that residents will be receptive to treatment if they are not given their constitutionally guaranteed rights. Treating inmates as slaves of the state or acting as if they left their due process rights behind upon entering the prison gates engenders a variety of angry emotions, none of which is likely to result in receptivity to the treatment process.

THE FUTURE OF CORRECTIONAL TREATMENT

The future of correctional treatment will vary from one subsystem of the juvenile and adult justice system to another. Programs in community-based corrections will probably be expanded because of the prohibitive expense of placing offenders in long-term institutions, while programs in correctional institutions—especially maximum-security prisons—may be more limited.

Probation

Both juvenile and adult probation will probably stress supervision of clients and the needs of victims of crime more in the future. In juvenile probation, the popularity of the logical-consequences model—which is essentially a deterrent model—will probably increase. Consequently, juvenile probation officers will try to discover more and more "costs" to the youthful offenders of law-violating behavior. The already widespread use of community service as a means of restitution will increase. Intensive "tracking" programs with juvenile offenders may be more widely adopted. Furthermore, juveniles who persist in law-violating behavior may be placed in group homes for longer periods of time.

In adult probation, the surveillance of probationers will be emphasized more than ever before in the history of probation. There will be less toleration of law-violating behavior, and offenders will be sent more quickly to residential programs. The number of residential facilities for probationers will dramatically increase in nearly every state and include probation centers, restitution centers, and therapeutic communities. In other words, while evidence of more criminal or antisocial behavior will be necessary to send a probationer to prison, less such behavior will be tolerated before he or she is sent to a residential program in the community.

The justice model will have considerable impact upon probation departments across the nation. Probation officers in more and more jurisdictions will look upon offenders as volitional and responsible human beings and, therefore, few excuses will be made for offenders who again violate the law. Probation officers also will place more emphasis on the due process rights of offenders, especially during the probation revocation process, and more stress on the needs of victims than on treatment of the client. Offender participation in rehabilitation will be regarded as strictly voluntary and will not affect the length of probation.

Correctional Institutions

In the 1970s, the correctional pendulum swung back to punishment, and the repressiveness of the utilitarian punishment philosophy is likely to be felt for the next decade or two in adult prisons. Treatment will be viewed somewhat differently. Few jurisdictions will regard treatment as mandatory for release from confinement. Most jurisdictions will adopt one of two positions on the feasibility of institutional treatment: (1) Involvement in treatment is voluntary and has nothing to do with the length of confinement, but the availability of programs is mandatory as a condition of humane confinement; or (2) treatment is a privilege an offender may receive but to which he or she is not necessarily entitled.

The current lawless and violent settings of maximum security prisons make the future of correctional treatment in such facilities bleak. Big House prisons will probably become repositories for hard-core offenders. Determinate sentencing structures will send offenders to these institutions for prolonged sentences. Inmates will be permitted less freedom of movement because the basic purpose of these repressive facilities will be to hold offenders while they are doing time. Treatment within these facilities will be looked upon as a privilege to be earned.

However, minimum- and medium-security prisons will continue to provide programs and to encourage inmates to participate in them. For those inmates willing to participate in the programs, the emphasis will be more on making the inmate a productive member of society than on dealing with his or her emotional adjustment of the inmate. Career planning and guidance counseling will encourage inmates to participate in educational and job preparation programs. Alcohol or drug abuse counseling, which aim at resolving specific problems, will also receive priority over treatment geared toward improving the inmate's general well-being.[19]

Juvenile correctional institutions will be characterized by less repressive measures than will adult institutions. Because juvenile institutions are smaller, and because of the recent reforms that have taken place within these facilities, their administrators do not have the same problems with lawless inmate societies as do administrators in adult prisons. Rehabilitation is more firmly entrenched in juvenile correctional institutions than in adult prisons. Thus, treatment will continue to flourish in training schools, but it will be less instrumental in determining when a youth is ready to be paroled than it has been.

Parole

In adult corrections, the parole board will be phased out in most state correctional systems as determinate sentencing replaces indeterminate sentencing. However, community supervision of exoffenders will continue. Some jurisdic-

---

[19]Peter C. Kratcoski, *Correctional Counseling and Treatment* (Monterey, Calif.: Duxbury Press, 1981), p. 427.

tions may require exoffenders to register at the police department when they return to the community and use the police to maintain surveillance of these individuals.

Community assistance programs are unlikely to be greatly expanded in the future because of fiscal constraints. Thus, unfortunately, exoffenders will continue to return to the community without adequate support networks and without assistance in finding employment and obtaining needed services.

Juvenile aftercare will probably continue to be a confused process because it faces two apparently insurmountable problems: the high recidivism rate for parolees and the economic infeasibility of returning youthful offenders to institutions. The likely resolution will be to refer more youthful offenders to the adult court if they return to law-violating behavior.

RECOMMENDATIONS FOR CORRECTIONAL TREATMENT

To expand the role of, and to improve the services of, correctional treatment in the future, several recommendations are in order:

1. Involvement in treatment should be entirely voluntary. Participation, or the lack of participation, in these programs should not be related to the length of institutional stay or to the length of supervision in community programs.
2. Adult inmates should have the opportunity to become involved in meaningful and adequately paid work during incarceration.
3. Both juvenile and adult inmates should have the opportunity for some degree of self-governance during confinement.
4. Safe environments must be provided for institutionalized offenders. Only when inmates feel safe can they be concerned about much more than personal survival.
5. A variety of programs should be offered in correctional institutions. These interventions should be grounded on good program design, implemented with program integrity, and evaluated on an ongoing basis with sophisticated research methods.
6. More care must be taken to ensure that common elements of effective programs thrive in correctional environments.
7. A progressive array of services must be established for offenders in the community. Such a network of support services, as therapeutic communities have demonstrated, is imperative to improve the positive impact of correctional treatment.
8. Career and economic incentives must be made available for persons who have the motivation and skills to become effective treatment agents so that they will be persuaded to seek out such employment and to stay involved in correctional service.
9. Only through well-planned and soundly executed research can further development of treatment concepts and practices take place; therefore, research on correctional treatment must be given a much higher priority than it presently has.

SUMMARY

As Chapters 1 and 2 indicated, perhaps we have promised too much with correctional treatment. Violent and inhumane prisons are certainly unpromising places for treatment. But even in community-based corrections, clients' histories of failure, inadequate skills, and drug and alcohol addiction result in far more failures than successes.

Yet the danger is to expect too little from correctional treatment. Some offenders do profit from treatment in community-based and institutional settings. The positive effect may be short-ranged—simply to make their present confinement more bearable—or it may be long-ranged—to provide them with a sense of mission or purpose so they can live crime-free. Some programs really are effective, and some treatment agents do have positive impacts on offenders. It would appear that this is particularly true for those offenders who have "hit the bottom" and are consequently more receptive to change in their lives. With these offenders the results are sometimes remarkable.

However, the social, economic, and political context against which correctional treatment is set does not make it easy to improve treatment. The "get-tough" mood of the public has contributed to increased use of incapacitation, has discouraged politicians from supporting treatment-oriented corrections, and has reduced the use of programs such as work release and home furloughs. In a time when economic resources are limited, correctional programs will continue to receive the last piece of the fiscal pie. The end of LEAA funding has meant that many promising community-based programs have been closed. Many other community programs will find it difficult to keep their doors open in the 1980s. As for correctional environments, overcrowded prisons result in unsafe settings in which victimization prevails and prisoners only become embittered. Inmates interpret sensitivity and kindness as weakness, and survival becomes the dominant concern.

The future of correctional treatment ultimately depends on three factors: funding research, so more effective technologies can be developed for the treatment process; the identification of what works for which group of offenders, so that offenders interested in treatment can be given the interventions most compatible with their needs and interests; and the creation of more humane correctional contexts so that the environment will not interfere with the treatment process.

The United States is not a pacesetter for corrections and has not been for a long time; merely being content with warehousing offenders will put our nation back in the Dark Ages of corrections. Considerable fanfare went into the burial of treatment in the mid-1970s, although treatment programs continue to exist in community and institutional settings. We need to put the same burst of energy into reemphasizing treatment, not as a panacea or as a condition of release, but as a viable option for those who are interested in change, growth, and positive movement in their lives. Any less will be cruel and unusual punishment.

DISCUSSION QUESTIONS

1. As you finish this book, are you more hopeful or more discouraged about the role of correctional treatment than when you started the book?
2. What are the possibilities and problems that correctional treatment is likely to face in the future?
3. What questions are raised about correctional treatment in this chapter? What answers are given?
4. What recommendations would you add to the ones found in this chapter?

Selected
Bibliography

ABRAMS, A. I. and SIEGEL, LARRY M. "The Transcendental Meditation Program at Folsom State Prison: A Cross Validation Study." *Criminal Justice and Behavior* 5 (1978): 3–19.

ADAMS, STUART. *Evaluative Research in Corrections: A Practical Guide*. Washington, D.C.: GPO, 1975.

———. "Evaluative Research in Corrections: Status and Prospects." *Federal Probation* 38 (1974): 14–21.

ALLEN, FRANCIS A. *The Borderland of Criminal Justice*. Chicago: University of Chicago Press, 1964.

———. *The Decline of the Rehabilitative Ideal*. New Haven: Yale University Press, 1981.

ALLEN, HARRY E.; CARLSON, ERIC W.; and PARKS, EVALYN C. *Critical Issues in Adult Probation*. Washington, D.C.: GPO, 1979.

American Friends Service Committee. *Struggle for Justice: A Report on Crime and Punishment in America*. New York: Hill and Wang, 1971.

BAILEY, WALTER C. "Correctional Outcome: An Evaluation of 100 Reports." *Journal of Criminal Law, Criminology, and Police Science* 57 (June 1967): 153–160.

BARTOLLAS, CLEMENS. "Sisyphus in a Juvenile Institution." *Social Work* 20 (September 1974): 364–368.

———. *Introduction to Corrections*. New York: Harper & Row, 1981.

BARTOLLAS, CLEMENS; MILLER, STUART J.; and DINITZ, SIMON. *Juvenile Victimization: The Institutional Paradox*. New York: Halstead Press, 1976.

BARTOLLAS, CLEMENS, and MILLER, STUART J. *Correctional Administration: Theory and Practice*. New York: McGraw-Hill, 1978.

BARTOLLAS, CLEMENS; MILLER, STUART J.; and WICE, PAUL P. *Practitioners in American Justice: The Promise and the Performance*. Englewood Cliffs, N.J.: Prentice-Hall, 1983.

BERLIN, ALEXANDER B. and BERLIN, LOUIS. *Treating the Criminal Offender.* 2d ed. Englewood Cliffs, N.J.: Prentice-Hall, 1981.

BERNARD, J. L., and EISEMAN, R. "Verbal Conditioning in Sociopaths with Spiral and Monetary Reinforcement." *Journal of Personality and Social Psychology* 6 (1976): 203–206.

BLACKMORE, JOHN. "Human Potential: Therapies, Behind Bars." *Corrections Magazine* 4 (December 1978): 28–38.

———. "Big City Probation: 'Treatment? There's No Treatment Going on Here.' " *Corrections Magazine* 6 (December 1980): 13–15.

———. *Community Corrections* 6 (October 1980): 4–14.

BOOKMAN, DAVID, et al. *Community-Based Corrections in Des Moines: An Exemplary Project.* Washington, D.C.: GPO, 1976.

CARLSON, NORMAN. "A More Balanced Correctional Philosophy." *FBI Law Enforcement Bulletin* 46 (January 1977).

COLSON, CHARLES W. *Born Again.* Old Tappan, N.J.: Spire, 1977.

CONRAD, JOHN P. "We Should Never Have Promised a Hospital." *Federal Probation* 49 (December 1974): 3–9.

———. "The Survival of the Fearful." In *In Fear of Each Other,* edited by John P. Conrad and Simon Dinitz. Lexington, Mass.: Heath, 1977.

———. *Justice and Consequences.* Lexington, Mass: Heath, 1981.

———. "A Lost Ideal, a New Hope: The Way to Effective Correctional Treatment." *Journal of Criminal Law and Criminology* 72 (November 1981): 1699–1734.

———. *Adult Offender Education Programs.* Washington, D.C.: National Institute of Justice, 1981.

CULLEN, FRANCIS T., and GILBERT, KAREN E. *Reaffirming Rehabilitation.* Cincinnati: Anderson, 1982.

EMPEY, LAMAR T. *Alternatives to Incarceration.* Washington, D.C.: GPO, 1967.

FEDO, MICHAEL. "Free Enterprise Goes to Prison." *Corrections Magazine* 4 (April 1981): 5–15.

FINCKENHAUER, JAMES. *Scared Straight.* Englewood Cliffs, N.J.: Prentice-Hall, 1981.

FOGEL, DAVID. ". . . We Are the Living Proof": *The Justice Model for Corrections.* Cincinnati: Anderson, 1975.

FOGEL, DAVID, and HUDSON, JOE. *Justice as Fairness.* Cincinnati: Anderson, 1981.

GENDREAU, PAUL, and ROSS, BOB. "Effective Correctional Treatment: Bibliotherapy for Cynics." *Crime and Delinquency.* 27 (October 1979): 463–489.

GERARD, ROY. "Institutional Innovations in Juvenile Corrections." *Federal Probation* 34 (December 1970): 38–40.

GLASER, DANIEL, "Achieving Better Questions: A Half-Century's Progression in Correctional Research" *Federal Probation* 39 (1975): 3–9.

———.*The Effectiveness of the Prison and Parole System.* Indianapolis: Bobbs-Merrill, 1964.

GLASER, DANIEL, and O'LEARY, VINCENT. *The Control and Treatment of Narcotic Use.* Washington, D.C.: GPO, 1972.

GLASSER, WILLIAM. *Reality Therapy.* New York: Harper & Row, 1965.

HALEY, PETER. "The Cookie Monster Goes to Prison." *Corrections Magazine* 4 (December 1978): 35–38.

HALLECK, SEYMOUR L., and WITTE, ANN D. "Is Rehabilitation Dead?" *Crime and Delinquency* 23 (October 1977): 379–382.

HARRIS, THOMAS A. *I'm OK—You're OK*. New York: Harper & Row, 1965.

HAWKINS, GORDON. *The Prison: Policy and Practice*. Chicago: University of Chicago Press, 1976.

HICKEY, JOSEPH E., and SCHARF, PETER L. *Toward a Just Correctional System*. San Francisco: Jossey-Bass, 1980.

JACOBS, JAMES. *Stateville*. Chicago: University of Chicago Press, 1977.

JACOBS, JAMES B. "Notes on Policy and Practice." *Social Service Review* 50 (March 1976): 138–147.

JESNESS, CARL F. *The Preston Typology Study*. Sacramento, Calif.: Institute for the Study of Crime and Delinquency, 1968.

JOHNSON, ROBERT, and PRICE, SUSAN. "The Complete Correctional Officer—Human Service and Human Environment of Prisons." *Criminal Justice and Behavior* 8 (1981): 343–373.

KITTRIE, NICHOLAS N. *The Right to Be Different*. Baltimore: Penquin, 1973.

KRAJICK, KEVIN. " 'Not on My Block': Local Opposition Impedes the Search for Alternatives." *Corrections Magazine* 6 (October 1980): 15–29.

———. "Probation: The Original Community Program." *Corrections Magazine* 6 (December 1980): 6–12.

KRATCOSKI, PETER C. *Correctional Counseling and Treatment*. Monterey, Calif.: Duxbury Press, 1981.

LILLYQUIST, MICHAEL H. *Understanding and Changing Criminal Behavior*. Englewood Cliffs, N.J.: Prentice-Hall, 1980.

LIPTON, D.; MARTINSON, R.; and WILKS, J. *The Effectiveness of Correctional Treatment: A Survey of Treatment Evaluation Studies*. New York: Praeger, 1975.

MACNAMARA, DONAL E. J. "The Medical Model in Corrections: Requiescat in Pace." *Criminology* 14 (February 1977): 439–440.

MARTIN, SUSAN; SECHREST, LEE; and REDNER, ROBIN; ed. *The Rehabilitation of Criminal Offenders: New Directions for Research*. Washington, D.C.: National Academy of Sciences, 1981.

MARTINSON, ROBERT. "What Works?—Questions and Answers about Prison Reform." *Public Interest* 35 (Spring 1974): 22–54.

MARTINSON, ROBERT. "California Research at the Crossroads." *Crime and Delinquency* 22 (April 1976): 180–191.

MARTINSON, ROBERT, and WILKS, JUDITH. "Save Parole Supervision." *Federal Probation* 41 (September 1977): 23–27.

MENNINGER, KARL. *The Crime of Punishment*. New York: Vintage Press, 1966.

MINER, JOSHUA L., and BOLDT, JOE. *Outward Bound USA: Learning through Experience in Adventure-Based Education*. New York: Morrow, 1981.

MITCHELL, GREG. "Voices from the New Literary Underground." *Corrections Magazine* 8 (February 1982): 43–50.

MITFORD, JESSICA. *Kind and Unusual Punishment*. New York: Knopf, 1973.

MORENO, J. L. *Who Shall Survive?* Rev. ed. New York: Beacon House, 1953.

———. *Psychodrama*. Beacon, N.Y.: Beacon House, 1969.

MORRIS, NORVAL. *The Future of Imprisonment*. Chicago: University of Chicago Press, 1974.

————. "Punishment, Desert, and Rehabilitation." Lecture at the University of Denver College of Law, Denver, Colorado, 12 November 1976.

National Advisory Commission on Criminal Justice Standards and Goals. *Corrections.* Washington, D.C.: GPO 1973.

————. *A National Strategy to Reduce Crime.* Washington, D.C.: GPO, 1973.

PALMER, JOHN W. "The Night Prosecutor." *Judicature* 59 (June–July 1975): 23–25.

PALMER, TED. "Martinson Revisited." *Journal of Research in Crime and Delinquency.* 12 (April 1976), 133–152.

————. *Correctional Intervention and Research: Current Issues and Future Prospects.* Lexington, Mass.: Heath, 1978.

POTTER, JOAN. "The Pitfalls of Pretrial Diversion." *Corrections Magazine* 7 (February 1981): 5–11.

————. "The Jaycees: Tapping Inmate Initiative." *Corrections Magazine* 8 (February 1982): 35–42.

QUAY, HERBERT C. "The Three Faces of Evaluation: What Can Be Expected to Work." *Criminal Justice and Behavior* 4 (December 1977): 341–354.

RACHIN, RICHARD L. "Reality Therapy: Helping People Help Themselves." *Crime and Delinquency* 20 (January 1974): 51–53.

Report of the Twentieth Century Fund Task Force on Criminal Sentencing. *Fair and Certain Punishment.* New York: McGraw-Hill, 1976.

ROGERS, CARL R., Ed. *Client-Centered Psychotherapy.* Boston: Houghton Mifflin, 1951.

ROSS, ROBERT R., and MCKAY, BRYAN. "Behavioral Approaches to Treatment in Corrections: Requiem for a Panacea." *Canadian Journal of Criminology* 20 (1978): 279–295.

ROSS, ROBERT R., and GENDREAU, PAUL. *Effective Correctional Treatment.* Toronto: Butterworth, 1980.

ROTHMAN, DAVID. *The Discovery of the Asylum: Social Order and Disorder in the New Republic.* Boston: Little, Brown, 1971.

————. *Conscience and Convenience: The Asylum and Its Alternatives in Progressive America.* Boston: Little, Brown, 1980.

SCHUTZ, WILLIAM C. *Joy: Expanding Human Awareness.* New York: Grove Press, 1967.

SCOTT, JOSEPH W., and HISSONG, JERRY B. "Changing the Delinquent Subculture: A Sociological Approach." In *Readings in Juvenile Delinquency,* edited by Ruth Shonle Cavan. Philadelphia: Lippincott, 1975.

SEASHORE, MARJORIE J., et al. *Prisoner Education: Project NewGate and Other College Programs.* New York: Holt, Rinehart, and Winston, 1976.

SECHREST, LEE; WHITE, SUSAN O.; and BROWN, ELIZABETH D., eds. *The Rehabilitation of Criminal Offenders: Problems and Prospects.* Washington, D.C.: National Academy of Sciences, 1979.

SERRILL, MICHAEL S. "Delancey Street." *Corrections Magazine* 1 (September 1974): 13–28.

SMYKLA, JOHN. *Community-Based Corrections: Principles and Practices.* New York: Macmillan, 1981.

STANLEY, DAVID T. *Prisoners Among Us.* Washington, D.C.: Brookings Institution, 1976.

TAFT, PHILIP B., JR. "Whatever Happened to That Old-Time Prison Chaplain?" *Corrections Magazine* 4 (December 1978): 54–61.

TOCH, HANS, ed. *Therapeutic Communities in Corrections.* New York: Praeger, 1980.

"Treating Sex Offenders in New Jersey." *Corrections Magazine* 1 (November–December 1974): 13–24.

VAN DEN HAAG, ERNEST. *Punishing Criminals.* New York: Basic, 1975.

VON HIRSCH, ANDREW. *Doing Justice.* New York: Hill and Wang, 1976.

VORRATH, HARRY H., and BRENDTRO, LARRY K. *Positive Peer Culture.* Chicago: Aldine, 1974.

WARREN, MARGUERITE Q. "The Community Treatment Project: History and Prospects." In *Law Enforcement Science and Technology,* edited by S. A. Yefsky. Washington, D.C.: Thompson, 1972.

————. "Correctional Treatment and Coercion: The Differential Effectiveness Perspective." *Criminal Justice and Behavior* 4 (December 1977): 355–376.

WEBER, GEORGE. "Conflict between Professional and Nonprofessional Personnel in Institutional Delinquency Development." In *Prison Within Society,* edited by Lawrence Hazelrigg. Garden City, N. Y.: Anchor, 1969.

WILSON, JAMES. Q. *Thinking about Crime.* New York: Basic, 1975.

WOODWARD, HARRY H., and CHIEVERS, FREDERICK M. "Teaching Motivation to Inmates." *Federal Probation* 40 (March 1976): 41–48.

YOUNG, CHARLES M. "Cell Block Theater." *Corrections Magazine* 2 (December 1976): 13–17.

ZIMRING, FRANKLIN E., and HAWKINS, GORDON J. *Deterrence.* Chicago: University of Chicago Press, 1973.

INDEX